Pauline E. Hopkins

Pauline E. Hopkins
A Literary Biography

BY HANNA WALLINGER

THE UNIVERSITY OF GEORGIA PRESS   ATHENS & LONDON

© 2005 by The University of Georgia Press
Athens, Georgia 30602
All rights reserved
Designed by Erin Kirk New and Sandra Hudson
Set in 10/13 Berkeley Medium by Bookcomp, Inc.
Printed and bound by Maple-Vail
The paper in this book meets the guidelines for permanence
and durability of the Committee on Production Guidelines for
Book Longevity of the Council on Library Resources.

Printed in the United States of America
09 08 07 06 05 C 5 4 3 2 1

Library of Congress Cataloging-in-Publication Data
Wallinger, Hanna.
Pauline E. Hopkins : a literary biography / Hanna Wallinger.
p. cm.
Includes bibliographical references and index.
ISBN 0-8203-2704-2 (alk. paper)
1. Hopkins, Pauline E. (Pauline Elizabeth)   2. Authors,
American—19th century—Biography.   3. Authors, American—
20th century—Biography.   4. African American women—
Intellectual life.   5. Women and literature—United
States.   6. African American authors—Biography.
7. African Americans in literature.   I. Title.
PS1999.H4226Z94 2005
818'.409—dc22
2005001135

British Library Cataloging-in-Publication Data available

Contents

Illustrations

Acknowledgments

Any academic undertaking involves a cooperative effort. This book could not have been undertaken or brought to its conclusion without assistance from various quarters, financial and personal.

First and foremost I am greatly indebted to the Austrian Fonds zur Förderung der wissenschaftlichen Forschung for granting me a two-year leave of absence for this research. The Charlotte Bühler-Habilitationsstipendium provided me with the financial support I needed for research, travels, and conferences. Thankfully, it also allowed me to work at my own pace without having to devote time to teaching or administration. With their support I was able to travel to Washington, D.C., and Nashville, Tennessee, for research and to attend conferences in Graz, Innsbruck, and Münster.

I thank the Institut für Anglistik und Amerikanistik at my home university in Salzburg for encouraging me in this project, writing letters of recommendation, and giving me space for a quiet withdrawal. I am much indebted to Leo Truchlar, who was dean of Humanities at that time, for his support and careful comments. I am also grateful to my colleagues at the Institut, Dorothea Steiner, Norbert Müller, Holger Klein, and Sabine Coelsch-Foisner. My colleagues from other disciplines, especially Elisabeth Schreiner, Gabriele Blaikner-Hohenwart, and Angela Birner, reassured me on this project every step of the way. I am indebted to Derek de Silva, incorruptible arbiter of literary quality. My thanks extend to Geoffrey Howes for invaluable advice. Without the help of Linda Reschen, expert reader, matchless stylist, and scrupulous copyreader, this manuscript would be in much worse shape.

I also thank Gudrun Grabher (University of Innsbruck) and Fritz Gysin (University of Bern) for the long and helpful reviews of the study. I wish to acknowledge my debt to the expertise of Nancy Grayson at the University of Georgia Press and her wonderfully competent editors Jon Davies, Jennifer Reichlin, and Daniel A. Simon. Many of their suggestions influenced the revision of the original manuscript.

Outside of Salzburg, I have found help at the Library of Congress and the

Moorland-Spingarn Research Center in Washington, D.C., the Fisk University Special Collections in Nashville, and Mugar Library in Boston. I give special credit to the expertise of Beth M. Howse at Fisk and Leida I. Torres at the Moorland-Spingarn Center. Help has been extended to me by John C. Johnson of the Special Collections department at Mugar Library and Alice Tucker of the Perkins Library, Duke University. The knowledgeable staff at the Salzburg University Library have been instrumental in facilitating access to the many books and articles I needed. I have also received funds from the Stiftungs- und Foerderungsgesellschaft der Paris-Londron-Universität Salzburg.

Special thanks go to my friends and colleagues from CAAR (Collegium for African American Research). Over the years, CAAR conferences have become to me important forums of communication, intellectual discourse, and stimulating talks. Maria Diedrich, Fritz Gysin, Justine Tally, Christopher Mulvey, Carl Pedersen, Giulia Fabi, Paul Spickard, Walter Hölbling, Clara Juncker, Geoff Pitcher, and many others have extended invaluable advice and encouragement. Ronald and Abby Johnson and John David Smith have helped with rare bibliographic items. At CAAR conferences, I have had the opportunity to present my ideas and defend my theses.

In the era of the Internet, e-mail correspondence has become vitally important as a source of information and a means of keeping in contact. The one message that turned out to be more important than any others was sent to me by John Cullen Gruesser, editor of the first collection about Hopkins. He offered his help and has never turned me down when I needed assistance. I thank him for reading the very first version of this book and sending it back with so many comments.

Many hours of writing were spent in my quiet attic in a busy household. It is my heart's desire here to include in my thanks five lovely children, all nearly of one age, who took over the kitchen and a lot of other chores so that I could be upstairs. And the most meaningful person always and ever continues to be Hans, unwavering in his loyalty and encouragement.

Earlier versions of parts of this study appeared as follows:
"Agitation in the Family: Charles W. Chesnutt's *The Marrow of Tradition* and Pauline E. Hopkins' *Contending Forces*," in *The Self at Risk in English Literature and Other Landscapes: Honoring Brigitte Scheer-Schäzler on the Occasion of Her Sixtieth Birthday*, ed. Gudrun M. Grabher and Sonja Bahn-Coblans (Innsbruck: Institut für Sprachwissenschaft, 1999), 61–73.

"Pauline E. Hopkins as Editor and Journalist: An African American Story of Success and Failure," in *Blue Pencils and Hidden Hands: Women Editing Periodicals, 1830–1910*, ed. Sharon M. Harris (Boston: Northeastern University Press, 2004), 263–98.

"Voyage into the Heart of Africa: Pauline Hopkins and *Of One Blood*," in *Black Imagination and the Middle Passage*, ed. Maria Diedrich, Henry Louis Gates Jr., and Carl Pedersen (New York: Oxford University Press, 1999), 203–14.

Pauline E. Hopkins

Introduction

On the first page of *Contending Forces: A Romance Illustrative of Negro Life North and South* (1900), the portrait of a beautiful and dignified Pauline Hopkins (1859–1930), one of the two pictures available to us, is inscribed "Yours for humanity." The author looks the reader directly into the eyes; her mien is serious, unsmiling, as was the custom of her time. The hat, decorated with ostrich feathers and a ribbon according to the fashion of her day, accentuates her stylish outfit, while her dark dress with the white collar that reaches up to her neck underlines the somberness and noble attitude. The reverse of this page of *Contending Forces* brings the reader right into the story. It is a picture, drawn by R. Emmett Owen, of the whipping scene from the book in which Grace Montfort lies on the ground in a puddle of blood with her back bare and marked by the lash, while one of her torturers looks down upon her, with one hand holding a whip and the other stuck in his waistband. His broad-brimmed black hat and his black leather boots emphasize his menacing attitude. The other man binds his whip into a hook, looking away from her as if wanting to demonstrate an utter negligence of the woman's pain. The caption of the drawing reads, "He cut the ropes that bound her, and she sank upon the ground again."

The photograph of the author and the engraving placed next to each other accentuate a duality between the present and the past, the African American author in her full right and the light-colored woman deprived of all her rights, the author who looks at you and talks to you and the woman whose face is turned away, who is powerless and dominated by the two men. The two images symbolize the passage of time from slavery to Boston at the turn of the century. The title page—with the full title, names of the author and illustrator, and date and place of publication—bears an epigraph by Ralph Waldo Emerson: "The civility of no race can be perfect whilst another race is degraded." Finally, the page preceding the table of contents bears a dedication: "To the Friends of Humanity Everywhere I offer this humble tribute written by one of a proscribed race." By identifying herself as "one of

1

Pauline E. Hopkins in her
feather hat on the first
page of *Contending Forces*
(1900), signed "Yours for
humanity, Pauline E. Hopkins."

a proscribed race," Hopkins clarifies her viewpoint right from the beginning. Her position is one of identification. She is one of the writers whose pen is, to use Anna Julia Cooper's phrase, "dipped in the life blood of their own nation." The literal flowing of blood from the woman's wounds highlights the "distinctive American note" of this thrilling story (*Voice from the South* 175, 224).

The creative writing of Pauline Elizabeth Hopkins is one of the most interesting rediscoveries of recent African American literary history. Virtually unknown for the better part of the twentieth century, Hopkins's remarkable achievements merit the revaluation and revisionism that characterizes so much of recent literary studies. Prompted by a desire to recover, republish, and make available to readers and critics the lost texts of literary history, the contemporary critic will find a rewarding subject in Hopkins. The concerns of Hopkins were the contending forces she alluded to in the title of her first novel. The difficult transition of the African American population from the time of slavery through Reconstruction into the twentieth century, the old strife between the North and the South, the legacy of the past, and the growing materialism and imperialism of the United States at the turn of the twentieth century were Hopkins's prime agenda. Her own fiction, journalism, historiography, and work as editor of the *Colored American Magazine* show

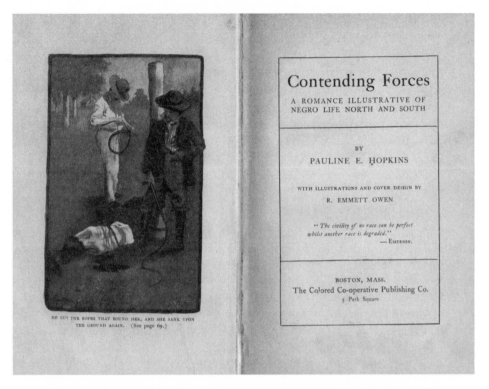

The title-page spread of *Contending Forces* (1900). The caption reads: "He cut the ropes that bound her, and she sank upon the ground again."

her to be passionately committed to righting the wrongs done to her race, investigating the past, and envisioning a better future.

Much of her fiction has been republished in the Schomburg Library of Nineteenth-Century Black Women Writers, under the general editorship of Henry Louis Gates Jr. In 1988 the Oxford University Press published in this series *Contending Forces: A Romance Illustrative of Negro Life North and South* (with an introduction by Richard Yarborough) and *The Magazine Novels of Pauline Hopkins* (with an introduction by Hazel V. Carby), which comprised her three serial novels: *Hagar's Daughter: A Story of Southern Caste Prejudice* (1901–2); *Winona: A Tale of Negro Life in the South and Southwest* (1902); and *Of One Blood; or, The Hidden Self* (1902–3). In 1991 the Oxford University Press reprinted seven of her short stories in *Short Fiction by Black Women, 1900–1920*, edited by Elizabeth Ammons. In addition, her play *Peculiar Sam;*

or, The Underground Railroad (1879) was included in *The Roots of African American Drama* (1991), edited by Leo Hamalian and James V. Hatch.

Pauline E. Hopkins: A Literary Biography is designed to be a comprehensive addition to the ever-increasing scholarship on Hopkins and is the first monograph devoted exclusively to her life and work. It contains groundbreaking new discoveries about her life, especially concerning her relations with famous men and women and the development of her thinking about race and class. It analyzes a set of letters recently discovered, letters that illuminate the role of Booker T. Washington with regard to the *Colored American Magazine*. It details the discovery of her writing under a pseudonym other than the known alias Sarah A. Allen. For the first time, her better-known novels and the texts that have so far received little attention are interpreted with an attempt to show continuities, similarities, and changes. Hopkins used elements of the sensational and sentimental novel, the melodrama, the western plot, and the tragic mulatto theme. She was an innovator in detective fiction. She was the first widely important African American editor, a biographer, and a playwright. She authenticated black speech patterns and presented new types of African American womanhood. With Elizabeth Ammons, we can now see that Hopkins, "far from being minor, flawed, or artistically incompetent, is one of the United States's great experimental novelists" ("Afterword" 213). This study also reprints *A Primer of Facts* (1905), a key text by the author that is extremely difficult to locate.

Hopkins's life, her literature, and her relations with black and white men and women are portrayed as negotiations, a term that implies issues of agreement and bargaining, of traveling over rough seas and terrain, and of completing or accomplishing what someone sets out to do. As an African American, Hopkins had to move through difficult territory; as a woman, she was often forced to achieve some kind of agreement. Above all, as a strong personality she certainly accomplished many of the things she set out to do. Hopkins had to negotiate her way, sometimes meekly, sometimes cunningly, but most often in a very outspoken and loud voice, across two centuries, and across boundaries and impediments that threatened to silence her. Her negotiations were not always successful (when she had to resign from her job as editor, for example), nor were they always completed (when she published her last novel only as a fragment, for example). Her failures and defeats were all the more bitter because she was honestly dedicated and passionately committed to her purposes: she never abandoned the hope that she would contribute to the progress of her race—the women of her race in particular—and to the improvement of America.

It is also enticing to consider the Latin origin of the word: *negotium* means "business" and is derived from *neg*, meaning "not" or denoting negation, and *otium*, meaning "leisure" (all uses of the word from *Webster's*). Despite the wide variety of their careers and choices in life, Hopkins, and with her a whole generation of African American women writers, would call themselves "not at leisure"; instead, they were restless, as Hopkins once said when she talked about the "resistless restlessness" of the "cultured intellect" ("Famous Women: Educators" 41). She had no leisure to let conditions be as they were; she and the women of her generation were writers, journalists, clubwomen, historians, teachers, and heads of households.

In my own understanding of literature, history, and literary history, Hopkins stands as much or as little for this time as many of the more famous writers and thinkers. There is simply no way to argue that a writer who left more records or was involved in more public offices or traveled more widely would represent his or her time or place more adequately than one who did not do so. It will always add to the understanding of gender, race, class, region, and period if the general aspect is explained through the particular and if so-called national issues are filtered through an individual experience. At the beginning of this study there was curiosity: curiosity to find out in the specific rather than the general how a woman's life was shaped along historical, social, racial, and literary lines. In an excellent article about William Wells Brown's novel *Clotel*, a novel that precedes Hopkins's *Contending Forces* by nearly half a century, Ann DuCille adequately describes her need to study this early African American novel: "*Clotel* remains a book in need of both reading and readings, an originary, enabling text in want of analysis and deep theorizing—perhaps in want even of a tradition" ("Where in the World" 451). Many recent critics, including myself, I would claim, have experienced a similar need to read Hopkins's novels, put them into some kind of tradition, and see them as texts in want of analysis and theorizing. Hopkins needs to be taken seriously as a political writer, a social critic, an influential editor, and a pioneer playwright and fiction writer. Her unconventional and manipulative voice was part of a tradition, her views and writings typical of her time and circumstances. This study is an effort to put Hopkins back into a context into which she belonged in the first place.

There are many possible ways of looking at the period between 1880 and 1920; many visions and angles provide useful insights. Movements and schools of criticism have always privileged one particular reading over another; often the choices were not based on conscious decisions to exclude or include certain groups and trends but were grounded in extraliterary motivations, such as the sociopolitical situation in general, cultural trends, demands of the marketplace, or developments in academia. As Stephen Greenblatt says in *Shakespearean Negotiations*, there is no "single, fixed, mode of exchange," because in fact "there are many modes, their character is determined historically, and they are continually renegotiated" (8). Initially, Greenblatt's investigations into the so-called minor figures of a given period and major texts from new perspectives led him to "look less at the presumed center of the literary domain than at its borders, to try to track what can only be glimpsed, as it were, at the margins of the text" (4). Eventually he developed a model for the analysis of texts valid for many cultures and periods. The movement Greenblatt instigated, new historicism, has made this study possible. Paying attention to modes of production, to political surroundings, to power structures, to see an author as an individual and at the same time as a product of collective exchange—these concerns have shaped my critical reading. A broad use of the term *negotiation* is useful in this context. It helps me through the texts across a century and over the Atlantic, and it always reminds me that, in the end, these are negotiations only and not conclusions or set and fixed answers that will "explain" the writer once and for all.

Information about the life of Hopkins continues to remain elusive. The available biographical data contain many blank spots, silences, and fragments of information. This book has been motivated in great part by a desire to discover more of the biography of Hopkins. In order to compensate for the lack of directly autobiographical material, her numerous journalistic pieces serve as indirect comment on the author's intellectual and literary development. Fortunately, her career as editor of Boston's *Colored American Magazine* from 1900 to 1904 can be documented quite fully, providing a key to the personality of Hopkins that would otherwise be sadly missing. From all available sources, I deem it safe to state that Hopkins led an uncommonly eventful and interesting life and that she was a woman of conspicuous significance in the Boston of her time.

Her life can be divided into three periods that result from her involvement in editing. The first part of this book, "Restlessness of the Spirit," focuses on the years from 1859 to 1900, the period in her life that set the tone for later accomplishments. "Background and Beginnings" treats her youth, her family background, her experiences as a pupil, her commitment to a career as singer and performer, and her experience in the 1890s as a stenographer. These years must be considered far more public and important than previously acknowledged. Her devotion to art and her involvement with famous men and women began early in life, and her touring of the country with the "Hopkins' Colored Troubadours" set the stage for later writing and activities. A discussion of *Peculiar Sam*, her stage drama first published in 1879, treats her interest in music and her commitment to stage performances and pays special attention to the phenomenon of minstrelsy.

Parts 2 and 3 of this study cover the years from 1900 to 1905, the most prolific time in her life. Part 2, "Negotiations in Race and Gender," deals with her public life as journalist, editor, writer, and political activist. In 1900 she began her career at the *Colored American Magazine*, which not only involved her in the business of magazine editing but also gave her a public voice as a journalist and allowed her to engage in the many issues of race and gender. After her dismissal from the magazine, she contributed to the *Voice of the Negro*, an Atlanta-based journal in which she published a five-part series, "The Dark Races of the Twentieth Century." In 1905 she self-published a historical treatise, *A Primer of Facts*.

The chapter devoted to the *Colored American Magazine* makes a comprehensive survey of her role at the magazine, of editorial politics, power struggles, and possible readers. It also shows in detail how the transition of the magazine under the indirect patronage of Booker T. Washington affected Hopkins's career. One discovery of my research about Hopkins's life is that she wrote under more pseudonyms than commonly acknowledged. Although it was known in her time that she wrote under her mother's name as Sarah A. Allen, it was not generally known that she also published a few articles under the name of J. Shirley Shadrach. This discovery and a close reading of the Allen/Shadrach/Hopkins essays raise questions about the use of pseudonyms in general and the purposes of this form of disguise.

Although Hopkins never gained a large national audience in the United States or elsewhere, her local fame in and around Boston provides access to a whole catalog of social, cultural, and political issues. One prominent example is her relationship to Booker T. Washington, one of the most influential race leaders of her time and a man who determined her career to a large degree. In the chapter "Booker T. Washington and Famous Men," I treat her dealings with "famous men of the Negro race," as she called one series of essays. Based upon a recently discovered set of letters, special emphasis is paid to the power play behind the scenes of the magazine, especially the role of John C. Freund, which eventually led to the relocation of the *Colored American Magazine* to New York. The focus is on Washington but also includes references to such famous race leaders as Frederick Douglass, William Wells Brown, W.E.B. Du Bois, and William Monroe Trotter. A treatment of Hopkins in relation to Booker T. Washington sheds as much light on the latter as on the former. It proves that if a period is seen from a perspective other than that of one of the allegedly great leaders, a novel way of looking at it unfolds. Hopkins evolves as an early African American woman whose feminist ideals sometimes collided with her race allegiance.

In a similar yet less controversial way, Hopkins interacted with a generation of women intellectuals, African American clubwomen, journalists, and creative writers such as Anna Julia Cooper, Gertrude B. Mossell, Ida B. Wells-Barnett, Josephine St. Pierre Ruffin, Fannie Barrier Williams, Mary Church Terrell, and Victoria E. Matthews. Hopkins's disappearance from literary history has damaged our historical understanding of a period that is now called the "Black Woman's Era" (also my chapter title) and encompasses the last twenty years of the nineteenth and first twenty years of the twentieth centuries. More than a generation of African American women writers produced numerous volumes of fiction, poetry, and essays; they were journalists, essayists, lecturers, historians, and educators. An analysis of this important era in the intellectual development of African American women sheds light on a period that empowered African American women to an unprecedented degree. At the same time, these women had to contend with the prevailing notions of the time that limited the sphere of the woman to the home more than to the public realm. They faced the antagonisms of white women and often those of black men in their negotiations as clubwomen, writers, teachers, and intellectuals. Hopkins was actively involved in and a contributor to the debates of her time.

Several of her journalistic pieces, especially her series in the *Voice of the Negro* and her self-published treatise *A Primer of Facts*, place Hopkins in the context of black cultural nationalism or Ethiopianism, with its religious optimism, its belief in the ancient glory of Egypt and Ethiopia, and its desire to instill race pride. The chapter "The Voices of the Dark Races" will analyze the scientific and historical context of her writing on race. Since Hopkins's *A Primer of Facts* is still largely unavailable to the interested reader, the appendix to this book reprints an annotated version of her 1905 text. Hopkins very often saw race in combination with class and treated the problem of labor and capitalism as equally important to the problem of race. There is sufficient evidence in her treatise and her race essays to claim that she was an early advocate of solidarity between the middle class and the working class.

Part 3, "Negotiations in Literature," concentrates on Hopkins as an author and provides an analysis of her novels and short stories in order to demonstrate their artistic value and their negotiations in issues of history, race, class, and gender. "The Values of Race Literature" shows Hopkins's involvement in the literature of her time. If we call Hopkins, as Elizabeth Ammons does, a "major, complex, serious American writer" ("Afterword" 211), then we have to justify this assessment by reading her literary achievements against the background of her time. This includes an examination of her interaction with a generation of writers and their discourse on the use and function of what they chose to call race literature: Anna Julia Cooper, Gertrude Mossell, Victoria Earle Matthews, and George Marion McClellan. When Ammons sees in her a writer who "borrows, innovates, invents, enjambs, and switches" (213), her position within the literary tradition and her deviation from that tradition have to be evaluated. As an innovator in detective fiction, as the first widely important African American woman editor, as biographer and playwright, the complexity and multiplicity of her talents must be taken into consideration and compared with the careers of her contemporaries.

When Hopkins published her first novel, *Contending Forces*, she set out to erase the "stigma of degradation" from her race (13). Neither her undertaking nor her style was entirely new, nor did they run totally against the literary grain of her time, but she aroused controversy with her type of race literature nevertheless, especially with the novels *Contending Forces*, *Hagar's Daughter*, *Winona*, and *Of One Blood*. Since she insisted that the occurrences she described were taken from real life, her novels became a criticism of past and contemporary race relations. The choice of light-colored heroines and her decision to write about very dark heroes and mixed-race villains also met with some criticism. Certainly, her combination of thrilling romance plots, sensational details, occasional veiled references to famous men and women of her time, and astute analysis of the political situation sparked the interest of her contemporary audience and fascinates readers even a hundred years later.

Four chapters of this study focus on the novels; each is organized around principles of negotiation and transition. Hopkins's main concerns are historiography, the discussion of the slave past and ancient Africa, and their legacy in the America of her time; the fate of the beautiful mixed-race woman; the heroism of her male characters, their manliness and civil courage; and ancient African glory and the future of race leadership.

Contending Forces, as discussed in "Contending Forces of the Slave Past," contains the transition in space from the West Indies to the United States and in time from the late eighteenth to the late nineteenth century. Synecdochal images—whipping for the slave past, lynching for contemporary Boston— stand in for a novel that combines middle-class aspirations with political ambitions and a sensational plot with realistic elements. The legacy of the past influences families and decisions and thus forms Hopkins's early concern in writing, a concern that governs most of her fiction. Racial issues fundamentally determine character and plot in all her novels. The chapter "Hagar's Beautiful Daughters" treats the figure of the mixed-race woman, a stock character in much of the literature of her time. Dramatic scenes of revelation are used as focal points for a discussion of the highly significant choice of this type of beautiful heroine, of melodramatic elements in Hopkins's fiction, of moral questions and tragic consequences. It will be shown that Hopkins decentered the tragic mulatta plot and envisioned new roles for her heroines. The same can be said about her male characters. When race is added to virtue and manliness, stereotypical roles have to be revised. "Winona, Manhood, and Heroism" concentrates on Hopkins's second serial novel and links the questions of manhood and heroism with considerations of race, color, and the international dimensions of slavery. "*Of One Blood* and the Future African American" deals with the last serial novel, *Of One Blood*, the only novel with a heroic mixed-race male character who passes for white. The plot moves from America to Africa and back again and contains the utopian setting of an underground empire. Although a great part of it is set in Africa, this can be seen as Hopkins's strategy of discursive displacement, her mode of displacing elements of plot, character, and setting to conceal her criticism of contemporary society.

Hopkins writes in *Contending Forces* about the rather well-to-do part of colored society in turn-of-the-century Boston or, in *Hagar's Daughter*, about the noble white society of Washington, D.C., in 1882, but at the same time she extends the romantic content of the novels into a discussion of a less exclusive part of society. Hopkins's careful balance between folk characters using black dialect and heroic characters using standard English shows her concern with the portrayal of an African American experience that is inclusive rather than exclusive. It also places Hopkins into a tradition of dialect writing, which even in her time elicited controversial views about the definition and role of race literature. The chapter "Folk Characters and Dialect Writing," therefore, concentrates on the various uses and different purposes of black dialect and folk characters in Hopkins's fiction.

Apart from the four novels, the short fiction constituted Hopkins's fame in her lifetime. Six stories were published in the *Colored American Magazine* from 1900 to 1903, and one later story appeared in the *New Era Magazine* in 1916. During the time of the magazine's existence, some fifty short stories were published altogether, enough to warrant the claim that there was a kind

of *Colored American Magazine* school of short-story writing that was decidedly influenced by Hopkins, as argued in my chapter "Short Stories in the
Colored American Magazine." Stories with related topics—such as Christmas
stories, stories about spiritual phenomena, dialect stories, and stories about
passing—constitute an organic whole. Hopkins contributed to all the topics
and probably initiated or encouraged the publication of many of the other
stories. An evaluation of her short fiction in the context of the general *Colored
American Magazine* canon is long overdue.

The years of Hopkins's prolific writing were numbered after she was
ousted from the *Colored American Magazine*. In 1905 her slow withdrawal
from the public began, and when she died in 1930, she was practically forgotten. Two chapters of part 4, "Voices and Silences," concentrate on the final
signs of her creativity and political activity. "On the Platform with Prominent Speakers" treats her public addresses in 1905 and 1911. "The *New Era
Magazine*" concentrates on her final attempts at publishing in 1916: her
fragmentary novel "Topsy Templeton" and "Converting Fanny," a story she
published as Sarah A. Allen.

Apart from the fact that she worked as a stenographer, there is scant information about her after 1916. "The Late Years" treats her fate as a neglected
and underrated writer who could not make herself heard in the Harlem
Renaissance, the period of a highly visible black presence in the arts, a fate
shared by many other African American writers of her generation. Although
they differ in relative fame and periods of productivity, Hopkins's career
can be compared to those of Charles W. Chesnutt, William Monroe Trotter,
Paul Laurence Dunbar, Alice Moore Dunbar-Nelson, Sutton E. Griggs, and
Anna Julia Cooper. All of them suffered—at some time in their lives and
in their reception as writers over the next one hundred years—from lapses
of visibility, neglect, or misreadings. Some examples from influential critics
are used in this chapter to show that changing times demanded a different
kind of literature and that Hopkins could not negotiate this transition. In
this context, Hopkins's life and career can be seen as typical rather than
exceptional.

This study would not have been possible without the groundbreaking work
of scholars and publishers in the field of African American studies from the
early 1970s onward. After *Contending Forces* was reprinted in a Mnemosyne
edition in 1968, the evaluation of Hopkins began to change with Ann Allen
Shockley's essay of 1972, entitled "Pauline E. Hopkins: A Biographical Excursion into Obscurity." She called her one of "the most neglected early black

women writers" and specified the biographical facts of her life (22), most of them based on an evaluation of the Hopkins Papers at Fisk University. This important archival work led to more and increasingly detailed biographical and bibliographical work. Shockley also included a chapter of *Contending Forces* and an extended biographical entry in her 1988 anthology and critical guide, *Afro-American Women Writers: 1746–1933.*

A further reprint of *Contending Forces* in 1978 by the Southern Illinois University Press shows the prominence of this text over her other work. The 1978 reprint was part of a series entitled Lost American Fiction and contained an afterword by the renowned poet Gwendolyn Brooks. This afterword and a review of the novel in the journal *Callaloo* show, however, that the time was still not ripe for a radical new reading of Hopkins. Writing in the wake of *Native Son, Invisible Man, Jubilee,* and *Roots,* Brooks calls her "not indignant enough," although she recognizes that "black fury invaded her not seldom and not softly." She grants her the right to voice her concerns in the manner of her time: "If she has not chosen from her resources words and word jointures that could make changes in the world, she has given us a sense of her day, a *clue* collection, and we can use the light of it to clarify our understanding and our intuition" (404). Still, she remonstrates her for proving herself "a continuing slave, despite little bursts of righteous heat" (405). Brooks takes special offense at the depiction of light-colored heroines and Hopkins's references to the higher race and Anglo-Saxon superiority. She objects to the narrative voice in the text, clearly associated with the author's opinion, which has aroused, as this study will show, much antagonism in other readers as well. Whereas, for many readers of her time, Hopkins went too far in her condemnation of past wrongs and present injustice, for Brooks and many of her generation, she did not go far enough. To do justice to Brooks, she recognizes that "only the squeaky wheel gets the grease of notice and empathy from the preoccupied, obsessed, self-honeying, self-crowned Editors of our world" (408).

During the next ten years the scenery changed significantly. *Contending Forces* and the serial novels were republished along with many other texts by women of this period. Lois Brown wrote an excellent doctoral dissertation that added many biographical details; influential studies by Nellie Y. McKay, Claudia Tate, Elizabeth Ammons, Hazel V. Carby, Ann DuCille, and several others included Hopkins in their analyses and set her into a wide variety of contexts.

A good example of this shift of paradigms is a comparative reading of Claudia Tate's "Pauline Hopkins: Our Literary Foremother" of 1985 and her

Domestic Allegories of Political Desire of 1992. In between these two dates, the Schomburg Library of Nineteenth-Century Black Women Writers published the three serial novels and *Contending Forces* and thus made these texts, especially the serial novels, widely available and visible. Tate can be credited in great part as being responsible for a revisionary look at Hopkins and her generation. Grounded in a feminist literary movement that challenged basic assumptions of literary criticism and questioned the validity of individual texts, genres, and a predominantly male-based and race-conscious canon, Tate sets out to evaluate the writings of Hopkins against her own social context, against a tradition of black women writers and the white sentimental and domestic novels (see "Pauline Hopkins" 56). She radically changes the interpretation of such a character as Sappho Clark in *Contending Forces*—who had had to take so much criticism because of her skin color, her middle-class values, and adherence to a strict moral code of white behavior—when she writes: "Her most important role, however, is not that of the 'tragic mulatto' but that of Hopkins's spokeswoman for the political rights of black Americans" (58). Finally taking Hopkins as a serious writer, she sees as her key message that "black men and women must be responsible for the course of their own advancement and that duty, virtue, carefully controlled emotions, the institution of marriage, and the vote are the key components for directing social progress and achieving results" (59). Yet in 1985 she still sees *Winona* as an "exercise in nostalgia" and "essentially an escapist, melodramatic romance" (61) and discusses *Of One Blood* in its "even more limited contexts," although it is an "extremely intriguing, imaginative, and provocative novel" (62).

Between the late 1970s and early 1990s, critics and historians, too numerous to include them here by name, wrote about the melodrama, the local-color/regionalist movement, the sentimental and domestic novel, the utopian novel, the detective plot, the romance, the African American women's club movement, and many other subjects revolving around a revision of the existing canon. In 1992 Tate could thus draw upon a large array of critical texts in general and the republication of key texts by African American women writers of the period between 1890 and 1920 in particular. The works of Frances Watkins Harper, Amelia E. Johnson, Emma Dunham Kelley-Hawkins, Katherine D. Tillman, Victoria Earle Matthews, Anna Julia Cooper, and Alice Moore Dunbar-Nelson proved particularly interesting for "close textual readings, cultural critique, and discourse analysis" of a new body of texts (*Domestic Allegories* 5). Reading eleven texts by Harper, Hopkins, Johnson, Kelley, and Tillman "against the cultural history of the epoch

of their production," Tate attempted to recover "much of the cultural meaning, values, expectations, and rituals of African Americans of that era, which
are symbolically embedded in these black Victorian love stories." Reading
Tate from the vantage point of more than a decade later, there is a kind of
relief that someone finally did justice to these writers and that old critical
opinions about them could be rephrased and thus critically challenged:

> These writers repeatedly wrote novels about the moral development, spiri-
> tual maturation, professional aspirations, and economic advancement of and
> of course social justice for black Americans. They inscribed these pursuits
> within the familiar marriage plot of nineteenth-century white women's senti-
> mental fiction, transforming that plot into the story of racialized, ideal-family
> (re)formation. Even in those instances when the racial designation of the char-
> acters was effaced to some degree, the author's racial identity or black cultural
> markers indirectly racialized the story. (11)

Only a "historicized interpretative model," Tate argues, will rescue these
texts from critical neglect (19). Although the reader might have noticed a
slight tone of reserve about Hopkins's serial novels, Tate's analysis of them
in the later full-length study is based on radically different parameters:

> Like *Hagar's Daughter, Winona* and *Of One Blood* also evolve as tests of true
> love; however, these latter serials are more explicit racial polemics although
> cast in highly symbolic format. Hopkins again relied on the popularity of the
> formula novels to entertain her readers with adventure and intrigue, while
> she manipulated the plot to incite the reader's sympathy for the virtuous mu-
> latta heroine and scorn for those harboring racist viewpoints who threaten
> the heroine's happiness. Rather than transparently reveal her frustration with
> the increasingly hostile racial climate of her era, Hopkins again depended on
> discursive displacements. (200)

The rather detailed presentation of Tate's viewpoint does not imply that other
critics did not contribute in large part to this shift in paradigms, but it is meant
to be taken as exemplary. Within the past few years, the MLA bibliography has
listed about forty dissertations that include Hopkins in their title. John Cullen
Gruesser edited *The Unruly Voice: Rediscovering Pauline Elizabeth Hopkins* in
1996, a collection of critical essays that can be taken as representative of new
possible ways of looking at her.

In the future, it is highly probable that the criticism of Hopkins's other
serial novels, short stories, and playwriting will increase. The ground has
been prepared by Elizabeth Ammons and Martha M. Patterson on *Winona*

and Claire Pamplin on *Hagar's Daughter*. When Janet Gabler-Hover wrote *Dreaming Black/Writing White: The Hagar Myth in American Cultural History*, one of the surprising facts about this well-researched book is that Hopkins's novel was her starting point. She read *Hagar's Daughter* first and then began to look for other Hagar texts, which in itself is a sign of the far-reaching consequences of revisionist readings.

Analyses of Hopkins's fiction are included in the studies of Ammons, Carby, Gruesser, Soitos, Sollors, Sundquist, Tate, and others. The comparative treatment of Hopkins and other writers in the many dissertations shows that, within two decades, the negotiations between Hopkins and her critics have become one of inclusion rather than exclusion. Her work is included in nearly all major anthologies and literary histories published after the early 1980s. One more example is sufficient to prove that today an interested scholar can find references to Hopkins under subjects largely unheard of before. In the recent *Oxford Companion to African American Literature*, Hopkins has her own entries under her name and under *Contending Forces* and receives extensive treatment under *Colored American Magazine*. Apart from this, she is also referenced under the following headings: black aesthetic, black female detective character, black nationalist novel, double consciousness, forms of address, magazine fiction, mulatto character, musical, novel, short stories, speculative fiction elements, strong female protagonists, violence against blacks, and Women's Era Club.

As these possible new approaches show, negotiations concerning the life and literature of Pauline E. Hopkins are not finished by any means. A comprehensive anthology of all her nonfiction writing, for example, would be most helpful. New angles of vision are being opened at conferences and in scholarly collections and journals. Hopkins has been made part of the canon of African American literature.

Restlessness of the Spirit
1859-1900

Hopkins's mother was a descendant of Nathaniel and Thomas Paul, who founded Baptist churches in Boston at the beginning of the nineteenth century. Thomas Paul's niece was Susan Paul, a notable Boston female reformer, life member of the Massachusetts Anti-Slavery Society, organizer of the Garrison Junior Choir, and temperance worker (Horton, *Free People* 45). Her great-uncle James Monroe Whitfield was born in Exeter, New Hampshire, in 1822. It is believed that he was a descendant of Ann Paul, sister of Rev. Thomas Paul of Exeter. His sister was Mrs. Elizabeth P. Allen, whose daughter Annie Pauline Pindell became a famous singer. From the available sources it is not entirely clear whether this Mrs. Elizabeth P. Allen is the same Elizabeth B. Whitfield Allen, the grandmother of Pauline Hopkins. If true, the singer Annie Pauline Pindell would be her aunt. Whitfield was an ardent supporter of Martin R. Delany's colonization project in the 1850s. By profession he was a barber, but he has survived as a poet of protest against racism and a writer of antiracist propaganda.[2]

Whitfield's second cousin was the poet Elijah William Smith (1830–95), whom Hopkins profiles in the December 1902 issue of the *Colored American Magazine*. She calls him "emphatically a race man" ("Elijah William Smith" 99). He was a one-time apprentice at Garrison's *Liberator*, later became the organizer of the Progressive Musical Union, and wrote a number of poems. Hopkins identifies him as the second son of Elijah and Ann Paul Smith, the famous Susan Paul's sister. Again she emphasizes the political, religious, and educational excellence of the Paul family: "The Paul brothers were educated in England and returned to this country to preach. They were all Baptist ministers, very eloquent and forceful in the pulpit" (97).[3] Elijah William Smith's sister was Mrs. Susan Paul Vashon, wife of George Boyer Vashon, an early African American abolitionist poet (Jackson 241–43).

Although the information in the biographical sketch highlights her remarkable ancestry and establishes an indirect link with the famous abolitionist leaders William Lloyd Garrison and Frederick Douglass, it does not give the name of her mother. Ann Allen Shockley, Dorothy Porter, and Lois Brown identify her as Sarah Allen, and she may have been only fourteen years of age when she gave birth to Pauline (L. Brown, "Essential Histories" 26). The writer Pauline Hopkins later paid tribute to her mother by using her name as her pen name. Her ancestry on her mother's side sets her firmly into a northern background and a family line that distinguished itself through religious, abolitionist, and literary prominence. The Paul family and their descendants were certainly a famous Boston family. Family connections, at that time, were as important to an African American as they were to white people and paved the way for her in many regards.[4]

There are also parallels between her own family past and that of the Smith family that she uses in her first novel, *Contending Forces*. The parents of her mother's father may have been Jessie Allen of Bermuda and Elizabeth B. Whitfield of Exeter, New Hampshire. In *Contending Forces*, the fugitive slave Jesse Montfort marries Elizabeth Whitfield, who lives in that same place. This is the most prominent example of the writer Hopkins trying to incorporate her own family history into her fiction. Later examples include her heroine Winona's disguise under the name of Allen Pinks in her novel *Winona* and the white character in her fragmentary novel *Topsy Templeton*, who bears the name of Mrs. Elizabeth Hopkins-Templeton. In the July 1903 issue of the *Colored American Magazine*, the "Editorial and Publishers' Announcements" advertise a portrait of Toussaint L'Ouverture, described as a "rare oil painting" (547), that was brought from the island about 1806 and was the property of Mr. William A. Hopkins, Pauline's father or stepfather. This can be seen as corroborating evidence of the Bermuda origin of the Allen side of her family.

There is some inconsistency as to the name and identity of her father. The biographical sketch names as her father "William A. Hopkins, a G.A.R. veteran of the Civil War, . . . a native of Alexandria, Va., . . . a nephew of the late John T. Waugh of Providence, R.I., and a first cousin of the late Mrs. Ann Warrick Jarvis of Washington, D.C." (218). Lois Brown assumes that this was her stepfather, whom her mother married when Pauline was about eighteen years old. On her death certificate her father's name is given as Northup, and he might have been William A. Hopkins's brother (L. Brown, "Essential Histories" 26). William A. Hopkins obviously fought in the Civil War in the Grand Army of the Republic ("G.A.R. veteran") and later migrated to Boston from Virginia, thus joining many other African Americans seeking a better life in Boston.[5]

Despite this somewhat obscure information, it can be proven that Pauline called herself Pauline E. Allen in her youth. For example, she signed her early play "One Scene from the Drama of Early Days," which treats the biblical story of Daniel in the lions' den, as "Pauline E. Allen." In 1879, however, she copyrighted the original version of *Peculiar Sam; or, The Underground Railroad*, a musical drama, under the name of Pauline E. Hopkins.[6] It can therefore be concluded that her mother kept her own maiden name of Allen up to some time before 1879, when she married William A. Hopkins and changed it to Hopkins. The conclusion from this that Pauline was born out of wedlock is plausible but cannot be substantiated. The names of both Sarah H. Hopkins and William Hopkins appear frequently on the playbills announcing and advertising "P. E. Hopkins' Colored Troubadours," a group of performers that toured the American North in the 1880s. Through her father's or her stepfather's side, Hopkins, despite her birth and education in the North, had a link to the American South and the slave past that later served as the subject of much of her fiction.

There is a strange reluctance on the part of the older Pauline Hopkins to spell out her relationships with famous people. In her article about Elijah W. Smith, she does not mention her family ties with him. In the "Phenomenal Vocalists" part of her "Famous Women of the Negro Race" series, she does not refer to her relationship to the great singer Annie Pauline Pindell. And when, in the same article, she writes about the Hyers sisters, she does not point out that they participated in her program at one time. It is difficult to account for this reluctance on her part. Hopkins was obviously proud of her family background but did not feel it proper to go into details about her immediate parental lineage. When she wrote this sketch, both her mother and father were still alive, and she had to be considerate of them. Most likely, given the self-confidence that she had as member of the *Colored American Magazine* staff, she wanted to be judged by her achievements and not only by her family background.

Early in her life the family moved to Boston, where she spent most of her life. The young Pauline attended public schools in Boston and graduated from Boston Girls' High School. At six years of age, Pauline must have witnessed the salute of a hundred guns and the ringing of church bells celebrating the passage of the Thirteenth Amendment by the House of Representatives on January 31, 1865 (Daniels 87). The date of her birth linked Hopkins to a nation divided on the question of slavery and on the brink of a civil war, while the place of her birth saved her from the immediate constraints and hardships of slavery, that "peculiar institution."

In 1850 Boston had a population of about 130,000 people, among them only about 2 percent African Americans. It was a thriving city, a financial, political, social, and cultural center of the North (Collison 61).[7] For African Americans Boston was the center of white abolitionism, the home of such famous figures as William Lloyd Garrison, Charles Sumner, and Wendell Phillips. An atmosphere of liberalism helped establish a firmly united African American community that produced leaders who were recognized throughout the nation. Boston became a relatively safe place for escaped slaves even after the passing of the Fugitive Slave Act in 1850 that allowed the capture of escaped slaves in the northern free states. According to Gary Collison, the story of the fugitive slave Shadrach Minkins, whose recapture by his former owner aroused widespread legal and social activity among free blacks and liberal white Bostonians, proves how effective and determined were the efforts of both white and black leaders to shelter slaves and protect them.

Adelaide Hill Cromwell states that between 1830 and 1870 the common cause of abolitionism brought about a closeness between whites and African Americans that gave rise to the myth of Boston as an ideal and model city for race relations. Although, as she argues, this was an illusion in many cases, numerous issues that were raised and resolved in Boston set the standard for action elsewhere. The issues were segregation, the efforts of the American Colonization Society, and the fugitive slaves (Cromwell 39–40). Later issues included equal rights in education, housing, and restaurants as well as the overriding concern of voting rights. Many of the black leaders who gained prominence in the years before emancipation served as role models for later generations and as exemplary figures in later historiography, including Pauline Hopkins's series about famous African American men and women. Frederick Douglass and Charles Lenox Remond visited Boston often and inspired its abolitionist sentiment. Certainly Hopkins was acquainted in a general sense with many other notable African Americans. Her ancestors, the Paul family, James Whitfield, and Elijah W. Smith were part of this tradition of resistance and activism.

Boston's African American population doubled in size from 8,215 in 1890 to 16,350 in 1920. As Mark Schneider points out in *Boston Confronts Jim Crow*, a study in which much background information is provided, this was still an insignificant portion of the national African American population, the majority of which lived in the South. From the 1890s onward this community inhabited the north and west slopes of Beacon Hill and the South End and Lower Roxbury districts. In 1920 about half of the city's African American population lived in South End's Ward 13 (Schneider 4–5).

Cromwell enumerates the positive and negative aspects of race relations in Boston between the Civil War period and the early 1900s. She sees business achievements and political gains immediately after the war as positive. On the negative side, she lists the frequently token Negro participation in public affairs, the lack of unity resulting from the loss of the common cause that the antislavery movement had provided before the Civil War, and the absence of a substantial radical protest movement. By the end of the century, Cromwell argues, "the problems of a deteriorating economic position, a weakened political voice, and adjusting to foreign- and southern-born immigrants created formidable strains in the Negro upper strata" (64).

In May 1904 the *Colored American Magazine* reprinted an article from the *Boston Sunday Herald* called "Boston as the Paradise of the Negro." In it four prominent African Americans were interviewed about the advantages of living in Boston. They were William H. Lewis, assistant United States district attorney and one of the most prominent African Americans of the time; James H. Wolff, lawyer and vice-commander of the Department of Massachusetts, G.A.R.; the Reverend Dr. J. H. Henderson, pastor of the A.M.E. Church on Charles Street; and J. H. Lewis, tailor and businessman. All four emphasized the climate of liberalism, the good understanding between the races, the relative freedom from segregation in Boston, and the general absence of a race problem. All of them, however, also pointed out that the industrial status (i.e., employment opportunities) was far from ideal and that only a few African Americans had been appointed to political positions. Around the turn of the century, Boston had about 11,500 African Americans, constituting about 2 percent of the population, which was about the same percentage as fifty years before (Thernstrom 179).

Despite the obvious discrimination she and her fellow African Americans had to contend with, Hopkins comes out as a fervent admirer of New England. In *Contending Forces*, Sappho Clark, a stenographer with southern origins, talks about the "liberty-loving community," and the narrator comments upon the advantages of living in this city: "Here in the free air of New England's freest city, Sappho drank great draughts of freedom's subtle elixir" (115). But Sappho Clark also talks about the problems she had in finding adequate employment. John Daniels titled *In Freedom's Birthplace* his 1914 study about Boston's African American population. He highlights the vital role of the Boston African Americans in the antislavery movement and discusses the social, religious, and political roles of Boston African Americans after the Civil War. In his analysis of the economic situation, he notes with regret the largely menial occupations they were able to find.

Hopkins calls out, for example, at the end of the second installment of her series about educators in "Famous Women of the Negro Race": "May my tongue cleave to the roof of my mouth and my right hand forget its cunning when I forget the benefits bestowed upon my persecuted race by noble-hearted New England" ("Famous Women: Educators [Continued]" 130). Pauline Hopkins lived most of her adult life in the Boston area, and her short relocation to New York City with the *Colored American Magazine* may have failed in part because of her deep rootedness in Boston.

In the late nineteenth century, Boston was renowned for its radical activism, a general frame of mind grounded in the proud memory of an antislavery past, of resistance toward segregation, and a tradition in self-organization.

Economic needs and a growing sense of danger coming from Jim Crow laws contributed to feelings of anger and protest and motivated many promi-nent African American families in a continuing spirit of rebellion (Schneider 1–26).

A tradition of radical activism centered in and around Boston went back to David I. Walker's *Appeal* in 1829, his uncompromising call to arms against the system of slavery. John Brown, whose life inspired Hopkins's novel *Winona*, received much support from Boston abolitionists. Lewis Hayden and Robert Morris risked jail for their help in freeing Shadrach Minkins. And Hop-kins's contemporary William Monroe Trotter, editor of the colored *Guardian*, continued the tradition of radical politics into the twentieth century. The histories and deeds of these public men were certainly known to Hopkins, whose articles display a wide knowledge of national and local history. They formed her own character, especially in her relationship to the more ac-commodationist attitude of Booker T. Washington, and became part of her writing. In a 1905 speech that she gave at the William Lloyd Garrison Cen-tennial in Boston's Faneuil Hall, she sets herself firmly in this tradition of New England activism, saying: "Yesterday, I sat in the old Joy Street church and you can imagine my emotions as I remembered my great grandfather begged in England the money that helped the Negro cause, that my grandfather on my father's side, signed the papers with Garrison at Philadelphia. I remem-bered that at Bunker Hill my ancestors on my maternal side poured out their blood. I am a daughter of the Revolution, you do not acknowledge black daughters of the Revolution, but we are going to take that right" (*Guardian*, 16 Dec. 1906, 4). Although she does not identify the ancestors she is talking about, this statement not only highlights her feminism but also proves the argument that she felt herself to be part of, through ancestry, the noble men and women about whom she wrote. As she writes in an article about Robert Morris: "We delight to honor the great men of our race because the lives of these noble Negroes are tongues of living flame speaking in the powerful silence of example, and sent to baptize the race with heaven's holy fire into the noble heritage of perfected manhood" ("Famous Men: Morris" 337).

Pauline Hopkins's writing started with the essay that she submitted for the contest sponsored by William Wells Brown and the Congregational Publish-ing Society of Boston. "Evil of Intemperance and Their Remedies" is one of the few items by the young Hopkins at the Fisk University Library Special Collections. The fifteen-year-old schoolgirl calls intemperance "the many headed serpent, whose poison fangs none can escape if once they become entangled" (box 1, folder 2, 7). Firmly grounded in the pro-temperance movement, Hopkins here echoes one of the main concerns of the black women's club movement that saw drunkenness as a sign of public disgrace. While she admonishes the father of a family to be upright and honest, she places the greatest duty on the mother, whose motherhood is a "monument of woman's holiest mission" and whose duty it is "ever to urge her children on, to the goal of rest and peace" (11). A seriousness of purpose, considerable writing skills, and an essential longing for a happy home life that might reflect a more general public welfare distinguish this early essay.

There is no known record that Hopkins went to college after she had grad-uated from the prestigious Boston Girls' High School. We cannot determine just how much of a grievance it was to a gifted woman like Hopkins that the necessary means were probably unavailable to pay for a college education, but her journalism gives a hint of that sentiment. Hopkins talks about the "resistless restlessness" of the "cultured intellect" that seeks out "the intri-cate laws of Nature" and "penetrates the form and passes the boundaries seeking the First Principle" of all "matter already formed and boundaries set" ("Famous Women: Educators" 41). In this she echoes the thoughts of her contemporary Anna Julia Cooper, who remembers her longing for a substantial and classical training: "I had devoured what was put before me, and, like Oliver Twist, was looking around to ask for more. I constantly felt (as I suppose many an ambitious girl has felt) a thumping from within unanswered by any beckoning from without" (*A Voice from the South* 76). She demanded money and scholarships for young African American girls to encourage them in obtaining higher education.

By far the largest part of her series "Famous Women of the Negro Race" contains three installments about educators. Apart from discussions about home life and the church, education is the most frequent topic in public discourse to test individual worth, public achievement, gender roles, and racial progress. The African American woman who wanted to succeed in obtaining a good education had to face many odds. The greatest problem for her was the legacy of the slave past, in which the slave was classified as a brute so that the benefits of education could be denied to him. To control the slaves, the masters had to prevent literacy because it led so often to liberty. After emancipation, brave and courageous educators often needed to fight racism, lack of money, and personal danger in their attempts to teach the colored race. For African Americans around the turn of the century, education was a sure path to middle-class status and a proof of the race's intellectual abilities.

In the second installment of this series, Hopkins discusses, for example, the life and career of Miss Maria Louise Baldwin, who was a teacher and later principal of the Louis Agassiz School at Cambridge. She mentions Baldwin's longing to be given an "opportunity" to prove her worth, an opportunity that came rarely to colored women of her time. In 1882, when Miss Baldwin was appointed a teacher, this moment gave her "the fulcrum, the one thing demanded by humanity—opportunity" (127). Hopkins continues in the vein that was influenced by her own life story: "Without this [opportunity], aspiration and ability may be said to resemble 'silent thunder'; youthful and unknown, deprived of opportunity, genius is baffled and sinks to earth never to realize its 'noble aspirations' " ("Famous Women: Educators [Continued]" 127). As before, when she speaks about exemplary lives, the case of Miss Baldwin inspires hope and shows African American civilization moving into a higher realm of esteem in the world's view. At times Hopkins sounds slightly defensive about the value of education being measured by college degrees. In her article about Lewis Hayden, she mentions his lack of formal training and adds: "But what of that? We have lived to prove the truth of the aphorism: Great minds are not made in schools" (473).

It is highly significant that the young Pauline Hopkins, at about the age of twenty, chose to enter the entertainment world rather than continue her formal education in college. In *What a Woman Ought to Be and to Do: Black Professional Women Workers during the Jim Crow Era*, Stephanie J. Shaw has investigated the lives of about eighty professional African American women between the 1880s and the 1950s. In one chapter, Shaw discusses schooling and especially the strict codes of behavior and dress, the moral and domestic teaching that schools and colleges offered to young black women in their efforts to develop leadership qualities and exemplary status. It is important to see that college training in the 1880s, as Shaw's study shows, would have pressed the young Hopkins more than any family background into a frame of moral thinking, decent behavior, and community-oriented conduct that was deemed proper for educated African American women. It can be safely assumed that her life as a playwright and performer and especially her popularity and success on the stage encouraged the development of a firm personality, a certain unconventionality, and above all her outspokenness about the rights of African Americans and the rights of women in particular.

There is no evidence, however, that her life as entertainer precluded an adherence to good manners, high morality, and basic Christian values. It would be an exaggeration to see the young Hopkins as some kind of bohème or minstrel type. Judging from the character portrayals in her fiction and her essays about the women's club movement, Hopkins thought highly of morals and manners and believed that individual effort should be conducive to community aims and not to personal advancement. Shaw's observation that the women whose records she studied were taught that privilege (in education, manners, wealth) always imposed responsibility upon those not so well-off can certainly be verified in Hopkins's life and career (91).

Performances and "Peculiar Sam"

*W*hile most studies of Hopkins so far have concentrated on her four novels, a few of the short stories, and the journalism, any in-depth analysis of her development as a writer is incomplete without an interpretation of her play *Slaves' Escape; or, The Underground Railroad*, later renamed *Peculiar Sam; or, The Underground Railroad*. A look at *Peculiar Sam*, as the play is now commonly referred to, entails references to Hopkins's interest in music and her background in theater, especially minstrelsy and musical drama. This text also invites general considerations of the legacy of William Wells Brown and Harriet Beecher Stowe in her writing. A discussion of this play and its literary and sociocultural contexts necessitates, therefore, an exploration of the negotiations and exchanges that shaped the career of the young writer.

By describing Hopkins's background in music and the stage, it is possible to set her later career into an earlier context. When she chose a form of publicity geared to a mass audience, she demonstrated her venturesome spirit and consideration for the public taste. This part of her life foreshadows the stages in her later career as journalist, editor, and writer of short stories and serial novels, all of which are connected to another mass medium. It can be shown that although she wrote within a tradition, she impressed her own half-beat on it.

Hopkins's affinity for music is shown in various aspects of her biography and writing. In her "Phenomenal Vocalists" essay of November 1901, she extols the divine power of music: "Music is one of the very elements of the soul and voice, implanted by an all-wise Creator, part of our God-given nature—sign—manual of the universal kinship of all races" ("Famous Women: Phenomenal Vocalists" 46). She emphasizes the unifying genius of musical talent that is not confined to the educated and white part of the population. She is also one of the early writers who claim that African American music is America's most original contribution to world music: "The genius of music, supposed to be the gift of only the most refined and intellectual of

30

the human family, sprang into active life among the lowly tillers of the soil and laborers in the rice swamps of the South. The distinguishing feature of Negro song is its pathos and trueness to nature. It is the only original music of America, and since emancipation has become a part of the classical music of the century" (46).

One of the most prominent examples of her predilection for music is found in the second chapter of her novel *Of One Blood*. Reuel Briggs, full of dark thoughts and negative feelings, is taken to a concert of the Fisk Jubilee Singers. The group is introduced by the narrator: "A band of students from Fisk University were touring the country, and those who had been fortunate enough to listen once to their matchless untrained voices singing their heart-breaking minor music with its grand and impossible intervals and sound combinations, were eager to listen again and yet again" (450). Although Hopkins's narrator was certainly mistaken in assuming that their voices were untrained, she captured very well the fascination these singers, who were taken to represent the potential inherent in a recently emancipated race, exerted on their audiences. As it is later said about them, "These were representatives of the people for whom God had sent the terrible scourge of blood upon the land to free from bondage" (452). Their outstanding musical talent, the beauty of their voices, and their repertoire of spirituals and concert music kept the audiences rapt. It was a fascination arising from the combination of the historical legacy of these singers as descendants of slaves and their artistic superiority.

Reluctantly, Reuel Briggs is drawn into a mood of expectancy when the choir begins the concert. The fame of its soloist preceded her, as is shown in the adoration of Reuel's colleagues who had heard her before. When Dianthe Luske sings "Go Down, Moses," the audience listens breathlessly: "There fell a voice upon the listening ear, in celestial showers of silver that passed all conceptions, all comparisons, all dreams; a voice beyond belief—a great soprano of unimaginable beauty, soaring heavenward in mighty intervals." Reuel is "dazed, thrilled." Some people in the audience weep: "Spell-bound they sat beneath the outpoured anguish of a suffering soul. All the horror, the degradation from which a race had been delivered were in the pleading strains of the singer's voice. . . . It pictured to that self-possessed, highly-cultured New England assemblage as nothing else ever had, the awfulness of the hell from which a people had been happily plucked" (453–54).

A description such as this was certainly typical of the time, when the Fisk Singers had acquired national fame. The predominantly black Fisk University in Nashville, Tennessee, was founded in 1866. As music historian Eileen

Southern recounts, the first concert of Fisk students took place in 1867 in Nashville, and soon after George L. White, a young white teacher, took the group on a singing tour in order to raise money for the university. Their nationwide reputation was made in 1872 during the World Peace Jubilee in Boston. Patrick Sarsfield Gilmore organized a chorus of twenty thousand singers and an orchestra of two thousand instrumentalists. Johann Strauss the younger was invited to direct the huge orchestra in the "Blue Danube Waltz." On the sixth day of the festival the Fisk Jubilee Singers attracted the attention during a rendition of "The Battle Hymn of the Nation," as Eileen Southern reports from contemporary sources:

> The local black chorus was to sing the verses of the song and the rest of the choral forces were to come in on the refrains. The orchestra began on too high a pitch, however, and the opening verses were a "painful failure." The Fisk Singers sprang to their rescue; singing out strongly with their well-trained voices, they easily reached the high notes. . . .
>
> The reputation of the Fisk Jubilee Singers was made! They went on to sing at places in the United States that had never before heard folk music of black America, before crowned heads of Europe, and before the common people in Germany, Switzerland, and Great Britain. Everywhere the Singers "carried their audiences by storm" and won acclaim from the critics. (*The Music* 229)

Hopkins was thirteen years old in 1872. It can be safely assumed that she was either present at this festival or that she heard about it at school or in her family. Later Hopkins was called "Boston's Favorite Colored Soprano" (Hopkins Papers, box 1, folder 11), which proves her own reputation as a singer.[1] Given the musical record in her family—her mother's sister was a professional singer and her mother performed with her on the stage—this festival may have given her an early impetus to pursue her later career as singer and playwright. After graduating from Boston Girls' High School, she spent the formative years of her youth in the entertainment world.

An evaluation of the single surviving early play, *Peculiar Sam; or, The Underground Railroad*, makes much more sense when Hopkins's personal and musical backgrounds are both taken into consideration. In the latter part of the nineteenth century, groups like the Fisk Jubilee Singers stood in competition with the predominant commercial minstrel groups. The performance of white entertainers in blackface dated from the 1830s, when Dan Rice performed the comic act "Jump Jim Crow." For more than sixty years minstrel performances enjoyed immense popularity because of dance numbers, jokes, catchy tunes, and the stereotypical portrayals of the comic darky, the ridiculous urban dandy, or the faithful but naïve Uncle Tom. A typical show consisted of four, five, or sometimes more white male performers with blackened faces who performed songs, some performances ("comic dialogues, malapropistic 'stump speeches,' cross-dressed 'wench' performances"), and some narrative, which were usually set in the South (Lott 5). Characteristically, the performers moved with shuffling feet and rolled their eyes, and their lips were painted to appear grotesquely huge. The Negro characters they played usually had to steal chickens and watermelons, were afraid of the dark, ghosts, or graveyards, and they generally showed only a minimum of intelligence and frequently mispronounced words for comic effect.

Whereas in later years many critics rejected minstrelsy as racial discrimination because of the stereotypical characters (see Toll; Huggins, *Harlem Renaissance* 11), today there are also those who see a mutual enrichment of white and African American culture through minstrelsy. Eric Lott, for example, says that it "was cross-racial desire that coupled a nearly insupportable fascination and a self-protective derision with respect to black people and their cultural practices, and that made blackface minstrelsy less a sign of absolute white power and control than of panic, anxiety, terror, and pleasure" (7). Lott sees blackface minstrelsy as "less a *repetition* of power relations than a *signifier* for them—a distorted mirror, reflecting displacements and condensations and discontinuities between which and the social field there exist lags, unevennesses, multiple determinations" (8). Berndt Ostendorf argues that minstrelsy "anticipated on stage what most Americans deeply feared: the blackening of America" (67). Despite all the caricatures, it brought black music, song, and dance into American popular culture.

African American minstrelsy began at the end of the 1860s with Lew Johnson's Plantation Minstrel Company and the first successful all-Negro company, the Georgia Minstrels. A later company, Strague and Blodgett's Georgia Minstrels, performed Hopkins's play in 1879. These and similar groups, many of them managed by white men but some of them owned by black artists, gave stage training to the performers Billy Kersands, Wallace King, to the songwriter James Bland, or singers like Sam Lucas, the Luca family, and the Hyers Sisters. "Although they were considered 'respectable and refined,' the Hyers Sisters, like Alexander Luca of the antebellum singing family, found that minstrelsy provided one of the few consistent salaried outlets for black musical talent" (Toll 210). As Ostendorf writes, all these artists had "to work within prefabricated roles and were up against a public which expected certain types of performance from them" (72). There was even the phenomenon of black artists blackening their faces and drawing lines around mouths and eyes. While white audiences were usually attracted by the gorgeous stage spectacles, a "subconscious desire to reaffirm white cultural dominance," and a "search for the primitive and pre-industrial life-style" (Ostendorf 82), black audiences were attracted by the artistry and non-sense of the performance. Ostendorf calls this a "type of shame management through hyperbolic self-presentation" (84). It is also clear that minstrelsy offered black artists the national stage they needed for the development of their art.

Pauline Hopkins was certainly aware of the minstrel performances. Robert Toll writes about a group called the Haverly Colored Minstrels, who created an entire plantation scene in an open field near a Boston theater in 1879–80. Quoting from contemporary newspaper reports, this scene was "complete with 'overseers, bloodhounds, and darkies at work.' It featured over one hundred Negroes appropriately costumed, 'indulging in songs, dances [and] antics peculiar to their people' " (205). Hopkins also must have known the self-derogatory stereotyping and racist connotations of this kind of enter-tainment. Although she turned away from many of the racist stereotypes in *Peculiar Sam*, she relied, at the same time, on some of minstrelsy's successful formulas: popular songs, famous singers, and great stage spectacle.

In *Playing the Race Card: Melodramas of Black and White from Uncle Tom to O. J. Simpson*, Linda Williams mentions five hundred so-called Tommer Shows in the 1890s, successful acting companies touring the country with stage versions of Harriet Beecher Stowe's *Uncle Tom's Cabin* (85; see also 45–95). This book was certainly a kind of mastertext for Hopkins's generation of writers. No doubt, she was familiar with the novel and the many pos-sible ways of adapting it for the stage. The best-selling novel *Uncle Tom's Cabin; or, Life Among the Lowly* (1852) led to "a veritable flood of Uncle Tom poems, songs, dioramas, plates, busts, embossed spoons, painted scarves, en-gravings, and other miscellaneous memorabilia" (Yarborough, "Strategies" 63) and a "great midcentury vogue of 'Tom shows' " (Lott 211). Numerous productions followed, written from "antislavery, moderate, and proslavery positions—the lot of them informed by the devices of the minstrel show." All this led to "offshoots, parodies, thefts, and rebuttals of every imaginable kind" and later to film adaptations, the first silent film being shown in 1903 (Lott 212, 214, 273 n.13).

To use a term coined by Henry Louis Gates, Hopkins and many other writers signify upon this text "with a black difference" (*Signifying* xxii). She subverts the text by referring to it with a new meaning. When she names, for example, the evil character in *Hagar's Daughter* St. Clair Enson, she reinterprets the role of the benevolent but weak slaveholder Augustine St. Clare in *Uncle Tom's Cabin*. St. Clare, much like Charles Montfort in *Contending Forces*, wreaks havoc upon the lives of his slaves although he never mistreats them. Benevolence here can be as cruel as whipping because, in the end, the results are the same. The slaves are sold and slave families are separated. The escape of George Harris and Eliza and their bitter diatribes against the system of slavery were certainly part of her mental makeup. The same holds true for Eliza's heroic crossing of the river with her child in her arms, the benevolent Quakers, the cruel mistress Marie St. Clare, and the cold but well-meaning northerner Miss Ophelia, the mischief of Topsy and the various other slaves, the holiness of Eva, the faithfulness of Uncle Tom, the cruelty of Simon Legree, and the diabolic role of the slave dealer. *Uncle Tom's Cabin* and the rewriting of it by William Wells Brown in the various versions of *Clotel* are a literary background readily available to a writer even fifty years after the original publication of these novels.

Many of the artists who performed in minstrel plays were highly talented singers and performers. Time and again, as Eileen Southern notes, they attempted more serious forms of stage dramas. The Hyers Sisters Company, for example, "one of the best opera bouffe troupes in America" (*Music* 254), staged more than seven musicals. Sam Lucas, a star vocalist, tried to move away from minstrelsy, as Toll reports: "Throughout his career he continually sought 'serious' non-minstrel parts that could diversify the images of the stage Negro, but until the 1890s he had to fall back on minstrelsy to support himself" (217).[2]

One of the musical dramas performed by Sam Lucas and the Hyers Sisters was Pauline Hopkins's *Peculiar Sam; or, The Underground Railroad* (subtitled *A Musical Drama in Four Acts*), written in 1879. Under this title, Leo Hamalian and James V. Hatch republished the manuscript that is included in the Hopkins Papers at Fisk University in *The Roots of African American Drama* (1991), as did Eileen Southern in *African American Theater* (1994). It is thus the most available version of the drama that was staged under various titles: *Slaves' Escape; or, The Underground Railroad* (subtitled *A Musical and Moral Drama in Three Acts*); *The Underground Railroad*; *Escape from Slavery; or, The Underground Railroad*; and *The Flight for Freedom; or, The Underground Railroad* (subtitled *A Musical Comedy in Three Acts*). The play was produced and performed by, among others, Hopkins' Colored Troubadours, a group that included Pauline Hopkins, who sang the lead; her mother; William A. Hopkins; Sam Lucas, a singer of considerable local fame; a chorus of jubilee singers; and, at least in several performances, the famous Hyers Sisters. Performed by Sprague's Underground Railroad Company, it then toured the Midwest, moving through "Illinois, Minnesota, Wisconsin, Michigan, Iowa, Kansas, and Missouri, playing one- and two-night stands in any places that offered accommodations, and returning by request for repeat performances to St. Paul, Chicago, and some of the other larger towns" (Southern, *Peculiar Sam* xxiv). As Eileen Southern has discovered, its East Coast premiere was on December 8, 1879, in the "opera-hall" of the Boston Young Men's Christian Union (xxiv). The most memorable performances must have been in July 1880 in Boston at the Oakland Garden, with the Hyers Sisters and Sam Lucas playing the leading role. It played for a week and attracted the attention of a large audience (xxv).

Peculiar Sam anticipates the deviation from norms and the negotiations with character depiction, plot construction, and the use of tradition as well as her concessions to the taste of her audience, all of which determine the later and more famous stages of Hopkins's career. She uses the minstrel model, exposes its ridiculous hyperbole, and subverts it with her own message. In order to prove this point, and especially because the play is not widely known, a summary of the plot is necessary. This discussion leads to a reevaluation of the early stages of her writing. (The text quoted from is the more widely available anthology of Hamalian and Hatch.)

In the fashion of a typical minstrel show, the play opens with Sam, Pete, and Pomp and another field hand singing lively tunes and Sam trying out the steps he has just invented. Since the play was written for Sam Lucas, it can be imagined that this opening gave him the necessary stage presence to show his art, while the other three characters were needed to complete the quartet. Upon leaving him, however, Pete warns Sam of imminent danger, his master's intention to marry Virginia to the black overseer. Since the death of the old master, times have changed. A portrayal of the helplessness of the individual slave regarding his or her personal choices, such as marriage, is certainly not part of most other minstrel shows. Sam, who speaks dialect throughout the play, now sings a solo, a love song to Virginia, who is an educated house slave. The stage directions even call him "thoughtful" (102), which is a state of mind usually not associated with the stereotypically comic role. It is obvious that Hopkins combines elements of the minstrel show (the dancing and singing) with elements of more serious forms of theater.

The thoughtful and bitter trait in Sam, the "peculiarity" in his character, becomes clearer in his dialogue with Mammy, who tells him that Virginia has already been married to Jim, the overseer. Sam now gives voice to his despair

HOPKINS'
COLORED TROUBADOURS

Guitar Players and Southern Jubilee Singers,

Will give one of their Pleasing Entertainments, consisting of Jubilee Singing, the sweetest ever heard,

UNDER THE AUSPICES OF THE ROYAL ARCANUM,

At ARCANUM HALL, ALLSTON,
Friday Evening, Nov. 24, 1882.

Miss PAULINE E. HOPKINS, Boston's Favorite Colored Soprano.
Miss ANNIE PARKS, Washington City Favorite Contralto.
Mr. JAMES FREEMAN, Tenor.
Mr. JAMES HENRY, Bass.
Assisted by Mr. GEORGE TOLLIVER, Camp Meeting Songster.
Mr. W. A. HOPKINS, Guitarist and Vocalist.
Miss CARRIE ALDEN, Pianist and Vocalist.

Despite the unfavorable weather the Hopkins Colored Troubadours had a very good audience at the City Hall, last Sunday evening. The programme was an appropriate one, and excellent in all respects, consisting of solos, duets, piano and guitar renderings, and chorus singing by the entire company. The company has left behind a very good impression, and will be heartily welcomed whenever they choose to visit our city again.—*Malden Press*, Jan. 28, 1882.

BOSTON, AUGUST 19, 1882.

Having employed the Hopkins' Jubilee Singers several times, I take pleasure in recommending them to societies, especially temperance organizations. No meeting of this kind is complete without good music. Miss Pauline E. Hopkins, the Soprano, has a sweet voice, and is a favorite wherever she sings,
JAMES H. ROBERTS.

PROGRAMME.

PART I.

1. OVERTURE, Piano, ... Miss Carrie Alden
2. "We are all hyar," .... Jubilee Singers
3. SONG AND CHORUS, "Sunny Home," .... Miss Hopkins and Quartette
4. "Blow Gabriel," .... Mr. Freeman and Jubilee Company
5. "I'll be dar," .... Mr. Tolliver and Jubilee Company
6. SOLO, Selected, ... Miss Hopkins
7. "Yellow Rose of Texas," .... Mr. Freeman and Jubilee Company
8. DUET, "Whispering Hope," .... Misses Hopkins and Alden
9. "Moses," .... Mr. Tolliver and Company
10. "Water chilly and cold," .... Company

PART II.

1. "Live Humble," old fashioned Camp Meeting Hymn, Mr. Tolliver and Com'y
2. "Magnolia," .... Mr. Freeman
3. "Children I'm gwine to shine," .... Mr. Freeman and Company
4. "Sweet Chiming Bells," .... Quartette
5. SPECIALTY, Exedus, ... Mr. Tolliver
   Ship of Zion, ... —liver and Company

Hopkins' Colored Troubadours: Program of a November 24, 1882, performance with Miss Hopkins as "Boston's Favorite Colored Soprano."
Hopkins Papers, Fisk University Special Collections.

and bitterness: "An' dats' de way they treats dar slabes! An' den they tells how kin' dey is, an' how satisfied we is" (102). Mammy, in her deep-rooted belief in the essential goodness of people and the Lord's justness, comforts him: "Don't yer gib up nor lose your spirits, for de Lord am comin' on his mighty chariot, drawn by his big white horse, an' de white folks hyar, am a gwine to tremble" (103). However simple her faith might be, Mammy is ready to join the flight to Canada as soon as she feels it necessary. As she has spent most of her life on Magnolia Plantation, despite the many hardships she has encountered there, she leaves it with sorrow and tears: "Good-bye ole home, de place whar my chillern war born, an' my ole man am buried. Ise ole now, I may neber see you 'gin, but my chillern's gwine, an' I'm boun' to go too" (108). When the new master threatens to sell them all down the river, her long patience and faithful service end and Sam's bitterness wells up.

The serious content of this first act is, however, only part of the performance. Sam's dances and songs, his comic speech to the overseer, and his disguise as a gentleman are stock ingredients of the minstrel show and certainly dominate this act. Hopkins well knows what her audience wants, and the subversive message is used to set her play apart from the usual comic minstrel show. One of the few reviews we have of the play mentions the reaction of the audience: "To say they were pleased, is to say the least—they were delighted. Sam Lucas, the comedian, is a host in himself, and caused the audience to explode with laughter at short intervals during the evening." In yet another review, it is said that Al Holden, who played the role of Sam in this particular performance, "carried off the honors of the evening, his rendition of the character showing a fine appreciation of the requirements of the impersonation and a keen sense of the humorous situations incidental to his role." In another review, a further detail is added: "The parts are taken with realistic effect, and the plantation songs are given with all their original spirit. Between the acts the La Rues appear in songs and dances, eliciting much applause. At the close of the drama the plantation scene is given on the lawn, with a steamboat race" (HP, box 1, f.11). Obviously, there was enough in the play to turn it into a successful stage spectacle.

Hopkins's strategy, the combination of minstrel show and serious drama, is continued in the second act. When the escaped slaves sing "Steal Away," for example, this song, a stock feature in minstrel shows, takes on the original and literal meaning of stealing away from slavery into freedom (Levine 52). On their escape from the plantation, their first stationmaster is Caesar, whom Mammy soon recognizes as a former slave from Magnolia Plantation. The scene between Sam (disguised as Caesar) and Jim is highly comical and makes use of the alleged fear of the supernatural of every Negro. As before, however, Sam outwits his pursuer, recognizes the ghost as Jim, and takes him along to their hiding place, a cave. His sister Juno, whose part is that of the simple slave, guards Jim with a pistol and frightens him dreadfully. The many disguises of Sam so far are certainly one of the main attractions of this leading role. In contrast to Sam, Virginia plays the more conventional role of the pretty female slave (with a few beautiful solos) who must be rescued by the heroic male figure. While this constellation was part of some slave narratives, it was certainly not part, at that time, of standard stage dramas.

The third act treats the final escape of the group across the river. Again Sam is the cunning, contriving sort of slave who not only poisoned all the bloodhounds in the vicinity but also stole some money to do this. When he boards the raft, he displays great relief: "I tell you chillern I feels so happy I doesn't kno' mysel'. Jes feel dis air, it smells like freedom; jes see dose trees, dey look like freedom. *(points across river)* an' look ober yonder chillern, look dar good, dat ar am ol' freedom himsel' " (118). At a time when most audiences were used to seeing a romantic side of the slave past, Sam's clever tricks and relief must have been greatly astonishing. This act seems short by comparison, but it offers some great songs and stage spectacle.

The final act is the most unconventional part of the play. The action takes place after the Civil War in Canada and thus becomes a version of the "northern escape story" of Eliza's and Harry's escape in *Uncle Tom's Cabin* or Frederick Douglass's *Narrative* (L. Williams 47). Mammy and Caesar are married now and wait for the return of Sam, who has just been elected congressman for Cincinnati. Virginia is a singer and Juno a teacher. Mammy and Caesar are proud of the achievements of the younger generation, but they also voice some sentimental remembrances of the sunny South and the old times. Caesar even says, "An' ol' 'ooman, ef de ol' man dies firs', bury me at ol' Marser's feet, under the 'Nolin tree" (119). This may be seen as a sign of conventionality, of Hopkins's concession to the expectations of her audience. It may also be seen as the very human reaction of an old couple who have not quite adapted to living conditions in the home they were forced to make in Canada.

In some way, the old couple's longing for the South is taken up in one scene in *Contending Forces*, when the guests at Ma Smith's boardinghouse conclude a social evening with the dancing of the Virginia reel. Although church stewardess Ma Smith was opposed to this pastime in her respectable home, she could not prevail against the determination of the young people to have a good time. The dance allowed the couples who participated in it a freedom of movement and invention of dance steps they obviously enjoyed: "Sam had provided himself with the lively Jinny for a partner, and was cutting grotesque juba figures in the pauses of the music, to the delight of the company. His partner, in wild vivacity, fairly vied with him in his efforts at doing the hoe-down and heel-and-toe. Not to be outdone, the Rev. Tommy James and Mrs. Davis scored great hits in cutting pigeon wings and in reviving forgotten beauties of the 'walk-'round.' Tommy 'allowed' he hadn't enjoyed himself so much since he came up North" (164). It is remarkable that even in these upwardly mobile northern city dwellers, a part of them longs for the emotional relief of dance and enjoyment that is here interpreted as a remnant of their southern roots. Hopkins obviously had the performance of her play in mind when she called the two characters who otherwise are not part of the main action Sam and Jinny and had them perform something of a stage dance.

In *Peculiar Sam*, Virginia is still not married to Sam because she feels she is legally bound in marriage to Jim. In the not unexpected conclusion, a visitor is announced who gives them a card: "Mr. James Peters, Esq., D.D., attorney at law, at the Massachusetts bar, and declined overseer of the Magnolia plantation" (121). Here even the character of Jim, who combines elements of the faithful slave and cruel overseer, experiences an unexpected turnaround. He tells the family that when he got back to his master without the fugitives and the money his master had given him, he was severely punished. But when his master later fled before the Union troops, he took all his valuables, made his way to Massachusetts, received an education and was admitted to the bar, and became "one ob de pillows ob de Massatoosetts bar" (123). He is married and has twin children, called Jinny and Sam. Virginia is thus free to marry Sam, and preparations are made immediately.

The clever and cunning side in Jim has served him well. He is the type of slave who sees an advantage in ingratiating himself with his master. This helps him pursue his own aims and gain some considerable benefits. He showed enough daring and cunning when he grasped the opportunity to help himself to his master's valuables and thus emerged a free man with some money on his side. The evil side in him, his taking sides with the master rather than his fellow slaves, is a demeaning stereotype that also fits Isaac in *Hagar's Daughter* and exposes the demoralizing effects of slavery. Although he is criticized for his unethical conduct, his later opportunism and his ability to adapt to the circumstances of postslavery times are treated with irony but not with condemnation. This latter character trait is also traceable in Ophelia Davis and Sara Ann White in *Contending Forces*. When their Louisiana mistress left them in the course of the war, the two slaves took what they could get hold of. Ophelia Davis emphasizes that she came by her decent dress and lace shawl honestly: "Yas'm, when my ol' mistis left her great big house an' all that good stuff—silver an' things—a layin' thar fer enyone to pick up thet had sense 'nough to know a good thing an' git it ahead of enybody else, I jes' said to myself: 'Phelia, chile, now's yer time!' Yas'm, I feathered my nes', I jes' did" (105). Ophelia and Sara Ann certainly had enough sense to know how they could take revenge for past drudgery. It is this common sense in combination with a shrewd business sense that helped the former slaves in their northern careers after the war. Both the positive and negative stereotypes show the complex discourse about the roles of African Americans of the time. Hopkins does not attempt to reconcile two seeming discrepancies in behavior resulting from the legacy of slavery. She holds a realistic albeit unflattering mirror up to her audience.

The message in the final act of *Peculiar Sam* must have been well understood by the audience and certainly constituted the attraction to such companies as the Hyers Sisters and such performers as Sam Lucas. When given the opportunity, the African American becomes respectable, pursues a career, and has success in his life. Sam the congressman, Virginia the singer, Juno the schoolteacher, and Jim the attorney represent the opposite of traditional stage roles despite their occasional comic acts. For their performers, these were roles more acceptable than those that accepted slavery as "amusing, right, and natural" (Lott 3) or that, as Ostendorf says, "forced one of the tragic figures of American history to accept a comic role on the American public stage" (68).

Apart from *Out of Bondage* by the white writer Joseph Bradford, which was written for the Hyers Sisters, and apart from the well-known and immediately recognizable general model of the Tommer Shows, there is only one other immediate precedent for *Peculiar Sam*. Hopkins's model as writer, activist, and lecturer, William Wells Brown, wrote *The Escape; or, A Leap for Freedom* in 1858. The play was never performed, but there were numerous occasions when Brown gave a reading of it. Hamalian and Hatch, who reprint this play in *The Roots of African American Drama*, suppose that Hopkins was present at one of these readings (39). It can be proven without doubt that she knew this play, as will be shown.

Like *Peculiar Sam* and *Out of Bondage*, *The Escape* consists of a part that takes place on a plantation and involves the escape of slaves with the help of abolitionists working for the underground railroad. Glen and Melinda, hero and heroine, both of them educated slaves, decide to flee because Dr. Gaines,

Melinda's owner, wants her as his mistress. The slave speculator Dick Walker threatens to sell them down the river. But Quakers help them, and a well-meaning white northerner, significantly called Mr. White, protects them and sees them to safety.

There are several connections and several verbatim borrowings between Hopkins's fiction and Brown's play. The slave trader Walker bears the same name as in *Hagar's Daughter*. In *The Escape*, he encounters the Reverend Mr. Pinchen, who tells him about the work of religion among slaveholders: "Now, there is Mr. Haskins—he is a slave-trader, like yourself. Well, I converted him. Before he got religion, he was one of the worst men to his niggers I ever saw; his heart was as hard as stone. But religion has made his heart as soft as a piece of cotton. Before I converted him, he would sell husbands from their wives, and seem to take delight in it; but now he won't sell a man from his wife, if he can get any one to buy both of them together" (59). This scene appears in *Hagar's Daughter* (12–13) and borrows heavily from Brown. The scene in which Walker examines the slaves repeats a similar scene in *The Escape* nearly verbatim (*The Escape* 62–63; *Hagar's Daughter* 11–12). To be sure, both are stock scenes, and Brown makes use of them several times, including in his novel *Clotel*. But the fact that Hopkins repeats two extended dialogues word for word must be seen as proof of Brown's influence on her. In *The Escape*, there is the figure of the cruel slavemistress who whips her house slave on every occasion. In *Winona*, there is cruel Mrs. Thomson, who shows no mercy to Winona. Mrs. Gaines tries to force Melinda to drink some poison, a scene that may have inspired Hopkins in *Of One Blood*. Also, Brown's comic slave Cato, who works as a doctor for his master and finally escapes in his master's best clothes, may have influenced the figures of Sam and Jim in *Peculiar Sam*. Hopkins's extensive borrowing from Brown shows, on the one hand, her admiration of him and her acceptance of his position as role model. On the other hand, it proves that the young writer needed some kind of master narrative to legitimize her own search for a voice as an early female African American writer.

According to all records, the performances of *Peculiar Sam* met with enthusiasm. "Despite the unfavorable weather," an 1882 reviewer writes, "the Hopkins Colored Troubadours had a very good audience at the City Hall, last Sunday evening. The programme was an appropriate one, and excellent in all respects, consisting of solos, duets, piano and guitar renderings, and chorus singing by the entire company" (HP, box 1, f.11). One of the playbills of August 13, 1880, from the *Cape Ann Weekly Advertiser*, praised Pauline Hopkins's voice and identified her as a writer: "The sweet voice of Miss Pauline E. Hopkins, soprano, showed wonderful expression and control, and painstaking culture. . . . In addition to her rare gifts as a vocalist, Miss Hopkins is the author of several successful musical comedies" (HP f.11).

Later reports of the performances of the P. E. Hopkins' Colored Troubadours, included in the program folder for a performance on February 26, 1882, date her appearances back to March 29, 1879, and April 19, 1879. These are two newspaper reports quoted in the program folder that praise these earlier performances as a "rare treat." In most performances, P. E. Hopkins is listed as soprano and as playing the lead role; her mother, Mrs. S. A. Hopkins, is usually listed as playing the mother of the heroine; and her stepfather, W. A. Hopkins, is listed as playing the overseer; it is also mentioned that he plays the guitar and performs as vocalist. In 1895 he is announced as a writer himself: "Guitar Player and Character Artist, in his very laughable Instructive Sketch of Southern Life, entitled 'Uncle Pete's Cabin'" (HP f.11).

An earlier recorded performance bears the title " 'Pauline,' or the Belle of Saratoga," and lists William A. Hopkins as part of the Committee of Arrangements. It can be assumed that the title of the performance refers to Pauline Hopkins herself, who, as Pauline E. Allen, played the title role. Another earlier play, now lost, was *Aristocracy* or *Colored Aristocracy*, a musical drama in three acts, which was performed by the Hyers Sisters Concert Company in 1877 (Southern, *Music* 253). Hopkins also wrote a five-act play, "Winona," of which a partial copy of only a few pages is included in the Hopkins Papers (the copyright date is 1878). Together with the various versions of *Peculiar Sam* and her early undated play about Daniel in the lions' den, these dramatic pieces make up a considerable amount of playwriting and certainly surpass juvenile attempts at writing.

Hopkins later writes about the Hyers Sisters and their performance in *Out of Bondage:* "The introduction of this drama, in which, for the first time, all the characters were represented by colored people, marks an era in the progress of the race. Never, until undertaken by these ladies, was it thought possible for Negroes to appear in the legitimate drama" ("Famous Women: Phenomenal Vocalists" 51). It is, therefore, possible to reevaluate Hopkins's career and success as a playwright and performer. She had a number of justly famous singers on her program. The Hyers Sisters, Sam Lucas, Fred E. Lewis, and Elijah William Smith were all very well known (see Southern 253–54). Her decision to write a colored musical comedy was virtually unprecedented in her time and shows her acute awareness of the tastes of her audience.

The bright and intelligent young Hopkins definitely showed a gift for writing. The production and successful performance of her play prove her talent for entertainment and her venturesome spirit. Many other performers tried their hands at musical plays in the tradition of the minstrel plays. Many, like her group, could earn some money in this way but could not make a living by it, one that would ensure financial stability for a longer period of time. Although the 1890s are the decade when relatively little is known about Hopkins, she was certainly not idle.

Hopkins gave recitals and concerts in Boston and lectured on black history. The biographical sketch of January 1901 mentions two lectures about Toussaint L'Ouverture, one at Tremont Temple in Boston, the other one delivered to a Friends School in Providence, Rhode Island. In 1892 she was asked to deliver a memorial address at the Charles Street A.M.E. Church. The first installment of her serial novel *Hagar's Daughter* bears the date 1891. Only the second installment was copyrighted in 1901, the year of its appearance in the *Colored American Magazine*. In 1899 she registered *Contending Forces* with the Library of Congress (HP, box 1, f.9). She lectured on African American history. All this proves that Hopkins was active as a performer, singer, writer, and public lecturer well before her better-known and more public involvement with the *Colored American Magazine*.

By the early 1890s, when Hopkins was past her thirtieth birthday, she left the entertainment world in search of greater financial security. She studied stenography and passed the civil service exam. Her desire to learn a trade was more than understandable.[3] Her contemporary, the writer Charles W. Chesnutt, saw the art of stenography "as the magic carpet to take him to the North, to the land of opportunity, to life" (H. Chesnutt, *Charles Waddell Chesnutt* 26).[4] The work of stenography certainly was a respectable and accepted occupation for a single woman of Hopkins's time and served her extremely well in her career as editor. A fictional representation of this autobiographical detail comes when Sappho works as a stenographer in *Contending Forces*. For four years Hopkins worked in the Bureau of Statistics, where she participated in the Massachusetts decennial census of 1895. This trade served her well until her death in 1930 at the age of seventy-one.

She chose to weather the "Nationalist Nineties," as John Higham calls this decade, with work largely not artistic. Since the 1890s were characterized by national and international unrest, this was a wise choice. On the international plane, the Spanish-American War, the military occupation of Cuba, and the annexation of Guam, the Philippines, Puerto Rico, Hawaii, and Wake Island demonstrate the imperialistic agenda of the time (Glazener 159). On the national level, the Homestead Strike of 1893, the Pullman Strike of 1894, labor unrest, rural upheavals, the restriction of immigration, the official closing of the frontier, and the restrictions of monopolies dominate this decade (Higham 68–105). The economic depression of 1893 to 1897 certainly made it harder for a performing group like Hopkins' Colored Troubadours to finance their programs. Racial strife in the United States considerably worsened in the 1890s. *Plessy v. Ferguson,* the Supreme Court decision that legalized segregation in 1896, was only one example of the many "Jim Crow" laws that aimed at segregation and a curtailing of voting rights. An estimated one hundred lynchings of Negroes per year between 1893 and 1904 (Gossett 269), often accompanied by atrocious tortures, speak of a decade that historian Rayford W. Logan has called the "nadir" of American race relations.

After this in-between period, Hopkins's ambition drove her to tackle the nearly unprecedented role of editor, journalist, and writer of fiction. Nellie Y. McKay interprets this choice in the following way: "But the security of such a livelihood did not put an end to Hopkins's ambitions to engage in more creative expression. She never gave up the ideal of becoming a writer; through the 1890s she continued to nurture that dream and also lectured successfully on black history in the Boston area" ("Introduction" 3). Claudia Tate writes about this period before the founding of the *Colored American Magazine:* "Although Hopkins wrote essays, poetry, and musical dramas before she was twenty, she did not try her hand at fiction until 1900, probably because there were few African American outlets for this genre until the advent of the *Colored American Magazine*" ("Hopkins" 366). It is indirectly known that at some point, she followed the advice of Fred Williams, the veteran stage manager of the Boston Museum ("Pauline E. Hopkins" 218), and turned from playwriting to fiction. It was her ambition to write fiction, "in which the wrongs of her race shall be so handled as to enlist the sympathy of all classes of citizens, in this way reaching those who never read history or biography" (219).

Negotiations in Race and Gender
1900-1905

The "Colored American Magazine"

*H*er reputation as a performer and writer, a certain financial stability, and "grim determination"—as R. S. Elliott, a white man in charge of the technical management of the magazine in its early years, chose to call it ("The Story" 47)—allowed Pauline Hopkins to grasp one of the few opportunities available to her when the *Colored American Magazine* was founded in Boston in 1900. Elliott includes this information probably upon her request: "Pauline Hopkins has struggled to the position which she now holds in the same fashion that ALL Northern colored women have to struggle—through hardships, disappointments, and with very little encouragement. What she has accomplished has been done by a grim determination to 'stick at it,' even though failure might await her at the end." Elliott then adds the laudatory sentence: "Let us have a few more Pauline Hopkins to help forward the brighter and better day for the race" (47).

In the following discussion, the first part will be devoted to the *Colored American Magazine* in general and Hopkins's involvement with it. It is necessary to know the basic facts about the *Colored American Magazine* in order to understand Hopkins's role at and contribution to the magazine. In subsequent chapters, I will treat her use of pseudonyms and establish the fact that Hopkins used more pseudonyms than commonly attributed to her; analyze her negotiations with the "famous men" of her race, in particular with Booker T. Washington, which entails a detailed description of the sale of the magazine and its removal to New York; and, finally, discuss Hopkins's involvement with the "famous women" of her race and investigate her opinions on race and racism. My premise is that Hopkins was at the center of crucial debates about the cultural politics of magazine editing, the cultural politics of radical activism, and the early feminist movement. She was on the scene when race consciousness was being redefined. I also argue that her negotiations of gender were never detached from her negotiations of race.

In 1900 the *Colored American Magazine* was founded by Walter W. Wallace, Jesse W. Watkins, Harper S. Fortune, and Walter Alexander Johnson. Both

Wallace, the managing editor, and Fortune, the treasurer, had a background in music. All four founders came from Virginia, the place of origin of Hopkins's stepfather and a sign of the migration north of many upwardly mobile African Americans. In his May 1901 article about the foundation of the magazine, Elliott describes them as exemplary men bent on achieving education and becoming successful businessmen ("The Story" 45–47).

The magazine was published by the Colored Co-operative Publishing Company, which also published four books, among them Hopkins's first novel, *Contending Forces*. Hopkins was involved financially in this publishing company and contributed her share to the initial launching of the magazine. It was located at 232 West Canton Street in the South End, moved to 5 Park Street later the same year, and ended up at 82 West Concord Street in May–June 1903. The magazine was first issued in May 1900 and declared itself to be "devoted to the higher culture of Religion, Literature, Science, Music and Art of the Negro, universally" ("Announcement"). The first editorial and publisher's announcement called for contributions from everyone interested in the race: "A vast and almost unexplored treasury of biography, history, adventure, tradition, folk lore poetry and song, the accumulations of centuries of such experiences as have never befallen any other people lies open to us and to you" ("Editorial," May 1900, 60). The political purpose of the magazine was defined plainly: "What we desire, what we require, what we demand to aid in the onward march of progress and advancement is justice; merely this and nothing more" (61). According to Abby Arthur Johnson and Ronald Maberry Johnson's *Propaganda and Aesthetics: The Literary Politics of Afro-American Magazines in the Twentieth Century*, the *Colored American Magazine* was "the first significant Afro-American journal to emerge in the twentieth century" (4).[1]

The *Colored American Magazine* set out to be a quality journal similar to the *Atlantic Monthly* and saw itself as a magazine dedicated to the needs of a particular reading group: African Americans and as large a number of white sympathizers as possible. In a letter to Booker T. Washington in 1901, Walter Wallace indicates that one-third of the subscribers were white and that the magazine had a circulation between fifteen thousand and sixteen thousand per month (*Booker T. Washington Papers* 6:184–85). Nancy Glazener writes about the connections between the *Colored American Magazine* and the *Atlantic Monthly*: "Few if any of the contributors to the *Colored American Magazine* (1900–1909) also published work in the *Atlantic* group, yet the magazine manifested a commitment to literature commensurate with the *Atlantic*'s. Not only did the magazine announce its sponsorship of 'the higher culture of Religion, Literature, Science, Music and Art of the Negro,' but

Front cover of the *Colored American Magazine*, September 1902.

The founders of the *Colored American Magazine* portrayed in R. S. Elliott's "The Story of Our Magazine" (May 1901): Walter W. Wallace, President and Managing Editor; Jesse W. Watkins, Secretary and Assistant Treasurer; Harper S. Fortune, Assistant Secretary and Treasurer; and Walter A. Johnson, Vice-President and Advertising Manager.

Part of an advertisement for the *Colored American Magazine*, March 1904.

also the decorum of its prose and the consistency of its attention to aesthetic refinement and social respectability echoed the *Atlantic* group's class-marked vision of culture" (8).

The *Colored American Magazine* contained elements of the mass magazine, such as articles that reflected evangelical piety (e.g., a long series of biblical stories) or addressed childrearing and health issues (e.g., an article about the importance of healthy teeth). At the same time, the *Colored American Magazine* catered to the interests of a kind of social elite with articles about particular social classes (e.g., about "Boston's Smart Set" in January 1901), with occasional fashion notes and even pieces about vacation traveling.[2] One of its main concerns was education and information about schools, educators, and famous graduates, an emphasis that increased after the magazine came under the control of Booker T. Washington. But with the inclusion of numerous poems, short stories, and serial novels, the *Colored American Magazine* truly turned into a quality journal. It offered literary access to such writers as Pauline Hopkins, who seized the opportunity and gained some degree of public prominence. When writing is, as Richard Brodhead sees it, an "acculturated activity,"[3] the many extraliterary factors that make the production and marketing of literature possible must be taken into account in order to explain the rise to prominence of a certain writer or a group of writers at certain times.

At the end of its first year, the *Colored American Magazine* claimed one hundred thousand readers (Elliott 43). It initially sold at fifteen cents a copy and $1.50 for a full-year subscription. A system of agents was established. They were promised a liberal commission and repeatedly encouraged to solicit new readers. In the January 1901 issue, there was a full-page advertisement for *Contending Forces* with the call "Agents Wanted Everywhere" opposite the table of contents. Beginning in February 1901, an engraving called *The Young Colored American* was offered free for a year's subscription. In February 1901 the "Editorial and Publishers' Announcements" informed the reader: "From present indications, our February edition will be entirely sold out by the middle of the month, and this in spite of the fact that we increased our printing order for February fifty percent over that of the January issue" (316). Another inducement was a gold watch free for the soliciting of eight subscriptions. A copy of *Contending Forces* was also offered free, although limited numbers restricted this offer to those who applied first (see "Editorial and Publishers' Announcements," May 1901, 79).

Taking a clue from the fact that the people who volunteered to distribute the magazine were also the most likely readers, it is useful to look at R. S. Elliott's "The Story of Our Magazine," in which he profiles owners, editors, contributors, and agents. He states as the magazine's goal: "To the encouragement of those who faint, or would slavishly bend under the weight of a mistaken popular prejudice; and to the inspiration and aid of all our noble men and women, who are fearlessly and successfully vindicating themselves and our people, THE COLORED AMERICAN MAGAZINE has been and is devoted" (44).

The nearly sixty agents who sent in their biographical sketches present a spectrum of African American society from schoolteachers, businesspeople, farmers, to people involved in numerous business, social, church, and political organizations. Very often an account of their lives includes references to prizes, scholarships, and business achievements, to pride in their family origin and children, to their ambitions in the fields of business and community work, and to their memberships in various organizations. Here is one example, quoted in full to represent the typical biographical sketch:

> MISS MAUDE ERMA WEEDEN, our agent at Brockton, Mass., is the daughter of Mrs. Mae Weeden, whom Dr. Wells Brown once recognized as a very able woman, and a writer of no mean order. Miss Weeden's education after leaving the high school was at the hands of special teachers at home. She has taught school in New Jersey in primary grades, also acted as vocal instructor. She is at present receiving instructions from a European graduate, also giving instructions to a number of white pupils. Her spare time is given to self-improvement, that in time may help the people of her race. She has time for neither society nor fashion, although belonging to families of both social standing and means. Her ambition is to be helpful to others. (70)

The reader easily detects the aspirations to a self-reliant, self-confident and proud middle-class status here and is clearly asked to share them. William A. Grigg of Petersburg, Virginia, is called "one of the most prominent young men of the race [who] has a sound mind in a sound body and might, in common parlance, be termed a 'hustler.' He is making things 'hum' about Charlotte and vicinity in the interest of THE COLORED AMERICAN MAGAZINE, having recently accepted agency for same" (75–76). A lack of schooling was sometimes mentioned as proof of even greater achievement. An example is Mrs. Anna Harrison Brown, agent at Richmond, Virginia: "She is a thorough business woman, a person of great ambition, an earnest churchworker and is possessed of a voice of great volume, being leader of the choir of the First Colored Christian Church. Mrs. Brown has never had more than three months' schooling" (75). Some of the agents represented the typical migrant from the South, as for example Nathaniel B. Dodson, general agent for New York (65–66).

Mr. Dodson also organized a Literary Agents' Business Club in order to "create among our people a taste for good reading matter suitable for the Home, that shall give inspiration and encouragement to our boys and girls to aspire to high ideals and high aims in life" (66). Since the Colored Co-operative Publishing Company was, as the name says, a cooperative enterprise, Dodson's initiative reflected the interest of the readers, contributors, and agents. His ideas are worth quoting in full because of the typical spirit of optimism and hope attached to the publication of this magazine: "To help build a Publishing House, that in time shall be the crown and flower of the Negro race in Literature and Art, and thereby leave to posterity a legacy that shall speak to coming generations in more eloquent terms than the most brilliant orator of our day. It is further the object of this club to give references to ambitious young men and women seeking positions of trust and responsibility in other lines of work, for the advancement of the race" (66). The pedagogic function of the magazine and its fiction and poetry were seen as a contribution to an advancement of the race. It must be added here that, of course, the literate portion of the African American population was relatively small and that the message was also addressed to a white audience, which was influenced to think in positive terms about the achievements and ambitions of African Americans.[4] As Elliott puts it, the reader should "consider Negro ambition, enterprise and culture in a serious sense" (43). He speaks to the white reader here because the African American community consistently described itself as industrious, honest, hardworking, and caring.

"The Story of Our Magazine" is accompanied by sixteen pages of portraits, including those of the founders and Hopkins herself. In her article about the African American home in the *Colored American Magazine*, Debra Bernardi sees the function of these pictures as a family album that acquaints readers "with other members of their 'racial brotherhood'" (209). This is a fitting description of these pictures, all of which show serious-looking, dignified African Americans in their best clothes. The half-page portrait of Hopkins is the same as in *Contending Forces*. Like Albreta Moore Smith next to her, she wears a hat and looks at us with a serious face. She wears a dark dress with a light color around her neck. It is one of only two pictures of Hopkins available to us, and the size allotted to it may illustrate her important position at the magazine.

Pauline Hopkins seized the possibility that the *Colored American Magazine* offered. Her interest in various forms of literature was clearly established

ALBRETA MOORE SMITH, CHICAGO, ILL.,
Our Chicago Correspondent.
(See page 47.)

PAULINE E. HOPKINS, BOSTON. MASS.
A Leading Race Author and Regular Contributor to our Magazine.
(See page 47.)

A portrait of Hopkins appears in "The Story of Our Magazine" (May 1901),
next to a portrait of Albreta Moore Smith, Chicago clubwoman and
correspondent of the *Colored American Magazine.*

before the year 1900, and her literary tastes and wide knowledge were certainly acquired in the formative years of her touring the country and writing various versions of the play she performed. She also wrote the first chapter of *Hagar's Daughter* and all of *Contending Forces* before she began at the *Colored American Magazine.* But without a channel for her literary activities, she would have been denied even the short-lived public prominence that she gained through her publications in the magazine. Her genius would have been lost to the annals of history.

Hopkins contributed numerous editorials and biographical articles; one chapter of her already published first novel, *Contending Forces*; and a total of seven stories and three serial novels to the magazine. The serial novels were *Hagar's Daughter: A Story of Southern Caste Prejudice* (1901–2), *Winona: A Tale of Negro Life in the South and Southwest* (1902), and *Of One Blood; or, The Hidden Self* (1902–3). Her four novels and her short stories, which will be analyzed later, demonstrate the main concerns of Hopkins around the turn of the century: the amalgamation of the races, ancient history, the women's

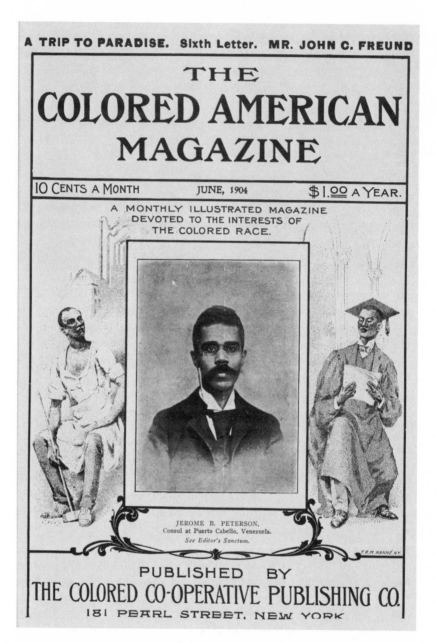

A TRIP TO PARADISE. Sixth Letter. MR. JOHN C. FREUND

THE
COLORED AMERICAN
MAGAZINE

10 CENTS A MONTH   JUNE, 1904 $1.00 A YEAR.

A MONTHLY ILLUSTRATED MAGAZINE
DEVOTED TO THE INTERESTS OF
THE COLORED RACE.

JEROME B. PETERSON,
Consul at Puerto Cabello, Venezuela.
See Editor's Sanctum.

T.R.M. HANNÉ N.Y.

PUBLISHED BY
THE COLORED CO-OPERATIVE PUBLISHING CO.
181 PEARL STREET, NEW YORK

Front cover of the *Colored American Magazine*, June 1904.

movement, the legacy of slavery, and the potential for heroism among African Americans.

The years 1900 to 1904 were her most prolific. Her novel *Contending Forces* was frequently praised in announcements and offered at a special rate to new subscribers. Some of her writings were published under the pseudonym Sarah A. Allen, her mother's maiden name. Another pseudonym she used was J. Shirley Shadrach. In all this, she and the entire staff of the journal strove to turn the *Colored American Magazine* into a "quality national journal" (Johnson and Johnson, *Propaganda* 4). Hopkins had considerable influence, as Johnson and Johnson note: "More and better fiction and poetry was published by the *Colored American Magazine* during the years Pauline Hopkins was editor than at any other time in its history" (*Propaganda* 6). Claudia Tate calls her a "leading proponent of activist black journalism during the post-Reconstruction period" ("Hopkins" 366). And William Braithwaite, a Boston poet and journalist, remembers later that Hopkins introduced the practice of paying for contributions in order to attract more and better fiction and poetry ("Negro America's First Magazine" 24–25). Carby concludes from the available evidence that she "had the power to influence the magazine's editorial politics" and called her position an "enviable place in the world of African American journalism" (4–5). McKay names as Hopkins's goals "the creation of an African American art and literature that would demonstrate the talents and skills of the group and prove to the rest of the world that black people, only recently released from slavery, were already as culturally advanced as other groups" (5).

To achieve this it was necessary at times to disguise herself so that she could contribute more to the magazine and convey her message. For a complete record of her career at the *Colored American Magazine*, it is therefore important to treat her use of pseudonyms in order to demonstrate that her position at the magazine demanded the constant vigilance of her position and voice. Although we cannot be sure that Hopkins limited herself to these two pseudonyms, it is significant to see that the use of pen names allowed her to publish more frequently and to voice her opinions more openly. The use of pen names was a survival strategy for the woman editor, who did not have a large support group to shield her against opposition nor role models to teach her survival schemes in a male-dominated corporate enterprise.

The Use of Pseudonyms

*H*opkins published her short story "The Mystery Within Us" in the first issue of the *Colored American Magazine* (May 1900). In the June issue it was announced that she would be in charge of the women's column. The September issue featured a long advertisement for her novel *Contending Forces*, which was forthcoming from the Colored Co-operative Publishing Company. In the next issue her short story "Talma Gordon" appeared. From then onward there was often more than one contribution by Hopkins in each issue of the magazine: usually one biographical sketch and often a short story or one chapter of her novel. In March 1901 the first installment of *Hagar's Daughter: A Story of Southern Caste Prejudice* was published. The serial ran each month through March 1902. The author was identified as Sarah A. Allen, and only a year later, when a new serial was about to begin, the editor announced that *Hagar's Daughter* was written by Pauline Elizabeth Hopkins under her mother's name ("Editorial," March 1902, 335). The use of this pseudonym allowed Hopkins to include up to three contributions in one issue. In the December 1901 issue, for example, she published one short story, one installment of *Hagar's Daughter*, and one biographical sketch. Hopkins continued to use this pseudonym off and on in future years.

In April 1901 she wrote a sketch about the life of Lewis Hayden, a fugitive slave who settled in Boston, became a successful tailor, was elected to the Massachusetts Legislature, and served in a position in the office of the secretary of state (see "Famous Men: Lewis Hayden"). Hayden was a famous and active abolitionist involved in the underground railroad, sheltering many fugitive slaves. One such fugitive, whose story Hopkins included in her profile, was a slave named Shadrach, whom Hayden helped to escape. Recently, the case of Shadrach Minkins was reconstructed by Gary Collison to exemplify the abolitionist movement in and around Boston in the 1850s. It can be safely stated that Shadrach was a famous name in Boston and that his capture under the Fugitive Slave Law was one of several that rose to public prominence in the immediate pre–Civil War period. In the August 1902 issue, an article entitled "Charles Winter Wood," by Sarah A. Allen, was announced. The article itself, however, appeared under the name of J. Shirley Shadrach. There is further evidence that J. Shirley Shadrach was another of Hopkins's aliases. The table of contents for the projected third issue of the *New Era Magazine* includes a story called " 'Butt-In' Bobby—An Easter Story, How a Boy Scout Saved His Mother" by S. Shadrach. Since Hopkins published "Converting Fanny" in the first issue of the magazine under the name of Sarah A. Allen, it is highly probable that Hopkins continued using her other pen name. In addition, there are repeated phrases that recur in other writings of Hopkins that make it more than probable that Shadrach was another of her pen names.

It is easy to understand why Hopkins chose her mother's name as a pseudonym. It is natural to use a name associated with oneself in some way, and it might show the good relationship between mother and daughter. The daughter pays tribute to the mother and lets her participate in her triumph. The choice of J. Shirley Shadrach is more difficult to explain. Hopkins positioned herself as a kind of female fugitive slave asking for protection. She established an imaginary bond between the fate of the heroic fugitive slave, forced to leave New England because of an inhuman law, and herself, a magazine editor under constant financial and ideological pressure. It was her form of self-protection against criticism from readers and the *Colored American Magazine* staff, which can be exemplified by an analysis of her contributions to the February and March issues of 1903. A discussion of the Shadrach/Hopkins essays also provides an essential clue to her thinking about race and miscegenation.

In general, the use of pseudonyms was not uncommon in the *Colored American Magazine* and African American periodicals. We find articles by "A. Gude Deekun" (A Good Deacon?), "Deesha," and "Fair Play" in the *Colored American Magazine* and a serial by Golden Gladsby in the *Voice of the Negro*. In "The Value of Race Literature," Victoria Earle Matthews identifies Augustus M. Hodges as "B. Square," John E. Bruce as "Bruce-Grit," W.H.A. Moore as "John Mitchell, Jr.," and Joe Howard as "Bill Nye" (182). Mrs. Matthews herself published as "Victoria Earle." Fanny Jackson was "Catherine Casey" (Perkins 184), and Claude McKay was "Eli Edwards" (Braithwaite, "Negro in American Literature" 39). Gladys Casely Hayford was Aquah Laluah, and Marita Bonner was "Joseph Maree Andrew" (see Roses 497, 514). Josephine Silone Yates was "R. K. Potter" (H. Brown 179), and Emma Dunham Kelley-Hawkins was "Forget-Me-Not." Frances E. Rollin Whipper published a biography of Martin R. Delany under the name

Frank A. Rollin (Loggins 259). Walter H. Stowers, author of the novel *Appointed* (1894), wrote as "Sanda" (Loggins 325).

In the announcement of "The Voice of the Negro in 1905," Gardner Goldsby is identified as a pen name: "He is a new aspirant for literary honors, but we feel sure, from what our office knows, that his first story will prove to be a winner." In a later issue, a writer identified only as "H." is announced:

> "The Southern Conspiracy" [i]s one of a series of short stories we are going to publish this summer. A young man whose father has done much in the literary world, and who himself is destined to become a great writer and author, writes "A Southern Conspiracy." He does not care to have his name divulged at this stage and so he writes under the pseudonym of "H." "H." has given us a charming and exciting short story in which he boldly uncovers the existence of a great Southern newspaper conspiracy to corrupt the northern public mind on the race question. "H." has been taking lessons under "M.V." of "International Underground History" fame, and here he has furnished us a tale that is more nearly fact than fiction. ("The Voice of the Negro for May, 1905")

Both announcements do us some service. They show that the practice of pen names was common at the beginning of the twentieth century and that readers knew or were directly informed about them (see Brodhead, *Cultures* 82ff.). The two items tell us that pen names were sometimes used for younger writers who either wanted to see how their fiction would fare in public or whose family connections put them under some considerable strain. The second announcement also tells us that the editors drop hints at the real identity that may seem obscure today but were probably relatively clear at their time. Although we wonder at the "M.V." of the "International Underground History" fame, the allusion might have been sufficient to enable certain readers to identify the author. The second announcement also shows that pen names served to obscure one's identity when the contents of the story, "more fact than fiction," were highly delicate and more than likely to elicit public indignation. A combination of these factors can also be applied to the case of the Allen and Shadrach pen names.

Hopkins found the use of a pseudonym very convenient. It allowed her to disguise her identity, publish more frequently, and avoid public criticism directed at herself. When in March 1902 Sarah A. Allen's alias was lifted, this revelation brought a considerable relief to readers of her time who were keen to identify a favorite author. The "Editorial and Publishers' Announcements" make this statement "in justice to Miss Hopkins, as well as in response to the general inquiry regarding the personality of the author of 'Hagar's Daughter' "

("Editorial," March 1902, 335). Whereas it was well known that she did use this pen name,[1] it is still challenging to find out why Hopkins used it for the first time and why and where she continued to use it.

She used her mother's name first in *Hagar's Daughter*, a novel that had the word daughter in its title and treated the many intricate familial race relations that connected the period of slavery with a more contemporary time frame. The subject matter contains the delicate matters of miscegenation, race strife in the South and in the nation's capital, and the position of mulatto women. Her decision to use a mainly white setting was certainly a choice that she recognized as questionable or at least problematic. It did not conform with her more outspoken and race-conscious nonfiction essays. Hagar, the prototypical fallen woman, may have been her way of tackling the difficult question of illegitimate birth. Whether this was prompted by any autobiographical background remains subject to conjecture.

The reason why she decided to publish the short story "The Test of Manhood" under the pen name Sarah A. Allen is practical. The same December 1902 issue already contains two other pieces of hers, one of them an installment of her novel *Of One Blood*. Since the story, as I will show in my short-story chapter, can be interpreted in close connection to Fannie Barrier Williams's short story in the same issue, it does not treat a more delicate subject than the Williams story; therefore, Hopkins cannot have been afraid of publishing it under her own name. The same may be said of the articles about "Mr. M. Hamilton Hodges" (a famous singer) in the March 1904 issue and "Mr. Alan Kirkland Soga" (a well-known South African contributor to the magazine) in the February 1904 issue. Practical considerations also account for the Sarah A. Allen short story "Converting Fanny" in the *New Era Magazine*, which comes in an issue that Hopkins dominates quite fully. There is only one issue in the *Colored American Magazine* in which Hopkins uses both of her pen names but does not publish anything under her own name. This is the issue of February 1904 that marks her removal from the magazine.

The use of a pen name in two other articles cannot be explained by practical considerations only. In the "Latest Phases of the Race Problem in America" (Feb. 1903), Allen/Hopkins voices an indirect criticism of the presidency of Theodore Roosevelt, about whom she feels only very cautiously optimistic. After the political appointment of an African American, there are high hopes for him, but Hopkins warns: "By this heroic treatment it seems that the President has broken loose from all restraints and declared war on the 'lily white' Republicans of the South, and that he intends to protect Negro federal

office holders in the South. This seems too good to be true" (247). It is understandable that she may not have wanted to voice this opinion too openly,
especially since Roosevelt had drawn much public approval (and, of course,
considerable disapproval from certain parties) after his dinner with Booker T.
Washington in 1901.

The second of the two articles is called "A New Profession: The First Colored Graduate of the Y.M.C.A. Training School, Springfield, Mass." (Sept.
1903). The strange fact about this article is that it includes some praise of
Booker T. Washington's industrial education and his demand for "a pure,
clean, Christian manhood" (662). Like most African Americans of her time,
Hopkins was capable of seeing the positive effects of industrial training
schools in the big cities that could help educate the young people and help
prevent crime, loitering, and immorality. It is also likely that in September
1903, as the next chapter will detail, Hopkins was under considerable pressure to include an article viewing Booker T. Washington in a positive light.
By using a pen name, she could at least avoid having to sign it with her
own name.

The name Shadrach is used in September 1903, in the issue following the
installment of *Winona* in which the heroine disguises herself as a boy, Allen
Pinks, and rescues the hero. The use of disguised identity here signifies
courage and superhuman love, because Allen Pinks poses as a fugitive slave
and risks being taken back into slavery at any moment. As a boy, Winona
can care for her white English lover Warren Maxwell who, strangely enough,
does not recognize her. It is, therefore, a very successful disguise that eventually leads to the reunion between the lovers. In *Hagar's Daughter*, the black
maid Venus disguises herself as Billy and contributes significantly to the
unraveling of the difficult plot and the rescue of her mistress. Again her
disguise across genders is successful and her actions as Billy are heroic. By
combining Shadrach, the name of an escaped slave, with Shirley, a first name
easily recognized as female, Hopkins also mixes male and female elements
and tries to recapture some element of the former heroism and activism
surrounding the various rescues of Shadrach Minkins.

The name was used between 1902 and 1904, with a later announcement
under this name in 1916. It can be assumed that it was not generally known
who stood behind it, although readers may have recognized it as a pen name,
mainly because the writer was never identified in any of the articles about
editors, writers, and agents of the magazine.

Two of the Shadrach articles deal with men who started in poverty and worked themselves up through a profession. One became a famous orator and teacher ("Charles Winter Wood," Sept. 1902), and the other became a famous orator who won the prestigious Yale award ("William Pickens," July 1903). Both articles contain some interesting arguments. In the article about Charles Winter Wood, Shadrach/Hopkins predicts that the "fate of the Negro is the romance of American history" and that the "future Walter Scott of America will find the border land of his romance" in the "thrilling incidents and escapes and sufferings of the fugitives, and the perils of their friends" (347). As the author of several of these thrilling tales, Shadrach/Hopkins knew what she was talking about. Her argument echoes the preface to *Contending Forces*, in which she writes: "*No one will do this for us; we must ourselves develop the men and women who will faithfully portray the inmost thoughts and feelings of the Negro with all the fire and romance which lie dormant in our history*, and, as yet, unrecognized by writers of the Anglo-Saxon race" (14). By repeating this idea in similar phrases, Hopkins chose a pen name to reiterate a message that was important to her. It is her appeal to African American writers to concentrate on material available to them and publish stories from their perspectives. This appeal goes hand in hand with her influence as an editor who encouraged publications that complied with these criteria.

In her article about William Pickens, she dares to criticize the orator's prizewinning speech because of his low estimate of his subject, the Haitians. She especially laments his view that the African American does not need the ballot, indirectly recognizing the influence of Booker T. Washington.[2] Her argument is clear and forceful: "Under a republican form of government, without the franchise men might as well be monkeys; the ballot makes the man" (521). Her call for agitation here comes in disguise, because it certainly aroused public indignation.

Ideological reasons explain the use of a pen name in two other central essays. In February 1903 Shadrach/Hopkins publishes the first of a two-part article called "Furnace Blasts." The title is taken from a poem by John Greenleaf Whittier and is mentioned in an earlier article about this poet by Hopkins ("Whittier" 329). The first part of the series is entitled "The Growth of the Social Evil Among All Classes and Races in America." Shadrach/Hopkins is concerned with the growth of crime that, in the public view, is mainly attributed to the innate depravity of the Negro. Shadrach/Hopkins quotes examples of the unfair treatment of the Negro in the courts, of dismal situations in the prisons and a female house of refuge, and of statistics about crime that set different standards for white and black criminals. She denounces the high divorce rate, the large amount of gambling, and a false system of education that values material wealth but not moral growth, all of which, however, are more visible in white than in African American society. When she turns to the delicate subject of unwed mothers and mulatto children, Shadrach/Hopkins lashes out against laws that fail to protect colored girls. She calls these social evils "a *national* sin" for which the dismal race relations in the United States are to be blamed (263). It is an angry article that clearly shows her disappointment with the present condition of society, with white society setting a bad example for African Americans.

Her most politically important statement in the second part of "Furnace Blasts" (March 1903) is her attitude toward social equality. In her words, the "greatest objection to Negro enfranchisement is found in the menace of social equality which it is contended will inevitably lead to amalgamation." Shadrach/Hopkins repeats the familiar and well-worn argument that every breach of racial etiquette and every violation of the strict separation between the races would lead to the chaotic intermingling of white and black. Political and civil rights could not be granted, it was commonly believed, because any sort of social equality would empower the position of the black man and thus threaten the so-called dominant race. Like many of her contemporaries, Shadrach/Hopkins is angry about the presupposition that every African American would crave the company of white Americans: "The truth is, the intelligent, self-respecting Afro-American finds every intellectual and social want more than filled among his associates of his own class" (348).

Shadrach/Hopkins then considers the serious problem of marriage outside one's race. Her short answer to the question, "Shall the Anglo-Saxon and the Afro-American mix?" is "They have mixed" (349). She defends this self-evident truth by pointing out the force of love defying all restrictions. In this manner she finds an argument about the relationship between the sexes rather than the races, an argument that is grounded firmly in her generally perceived bond of all humankind and the power of true love that surpasses boundaries and negotiates differences in class and race. Treading a more delicate ground, she continues to write about a union between the races based on moral and intellectual equality and, of course, on mutual consent. More often than not, the union of a black woman with a white man was "an alliance of shame" rather than one of love (350). She calls for character-building to raise the esteem of black women in the eyes of white men and also in the eyes of her white sisters.

What she calls unhappiness in marriage arising from a disharmony of "tempers, talents and dispositions" is a warning against interracial marriages when they are ill-matched, oriented toward financial improvement, or for the purpose of lightening the skin color of the offspring (350). She writes that "the lust of the eyes after the fleshpots of Egypt meshed in the gleam of floating golden hair and the glint of ethereal blue in the orbs of the Anglo-Saxon, must be suppressed" (352). She does not, however, denounce intermarriages as such; in fact, she uses them as one possible model for conjugal bliss in *Hagar's Daughter*.

Shadrach/Hopkins's advice to the hesitant, however, is clear: " 'Don't!' The time for amalgamation is not yet. In the company of the beautiful, virtuous and intellectual of your own race, lie health, happiness and prosperity" (352). Her argumentation is logical: when the African American woman is despised by her white sister and abused by the white man, who but the colored man can offer her a respected position in the world? Upon the premise of mutual consent, her advice is consistent with her earlier article about Charles Winter Wood, which voices the bold assumption that amalgamation will lead to the "future American" (347). This was a daring thought indeed, because amalgamation was usually perceived as the greatest hindrance to a peaceful coexistence of the races. Amalgamation was equated with pollution of the so-called pure Anglo-Saxon blood and had to be avoided at all costs. When Hopkins herself warns against it in one case and approves of it in another, it is clear that she separates the national and international question from the individual one and thus gives an example of the complex and contradictory public discussion about the race problem of her time. Still, she felt safer propagating the question of intermarriage at all under the use of a pen name. There would have been criticism of whichever position she had chosen to take. If she publicly favored amalgamation, as Charles Chesnutt did in his "Future American" series,[3] her fellow African Americans might call her a traitor to the race; if she denounced intermarriage, this would offend the many light-colored African Americans, especially the women she herself writes about in her fiction, who hoped to be able to legitimate their relationships at some point.

The same March 1903 issue includes a letter by a white reader criticizing the trend toward propagating interracial marriages in her fiction. Hopkins defends interracial unions in an angry tone, as will be analyzed in detail later. In this way, the Shadrach/Hopkins essay serves the purpose of emphasizing an argument and elaborating it from various angles and presumably from more than one writer. The same issue also contains another installment of her novel *Of One Blood*, in which there are instances of voluntary and involuntary passing. It also contains the second installment of "Reminiscences of the Life and Times of Lydia Maria Child," written under Hopkins's own name, in which she praises as exemplary the courage, care, and active involvement of this early abolitionist, one of her white sisters, on behalf of the African American.

The conclusion that Shadrach/Hopkins draws from all this in "Furnace Blasts II" is daring. She postulates the creation of a new type of man, the *Afric-American*: "The *Afric*-American has arisen, essentially American in every characteristic, in whom the blood of the Southern white has been contributed as the cement that binds these African tribes as one in the new genus homo" (352). The statement is reminiscent of Du Bois's more famous postulation about the essential twoness of the American Negro: "an American, a Negro; two souls, two thoughts, two unreconciled strivings; two warring ideals in one dark body, whose dogged strength alone keeps it from being torn asunder" (*Souls* 215).[4] While both writers see the existence of the special type of African American, Du Bois emphasizes his split and torn nature, whereas Shadrach/Hopkins points out the essentially homogeneous creation of this "new genus homo." She sees amalgamation, the mixture of the two races, as the constitutive and binding force that unifies African Americans in the United States.

Further textual evidence of the unity of Shadrach and Hopkins can be found in a long passage from her article about Charles Winter Wood, in which she voices her ideas about the "future American" who will be represented "by the descendants of men whose cosmopolitan genius makes them the property of all mankind" (347). This and four more paragraphs reappear verbatim in the *Primer of Facts*, Hopkins's treatise of 1905 (28–29).

Apart from the contents and the various intricate arguments in the Allen and Shadrach essays, the ideas about the progress of the races and the repetition of history appear in several of these articles, becoming familiar signs alerting the reader time and again to her characteristic race consciousness. In the Shadrach/Hopkins essay "Mrs. Jane E. Sharp's School for African Girls" of March 1904,[5] a theory about the progress of civilization keeps coming up repeatedly in her writing and receives a more sustained treatment in her *Primer of Facts* and in her novel *Of One Blood*. It is based upon the westward movement of civilization: "From the day of Africa's decline, the tide of progress has swept westward from Meroe to Egypt, to Greece, to Rome, to Briton [*sic*], to the undiscovered lands of the Western World." Now that civilization has circumnavigated the globe, Africa must be restored to its ancient glory. The quotation from the Bible, which she uses frequently, also appears here: "Princes shall come out of Egypt; Ethiopia shall soon stretch forth her hands unto God" (181; Psalms 68:31). Attentive readers of *Of One Blood*, which had ended in November 1903, must have recognized this phrase immediately because of its prominent position in this novel. Her pan-African standpoint and pride in the ancient greatness of Africa apparent in the novel is echoed in the short essay, in which she quotes Mrs. Sharp as saying: "If the colored race in America only knew their African antecedents, instead of regarding themselves as being descended from savages or slaves, they would have more self-respect, and would be encouraged to higher effort" (184).

The same idea appears in the Shadrach/Hopkins essay about Reverend Dorsey (October 1902). She attributes the downfall of the Roman empire to bribery and corruption, as she does later in her *Primer of Facts*. She ends with the observation, "History repeats itself. There is nothing new under the sun. Decay stands with tottering limbs and feeble breath, I fear me much, at the doors of the great American Republic, and lisps that we draw near the gates" (417). Shadrach/Hopkins ends the first part of "Furnace Blasts" in a familiar way, alluding to the rise and fall of civilizations that threaten American society as much as the Roman empire with decay, injustice, and corruption: "The American people are not less brutal and unjust to the Negro than was the Roman patrician to the common people of his day." She is convinced that "malice defeats itself" and that Rome fell because "omnipotence was wearied by the injustice of man. History repeats itself" (263). The latter phrase had by then become a kind of signature of hers. It can be found in a number of the biographical essays that were published under the name of Hopkins.

In the chronology of her involvement with the *Colored American Magazine*, these six Shadrach essays appear between September 1902 and March 1904. The "Furnace Blasts" essays precede the change in management that was then announced in the May–June issue of 1903 (there is no April issue of this year); a seemingly neutral essay about the African involvement of a prominent race leader of March 1904 treats a pan-African sentiment that had fallen out of favor with the new management and the indirect ownership of Booker T. Washington. Her use of pen names, especially that of Shadrach, thus helped her propagate her ideas but protected her as a person from criticism.

Booker T. Washington and Famous Men

*H*opkins's journalistic essays at the *Colored American Magazine* shed light on her biography, although the references are often indirect. Her "Famous Men of the Negro Race" series, running from November 1900 to October 1901, is the best starting point for a discussion of her negotiations with one of the most influential race leaders, Booker T. Washington, and of her position as a radical African American in the Boston of her time. Similar to most women who aspired to obtain positions of prominence, Hopkins faced a power structure working against her.

In November 1900 Hopkins started her series "Famous Men of the Negro Race" with a statement of purpose: "Races should be judged by the great men they produce, and by the average value of the masses" ("Toussaint" 11). Hopkins's view of the famous men of her race was shaped by her era's concepts of perfect manhood and her own beliefs in a common descent and a common purpose, which she once called "the vision of the Holy Grail" ("Robert Morris" 337). Like many of her contemporaries, Hopkins felt the need to move away from the definition of races as inferior or superior, civilized or uncivilized, of races as determined only by skin color, shape of the head, texture of the hair, or shape of the nose.[1] Famous men and women, according to her and most other African American intellectuals of her time, possessed reliable and verifiable records of achievements that could be documented. In writing these sketches, Hopkins drew upon her profound knowledge of the political and social climate of her immediate surroundings, Boston, and of African American history in general.

The idea of the "average value of the masses" that she mentions repeatedly in her essays came out of her deep conviction that the members of one race were not homogeneous as to educational standards, achievements, and moral advancement. This fundamentally class-based concept reflected the belief of many African Americans that "social equality" did not necessarily mean that the poor rural Negro should be judged the same as the well-to-do African American businessman or Harvard-educated race leader. Hopkins,

70

however, never conveyed the feeling that she looked down upon the uneducated African American. Instead, she thought it the moral responsibility of the wealthier and better-educated part of the population to uplift the race. The many intricate manifestations of class consciousness in her fiction, especially her nonpatronizing portraits of folk characters, will be treated later. In her dealings with famous men of the race, at this point it must be emphasized that she always judged the individual according to his value for the race in general. She regarded individual achievements as the results of social and racial circumstances, which put the individual, who profited from them, under an obligation to work for the welfare of all.

Hopkins's biographical essays may be read as comments on the contemporary situation of African Americans. The many references to Booker T. Washington reflect her and the journal's dependence on his support and goodwill. Since Booker T. Washington was a very controversial figure, provoking wholehearted approval or bitter disapproval, she could not avoid taking sides. It will be observed that she did so, often indirectly, and tried to prevent an open conflict, but lost her position as editor despite her caution.

The first editorial of the *Colored American Magazine* advocates the "bonds of that racial brotherhood, which alone can enable a people, to assert their racial rights as men, and demand their privileges as citizens" ("Editorial," May 1900, 60). While calling for progress, activism, and justice, it also carefully praises the aims and personality of Booker T. Washington. The editorial ends, for example, with the following comparison of Washington and Christ: "Surely whatever else he deserves, he does not deserve censure, criticism and calumny. Sad would it be, indeed, if it were said of him as it was said of another of earth's greatest benefactors 'He came unto his own and his own received him not'" (62; see also Schneider 64).

Booker T. Washington was the "wizard" of Tuskegee, the founder of the Tuskegee Institute in Alabama, an institution dedicated mostly to industrial education, and its principal from 1881 till his death in 1915. Controversial as a race leader, he warned African Americans against political agitation and promoted industrial education and agricultural expertise, which would guarantee them a secure position in society. From his humble southern origin he achieved a place of prominence in part through clever maneuvers, which were not always publicly known, that won him support at Tuskegee and gave him considerable political influence.[2] Washington published his autobiography, *Up from Slavery*, in 1901; it included a lengthy description of his "Atlanta Exposition Address," given only six years earlier. In this speech Washington called upon African Americans to work for their salvation through industrial

AN EXCELLENT PORTRAIT
OF
BOOKER T. WASHINGTON
GIVEN FREE WITH EACH YEARLY SUB-SCRIPTION TO THE "NEW ERA MAGAZINE"

Portrait of Booker T. Washington in the *New Era Magazine*, February 1916. Courtesy of Black Print Culture Collection, Special Collections and Archives, Robert W. Woodruff Library, Emory University.

progress and, to repeat his well-worn metaphor, to cast down their buckets where they were, in the American South. Agriculture, mechanics, commerce, domestic service, and the professions were the fields they should work in. Southern white people were asked to help this "most patient, faithful, law-abiding, and unresentful people" (*Up from Slavery* 148). In an attempt to assure the support of his white audience, he spoke against civil equality: "In all things that are purely social we can be as separate as the fingers, yet one as the hand in all things essential to mutual progress." His politics of racial accommodation through segregation alienated many contemporary African Americans who thought that voting rights, higher education, and equal opportunities were essential to the progress of the race. His disdain of political activism and his conciliatory attitude about voting rights guaranteed him, however, the prominent position and political influence that helped him maintain the Tuskegee Institute and pursue a number of other political aims. The fact that he had many followers is also reflected in the political climate that preceded the passing of *Plessy v. Ferguson* in 1896, the Supreme Court decision that legalized segregation on a large scale.

There are numerous examples of African Americans involved in education, politics, and journalism whose careers depended on the approval or disapproval of what is now called the "Tuskegee Machine." In his substantial study of Booker T. Washington's life, Louis R. Harlan claims that Washington "actually entered patronage politics with gusto and with a remarkable talent for its trivial details" (*Wizard* 6). Harlan quotes examples of Washington's influence on President Roosevelt and his power to further or quash the career of an African American politician or intellectual. He lists names of famous African American men and women who were directly or indirectly on the payroll of the "Tuskegee Machine."

One of Washington's opponents was William Monroe Trotter, Hopkins's contemporary in Boston, owner and editor of the *Guardian*, Boston's African American newspaper. Trotter was one of the founders of the Boston Literary and Historical Association, which, according to Elizabeth McHenry, was "a direct attack on the leadership and racial politics of Booker T. Washington" (144). Trotter was the head of the so-called Boston riot, when he and some fellow Trotterites disturbed a meeting of the National Negro Business League in July 1903. In retaliation, Washington began to discredit the reputation of Trotter's coeditor and eventually ruined the journal.[3] Hopkins, a member of the Boston Literary and Historical Association (see McHenry 184), agreed with Trotter about political radicalism. In a 1905 letter to Trotter (details about which will follow), Hopkins appeals to him for a "respectful hearing and judgment as to the best way to deal with this complicated case" because she felt she was "persistently hedged about by the revengeful tactics of Mr. Washington's men" (1).

Later opposition to the Tuskegee Machine was spearheaded by W.E.B. Du Bois, author of *The Souls of Black Folk*, one chapter of which—"Of Mr. Booker T. Washington and Others"—caused much public controversy. Du Bois was a graduate of the universities of Fisk, Berlin, and Harvard, and professor of economics and history at Atlanta University. He then became one of the founders of the Niagara Movement, which later merged into the National Association for the Advancement of Colored People (NAACP).[4] As editor of *Crisis*, Du Bois established himself definitely as successor to Booker T. Washington and replaced his accommodationism with a radical political agenda.

Although Du Bois was the most prominent opponent of Booker T. Washington on the question of industrial training versus the classical curriculum, the ramifications of this controversy can be detected in many other places and careers. The high-profile careers of Anna Julia Cooper, writer and educator in Washington, D.C.; Ida B. Wells-Barnett, radical antilynching crusader, civil rights activist, and suffragist in Chicago; Fanny J. Coppin, educator and school principal in Philadelphia; and Mary Church Terrell, famous clubwoman and wife of Judge Robert Terrell, a loyal follower of Booker T. Washington, were all dependent upon the goodwill of Washington.[5] In these cases, an ideological difference was infused with gender problematics. Pauline Hopkins offers a good example of the merging of race, class, gender, and ideology. She was one of the few prominent women to oppose Booker T. Washington. Although she had to choose oblique criticism rather than open confrontation, she risked her career because of her political views.

In her role as race historian in "Famous Men of the Negro Race," Hopkins judges the knowledge of exemplary lives as absolutely necessary for progress. When she writes about Robert Morris, the first practicing African American lawyer to influence the American bar, she precedes a discussion of his life by saying: "The contemplation of the life-work of these men is about all that we have to cheer and encourage us in our strivings after high ideals, and to appease our longings for the perfect day of our true emancipation,—the black man's sweet but ever-vanishing vision of the Holy Grail" ("Robert Morris" 337). The mythical rhetoric is subsumed under a more biblical rhetoric in many other instances: "We delight to honor the great men of our race because the lives of these noble Negroes are tongues of living flame speaking in the powerful silence of example, and sent to baptize the race with heaven's holy fire into the noble heritage of perfected manhood." Both the mythical and biblical language suggest that God and some mythological past have reserved a degree of greatness for the African race and its African American descendants. Her repeated emphasis that we are all "of one blood" allows her to get away from a dominant Anglo-Saxon supremacist standpoint and to apply the same standards ("perfected manhood"), descent ("of one blood"), and quest ("the Holy Grail," "true emancipation") to her race. This emphasis allows her to undermine white claims to supremacy because white Americans did not recognize the hardworking and fast-moving progress of the African American race.[6]

A good example of this strategy appears in the first part of her series. She begins with Toussaint L'Ouverture, whom she portrays as noble, heroic, paternal, merciful, and a natural leader of the people.[7] Toussaint L'Ouverture (1743–1803; spelled Overture by Hopkins) was a self-educated former slave who joined the Haitian Revolution in 1791 and became its foremost general, defeating both the French and British forces. In 1802 he was betrayed and captured, and died imprisoned in France. In her discussion of the life of this early black hero, Hopkins points out the lesson that African Americans can learn from the history of Hayti (Hopkins's original spelling) and solicits the acknowledgment of a bond with other African peoples; "we should clasp our hands in friendship" (24). In her analysis of Hopkins's race rhetoric, C. K. Doreski calls this "an act of Pan-African revelation" (10). Indeed, Hopkins emphasizes the belief in an all-encompassing race understanding based upon a deep Christian background: "Let us not fear for the future of Hayti or for the future of the whole race; the same God rules today who ruled in ages past. As a race we shall be preserved, although annihilation sometimes seems very near" ("Toussaint" 24). Toussaint, "Napoleon's black shadow" (11), commits heroic deeds, reminiscent of Greek heroism at "Thermopylae and Marathon and Platea" (24), but is expelled from his Haitian paradise and betrayed by Napoleon. His heroism needs to be remembered and recorded by African Americans, because it is not only a record of his suffering but shows the participation of a man of African descent in world history.

When we read her biographical sketches with an eye on Booker T. Washington, the choices she made about whom to include in her series and the order of appearance are significant. To begin with Toussaint L'Ouverture was certainly an excellent choice because he was recognized by most of her contemporaries as an exemplary man. She continued the series with a loving and reverent portrait of Frederick Douglass, and she placed this portrait in the December 1900 issue, at the beginning of the new century. Hopkins portrays him not only as a national heroic figure but also as her personal hero. There is no doubt that he influenced her decisively. In the introduction to a pamphlet that he and Ida B. Wells-Barnett wrote for the 1893 World's Columbian Exposition in Chicago, Douglass states: "We are men and our aim is perfect manhood, to be men among men. Our situation demands faith in ourselves, faith in the power of truth, faith in work and faith in the influence of manly character" (qtd. in Bederman 39). Hopkins pays her respect to the man, whom she admired and whose activist political ideals she tried to emulate. She certainly had him in mind when she put down her views on "perfected manhood."

In the next issue (January 1901), she discusses William Wells Brown (1814–84), who had influenced her early writing so much. Typical of the organizing principles in her biographical sketches, she narrates his life partly by giving facts and partly by telling anecdotes that point out the subject's brave soul or his wit or humor.[8] Her conclusion about Brown is that such self-made men of the race are still needed today: "How many of us today can occupy and fill their vacant places? Not alone *occupy*, but *fill* them. Alas! how few, when we consider our advantages. If much is given, much is required. An ignorant man will trust to luck for success; an educated man will *make* success. God helps those who help themselves" (236).

Given Hopkins's divided attitude toward Booker T. Washington, it comes as no surprise that she did not immediately name him as one of those who could "fill" the place of Brown. Yet considering that in 1901 readers might have expected Booker T. Washington to be at least fourth in this series, it is remarkable that months would pass till she would write about Washington in her essays about famous men of the race. Instead, she continued with a discussion of Robert Browne Elliott, a politician and race leader, whose life gave her the opportunity to analyze more recent history and criticize racism and intolerance. There is an indirect reference to Washington in her essay about Elliott that might explain Hopkins's attitude toward him at this time. Her point of departure is the much heralded "industrial development," a concept that is often synonymous with Washingtonian accommodationism: "The phrase 'industrial development' is greatly misunderstood by our white friends. To them it means an excuse, gladly hailed, to force the Negro to retrograde. To us it means, education of head and hand, not confining the Negro to any particular line of employment, certainly with no intention of curtailing his efforts to raise himself into any business, profession or so-cial condition that intrinsic worth and fitness may warrant him in seeking" ("Famous Men: Elliott" 300). This is an indirect criticism of Washington, whose ideas were often interpreted as restricting the educational possibilities of African Americans. Hopkins comes back to this point when she writes about Elliott's early death and the loss to his race and his country: "By his achievements we prove that it is possible for a Negro to rise to great political eminence as well as a white man, if the desire for his 'industrial development' does not blind our eyes to other advantages in life" (301).

Hopkins proceeds to discuss Edwin Walker, a lawyer; Lewis Hayden, a famous abolitionist and successful tailor; Charles Lenox Remond, another well-known abolitionist; Sgt. William H. Carney, who served in the famous Fifty-fourth Regiment of Massachusetts; John Mercer Langston, orator, lawyer, and statesman; Senator Blanche K. Bruce, politician and statesman; and Robert Morris, a lawyer. Most of these men lived in Boston or had ties to Boston and, as Doreski remarks, "most of the careers originate in the Oberlin-Boston nexus of liberal reform and abolitionist fervor" (14).

In the biographical sketch about Washington that finally appears in October 1901, Hopkins writes that no one will question "that Dr. Washington and Tuskegee are one" (436). Now this is no surprising statement, but what follows takes it literally: "Tuskegee is the soul of the man outlined in wood, in brick and stone, pulsating with the life of the human hive within on whom he has stamped his individuality." The guiding images here, that of the soul as brick and stone and that of the beehive, indicate the hardness of the man's soul and the busyness of the bee that works hard. Although the image remains within the realm of convention, it takes on extra meaning when we know that Washington's enterprising activities and influence, his individuality, which left its mark on many who depended on him, would eventually be directed against the journalist and oust her from her position as editor. It is also interesting to note that Hopkins gives two long quotations from a 1895 speech by Washington entitled "Industrial Education," which emphasized the achievements of black people in America, but that she does not quote from his more famous "Atlanta Exposition Address." She only refers to it as "his great speech" and says that it "received many flattering encomiums from leading men all over the country" (439). She returns to this point when she says that Washington is "without a peer" in "attracting the attention of the monied element."

Hopkins emphasizes his wealth once more when she calls him one of the most remarkable men of this age and mentions "his humble birth and rise to eminence and wealth" (441). The entire essay is permeated by references to money and wealth, mainly payments he received for Tuskegee, for his lectures, or the amount of money invested in such and such a part of Tuskegee. In her essay about John Mercer Langston, by contrast, there is wholehearted praise of his achievements but no reference to financial matters. In comparison to her unambiguous and genuine praise of Langston, her praise of Washington sounds flat and forced, at least to readers who read between the lines. Unlike the earlier essays, there are no references to "perfected manhood," common descent ("of one blood"), or the quest for the Holy Grail.

Toward the end of this five-page sketch of Washington, she writes: "View his career in whatever light we may, be we for or against his theories, his personality is striking, his life uncommon, and the magnetic influence which radiates from him in all directions, bending and swaying great minds and pointing the ultimate conclusion of colossal schemes as the wind the leaves of the trees, is stupendous" (441). Syntactically, her praise of his striking personality and uncommon life is all but subsumed by the second part of the sentence, where his magnetic influence is compared to the force of a storm. Hopkins leaves it to the reader to conclude who the great minds were that Washington bent and swayed. The "colossal" influence of the man would not only strip the trees of leaves but force many of his contemporaries to succumb to his views. When she finally compares him to Napoleon, the reader is reminded of the opening essay of the series about Toussaint L'Ouverture and Napoleon, the man who betrayed him: "When the happenings of the Twentieth Century have become matters of history, Dr. Washington's motives will be open to as many constructions and discussions as are those of Napoleon today, or of other men of extraordinary ability, whether for good or evil, who have had like phenomenal careers" (441). The cautious note in this essay about such an eminent figure hints to readers that they should scrutinize Washington's motives. For Doreski, Hopkins here bends the biographical conventions to her own purposes: "By its very nature, biography demands belief in the subject-embracing rhetoric, and this portrait must bear the polemic weight of the entire series. Whereas Toussaint's and Douglass's lives seemed divinely inspired, Washington's . . . seems decidedly secular, deliberate, and forced" (13).

The essay highlights Hopkins's dilemma of criticizing a man who she felt was taking African Americans in a wrong direction, while in general praising him as a race leader who had achieved a position of wealth and prominence. While she repeatedly argued that the identity and power of the race depended on its manly men and worthy women, she could not fully condemn one of its most prominent contemporary leaders. At the same time, she could not wholeheartedly endorse his program and, as early as 1901, must have felt her own position at risk because of this.

Hopkins's "Famous Men" series concluded in October 1901, but her dealings with Washington did not. Her career continued to be shaped by dealings with men who rarely showed an appreciation of her efforts and achievements. The question of Hopkins's attitude toward Booker T. Washington is not whether she was right or wrong from a historical standpoint in her assessment of his role and influence. Even if Booker T. Washington was perhaps less of an accommodationist than is usually acknowledged, since he organized legal battles against segregation and disfranchisement behind the scenes,[9] Hopkins could not have known about it at the time. To her, it appeared that Washington was the driving force behind people who sought to antagonize her.

In January 1903 she started what seemed to be the beginning of another series, "Heroes and Heroines in Black" with the subtitle "I. Neil Johnson, American Woodfolk, et al." For unknown reasons she did not continue this series, although it contributed to the overall tone of the magazine as praising the race and projecting a generally hopeful view of the future: "We propose in this article to touch upon the noble trait of heroism, in the Negro race, which is defined as gallantry, valor, courage" (206). She asserts that the heroic spirit is "the foundation of universal history, history itself being but an account of the deeds of men who have been the models and pattern for the great mass of humanity in past centuries from the beginning of the world." Heroism for her is "a military attribute of the soul; a fine contempt for safety or ease; a mind of such chivalric mold that thoughts of danger cause no disturbance; the highest degree of natural enthusiasm which the world profoundly venerates." Her examples of heroism are well chosen and interesting, giving testimony to the brave and fighting spirit of the Negro. She started the year 1903 with hopes for the welfare of the African American race in general: "The dawn of the Twentieth century finds the Black race fighting for existence in every quarter of the globe. From over the sea Africa stretches her hands to the American Negro and cries aloud for sympathy in her hour of trial" (211). Her personal outlook for the future is still optimistic: "But the Negro still lives, and while life remains, Hope lifts a smiling face."

As it turned out, however, the year 1903 proved to be very difficult and disappointing. Growing financial problems forced Walter Wallace to sell the magazine. As early as August 1901 he appealed to Booker T. Washington for financial help, writing about the "critical condition" because of the "expensive luxury" of also publishing books and because of outstanding subscription money (*Booker T. Washington Papers* 6:184–85). The *Colored American Magazine* was bought by William Dupree, a Civil War hero and leader in civic organizations, who was assisted by William O. West and Jesse W. Watkins. Hopkins was officially listed as literary editor in the May–June issue of 1903. The magazine functioned as the journal of the Colored American League, founded the same year in order to raise more money. However, the financial situation of the *Colored American Magazine* was not stabilized permanently, and, therefore, Dupree's ownership turned out to be only a transitional solution that did not guarantee its continued existence.

Dupree is profiled in an anonymous article, "Colonel William Dupree," in July 1901 as honorable, brave, an astute businessman, and full of integrity. Reminiscent of Hopkins's essays about famous men and women in style and tone, the profile includes a call to fight for the rights of men. When Dupree took over the magazine in May 1903, he was obviously pleased with Hopkins's work, as she remembers proudly: "I was engaged as literary editor because I was well-known as a race writer, had gained the confidence of my people, and also because there seemed to be at that time, no one else as well qualified to fill the position, for as yet the editing of a high-class magazine was puzzling work even to our best scholars" (Hopkins-Trotter letter 1). In the May–June 1903 issue, the three owners and editors are profiled in an article, "Biographies of the Officers of the New Management of Our Magazine," which is written in Hopkins's style, although it is not signed with her name. This article emphasizes the need to "renew the battle for equal and exact justice for all races and all men" and to present exemplary lives (such as that of William Dupree) that may serve to prove the "integrity, industry and character" of the race ("Biographies" 443). The "Editorial and Publishers' Announcements" in this same issue detail the possible hardships and months of doubt and uncertainty that preceded the reorganization and show the dedication of the managers to the publication: "At the cost of many anxious moments and sleepless nights, when not a star of hope was visible in the horizon, God has permitted us to save this enterprise to our race. Envy and covetousness have sat with us in council, but even as did the Christian martyrs of old forgive their tormentors the tortures inflicted upon them, so do we forgive our enemies. At some future day we hope to be able to tell our true story to our readers, who will then give us the full sympathy of their warm hearts" (466). In November 1903 Dupree suggested to Hopkins that he could solicit the white New York publisher and music critic John C. Freund for a series of articles on Jamaica. In the earlier months of his involvement with the magazine, Freund won Hopkins's confidence because she saw his engagement as "a case of pure philanthropy, one of those rare cases which are sometimes found among wealthy, generous and eccentric white men" (Hopkins-Trotter letter 2). She soon learned that he was instrumental in maligning and discrediting her as editor. Within months it became clear to her that Freund was backed by Booker T. Washington and was striving to transfer the magazine to New York.

This evaluation is based on the April 16, 1905, letter from Hopkins to Trotter that Ann Allen Shockley has located at Fisk and included in the Hopkins Papers. In the ten pages of this letter, Hopkins clarifies the background information about the sale of the magazine from the original owners to William Dupree in the spring of 1903, the constant financial and organizational problems this change entailed, and then moves on to discuss the involvement of John C. Freund, the foundation of the Colored American League, and the eventual transfer of the magazine to New York under the editorship of Fred R. Moore. The general tone of this long letter is one of despair and bitter disappointment about the treatment she received from the white patron and her African American colleagues.

Within the letter there are references such as "See accompanying letter marked with the number 1." These accompanying letters, twenty in number, are now available for study.[10] All of them are from John C. Freund; five of them are addressed to William Dupree, the rest to Hopkins herself. Although their numbering does not always correspond to the numbering mentioned in the Hopkins-Trotter letter, it is necessary to list them by writer, addressee, and date so that they can be identified more easily.[11] Three letters are written by John C. Freund to Mr. William L. Dupree, Superintendent, Station A, Post Office, Boston, Mass., dated November 19, 1903; January 27, 1904; and January 28, 1904. Letters marked 4 to 15 are from Freund directed to Miss Pauline E. Hopkins, Editor, "The Colored American Magazine," 82 West Concord St., Boston, Mass., with the following dates: Feb. 11, 1904; Feb. 18, 1904; March 5, 1904; March 12, 1904; March 14, 1904; March 16, 1904; March 17, 1904; March 18, 1904; March 24, 1904; March 25, 1904; and March 28, 1904. Letters 16 and 17 are from Freund to Dupree, dated March 31, 1904; and April 6, 1904. Three more letters are addressed to Hopkins on April 7, April 11, and April 16, 1904. The last two are directed to her home at 53 Clifton St., North Cambridge, Mass. In the Hopkins-Trotter letter there are additional references to the March 1904 issue of the *Colored American Magazine*, especially Hopkins's article about the foundation of the Colored American League, "How a New York Newspaper Man Entertained a Number of Colored Ladies and Gentlemen at Dinner in the Revere House, Boston, and How the Colored American League Was Started."

Hopkins's motivation for documenting her experiences at the *Colored American Magazine* and for sending the accompanying letters to Trotter a year after all this had happened is stated in her opening paragraph:

> Herewith I send you a detailed account of my experiences with the *Colored American Magazine* as its editor and, incidentally, with Mr. Booker T. Washington in the taking over of the magazine to New York by his agents. It is necessarily long and perhaps tedious at the outset, but I trust that you will peruse it to the end. I have held these facts for a year, but as my rights are ignored in my own property, and I am persistently hedged about by the revengeful tactics of Mr. Washington's men, I feel that I must ask the advice of some one who will give me a respectful hearing, and judgment as to the best way to deal with this complicated case. (1)

This opening passage shows Hopkins's bitterness and her understanding of the role Booker T. Washington played in this transaction.

The letter does not give information about how she got hold of the letters to Dupree, but it can be assumed that Dupree had given her a copy of them because he wanted her to understand the role Freund had played from the outset. She names him and Jesse Watkins and William West as potential witnesses, who would substantiate the truth of her testimony if Trotter asked them. About the position of Dupree, she adds: "Mr. Dupree, of course, knows more of the facts than I do, and I have no doubt would be willing to tell all that he knows if he were guaranteed protection from the malice of Mr. Washington's friends" (Hopkins-Trotter letter 10). This latter assessment shows that she still felt Dupree to be sympathetic toward her position and that she trusted him.

When John C. Freund first joined the *Colored American Magazine* with a series of articles on Jamaica, he seemed to be genuinely interested in the publication. In the second letter to Dupree (January 27, 1904), he uses the collective first-person plural ("to get us clear by the First of March") to show his identification with the editors. He suggests the formation of a league to raise money and support the magazine's goals. Yet there is already a hint of his attempt not only to finance the magazine but also to exercise control over its content. He informs Dupree: "I have also written to Miss Hopkins urging her to do her utmost to keep out of the magazine anything that might be construed into antagonism to the whites. We must take high ground in order

(*no. 17*)

(COPY)

New York, April 6th, 1904.

Colonel William H. Dupree,
    Station A,
        Boston, Mass.

My dear Colonel Dupree:-
        I have a prospect of help before long, but do not care
to speak of it as yet. A very prominent gentleman was at my
house last night, discussing the magazine, who is going to bring
the matter to the immediate attention of men who, he thinks, may
give some aid.   This was Booker T. Washington.

        There is, however, one rock right squarely ahead of us.
That is the persistence with which matter is put into the magazine,
which has no live interest, and furthermore, is likely to alienate
the very friends who might help us. Now, I have spoken of the
subject already more than I care to. Either Miss Hopkins will
follow our suggestion in this matter and put live matter into the
magazine, eliminating anything which may create offence; stop
talking about wrongs and a proscribed race, or you must count me
out absolutely from this day forth. I will neither personally
endorse nor help a business proposition, which my common sense
tells me is foredoomed to failure. Every person that I have spoken
to on the subject is with me. IT IS MR. BOOKER WASHINGTON'S IDEA.
        If you people, therefore, want to get out a literary
magazine, with articles on the Filipinos, I refuse to work one
minute longer with you. That is my ultimatum and I shall say no
more on the subject.

                Very truly yours,

                    (Signed) *John C. Freund.*

Letter dated April 6, 1904, from John C. Freund to Colonel William H. Dupree,
in which Booker T. Washington's work behind the scenes of the
Colored American Magazine is revealed. Reproduced by permission of
the Fisk University Franklin Library Special Collections.

to disarm opposition and bring out the good will of the white people who
are not only with you now, but have always been with you only you have
not known it." In addition to constantly urging Dupree and later Hopkins
to be more astute about business matters, the third letter to Dupree reveals
his belief that the magazine should contain news, essays about famous men

and women, organizations and universities, rather than literature and critical articles. He assumed the role of spokesman for all the editors: "What we want to do is to get to work and show what the colored people are doing for themselves; how they are raising themselves up, and to do this, not by means of glittering generalities, but by making up individual cases" (Freund-Dupree, Jan. 28, 1904). He presses his argument again in his February 18, 1904, letter to Hopkins: "The magazine should therefore, in my judgment, contain some fiction, some interesting articles which will appeal to the general mass of the colored people, but particularly, it should treat of the work being done by the Negro people." All this entails a curtailing of the editors' rights to "argue and fight prejudice on general lines or with glittering generalities, but it must prepare the way for a better order of things by demonstrating persistently what the colored people have already done for themselves, and thus prove beyond controversy that they can be uplifted, and that their future is assured, provided only they obtain opportunity and justice." Hopkins recognized Booker T. Washington's rhetoric in this letter, although it obviously took her some time to find out Freund's motives and his connections. Freund continued to compliment her on her ability and competence, although she could not but doubt his intentions after the receipt of these letters.

At about the same time, in January 1904, Freund invited her, Mr. and Mrs. Dupree, as well as some other people engaged in the *Colored American Magazine* to a dinner at the Revere House, Boston. This event is described by Hopkins in "How a New York Newspaper Man Entertained a Number of Colored Ladies and Gentlemen at Dinner in the Revere House, Boston, and How the Colored American League Was Started," a most interesting article documenting her views and the role of John C. Freund in the magazine to the readership. The article contains Freund's speech at the dinner, which not only illustrates his motivations but also the often difficult relationships between white patrons and African American entrepreneurs and artists.

Freund justifies his participation in this enterprise: "I took an ever increasing interest in what is called the colored race problem, not because, let me be frank, I have any particular interest in the colored people as such, but because of the principles which had appealed to me, and because I believed that a man should be what he makes himself, whether his face be white or black, his hair straight or kinky, his eyes blue or brown, whether his nose curves one way or the other" (153). Despite the lack of personal interest, Freund, in openly paternalistic rhetoric, proceeds to give good advice to the colored race in general and points out the important educational function of the magazine: "What you have to do is to put up such a proposition to the heart, the conscience, the chivalry, not only of the South, but of the people of the whole United States, that justice must—and will be done you" (154).

Thus far Freund does not differ from any other liberal white who thinks that the problem can be solved with good will and a determined effort on both sides. Then he criticizes the editor, Hopkins:

> I notice, in one of the articles written by your worthy, most talented and self-sacrificing editress, Miss Hopkins, a tendency to refer to her people as a "proscribed race."
>
> You must cease to speak of yourselves as a proscribed people. You must cease to dwell upon your wrongs in the past, however bitter, however cruel.
>
> How shall the barriers that hold you in be broken down, if you insist upon living behind them? Your duty is to forget the past, at least, to put it behind you and to advance bravely, with your faces to the dawn and the light. (155)

Freund here attacks not only Hopkins herself but an entire generation of writers who insist on dealing with past cruelty to explain the present situation and who think that "to advance bravely" involves the backward glance as well. This is a generation of writers refusing to forgive the nation's wrongs by politely talking about future possibilities instead of demanding a collective responsibility. His praise of Hopkins as a talented and self-sacrificing editor sounds more than perfunctory when he then attacks her fiction. The term *proscribed race* features prominently in her novel *Contending Forces*, which begins with this dedication: "To the Friends of Humanity Everywhere I offer this humble tribute written by one of a proscribed race." Hopkins correctly understood Freund's intention: " 'Proscribed race,' was a hit at my book *Contending Forces* and my serial story *Hagar's Daughter* both of which had aroused the ire of the white South, male and female, against me many of whom had paid me their compliments in newspaper squibs and insulting personal letters sent to the old management of the magazine" (Hopkins-Trotter letter 6).

Freund then urges colored people not to consider their position as unique in the world and not to think that all they need to do is to make it known to the white people how far they have advanced in the arts, sciences, and education. He points out that the race problem gets adequate coverage in some of the leading white journals. He speaks about the brave and noble president, Theodore Roosevelt, and the people's great interest in and aid to Tuskegee. His solution to the problem is self-help. Safe and sound in his white skin, Freund closes by talking about the fact that every race has had to struggle but that it can win and overcome adversity when it applies itself diligently enough.

It is difficult to imagine the reaction of the audience to this speech. Hopkins only notes that it was "cordially received" (158). The other speeches are not reprinted in full. She only mentions the speech of Mr. Butler R. Wilson, a lawyer, "who said that it gave him great pleasure to be present, and while he would not agree with all that had been said, he readily admitted that there was much food for thought" (158–59). Behind the scenes, Hopkins writes to Trotter, there was strict opposition to Freund's plan to transfer the magazine to New York (Hopkins-Trotter letters 2–3). Given Hopkins's writings, it is safe to assume that she was offended by the paternalistic tone of Freund's address and especially did not like its blunt praise of Booker T. Washington. The friction between Freund and Hopkins may be seen as well in her letter to Trotter, in which she laments that he "held with each one of us the patriarchal relation of ancient days" (Hopkins-Trotter letter 3).

The problems of financing and running the *Colored American Magazine* were acute most of the time. At the same foundational meeting of the Colored American League, at which Freund hinted at the new editorial policies, Hopkins addressed the audience, and her report is summarized in the following way: "Miss Pauline E. Hopkins, the editress of the Magazine, gave a most eloquent and touching account of the struggles of the magazine, with which she has been connected almost from its inception. She said that there were times when there was not a dollar in the treasury, and when the darkness of despair settled upon the little band of men and women who had devoted themselves to the cause, but even in the worst days, when everything seemed to have gone against them, they never despaired" ("How a New York Newspaper Man" 159). Freund is an early example of the white patronage of African American arts and artistic enterprises that would bloom during the Harlem Renaissance. *Negrotarians* was Zora Neale Hurston's word for whites who specialized in the uplift of the race. The list that David Levering Lewis gives in *When Harlem Was in Vogue* is long and reaches from columnist Heywood Broun and his wife Ruth Hale, to Pearl Buck, Fannie Hurst, Dorothy Parker, T. S. Stribling, Carl van Vechten, Vachel Lindsay, Julia Peterkin, and Charlotte Mason, the notorious patron of Langston Hughes, Zora Neale Hurston, Claude McKay, and Alain Locke.[12]

Problems of financing and running a small African American periodical were not confined to the *Colored American Magazine*. The Boston *Guardian*, founded in 1901 by William Monroe Trotter, was run initially out of Trotter's personal fortune and later had to be financed on a day-to-day basis. Trotter lost most of his investment, but he was able to publish the *Guardian* nearly without interruption up to his death in 1932 by displaying a singular obstinacy, persistence, and an incredible discipline. In contrast to the editors of the *Colored American Magazine*, Trotter steadfastly refused to open his paper to advertisements for tobacco, liquor, skin lighteners, and hair straighteners (Fox 207). Despite this lucrative commercial income, the *Colored American Magazine* was nevertheless shorter-lived than the *Guardian*, since it was not backed by a large personal fortune.

A similar fate befell the *Voice of the Negro*, the first magazine edited in the South by African Americans.[13] Throughout its existence (1904–7), Washington regarded the fame and quality of the *Voice* as dangerous to his own political position. The treatment of its editor, J. Max Barber, is especially revealing of Washington's tactics. For some time the outspoken and radical Barber had Washington's personal secretary, J. Emmett Scott, as associate editor. After Scott's resignation, Barber made it clear that he endorsed the formation of the Niagara Movement and the politics of W.E.B. Du Bois. Hopkins notes that this "organ has offended Mr. Washington deeply by adopting an independent course. The *Voice* has caught the New York trade and Mr. Moore is swearing vengeance" (Hopkins-Trotter letter 8). After his forced withdrawal from Atlanta, Barber strove hard but failed to maintain the magazine in Chicago. As Louis R. Harlan writes about his further career, "Barber also lost positions as a newspaper editor in Chicago and teacher in Philadelphia. Seeking a career in which Booker T. Washington could not hound him, he worked his way through dental school and set up a practice in Philadelphia."[14]

Du Bois's short-lived *Moon Illustrated Weekly* ceased publication after only a few months in 1905 because he refused to accept funding that was given to influence his editorial politics, and his *Horizon*, published in Washington, D.C., between January 1907 and May 1910, was also unable to survive (Johnson and Johnson, *Propaganda* 24–29).

Washington's clever strategy of winning over famous journalists can also be shown in his dealings with T. Thomas Fortune, the owner and editor of the *New York Age*, who started his career with a reputation as a militant and radical leader. His financial problems, however, drove him into the camp of Booker T. Washington, who bought the *Age* and used Fortune for his own purposes. Hopkins even claims that she learned that Fortune wrote Washington's *Up from Slavery* and many of his other articles (see Hopkins-Trotter letter 7). "All of these facts," she concludes, "go to show that the *New*

York Age is a subsidized sheet[,] for its editor is under money obligations to
Mr. Washington, and a man so situated is not a free agent by any means"
(Hopkins-Trotter letter 8).

In February 1904 Hopkins received a bouquet of violets, a book, and a
twenty-five-dollar check from Freund. She was greatly puzzled by this preferential treatment because it made her position in the office uncomfortable.
In her account of this she offers us a rare glimpse of her personal situation
at this time. She refers to her bedridden mother as one of her "burdens at
home" and says of herself: "As I am not a woman who attracts the attention
of the opposite sex in any way, Mr. Freund's philanthropy with regard to
myself puzzled me" (Hopkins-Trotter letter 3). In time Hopkins realized
that the gifts must have been meant as a bribe, just as she would later be
offered an increased salary to cover up Washington's role in the purchase of
the magazine and its relocation to New York. In terms of gender relations,
Freund's attempt to buy her so cheaply reflects his utterly condescending
attitude toward her.

In order to solicit contributions and advance sales, at the beginning of
1904 the *Colored American Magazine* started a series called "Industrial Education; Will It Solve the Negro Problem? Answered Each Month by the
Greatest Thinkers of the Black Race" (Jan. 1904). Basically this series is a
discussion of Washington's policies, and if a contributor did not want to
avoid the issue, as John Edward Bruce did by concentrating instead on the
problem of what the Negro question really was, he or she had to take sides.
According to Hopkins, these articles "created consternation in the ranks of
the Southern supporters because they were written by writers of so high a
standing in the literary world as to prove that the policy of industrial education solely for the Negro was not popular, and was doomed to failure in the
end" (Hopkins-Trotter letter 9).

From the beginning, Booker T. Washington thus seemed to be behind
the attempt to destroy the *Colored American Magazine* and transfer it from
the supportive environment of Boston to New York, although it could not
have been obvious to all that he was involved. In March 1904 Freund asked
Hopkins to write a letter to introduce Freund to Washington, and Hopkins
reluctantly did so: "Mr. Dupree and the staff requested me to comply strictly
with Mr. Freund's request, so, although I had NO PERSONAL ACQUAIN-
TANCE WITH MR. WASHINGTON, I wrote a letter to him detailing our
situation, recounting Mr. Freund's kind acts and craving Mr. Washington's
good offices as a race man in our favor" (Hopkins-Trotter letter 5). On March

25 and March 28, Freund informed Hopkins that he had met Mr. Washington and, in a letter referred to but not included in the available material, he told her that Washington had called upon him. In her own résumé of this part of her acquaintance with Freund, Hopkins doubted the fact that Freund and Washington had not met before: "The great question is,—Did Mr. Freund intend to help the enterprise when he took it up at the beginning and was he turned from his purpose by the influence of Mr. Washington's expressed views and desires, or was it a mutual understanding between these gentlemen from the beginning?" (Hopkins-Trotter letter 9).

Letter number 16, dated March 31, 1904, was dubbed by Hopkins "The Washington Letter" and was written by Freund to Dupree. In this letter Freund frankly admits his aversion to literary work and what he calls "political arguments." The magazine's aim should be "first—to record the work the colored people are doing; second—to make the whites acquainted with it." In the final paragraph Freund writes, "With any literary magazine, let me tell you frankly, Booker Washington has absolutely no sympathy. Neither he nor I have the least hope for its future, but for a magazine which will do as I say, there is every hope and certain help." The following letter, April 6, 1904, again addressed to Dupree, sets down the law: "Either Miss Hopkins will follow our suggestion . . . and put live matter into the magazine, eliminating anything, which may create offense, stop talking about wrongs and a proscribed race, or you must count me out absolutely from this day forth. I will neither personally endorse nor help a business proposition, which my common sense tells me is foredoomed to failure. Every person that I have spoken to on the subject is with me. IT IS MR. BOOKER WASHINGTON'S IDEA" (also quoted in Hopkins-Trotter letter 5). Hopkins notes that this letter "threw a firebrand into the office and made [her] position unbearable" (Hopkins-Trotter letter 5). The letter confirmed to her what she had suspected, namely that Freund "was curtailing my work from the broad field of international union and uplift for the Blacks in all quarters of the globe, to the narrow confines of the question as affecting solely the Afro-American" (Hopkins-Trotter letter 4). She suspects that Freund and with him Washington were offended by a number of solicited articles on President Roosevelt's Philippine policy and William Lloyd Garrison's criticism of industrial education in the April issue of 1904. She notes that she had committed herself to these articles previously and did not want to alienate and offend these renowned contributors to the *Colored American Magazine.*

The relationship between Hopkins and Freund turned from one of benevolence on Freund's side and tolerance and gratitude on Hopkins's side to one of mutual reproach and distrust. On March 24, 1904, Freund writes to her: "I note your amiable disposition to crown me, if not here then hereafter. You are like all your people; your heart's blood isn't good enough for anybody who gives you a kind word or does you a friendly act." In later letters he questions her competence as editor and criticizes her for her lack of business sense and her obstinacy.

Hopkins's assessment of the fate of the magazine unequivocally places the blame at Washington's door. Her final words in the ten-page letter condemn his role and character:

> With the knowledge which we possess, can we be expected to worship Mr. Washington as a pure and noble soul?
>
> Can we be expected to join in paeans of praise to his spotless character and high principles?
>
> One cannot help a feeling of honest indignation and contempt for a man who would be a party to defraud a helpless race of an organ of free speech, a band of men of their legal property and a woman of her means of earning a living. (Hopkins-Trotter letter 10)

Ironically, the March 1904 issue published two articles under her pen names, one under her own name, and proudly announced her as the editor of the journal, which is still called the journal of the Colored American League. The prospectus reads as an attack against racism and discrimination: "The recent attacks made by many prominent persons upon our race, and the efforts which have been made in some states in the South to deprive our people, by legislation, of the political and other rights guaranteed us by the Constitution, make it imperative for us everywhere to appeal to the conscience and heart of the American people" (unpaginated).

In late April/early May of 1904 the magazine was sold again, and Fred R. Moore, the national organizer and recording secretary of the National Negro Business League, which was financed and backed by Booker T. Washington, assumed the position of owner and editor. Although Washington's exact involvement in the purchase and restructuring of the *Colored American Magazine* was kept a secret, rumors of his having invested a large amount of money in a number of African American magazines had been spread in 1903 and denied by him fervently.[15]

Hopkins decided to move to New York, accept a salary of twelve dollars a week, and "succumb to the powers that were, and do all [she] could to keep the magazine alive unless they asked [her] to publicly renounce the rights of [her] people" (Hopkins-Trotter letter 7). The new owner of the magazine also held the rights to her novel *Contending Forces*, and she was not willing to forsake the money still promised to her. In New York she learned the system of manipulation behind the scenes of magazine publishing. She recapitulates the activities of Washington's active agents and trusted allies: "Plans are laid for 'downing' opposing Negroes, wires are pulled for paying political jobs, and 'ward-heeling' schemes are constantly resorted to" (Hopkins-Trotter letter 8).

The May 1904 issue is the first in which we find no article attributed to Pauline Hopkins or any of her pseudonyms. In the next issue, Fred R. Moore appears solo on the masthead of his "Publishers' Announcements." The address given is now Pearl Street in New York, with Moore as the general manager. The struggle for leadership had obviously been decided. Simultaneously, with a new layout of the title page, Hopkins's name disappeared from the magazine until November 1904, when Moore reported that she was in "ill health" ("Publishers' Announcements," Nov. 1904, 700). The same announcement names as associate editor Roscoe Conkling Simmons, who was Mrs. Margaret Murray Washington's nephew and a zealous supporter of his "Uncle Booker."[16] In a later retrospective detailing the development of the magazine under his editorship, Moore mentions that Miss Hopkins and Jesse W. Watkins "rendered good service until September 1904" ("Editorial," June 1905, 342), when Hopkins left because of ill health and Watkins was dismissed for undisclosed reasons. Hopkins most probably stayed in New York for another few months to prepare the essay about the city's subway system, which she published in the *Voice of the Negro* in December 1904.

The change in editorial policy is apparent in the column "In the Editor's Sanctum" of May 1904: "What the nation desires to know about the Southern Negro is not how many votes he casts so much as whether he is bringing himself into such a position that he can discharge his social and personal duties as an American citizen" (382). Civil rights here are discarded for material wealth because it is more important to become a "peasant proprietor of the soil" than to vote. The white man is asked to become a brotherly and protective friend of the black man: "We implore the white men of the North and the white men of the South to deal with the Negro question soberly, tenderly, discerningly; and throw their strong arms about the Negro, and protect and counsel him, and be his elder brother, and help him get education, and pour soothing oil into his wounds, and work hand in hand with him, and employ him, and put him on his feet, and teach him that he is a man" (383). This paternalistic rhetoric must have alienated many readers who were used to race pride in the magazine. It is interesting to find this editorial statement in the same issue that contains an article by Du Bois, "The Training of Negroes for Social Power," in the "Industrial Education" series. In it Du Bois advocates higher education so that educated African Americans will work for their race "to stamp out crime, strengthen the home, eliminate degenerates, and inspire and encourage the higher tendencies of the race not only in thought and aspiration, but in every-day toil" (339). Ironically, the same issue also contains an article about Boston as the "Paradise of the Negro."

Moore's editorial in the June 1905 issue, one year after the magazine relocated to New York, is even more explicit about the new editorial politics: "We shall support the policies of Dr. Booker T. Washington, irrespective of harping critics, because we believe in them, and we shall endeavor to make friends for the race wherever possible. We shall continue to publish the doings of the race in business and what is being done along educational lines; and at all times we shall reserve the right to criticise, in a dignified way, those policies that do not seem to be for our best interest" (342). While the emphasis of the magazine shifted from literature to current affairs, news of fraternal orders, education, and business affairs, it lost a great part of its readership (Bullock 113–15). Its circulation dropped considerably. While sales used to average from 800 to 1,500 copies in New York, they soon dropped to 200 a month (Hopkins-Trotter letter 8). Now, the new motto was: "Prejudice will be erased through education, character and money" ("Publishers' Announcements," March 1905, 164). Hopkins's political positions and commitment to African American literature clearly conflicted with the magazine's new editorial policies.

Perhaps the change in outlook and editorial politics can best be seen in a comparison between two sales strategies for the magazine. The first one is taken from its issues between October 1900 and February 1901, in which the editors announce that whoever subscribes for a year will receive for free a beautiful photogravure, *The Young Colored American*. Later, in May 1901, the gift was Hopkins's novel *Contending Forces*. The final gift, attached to a subscription to the magazine in 1909, was neither a beautiful race engraving nor a race novel, however, but a hair tonic that promised to "prevent, remove and cure Dandruff, stop Itching Scalp, cure Scaly Eczema of the Scalp, remove Tetter and Scurf, stop Falling Hair and cause the Hair to grow Long, Soft and Glossy" ("Advertisements," Nov. 1909). The move from culture to consumer society also rang the death knell of the magazine.

Hopkins's outspoken views and radical tendencies were no longer accepted. In 1928 Charles S. Johnson recapitulated Hopkins's failure as editor because of her uncompromising attitude: "The editor made no attempt to modify the magazine's expressions out of consideration for the white persons from whom most of the support was obtained" ("Rise" 13). In an essay written in 1947, William Stanley Braithwaite, a frequent contributor to the *Colored American Magazine*, writes about Hopkins's "outstanding contribution" but also about some kind of "friction" that evolved between the "temperamental editor" Hopkins and the "quiet but effective" R. S. Elliott ("Negro America's First Magazine" 24–25). Braithwaite's attitude toward Hopkins mirrors the arrogance of a male writer and probable rival toward a successful woman. Although he writes with the benefit of hindsight about what happened then, he cannot find any appreciative words for Hopkins's contribution. His downplaying of her role is worth quoting in full: "As a novelist Miss Hopkins regarded herself as a national figure, in the company of Charles W. Chesnutt and Paul Lawrence [*sic*] Dunbar and as such felt free to impose her views and opinions upon her associates in the conduct of both the book and magazine publications. Miss Hopkins resented bitterly Elliott's veiled authority, and was generally critical of Wallace's literary incompetence though it was chiefly due to his vision and enthusiasm that her own literary ambition had found its opportunity" (25). Braithwaite thus criticizes her for what he considers her thankless attitude toward Wallace. Braithwaite was also well aware of Booker T. Washington's influence on Freund, but he can only guess about Freund's initially taking a financial interest in the magazine as a result of Washington's initiative.

Johnson and Johnson point out that the devolution of the magazine into largely a party journal is of particular interest for the literary historian "because it suggests an incompatibility between accommodationism and the development of a healthy minority literature" (*Propaganda* 16). Booker T. Washington himself unfavorably compared the magazine to the *Voice of the Negro* in a 1906 letter to Moore: "I think I ought to say to you that which many of your best friends are constantly expressing, however, and that is that for the same money and strength you can get out a magazine that in dignity and power will be quite different from the one which you are now publishing. I do not believe that it will cost you a single dollar more to get out a really high toned magazine. . . . In magazine breadth, dignity and form, your best friends will tell you that it does not come up to the *Voice of the Negro*" (*Booker T. Washington Papers* 8:571). His own strategy had backfired, and the new editor was far less competent than the former one.

Although a number of excellent short stories were published in the magazine after 1904, its serials underwent significant changes. Hopkins's three serial novels, all of them about aspects of intricate race relations in the United States, gave way to Harriet Martineau, a white British writer, and her novel about Toussaint L'Ouverture, *The Hour and the Man* (1904–5), and to the Arabian romance "The Love That Could Not Sin" (1908), by Ralph W. Tyler, an African American writer. The Martineau novel was certainly an excellent choice by an internationally renowned writer, but there were several African American writers who could have been included. Tyler's romance is set in the past, depicting a love affair involving the prophet Mahomet (Muhammad), his wife Ayesha, and the youthful rebel Safwan. Much action, many battles, and a romance make up this story that does not directly comment upon race relations in the United States. In the June 1906 issue the editor called for literature with a "new style" that would raise up a new race of writers ("Publishers' Announcements," June 1906, 435), but the years 1906 and 1907 saw hardly any fiction and featured only a few poems.

What the controversy between Hopkins, Moore, and Washington shows more clearly than anything else is that despite her competence and popularity, Hopkins lacked the financial backing, political influence, and right gender that would have ensured a longer career. As a woman undertaking the nearly unprecedented career of editor, she was at a further disadvantage. The *Colored American Magazine* gave her access to the public, advertised her writings, and published her fiction and nonfiction, but it also effectively ended her career when she was ousted from it.

It is no surprise then that Booker T. Washington also figures in Hopkins's fictional writings. Dr. Arthur Lewis in her novel *Contending Forces* is a thinly veiled portrait of Washington. He believes in the value of industrial schools and even builds one that closely resembles Tuskegee Institute. His rather old-fashioned attitude toward women is shown when he completely dominates Dora Smith's opinions. One cannot say that Arthur Lewis is a villain, but he is certainly not heroic in anything he does. In her short story "A Dash for Liberty," which is based on historical facts, the name of the main character, the heroic slave who captures a slave ship and frees the slaves, is changed from Washington Madison to Madison Monroe. John C. Gruesser sees the name change in part as an indirect comment on Booker T. Washington ("Taking Liberties" 104). By dropping the name that would have reminded everyone of the prominent race leader, Hopkins disassociates the name Washington from an act of black heroism.

One of the ideas that irked Hopkins most was Washington's view of history, in particular his idea that the large slave plantations resembled industrial schools. His contribution to the "Industrial Education" series in January 1904 is a slightly weakened version of his argument in *Up from Slavery*, in which he writes that the Negroes "went through the school of American slavery" and that "the black man got nearly as much out of slavery as the white man did"

(37). Bethany Johnson sees Washington's policy as one example of "the lauda-tory defense of slavery for having brought real benefits to African Americans" (59). His "slavery-as-school" idea stresses the cultural advantages accrued by African Americans "in spite of the system" (51). Washington emphasizes, "I would be the last to apologize for the curse of slavery" ("Industrial Ed-ucation" 88), but this statement is belied by the otherwise positive picture of slavery he paints. One of Hopkins's most outspoken denunciations of this idea comes in her May 1902 essay "Famous Women," in which she writes: "By the toleration of slavery, the great American government lowered its high standards and sullied its fair fame among other nations. Though slaves were introduced by the fathers across the seas, this was not accepted as an apology for crimes worse than murder. . . . Slavery was the sum of all villainies, and the slave-holders the greatest of villains" ("Famous Women: Educators" 41).

By regarding slavery as contributing to the progress of the African Amer-ican and by emphasizing an attitude geared toward future development through hard work and manual training, Washington could not but antag-onize other prominent race leaders who were determined to propagate a history of the race. For Booker T. Washington, as Ross Posnock has argued, "black intellectual became a repugnant oxymoron, a corrupt and decadent monstrosity" (58). Washington called the men who interrupted his speech during the Boston riot of 1903 "artificial" men, "graduates of New England colleges" (qtd. in Posnock 59). Deeply involved as she was with the New England abolitionist ideals and its rich educational environment, Hopkins could not but disagree with Washington. Her choice to include the slave past in her fiction and her choice, especially, to see the woman's side of slavery set her at odds with this race leader.

When John C. Freund remonstrates Hopkins for using the phrase "a pro-scribed race," he reflects Washington's general belief that the history that proscribed the race had to be deemphasized in favor of a belief in progress and a better future. This is why Hopkins's decision to include the slavery past in *Contending Forces*, to set *Winona* in the South in the 1850s, to include Africa as the setting of *Of One Blood*, and to explain present action through the legacy of slavery in *Hagar's Daughter* can be seen as indirect reactions to Booker T. Washington's positions.[17]

Even the fragmentary *Topsy Templeton* in the 1916 *New Era Magazine* shows Hopkins's continuing preoccupation with Washington when two white philanthropic ladies, presented as rather eccentric and quixotic, could immediately have answered Washington's call for money to help in the "en-vironmental and moral uplift" of the Negro race (12). Their paternalistic rhetoric reminds the reader of his ideas about the proper education of young African Americans, but they lack a deeper understanding of the needs of their spiteful ward, Topsy Templeton. Pauline Hopkins's growing feminist self-confidence is also shown in "Converting Fanny" (1916), a story that asserts her rights as a woman to defend her position by any means.

Booker T. Washington certainly haunted Pauline Hopkins. She was not only directly confronted with him in her work as editor but also had to deal with him indirectly. As the following chapter will show, her relationship with several of the leading clubwomen can be traced back to the same conflict between conservative accommodationism and political activism. Hopkins here shared the experience of many other women of her time. The development of her career was also shaped by the historical development of the woman's era, 1880 to 1920, which was strongly influenced by the women's club movement.

The Black Woman's Era

*T*he black woman's era was the age of a generation of famous race women. Between 1880 and 1920 African American intellectuals, educators, public lecturers, and artists of all branches found recognition in the club movement. Hundreds of African American women were eager to uplift the race through motivations to self-help and race pride. The rise to prominence of several leading personalities is documented in Hopkins's essays, which provide the public awareness these women needed and deserved. It was not a homogeneous movement that united all the women involved in it; discord often predominated over agreement. Hopkins was aware of the various positions, knew the women involved in it, and negotiated the contradictions between white and African American women and the gender animosities between African American men and women. In her role as recorder of histories and biographies, she found her place in this movement.

Before, during, and after her time at the *Colored American Magazine*, Hopkins was active in the local women's club movement. Boston vied with New York City and Washington, D.C., for the lead in the organization of a national African American women's club movement. In 1893 Josephine St. Pierre Ruffin, a prominent social reformer and community worker, her daughter Florida Ruffin Ridley, and Maria Louise Baldwin, the first African American principal in a Massachusetts public school (Agassiz School), founded the Woman's Era Club. The club's activities included community work (orphanages, day nurseries, lodging, job placement, night classes, support for hospitals for black people, homes for the aged, homes for young working girls), church activities, literary societies, and other social gatherings dedicated to the goal of uplifting the race and protecting the rights of colored women. The club's journal, *Woman's Era*, was an early publication effort of colored women and included articles about fashion, health issues, legislation, and social activities.

The Colored Women's League was organized in Washington, D.C., in 1892 by Mary Church Terrell, Anna Julia Cooper, and Mary Jane Patterson. The Woman's Loyal Union was led by Victoria Earle Matthews in New York, and the Chicago Women's Club was founded in 1893 upon an initiative by Ida B. Wells-Barnett. Clubs were organized all over the country, led by active and engaged women to support suffrage, fight lynching, or work for racial uplift through social reform in general. In 1895 in Boston, the National Federation of Afro-American Women united thirty-six clubs in twelve states; its president was Margaret Murray Washington. This organization merged with Terrell's Colored Women's League under the name of the National Association of Colored Women (NACW), with Terrell as its first president.[1] These names of clubs and individual prominent women form the necessary background of Hopkins's own engagement as a clubwoman. Since Hopkins was involved in the Woman's Era Club of Boston, she knew the clubwomen and most probably also knew the various power plays, friendships, and animosities among them. It is highly probable that she attended the First Congress of Colored Women in Boston in 1895. There she may have met Anna Julia Cooper and Victoria Earle Matthews, who both delivered addresses (see Shirley Wilson Logan, esp. 48 and 121–22).

There is evidence that Hopkins gave one or more readings of her novel *Contending Forces* at the Woman's Era Club. In *Forgotten Readers*, Elizabeth McHenry cites a report in the *National Association Notes* of April 1900. It says that "an entertaining and interesting afternoon was spent at a Japanese Tea, given to Miss Pauline Hopkins, to aid her in the publication of her novel, *Contending Forces*, portions of which she read" (qtd. in McHenry 370 n.85). In this report she is also listed as the secretary of the Woman's Era Club. McHenry uses this incident as evidence of her general claim that women's clubs were committed to public literacy and that they provided an interested audience for African American women writers (231, 241).

In September 1901 Hopkins reports on the visit to the house of the poet John Greenleaf Whittier, during which she presented a historical sketch of his life ("Whittier" 327), a sketch that was reprinted in her Whittier essay. Hopkins was also first vice-president of the "Women's Auxiliary," as she notes in the first essay focusing on women's club issues in the second issue of the *Colored American Magazine* ("Women's Department" 121).

Hopkins's negotiations in gender were never detached from her negotiations in race. What Wilson J. Moses recapitulates about the women's club movement in general is certainly true for Hopkins as an individual. Moses argues that the NACW was "something more than a women's organization that was incidentally black" (*Black Nationalism* 129). Despite the many attempts to define race along biological and scientific lines, Evelyn B. Higginbotham offers a much more logical explanation when she defines race in allegiance with gender and class as "a social construction predicated upon the recognition of difference and signifying the simultaneous distinguishing and positioning of groups vis-à-vis another" (253). She brings into consideration the power constructions deriving from racial identification when she says that "race is a highly contested representation of relations of power between social categories by which individuals are identified and identify themselves." Race tends to blur and distinguish boundaries of class, region, and gender: "It precludes unity within the same gender group but often appears to solidify people of opposing economic classes" (255).

Confronted with racism in addition to sexism, challenged by the influence of the Tuskegee spirit, confronted with white women as antagonists rather than as sisters, and concerned with the public image of black women, Hopkins and her contemporaries could never see the woman's side only; they had to negotiate race as well.

In an announcement for 1902, Hopkins's series "Famous Women of the Negro Race" was advertised as a unique feature. The African American woman had to strive against peculiar adversities: "She is constantly called upon to combat not only caste, but disbelief, among the whites, in her morality, and in her possession of any of the gentler virtues of womanhood. There is no denying the overwhelming social and civil influence of woman; it is of vast extent. We have hundreds of virtuous, intelligent, cultivated, christian [sic], young colored women who have risen to take their places in society as wives and mothers, who have done much and are still doing much to lift the race and its homes" ("Announcement for 1902" 413). This statement reflects the subject of this chapter. It is Hopkins's concern with the "gentler virtues of womanhood" that the African American woman had to defend against all prejudices. Her concept of "perfect womanhood" included the possession of virtue, intelligence, Christianity, culture, and refinement and directly answered the many charges leveled against the morality of the colored woman ("Famous Women: Educators [Concluded]" 208). Like the "perfected manhood" she described earlier, ideal womanhood could be made apparent in achievements: names and careers, individual feats and group accomplishments had as prominent a place in this series as in the one about famous men. According to common belief, the colored woman was called upon to prove that she possessed the virtues of true womanhood, as they were defined at that time: purity, domesticity, religion, and submissiveness.[2]

Repeatedly, Hopkins spoke of "organized intelligence" ("Echoes" 711), by which she meant the many various individual clubs and the general club movement that offered career opportunities to many women. "Lifting as we climb"—the club's motto—reflected the obligation of the club movement for race work, be it the practical organization of a kindergarten or mother's club, the ideological teaching of race pride, or the call to political agitation. For more conservative race leaders, "to lift the race" implied lifting its homes. Race work was combined with attempts to improve the living conditions in the homes, to emphasize cleanliness and a certain standard in furniture and social manners, and to strive for an intact family structure. In her study of African American professional women, Stephanie J. Shaw summarizes the importance of domestic training for women at schools and colleges, because the African American community held the belief that "well-trained black women could also lift up the black community through the example they set in maintaining clean, orderly, and well-cared-for homes and families" (78). Apart from intellectual training, domestic skills were thought to lead to community work and race leadership. More radical women, like Hopkins, did not always approve of this interpretation of the motto, because it did not endorse political activism. The club movement thus reflected the general ideological controversy of the time between the conservative and radical views of race leadership.

A definition of the women's movement is given in the June 1900 issue of the *Colored American Magazine*, an issue that contained the first full treatment of the club movement edited by Hopkins. "We believe it to be the club women's task to 'little by little turn the desire of the world from things of the flesh to things of the spirit. She must make the world want to do things that raise it higher and higher' " ("Women's Department" 121). This ideology of selfless help based on Christian principles that informed the movement (to "turn the desire of the world from things of the flesh to things of the spirit") was commonly held to contribute to an improvement of the world ("to raise it higher and higher"). It was, therefore, typical of her time that Hopkins saw woman as the moral agent of the world: "Women are so active in advancing the cause not only of women, but of men, and in fact of the entire human family" ("Famous Women: Literary Workers" 277). It was commonly believed that lifting the homes equaled lifting the race, an opinion that was often extended to mean that the welfare of the individual family would lead to the welfare of the state in general. Echoing the central thesis of Claudia Tate's *Domestic Allegories of Political Desire* about the powerful political force of domesticity and literacy, Debra Bernardi sees that the "private domestic sphere becomes an extension of national action" (212).

In Hopkins's view the great responsibility of the educated race woman was "the broadening and deepening of her race, the teaching of youth to grasp present opportunities, and, greater than all, to help clear the moral atmosphere by inculcating a clearer appreciation of the Holy Word and its application to every day living" ("Famous Women: Literary Workers" 277). As an active clubwoman herself, she adheres with conviction to the general motto, "Lifting as we climb": "Let the women then, without adverse criticism, continue to help raise the race by every means in their power, and at the same time raise our common country from the mire of barbarism" ("Literary Workers" 278).

Her statements remind the reader of an earlier treatment of this topic in Anna Julia Cooper's *A Voice from the South*. In 1892 Cooper argued in "The Status of Women in America" for the important position of women in building up and maintaining civilization and for the important role colored women would be able to play. For her, the woman stands "at the gateway of this new era of American civilization" because: "In her hands must be moulded the strength, the wit, the statesmanship, the morality, all the psychic force, the social and economic intercourse of that era. To be alive at such an epoch is a privilege, to be a woman then is sublime" (143). Certainly her sentiments foreshadow those of Hopkins, especially when she sees woman as the morally uplifting agent, capable of elevating the race: "What a responsibility then to have the sole management of the primal lights and shadows! Such is the colored woman's office. She must stamp weal or woe on the coming history of this people. May she see her opportunity and vindicate her high prerogative" (145). Cooper's and Hopkins's views are also endorsed by two women who left sustained documents on such matters, Mary Church Terrell in her autobiography, *A Colored Woman in a White World* (1940), and Ida B. Wells-Barnett in *Crusade for Justice* (1928, edited in 1970 by Alfreda M. Duster).

Hopkins undertook the task to achieve this constant movement toward perfection and woman's moral excellence. She includes, in one part of her "Famous Women of the Negro Race" series, a short overview of the history of women throughout the centuries. In her opinion, a high mark was reached in the nineteenth century, a century that opened the door of opportunity for the African American woman. Hopkins emphasizes this fact: "It seems almost as if the inspiration of the times had created a new race of colored women, a new tide set in, new forces called into play, a new era in the world's history and through all this the moral and social regeneration of a race" ("Famous Women: Higher Education" 447). The woman's era, as Frances Ellen Watkins Harper called this time,[3] ushered in the full claim of the colored woman to

true womanhood and that of the colored man to civil manhood. The great
number of portraits of worthy men and women that were part of the *Colored
American Magazine* were necessary to attest to the fact that these people really
existed and could be represented in impressive pictures and that the deeds
of these men and women should be made public. They could be identified
by name, location, family affiliation, educational career, occupational career,
and often even the exact amount of their wealth. As Hopkins writes, "The
only proof of competence is performance" ("Higher Education" 447), and
performance could be recorded in the written word. In that sense the work of
the journalist is also that of a recorder of deeds, biographies, civil functions,
and professional, educational, or artistic excellence. As C. K. Doreski puts it,
this effort makes Hopkins the mediator "between the individual heroic soul
and the grander racial and cultural tapestry" (7).

Hopkins singles out the lives of Sojourner Truth and Harriet Tubman
for special treatment, national heroines whose experiences under slavery,
whose religious ideas, and whose strong feminist voices continue to fasci-
nate readers. With the telling of Sojourner Truth's life under slavery in the
North, Hopkins emphasizes that the North committed as many crimes in
the treatment of colored people as the South because the South forced its
principles upon the entire nation.

Hopkins begins her essay on Harriet Tubman with the life of Jesus Christ
as our model of endurance, selflessness, and sacrifice. Tubman's life remarkably embodied these Christian virtues and made her a heroic, venerable, and
remarkable woman. Under other circumstances Tubman would have gained
the same prominence as Joan of Arc or Florence Nightingale. Sojourner Truth
and Harriet Tubman are thus Hopkins's female role models. Their achievements prove the inherent worth, virtue, courage, and stamina of the African
American woman. Their life stories show the passage from slavery to emancipation and reconstruction and prove the intricate connections between
northern and southern hardships endured by the African American race.

Hopkins argues, therefore: "Maligned and misunderstood, the Afro-
American woman is falsely judged by other races. Nowhere on God's green
earth are there nobler women, more self-sacrificing tender mothers, more
gifted women in their chosen fields of work than among the millions of
Negroes in the United States" ("Famous Women: Vocalists" 46). As with
Sojourner Truth and Harriet Tubman, Hopkins tries to prove this statement
by telling her readers about "Phenomenal Vocalists," "Literary Workers,"
"Educators," and clubwomen. Except for Truth and Tubman, the women are
dealt with in groups rather than as individuals. Doreski calls this "group

portraits of community endeavor, privileging the public and spirited contributions of African-American women to culture and society" and points
out the fact that Hopkins has decided to give them "a contextualizing group
identity" (17).[4]

Several times, Hopkins raises the tricky question of ancestry. Writing
about the educator Maria Louise Baldwin, she argues that most African
American women would be "content to draw their ancestry from our common father Adam, and their talent from the bestower of all good things—
our Creator" ("Educators [Continued]" 126–27). But where there is a family
history that could be told and shown—as, for example, in her portrait of
the educator Joan Imogen Howard—Hopkins presents this as a remarkable
fact. Her life is discussed in close connection with that of her parents and
other members of the Howard family. She might be cited as proof of the
great influence of a stable and educated home life upon the future career
of the children. Miss Howard's many merits and appointments attest to her
achievement of "perfect womanhood" ("Educators [Concluded]" 208).

As could be expected from the great number of women who were involved in the club movement, there were considerable differences regarding the course the movement should take. A rather conservative number
of prominent clubwomen emphasized the aspects of culture, refinement,
good taste in clothing, strict morality, and restraint in the dealings with
white and black men in public. Margaret Murray Washington, for example,
third wife of Booker T. Washington, dean of women at Tuskegee College,
and active clubwoman, emphasized the ideals of a true home life: "a broadening of the family circle, tasty furnishings, order, cleanliness, softer and
nicer manners of the younger children, a more tender regard for parents, a
stricter idea of social duties and obligations in the home" ("Advancement
of Colored Women" 185). It is interesting to note that articles by Margaret
Murray Washington and Josephine Silone Yates, another rather conservative
race leader and president of the NACW from 1901 to 1906, dominated after
Hopkins had left the Colored American Magazine. Their positions resembled
closely the ideology of Booker T. Washington and spoke of a noteworthy
conservative element in the women's club movement. Although distinctions
were not always clear, women who could be seen in the camp of Washington's
antagonists included Ida B. Wells-Barnett (1862–1931), ardent advocate of
civil rights, women's rights, and economic rights; Josephine St. Pierre Ruffin
(1842–1924), activist, journalist, and suffragist from Boston; Victoria Earle
Matthews (1861–1907), active in settlement work, social welfare, and club
organizations; and Anna Julia Cooper (1858–1964).[5]

In an encyclopedia published in 1902 by Donald W. Culp called *Twentieth Century Negro Literature: A Cyclopedia of Thought on the Vital Topics Relating to the American Negro*, one hundred African Americans write about the vital topics (thirty-eight in number) of the time. Six of them discuss education: "Should the Negro Be Given an Education Different from That Given to the White?"; "Will the Education of the Negro Solve the Race Problem?"; "What Role Is the Educated Negro Woman to Play in the Uplifting of Her Race?"; "Did the American Negro Prove, in the Nineteenth Century, That He Is Intellectually Equal to the White Man?"; "What Is the Negro Teacher Doing in the Matter of Uplifting His Race?"; and "The Negro and Education." Apart from the fact that the topics in themselves represent a spectrum of the burning questions of the time, the individual answers encompass a wide variety of possible positions. In her contribution to the topic of the educated woman in connection with the uplifting of the race, Rosa D. Bowser, distinguished educator and clubwoman, says after referring to the admirable work of Mrs. Booker T. Washington and others: "Such are the women needed to-day. Women who teach by doing. Women who can take a basket of soap on the arm, and in a gentle, winning way present it to homes that need it, while at the same time extol its merits in a pleasant manner. Women are needed who can teach the lesson of morality, cleanliness of soul and body, and the hygienic and economic management of the humble home, by showing them how to perform these acts, and furnish examples" (181). The educated woman becomes a synonym for the leading clubwoman who must set an example. The quotation implies, of course, the notion of a class of women who needed this sort of uplifting because they did not meet moral and physical standards of excellence.

A similarly conservative position is advocated by Mary Church Terrell, one of the most prominent clubwomen. The daughter of a Memphis millionaire, she was married to Judge Robert Terrell, one of the few African American officeholders under the Roosevelt administration.[6] She answers for the conservative opinion when she writes, "Home life is the citadel and bulwark of every race's moral life" (183). And she probably knew what she was talking about when she wrote, "An educated wife formulates the political opinion of husband and son and though she may remain at home on election day, her views and opinions will find expression in the ballots of the male members of her household" (184).

Whereas most women agreed upon the necessity of social reforms, they did not always agree upon political activism. And as usual, the more conservative policy, as advocated by Margaret Murray Washington, Rosa D. Bowser, or in part by Mary Church Terrell, was challenged by women who demanded more rights in all aspects of life. Hopkins, single woman and journalist, was firmly convinced of the importance of engaging in politics: "We know that it is not 'popular' for a woman to speak or write in plain terms against political brutalities, that a woman should confine her efforts to woman's work in the home and church" ("Famous Women: Some Literary Workers" 277). Gender-based role assignments imposed restrictions upon all women of her time, and race put an additional stress on women that, Hopkins argues, had to be counterbalanced by extra care and awareness: "The colored woman must have an intimate knowledge of every question that agitates the councils of the world; she must understand the solution of problems that involve the alteration of the boundaries of countries, and which make and unmake governments."

Hopkins had neither an influential husband nor a family background of great wealth. This may account for her rather ambiguous attitude toward women such as Washington and Terrell. For this reason, the portrayal of Dora Smith in her *Contending Forces* seems less sympathetic than that of Sappho Clark. Dora argues that "I generally accept whatever the men tell me as right" and defends Arthur Lewis, her friend modeled upon Booker T. Washington, who thinks that "women should be seen but not heard, where politics is under discussion" (125, 126). Sappho Clark reacts to this statement with indignation and calls a man like Arthur Lewis an "insufferable prig!" (126). Her portrayal of the clubwoman Mrs. Willis in the same novel is also not totally positive. The heroine Sappho especially resents Mrs. Willis's attempt to meddle in her affairs, her effusive and inquisitive manner and her officiousness. Sappho Clark's outspoken advocacy of the rights of women clearly reflects Hopkins's own feminist and self-assertive views.

Mrs. Willis is the widow of an influential politician. She is presented as a typical woman of her time, "not a *rara avis*, but one of many possibilities which the future will develop from among the colored women of New England" (144). She is a shrewd businesswoman, a tireless organizer, and gives the impression of being very educated and cultivated "whereas a high-school course more than covered all her opportunities" (145). She started her career as clubwoman out of necessity after the death of her husband left her without adequate means of support. But she is also a cunning manipulator, who has influenced the vote more than once in the direction she desired. She holds her position by force of a tyranny that no woman dares to resist. She is the "pivot about which all the social and intellectual life of the colored people of her section revolved" (148).

Most likely, Hopkins modeled Mrs. Willis upon Josephine St. Pierre Ruffin, the influential and well-known Boston clubwoman and activist. Ruffin was born in 1842, and her age around 1900 thus corresponds with that of Mrs. Willis in the novel. Ruffin was married to George Lewis Ruffin, the state legislator, city councilman, and Boston's first African American municipal judge who died in 1886. Ruffin, much as Mrs. Willis, had to support herself and her family through speeches, clubwork, and political involvement (see Arroyo; Streitmatter). It may be assumed that Hopkins's Boston readers recognized Mrs. Willis as a thinly disguised Mrs. Ruffin and were amused at this. Clearly she is meant to represent the exemplary character of the race woman, although this was made with some reluctance because it can be assumed that Hopkins also suffered from Ruffin's manipulative and rather domineering personality. Hopkins never became a very prominent member of the Woman's Era Club, nor did she ever publish in the *Woman's Era*, the club journal.

Apart from the fact that Hopkins understood the powerful position of a coordinated movement of intelligent women, she may have underestimated its potential to antagonize the male race leaders who saw themselves confronted with accusations of failure and passivity. When feminism is defined in this case as the conviction of women that only they could save the black race, then this belief, as Deborah Gray White argues in *Too Heavy a Load: Black Women in Defense of Themselves, 1894–1994*, risked driving a wedge between black men and women: "At the heart of these feelings lay a sad loss of confidence in the ability of most black men to deal effectively with the race problem" (36). White cites the examples of Anna Julia Cooper, Fannie Barrier Williams, and Victoria Earle Matthews, all of them women Hopkins knew and appreciated, to prove her argument: "Although NACW leaders did not deliberately mount a malevolent campaign against black men, their rhetoric and that of their supporters juxtaposed the abilities of black men and women in such a way as to generate tension between them" (59). White sees a direct relationship between the women's criticism and the men's attempt to exclude them from positions of influence: "When club leaders criticized and ridiculed the political methods of black men, and vowed that black women would not sell votes, make deals with party bosses, pass endless resolutions that resulted in no action, . . . they laid the groundwork for new criticism from men" (64). Hopkins did, indeed, criticize and ridicule the political methods of black men, especially in her treatise *A Primer of Facts*, which contains a bitter statement about colored race leaders who sit silently in public discussion about lynching or disfranchisement and listen in "abject submission" (*Primer* 28). In her speech at the Garrison centennial in 1905, she also directs her criticism at this materialistic age, "when the price of manhood is a good dinner, a fine position, a smile of approval and a pat on the back from the man of influence, of a fat endowment" ("Speech" 4). Her severe criticism of the political methods of John Langley in *Contending Forces* likewise shows her low opinion of male race leaders to effect political change.

In "The Higher Education of Women," Cooper is also openly sarcastic about the role of men in uplifting the race. "The problem . . . now rests with the man as to how he can so develop his God-given powers as to reach the ideal of a generation of women who demand the noblest, grandest and best achievements of which he is capable" (70–71). She ridicules male contempt for female intelligence: "It seems hardly a gracious thing to say, but it strikes me as true, that while our men seem thoroughly abreast of the times on almost every other subject, when they strike the woman question they drop back into sixteenth century logic" (75). Both Cooper and Hopkins suffered from a social and political climate that gave more power to men and demanded more achievements from women. Their involvement in the club movement must be seen as a logical result of their self-definition as capable of leading and coping with problems on their own.

In addition to the sometimes strained relationship with the male leaders of the race, black clubwomen were often confronted with adverse reactions by white clubwomen. Anna Julia Cooper, Ida B. Wells-Barnett, and Mary Church Terrell have left extensive evidence of the problematic relationship between white and African American women. The prominent position Hopkins gave to the question whether the colored clubs would be accepted into the white women's club movement shows the significance of this issue and her preoccupation with it. Paula Giddings points out the basically similar goals of black and white women's clubs: "Neither group questioned the superiority of middle-class values or way of life, or had any romantic notions of the inherent nobility of the poor, uneducated masses; education and material progress were values that Black and White women shared. Both also believed in the importance of the home and the woman's moral influence within it. Black and White women saw the family as a microcosm and cornerstone of society" (97). But a difference in skin color overturned most similarities in opinion.[7] As mentioned before, the African American women's club movement was something more than an organization of women who happened to be black. Deborah White draws the conclusion that for black women, white women were part of the problem: "Black membership in national women's organizations would give black women recognition of their role in national progress and an institutional voice in affairs regarding all women. They were bitterly disappointed, therefore, when so many white women's groups endorsed the same malicious stereotypes as their men" (40). Hopkins clearly recognized this and raised this issue in her articles. In contrast, for example, to someone like Josephine Silone Yates, Hopkins is uncompromising and open in her criticism. In 1905 Yates even includes thanks to the national council for finally accepting the NACW into its ranks, but she does not mention at all previous discrimination and struggles ("Report").

In her report about the debate concerning the admittance of colored clubs into the General Federation of Women's Club at the Los Angeles convention in 1902, Hopkins cannot be conciliatory on the issue of sisterhood. One white member, a Mrs. Gallagher of Ohio, openly uttered words that hurt because of their deep and unreflected racism: "This is not a question of color," Mrs. Gallagher is on record to have said, "it is a question of an embryonic race, not yet strong enough to stand with us. The Negroes are by nature imitators. . . . They have not yet reached a plane on which they can compete with us and maintain their own independence" ("Famous Women: Educators [Concluded]" 210). Hopkins's reply contains, with her usual rhetorical emphasis, the enumeration of eminent, eloquent, and educated women of color, all of whom prove that they are not inferior.

In her account of the Los Angeles convention,[8] Hopkins takes her time to describe the lovely, highly cultured, and refined setting and the opening prayers in order to prepare the ground for her devastating and bitter remarks about the hollow and hypocritical nature of these lofty ideals: "What a mockery such a prayer must have seemed to the Almighty Father as he looked into the secret hearts of a majority of the members of that convention and saw their determined denial of the fatherhood of God and the brotherhood of man!" ("Famous Women: Club Life" 274). And then again, after the opening remarks by the delegate from Georgia, she writes in frustration that " 'greater things' were done there for the betrayal of law, order and peaceful government, not to speak of the degradation of a race of people, than have been attempted since the Missouri compromise." What follows is an in-group revelation of what took place behind the scenes, what the reactions were, how the white delegate representing the Boston Woman's Era Club was treated; information that certainly interested a large part of the female readership of the *Colored American Magazine*, most of whom would agree with Hopkins's judgment upon the southern white woman: "Meanwhile, tears and sorrow and heart-burning are the Southern white woman's portion and like Sarah of old, she wreaks her vengeance on helpless Hagar. Club life has but rendered her disposition more intolerable toward the victims of her husband's and son's evil passions" (277). Certainly readers were reminded here of Hopkins's treatment of the fate of Hagar and Hagar's daughter in her novel.[9]

The colored women's club movement and Hopkins's involvement in it can be characterized by their mutual, albeit sometimes controversial, views of the nature of "perfect womanhood," the exact nature of uplifting the race, and their positions toward each other, black men, and white women. It must be emphasized that the movement was a solidly middle-class phenomenon and that the motto of uplifting the race included a class concept of "other" women, rural or poor, who needed the moralizing agency of "us," the virtuous and impeccable clubwomen. In the phrase of Fannie Barrier Williams, the club movement is an effort "of the few competent in behalf of the many incompetent" ("Club Movement" 101). White argues that the different classes of colored women were "allied not united" in the club movement, the motto "presumed race and sex sameness, but social and cultural distance" (78). The enormous popularity of Margaret M. Washington, who was also the founder of the Southern Federation of Club Women, added the aspect of regional difference. This same aspect lay at the heart of the controversy between Booker T. Washington and W.E.B. Du Bois and certainly also influenced Pauline Hopkins's relations with both Washingtons.

Class, gender, and regional differences among the leading clubwomen added to the slow fading of the movement into relative unimportance. Hopkins's later neglect and fall from prominence was due not to any possible individual marginality but in part to the gradual disappearance of this organized activity that was eclipsed, as White says, after the turn of the century by the more spectacular and more male-dominated New Negro movement. This development, as White writes in her study, began in full after the return of black soldiers from World War I and the beginning of Marcus Garvey's Negro Improvement Association. A new militant black manhood and Garvey's promise to exalt the women of his race looked more promising than the old ideals of Victorian womanhood and the class-conscious club movement. Virile masculinity and a budding drive to sexual liberation for the women were at odds with such club activities as better homes or employment improvements (see White 110–41).

The clubwoman and journalist Hopkins was passionately committed to the goals of the movement and the concerns of women in general. She invested her time and energy in work destined to change existing views, habits, conditions, and institutions. Although she never rose to a position of great national prominence like some of her contemporaries who became presidents of the National Association of Colored Women (Mary Church Terrell, Josephine Bruce, Margaret Murray Washington, Josephine Silone Yates), the club movement offered her a degree of public prominence and an opportunity to become involved that was largely unknown to African American women of earlier generations. Her discussion of "perfect womanhood," the club movement, and the antagonism between black and white women places Hopkins firmly within the discourse of her time.

The Voices of the Dark Races

*H*opkins tried to stay with the *Colored American Magazine* for a short time after its transfer to New York. Due to ill health, incipient arthritis, and disagreement with the new editorial policies, however, she returned to Boston after a few months. Whatever the case, her health did not prevent her from writing for the *Voice of the Negro*. Its editorial policies under J. Max Barber were rather radical and close to the position of W.E.B. Du Bois and thus agreed more with her own preferences. In late 1904 and early 1905 Hopkins published an essay, "The New York Subway," and a six-month sociocultural survey, "The Dark Races of the Twentieth Century." The editor announced her association with the journal in the November issue of 1904 by saying: "Miss Pauline E. Hopkins is a well-known literary star among the Boston magazine writers. By any amount of coaxing and begging and paying we have been able to secure her services as one of our regular contributors." He adds, "Miss Hopkins was by far the best staff writer on the *Colored American Magazine* when it was published in Boston. She has made her mark and is entitled to be considered as one of the best young writers in the race. Be sure to see her first article. Miss Hopkins is no longer connected with the *Colored American Magazine*" ("Our Christmas Number," Nov. 1904, 467). Hopkins ceased to publish in the *Voice of the Negro* after the July issue of 1905, but there is no explanation for this in the magazine itself.

The *Voice of the Negro* repeated some of the successful editorial policies of the *Colored American Magazine*. It included, for example, a large number of articles by famous African American women. The July 1904 number even announced an entire issue devoted mainly to the voices of African American women in which they could answer "Mrs. Felton, Thomas Nelson Page, William Hannibal Thomas" and others about their unfair accusation of a lack of morality among colored women.[1] There was also a large number of portraits of notable men and women, some fashion and society notes, and a serial novel by Gardner Goldsby called *The Welding of the Link* (July 1905 to July 1906). After the Atlanta Riot of 1906, the editors of the magazine were accused of instigating racial violence. The October 1906 issue asked on its opening page, "Shall the Press Be Free?" and stated: "In certain parts of this country Truth is literally gagged and bound and lies dumb and helpless in the dust while the lie is haughty and mighty and wields the sceptre in all the regions round about" (391). J. Max Barber defended himself: "The *Voice of the Negro* has told the truth, the plain unvarnished truth for nearly three years in the city of Atlanta and the heart of the South. The time came when that section could no longer endure sound doctrine" (391).

At the same time that she wrote for the *Voice of the Negro*, Hopkins self-published her historical treatise, *A Primer of Facts Pertaining to the Early Greatness of the African Race and the Possibility of Restoration by Its Descendants—with Epilogue*. This treatise is Hopkins's call for black nationalism and establishes her place in a line of writers who became famous for their Ethiopianism, a movement that tried to vindicate the early greatness of the African peoples and explain their achievements in the diaspora. In her "Dark Races" series and *A Primer of Facts*, Hopkins combines the gender question with the race problem and tries to negotiate her way within a central paradox of her time: the denial of race difference coupled with an emphasis on the special role of the African American.

Hopkins must be seen as part of a pan-African, Ethiopianist, black nationalist movement, one of the few female writers who joined this discourse. With only a few women preceding her and only a few following her, Hopkins was a lonely female voice in the discourse about the negotiations between the past glory of the race, the many famous figures evolving from it, and the attempt to reconcile the present system of discrimination and injustice in the United States with signs of slow progress in race relations all over the world. In her writing about this subject, the racial idea always ends up being closely tied to the gender question.

Several terms must be clarified so that she can be put into the proper historical context. It is not the purpose, however, of this chapter to engage in the intricate literary and historical debate about the exact origins, uses of, and differences between the terms *black nationalism, pan-Africanism, Ethiopianism, afrocentricity,* or *africanist discourse* prevalent in the later twentieth century.[2] The debate will be recapitulated only inasmuch as it pertains to the writing of Hopkins, especially her *Primer of Facts*, and enables the reader to place her into a tradition.

In his contribution to *The New Negro* anthology of 1925, Arthur Schomburg opens his "The Negro Digs Up His Past" by summing up a dominant sentiment of past and present generations of African American historians and artists: "The American Negro must remake his past in order to make his future" (231). Relying on black nationalist rhetoric, Schomburg calls for a preservation of the collective cultural past in order to correct and rewrite history: "The Negro has been a man without history because he has been considered a man without a worthy culture" (237). To refute this widespread belief, writers have professed ideas about the ancient glory of Africa and a pan-African sentiment from the early 1800s onward. Despite differences in ideology and belief, Martin R. Delany, Alexander Crummell, Henry Highland Garnet, Frederick Douglass, Edward Wilmot Blyden, Bishop Henry McNeal Turner, William Wells Brown, Rufus L. Perry, and W.E.B. Du Bois have similar goals in mind: to emphasize a unity among the people coming out of Africa, to achieve some form of racial uplift, and to instill race pride and a belief in the message of the black race to mankind. Back to Africa, separatism within the United States, assimilation, and cultural nationalism were all movements that at some time attempted to answer the question about the origin, the message, and the legacy of the black person in America.

Turn-of-the-century and earlier black writers usually dealt with Africa under the heading of *Ethiopianism*, which is a glorification and dramatization of the African past but invested with a decidedly Christian background. It is a more narrow term than *classical black nationalism*, which is defined by Wilson J. Moses as including the Back-to-Africa movement and segregationist efforts to found an African American colony within the United States, a "spirit of Pan-African unity and an emotional sense of solidarity with the political and economic struggles of African peoples throughout the world," and a very general feeling of pride in a distinctive tradition in the arts (Moses, *Classical Black Nationalism* 20). With its Christian background, Ethiopianism suited Hopkins's occupation with history and the lessons history teaches. In principle a biblical view of Africa, Ethiopianism takes its name from the verse "Princes shall come out of Egypt; Ethiopia shall soon stretch out her hands unto God" (Psalms 68:31). Moses identifies as the two components of Ethiopianism the themes of "Rising Africa" and of the "Decline of the West," which he summarizes in the following way: "Ethiopianism may be defined as the effort of the English-speaking Black or African person to view his past enslavement and present cultural dependency in terms of the broader history of civilization. It serves to remind him that this present scientific technological civilization, dominated by Western Europe for a scant four hundred years, will go under certainly—like all the empires of the past. It expresses the belief that the tragic racial experience has profound historical value, that it has endowed the African with moral superiority and made him a seer" ("Poetics of Ethiopianism" 416). Eric J. Sundquist recapitulates that this reading of Psalms 68:31 "portrayed colonized Africa or enslaved Africans in the diaspora as prepared for providential delivery from bondage." It could be seen "to prophesy a black millennium, a violent seizure of freedom through acts of revolt sanctioned by God and led, literally or figuratively, by a black redeemer from within Africa or, in some interpretations, from America" (553).[3]

In his historical survey of the development of Ethiopianism, John Gruesser names as the four dominant elements of Ethiopianism "a common heritage linking black Americans and Africans, a cyclical view of history, the prediction of a bright future for Africa, and monumentalism." He adds that a fifth component was "African American exceptionalism," which is "the belief that because of their experiences in the West and adoption of Christianity black Americans were the people best qualified to lead Africans and members of the diaspora to the bright future foretold for them" (*Black on Black* 5–6).[4] In Hopkins's novel *Of One Blood*, many of the aforementioned elements are apparent: the view of history is fundamentally teleological; Africa and America are intricately linked in the family of Reuel Briggs; there is a belief in the cyclical view of history; the past of Africa is presented as glorious and the future looks bright, but the present reality is seen as dismal; the ancient ruins of Meroe and the hidden city of Telassar speak of great monuments and buried treasures; and Reuel Briggs is regarded as the future leader of an ancient Ethiopian/African people.

Hopkins concentrates on the questions of color and race in a five-part series published in the *Voice of the Negro* from February to July 1905.[5] The series is called "The Dark Races of the Twentieth Century" and shows her continual concern about the "unreasoning insanity on the question of color" ("Dark Races, I" 108). She was also increasingly concerned with questions of labor as a determining force for the twentieth century. As the editors announce for the July 1905 issue, her articles met with much approval: "Many people have written us and spoken to us about Miss Hopkins' articles. Evidently they have awakened great interest in the history of the colored people of the world" ("Voice of the Negro for July, 1905").

Hopkins begins her series with a quotation from Shakespeare's *The Merchant of Venice* and a reference to *Othello*, which leads her to remark that Shakespeare articulated "a silent protest against the unjustness of man to man" ("Dark Races, I" 108). In subsequent paragraphs she treats the problematic question of the origin of color, quoting from Delany's *Principia of*

Ethnology, the Bible, and some social scientists. Her favorite quotation from the Bible is "God hath made of one blood all the nations of men for to dwell on all the face of the earth" (108; Acts 17:26). Except for the Shakespeare quotation, the sources she uses, especially Delany and the Bible, are the same as in *A Primer of Facts*, which reinforces the idea that both the *Primer* and the series were written at the same time.

Her motivation for writing both *A Primer of Facts* and the "Dark Races" series is stated here, however, in very simple terms: it is her conviction that if the writing of history were left to white people, the history of African Americans would be distorted. Since there can be no doubt about the fact that the Anglo-Saxons desire "the complete subjugation of all dark races to themselves" ("Dark Races, VI" 461), the telling of the story cannot be left to them: "The presumption of superiority by the Anglo-Saxon race is insolently arrogant. We mark the insinuating patronage of other races by them, the slogan of social equality, the gospel of racial purity, the dangers of the Ethiopian Movement, as the outcome of a dread fear that is ever present with them and tugging at their very heartstrings. This is caused by the steady uplift of thousands of Blacks, Yellows and Browns. If we let them tell it, the slightest advancement in art, science and government removes all traces of Negro origin." Considering that this statement was made in 1905, it is a bitter observation of the geopolitical situation at the beginning of the new century. It is also a very frank denouncement of white supremacy unusual for the time and the journal for which it was written. The *Voice of the Negro* always had to negotiate between political and ideological independence and the dreadful political reality of southern Georgia in the early decade of the century (see B. Johnson, esp. 40–42). Du Bois said in 1903 that "the problem of the twentieth century is the problem of the color line" (*Souls* 209). Hopkins takes her stand on this important issue by enumerating facts and by quoting from as many sources as possible.

Her treatment of the South African Kaffirs may illustrate her typical struc-turing of the material available to her. She distinguishes the people she talks about as closely as possible with references to their geographical and political situation and then proceeds to describe their outward appearance and moral characteristics. She writes, for example: "The Kaffirs are one of the widest spread of the African families. The Kaffirs are blackish-red in complexion and the hair crisp. The men are a handsome set, very tall with an intellectual cast of countenance. They show much aptitude for civilization, but their origin is a mystery to scientists. The Kaffirs are great warriors" ("Dark Races, IV" 417).

This and similar descriptions and the quotation about the insolent arrogance of the Anglo-Saxon race cannot be cited without an analysis of the contradiction behind them. Hopkins's negotiations with race are a clear case proving H. Aram Veeser's premise of new historicist theory: that "every act of unmasking, critique, and opposition uses the tools it condemns and risks falling prey to the practice it exposes" (xi). Although Hopkins quotes from Johann Friedrich Blumenbach that there is not one "single bodily characteristic which is at once peculiar to the Negro, and cannot be found to exist in many other and distant nations" ("Dark Races, IV" 417), she always uses physical description to categorize races and tribes.[6] She could not possibly move away from the dichotomy of primitive versus civilized races, so she talks about "untutored savages" ("Dark Races, I" 108), the cannibalism of the Papuans ("Dark Races, I" 111), the easygoing nature of the Malay ("Dark Races, II" 188), the "Chinaman" who is "not endowed with much imagination" ("Dark Races, III" 332), and employs other generalizations.[7] These include her occasional uttering of a belief in the superiority of the Anglo-Saxon race: "But always predominating, we find the incisive Anglo-Saxon marching along triumphantly toward the sovereignty of the world" ("Dark Races, II" 188). The exact sources of her information remain unstated, but all her ideas remain within the realm of a general background in reading about race of the time.[8]

The fact that "Hopkins never challenges the basic assumption that races can be ranked qualitatively," as Richard Yarborough puts it in his introduction to *Contending Forces* (xxxvi), has been noted by most readers and critics of the late twentieth century up to now. It may seem contradictory to read about her belief in the superiority of the Anglo-Saxon race and her condemnation of racism in the same series within a very short time, but it is not a contradiction that she would have noticed at all. When she says she believes in Anglo-Saxon superiority and the less civilized state of many other races of the earth, she combines two ideas: she criticizes white supremacy because it takes unfair advantage of its "high" civilized status and suppresses other races, but she does not question its existence in itself. In *Classical Black Nationalism*, Moses notices a similar trend in other black nationalist texts of the period in contrast to those of the later twentieth century: "The nationalism of Alexander Crummell and Marcus Garvey was situated in a 'high culture' aesthetic, which admired symbols of imperial power, military might, and aristocratic refinement. Post-Garveyite nationalism, reflecting the influences of twentieth-century anthropology, has tended to idealize African village life, sentimentalize the rural South, and romanticize the urban ghetto" (3). Hopkins implicitly and thus typically endorses many cultural ideals of white Americans without questioning them profoundly. She condemns, for example, the United States for maintaining friendly relations with the Abyssinian emperor Menelik II, while it deals "severely with its own Negro population" ("Dark Races, IV" 415). On the other hand, she regards the American Negro as the epitome of the possible development and advancement of the dark races. Typical of the Ethiopianists of her time, she sees the African American embodying all the advantages of the contact between the Anglo-Saxon civilization and the ancient glory, rapid development, as well as the wide diversity of Africa:

> When Africa is mentioned, people instantly associate the tribes as one vast mass of hideous ignorance. Such is far from the case. Some of the tribes are as fine specimens of manhood as one could wish to meet. In proof of the versatility of its people we have but to refer to the great advance of the Negroes of the United States—a heterogeneous mass composed of contributions from nearly all the tribes of the fatherland. In America a great problem has been worked out—the problem of the brotherhood of man, represented by the highest intellectual culture among Negroes, that can be shown by any other race in our cosmopolitan population. ("Dark Races, IV" 417)

Consistent with her belief in the cyclical nature of civilizations, she sees the darker races as rising and the white race as deteriorating because of its racism and materialism. The future will be the combination of the best characteristics of all the races, and the American Negro will embody this type. The tension in her writing, therefore, is nonexistent because it is consistent with her belief in Ethiopianism, amalgamation, and the cyclical view of civilization.

The same dichotomy between civilization and primitivism appears in Hopkins's treatment of the question of colonialism. In her *Primer of Facts*, Hopkins asks herself if she believes in the fulfillment of the prophecy that princes shall come out of Africa. Her reason for believing in the prophecy can be found in the many significant happenings of the immediate past, namely the "establishment of the Liberian Republic, the Anglo-Boer war in South Africa and the rapid opening up of the Continent of Africa by civilized powers during the nineteenth century and the rapid intellectual improvement of Africans and their descendants in all parts of the world" (19). It is predictable that she sees the civilizing power of the colonization of Africa in a positive light. Moses writes that "black writers, even those opposed to African resettlement, believed that Africa must be redeemed from paganism, and barbarism, before it could be redeemed from European colonialism"

(*Afrotopia* 26). Hopkins opposes emigration, the movement that sought to send American blacks back to Africa, but endorses a general pan-African sentiment manifesting itself in a knowledge of Ethiopian history and in the fostering of race pride and of a friendship with the African peoples.

One example of a superior Anglo-Saxon, a gentle conqueror who governs in a firm and just way, is Sir James Brooke in Borneo: "The great thing is not to be in a hurry; to avoid over-legislation, law forms and legal subtleties; to aim first to make the people contented and happy in every way, even if that way should be quite opposite to European theories of how they ought to be happy" ("Dark Races, II" 188).[9] Her conclusion from this is simple: "If our powerful American leaders might be brought to emulate the example of Sir James Brooke in dealing with the race question in the United States, how matters would be simplified, and peace take the place of suspicion and hatred. But greed and the desire for high place will eventually override all humane suggestions for the upbuilding of humanity, and we may expect to see the present state of things continue to the end" ("Dark Races, II" 189). Her belief in this kind of gentle colonialism is represented in her fiction by Reuel Briggs, the protagonist of *Of One Blood*, who is depicted as a savior coming out of America and bringing progress to the African people. Her counterexample of the colonizer who economically exploits East India in piratical trade instead of bringing superior civilization is Captain Gordon, a central character in her short story "Talma Gordon."

In the fifth and concluding installment of "The Dark Races," Hopkins develops the racial antagonism further by including the question of labor versus capitalism. Since this series is one of the last public utterances by Hopkins, it may point to the development in her thinking at that time. She states, "The most serious questions of the hour are the Negro Problem and its fellow—Capital versus Labor. These are the factors which in a future generation will change the current of events and the deductions of science" ("Dark Races, VI" 462). The same idea is also set forth in the *Primer of Facts*, when she writes: "When labor and capital become contending forces, the Black will float into the full enjoyment of citizenship. Blood will flow, for humanity sweeps onward, and God's purposes never fail" (30). And she sounds prophetic when she writes, "But in the great labor contest which will inevitably come to our common country we take a stand with the vast human tide and 'sink or swim, live or die, survive or perish' with the great majority" ("Dark Races, VI" 463). By applying the term "contending forces" to the labor question, she puts extra emphasis on the idea behind it. The term "contending forces" was well known to her readers from the title of her first novel. Its more explicit use in *A Primer of Facts* is foreshadowed by Luke Sawyer, the very dark African American in his famous speech denouncing racism, in which he says that "conservatism, lack of brotherly affiliation, lack of energy for the right and the power of the almighty dollar" are the *"contending forces that are dooming this race to despair"* (*Contending Forces* 256). As it stands in the context of the novel, Luke Sawyer's speech is Hopkins's most radical and outspoken statement about race relations and condemnation of American capitalism. The ending of the fifth part of the "Dark Races" series even goes one step further in denouncing materialists and capitalists who will lose their manhood if they do not defend the poor, the weak, the downtrodden: "We want men with red blood in their veins and not the sluggishness of the cold materialist who scorns the 'dreamers' who make up the world's best people. Men of the times and for the times who will serve nobly their day and generation. Men who will teach the Anglo-Saxon that 'all men were created equal' and *'all men'* are not *white* men" (463).

Here, in 1905, Pauline Hopkins introduces a way of thinking about the race problem that would gain much public prominence later. Although practically unacknowledged, she may be regarded as a forerunner to Du Bois's writing on the labor question. In "The Negro Mind Reaches Out," an article that was included in Alain Locke's *New Negro* anthology of 1925, Du Bois takes up his earlier statement on the problem of the twentieth century being the problem of the color line. In the wake of the First World War, he explains economic and colonial imperialism: "Most men would agree that our present problem of problems was not the Color Problem, but what we call Labor, the problem of allocating work and income in the tremendous and increasingly intricate world-embracing industrial machine that our civilization has built" (385). By equating imperialism and industrialism, he traces what he calls the "dark colonial shadow" of Portugal, Belgium, France, and England. Nation-building, education, and democratic rule were, in his mind, all dependent upon industrial profit. Thus it would be labor unrest that would eventually bring about political change. Du Bois warns the white governments in power: "Future economic imperialism can only be held together by militarism" (410).

Du Bois's other articles about the labor problem—"Brothers, Come North" (1920); "The Negro and Radical Thought" (1921); "The American Federation of Labor and the Negro" (1929); "Marxism and the Negro Problem" (1933), and "Behold the Land" (1947)—all come later than Hopkins's *Primer of Facts* and "Dark Races" series.[10] Although one must keep in mind that Hopkins's work may not have been known to Du Bois, one must realize that her visionary powers and insight into geopolitical agendas included a consideration of the labor question as one of the important forces of the twentieth century.

In this context, Hopkins's *Primer* stands as a little-known document of her political and historical concerns, her feminist views, and her personal situation after leaving the *Colored American Magazine*. In 1905 Hopkins published a thirty-one-page treatise on the history of races, *A Primer of Facts Pertaining to the Early Greatness of the African Race and the Possibility of Restoration by Its Descendants—with Epilogue Compiled and Arranged from the Works of the Best Known Ethnologists and Historians*, which is reprinted here in the appendix. It was self-published in Cambridge, Mass., by P. E. Hopkins and Company and was the first part of what was probably planned as a comprehensive Black Classics Series. In it Hopkins lays down her thoughts about the early greatness of the African people in Ethiopia and Egypt, professes her belief in a fundamentally Christian teleology, and writes about the present situation of African Americans in turn-of-the-century America. She formulates her theory in the manner of a school primer with questions such as "Who Built the First City?" or "What Was the Original Man?" followed by condensed answers that could easily be memorized. Her style is didactic, her message clear: African Americans should be proud of their past and optimistic for the future.

Hopkins's endorsement of cultural nationalism and Ethiopianism rests, therefore, mainly upon three pillars. First of all, there is her deeply felt and often repeated need to interpret history according to biblical sources. The quotations that she most often uses are Psalms 68:31 and Acts 17:26. Her endeavor to reinterpret the biblical history of Noah and his sons moves her to presuppose a common descent of mankind and leads her to conclude from it the coming of a redeeming figure out of Africa, an early greatness of the Negro civilization, and a distinct tradition in literature and the arts. Second, she relies on classical sources to prove her arguments, although it is not her aim to write a scholarly historical study. She often does not identify quotations, which makes it sometimes hard for a later critic to determine how much she actually appropriated from other writers. Third, she relies on nineteenth-century black nationalist texts, especially the work of Martin Delany, William Wells Brown, Rufus L. Perry, and George Washington Williams, to substantiate her historical treatise.

Her treatment of the topic is not new, as she notes in the subtitle of her study. It is compiled from the arguments of early black nationalists and

Ethiopianists, while much of the Christian explanation of the development of different races or scientific explanations of race distinctions rests on much-used sources. The Bible takes first place and manifests itself in numerous passages of biblical interpretation and quotation. Without identifying many of her quotations correctly, she also cites directly from at least three books: William Wells Brown's *The Rising Son* (1874), Martin R. Delany's *Principia of Ethnology: The Origin of Races and Color* (1879), and Rufus L. Perry's *The Cushite; or, The Descendants of Ham* (1893).[11] She may also have known George Washington Williams's *History of the Negro Race in America, 1619 to 1880* (1883). In this sense, *A Primer of Facts* becomes as much a document of the popular reception of these earlier texts as a document of its own.

Hopkins prefaces her treatise by saying that "The standing of any race is determined by its mighty works and its men of genius" (4). As the author of two series about famous men and women of the Negro race, Hopkins was well qualified to judge the prominence of African American men and women of genius. In *Afrotopia*, Moses refers to the sociologist Orlando Patterson, who called this attempt " 'contributionism,' a concern among historians with demonstrating that black or African peoples have made a contribution to the progress of mankind" (23). This movement is also called "vindicationism," which is "the project of defending black people from the charge that they have made little or no contribution to the history of human progress" (Moses, *Afrotopia* 21).

In her line of argument, Hopkins sets forth a strictly biblical explanation of the common origin of all people, especially of Acts 17:26: "Of one blood have I made all nations of men to dwell upon the whole face of the earth." She writes, "Man began his existence in the creation of Adam, therefore all races of mankind were once united and descended from one parentage" (5). Since the Hebrew word *Adam* means red, his color "must have been clay color or yellow, resembling that of the North American Indian." In this Hopkins repeats Martin Delany's argument in *Principia of Ethnology* and William Wells Brown's argument in *The Rising Son*. Such statements try to reconcile the colors of the various races with the Christian doctrine that all mankind descended from Adam. "Until the entry of Noah's family into the ark, all people were of the one race and complexion" (5). The familiar Christian explanation of the division of mankind into races comes in her second chapter, when she talks about Noah's sons, Shem, Ham and Japheth, and the yellow, black, and white races. Like Delany and Brown before her, Hopkins relies on the most accepted, widely available, and authoritative source to give weight to her arguments. At her time biblical exegesis had had a long tradition, and the

Bible had been used for arguments both for and against slavery, emancipation, or racial discrimination.[12]

To reinforce her Christian argument, Hopkins, like many of her contemporaries, cites biological evidence to prove that basically the same red fluid runs in the veins of all races: "There is but one color, modified and intensified from the purest white to the purest black" (9). She also cites evidence that a different climate might produce different skin color. The deeper reason for this, however, is that God ordered it: "It is in accordance with the economy of the Creator to give an unerring reproductive system to each race whereby it should always be known by its own peculiar characteristics" (8). Hopkins here acknowledges the concept of a difference between the races, but it is a biological difference only, which, ordained by God, constitutes the brotherhood of all mankind because traces of the colors white, black, red, blue, and yellow appear in every single human being. Many of her phrases are taken verbatim from Delany and Brown. The sources that, for example, Brown himself quotes from, however, are not mentioned by Hopkins. Her unscholarly attitude toward the historical sources serves to enhance the genre of the text as a primer, an introduction to a subject with facts that she considers common knowledge. She does not intend to question the veracity of her data; she is not interested in a scientific debate. This is a primer presumably written for younger black people, instructing them about their origin and instilling race pride in them.

After stating the common origin of all races, Hopkins, like many other writers, concentrates on the early greatness of Ethiopia and Egypt as African civilizations that were settled by Cush, the son of Ham and the grandson of Noah: "That the rule of Cush extended from the Nilotic borders of Egypt in toward the interior of darkest Africa, and known as Ethiopia, is not to be disputed, all historians of ancient history agreeing on this point. In the early settlement of these countries, Ethiopia and Egypt were united kingdoms under the rule of three princes—father and two sons" (11). Hopkins here relies heavily on both Delany (see 48) and Wells Brown. In addition, she also goes back to Perry and George Washington Williams's two-volume history. The classical sources that Hopkins cites are Pliny, Diodorus Siculus, and Herodotus, and, as before, these sources are appropriated from her models nearly verbatim. Their accuracy is never questioned or examined.

The great cities of the ancient African empire were Meroe in Ethiopia and Thebes in Egypt. Of these two, Meroe gets special attention as "the seat of all ancient greatness" (12). It was an important trading center ruled by kings, one of whom, familiar to readers of her novel *Of One Blood*, was

Ergamenes, "who lived in the reign of the second Ptolemy" and became the founder of a new religion (13). Among the famous queens of ancient Ethiopia were Candace (also familiar from *Of One Blood*), Aahmes (wife of Amoris of Egypt), and the queen of Sheba.

As to the religious belief of ancient Ethiopia, Hopkins thinks there was a "Three-One-God" (14), the trinity manifested in Ham, Noah's son, who was also called Rameses I and was identical with Jupiter Ammon. "He is represented as the body of a man with the head of a ram seated on a great white throne of gold and ivory." The ram's head has a double significance, as she says in one of the passages taken directly from Delany, "combining the innocence of the sheep and the caution in the horns not to approach too near, illustrating the biblical declaration that 'no man can look upon God's face and live'" (15; Delany 65–66). A phoenix with extended wings sits at his right side, which illustrates "the essential attributes of the Christian conception of God, as a self-created being without beginning and without end." Like Delany, Hopkins attempts to read a Christian interpretation into ancient belief, so that she can combine a Christian worldview with a need to recapture greatness in early pagan Africa.

To her mind, the contribution of ancient Ethiopia to world civilization lies in the fields of "wisdom and Literature" (15). The pyramids, for example, were "architectural structures built in Ethiopia and Egypt, begun under Ham, Cush and Mizriam." These pyramids and other temples proved early proficiency in natural science, geometry, and the mechanical arts, in particular. The Ethiopians also excelled in literature and invented astronomy and astrology, "and communicated these sciences to the Egyptians" (17). In addition, the literature of the Israelites, "in letters, government and religion, was derived from the Africans, as they must have carried with them the civilization of those peoples in their exodus."

The concept of the cyclical view of history in Hopkins can be traced back to Brown's *The Rising Son*, in which he writes: "Every one knows that Rome got her civilization from Greece; that Greece again borrowed hers from Egypt, that thence she derived her earliest science and the form of her beautiful mythology" (43). The origin of all civilization thus lies in Africa and was shaped by Africans. Further back, this civilization came from Thebes and before that from Meroe, "the queenly city of Ethiopia, into which all Africa poured its caravans laden with ivory, frankincense, and gold. So it is that we trace the light of Ethiopian civilization first into Egypt, thence into Greece, and Rome, whence, gathering new splendor on its way, it hath been diffusing itself all the world over" (Brown 44). In the *Primer of Facts*, Hopkins takes up this idea and writes in her concluding message: "Ethiopia fell because of her arrogance and stiff-necked idolatry. Scarcely a sign of her ancient splendor can be found today, and low in the dust of humiliation lie her suffering children. Egypt fell, and so did Greece. Rome fell" (31). Hopkins admonishes her readers that history may repeat itself and that, if such great civilizations as Ethiopia and Egypt fell, the same fate may await the great modern Western civilization. God will certainly vindicate the poor and downtrodden races of the Earth.

Of course, Hopkins knew that her view of the African origin of all great civilizations was not commonly accepted in her time, so the question she poses in her treatise is, "How have the blacks of modern times demonstrated the fact that they are descended from the once powerful and learned Ethiopians?" (17). Her answer takes up the theme of her preface, namely because of the number of "phenomenally intellectual men produced in Africa and America." What follows is a list running through two pages of famous men and women in science, art, and literature, and a number of famous patriots from the Revolutionary War and the Civil War. Many of the people she mentions are the subjects of her "Famous Men" and "Famous Women of the Negro Race" series. The notable exception is Booker T. Washington, who is not included in her list. Thus her text also becomes a political statement, in which the past is made to reflect on the present situation.

The epilogue to the *Primer of Facts* functions as Hopkins's transition from a glorification of the past to a condemnation of present-day racism, especially as it is manifested in southern white racists. She quotes an astonishing six pages of the racist book by white southerner Jeannette Robinson Murphy, *Southern Thoughts for Northern Thinkers*.[13] While her treatment of the black women's club movement is never that of a woman's movement with the simple addition of race, this excerpt now proves that her treatment of race cannot be separated from her treatment of women.

The long excerpt highlights the racist and extremely one-sided view of history of Mrs. Murphy. She writes about happy Negroes under slavery, courteous white men, the southern lady on a pedestal, a sound and honest Christian belief, the Christianization of African savages, abolitionists tempted by Satan, lies of runaway slaves, and the "African in his present illiterate, irresponsible, shiftless state" (25). She insists upon the "utter segregation and social isolation" (24) of the Negro from society and rails against Harriet Beecher Stowe and northern missionaries. There will be race war in the North when the Negroes move there to find social equality. She suggests that instead of in higher education, all money should be invested in a colonizing project, with a special colony of Negroes somewhere in New England. Mrs. Murphy's extremely racist account of the past and present situation of African Americans must be seen as a counterhistory to the one Hopkins has just presented herself. It implies that if this one white woman can distort history to such a degree, even claiming that black mothers begged their masters to sell their own no-account children away from them ("not infrequently the master had to protect children from their savage mothers' rage" [25]), how then could other, trained historians distort history whenever they wanted to? There is no doubt that Hopkins expected her readers to understand her sarcasm and share it.

Mrs. Murphy's astonishing remarks certainly contributed to Hopkins's firm belief in the power of political agitation, especially for universal suffrage. Hopkins then replies to various parts of Mrs. Murphy's book and refutes one charge after the other: the so-called southern chivalrous man is responsible for the mixture of blood by the raping of black slavewomen; amalgamation, the mixture of black and white blood, cannot be prevented any more and need not lead to disaster: "Anglo-Saxon blood is already hopelessly perverted, with that of other races, and in most cases to its great gain" (29). She ridicules Mrs. Murphy's idea that blacks should give testimony in court that they were treated fairly during slavery, because blacks at this time were not allowed to give testimony in court at all. Her severest criticism is then directed at the white woman's denigration of black womanhood. "Our mothers are the bulwarks of the race whom we love, revere, and delight to honor" (30). Parental brutality came from the fathers who sold their quadroon or octoroon daughters in public auction sales. In conclusion, Hopkins talks about the "lamentable ignorance of the commonest scientific and historical facts" on the part of Mrs. Murphy, who, as a woman, should set an enlightened example of Christian principles (31).

This part of the *Primer* highlights the extreme racism, distortion of historical truth, and white-supremacist standpoint that writers like Hopkins had to contend with in her time. Advocating "utter segregation and social isolation of the colored man" (24), Mrs. Murphy idealizes the southern slavery past and speaks out for a segregated Negro state in New England. Hopkins includes a very pertinent example of how her nemesis, Booker T. Washington, to whom Mrs. Murphy refers to without quoting him directly, and his idea of industrial education could be appropriated by this racist white woman, who writes: "Instead of the South wasting any more of its hard earned money upon the impossible higher education of the Negroes, let us give them as a whole domestic training and sound Bible teaching, employing white ministers to lead them, as in the old regime, and then later on expend all our surplus money and energy in colonising the race somewhere as Abraham Lincoln suggested, and give it a chance to show if it is really capable of self-government and higher culture" (26). Lumping together Washington's industrial project with old-style religious preaching and plans for segregating the race entirely, this part of her epilogue serves as direct political criticism of the most powerful race leader of her time. Her call for agitation and the capitalization of her central message—"NEVER SURRENDER THE BALLOT" (27)—put her firmly into the radical camp.

Hopkins's conclusion from all the previous material is her vision of the "future American" (28), the mixed-race descendant of the best southern families. Amalgamation, the mixing of races, is seen as a positive force. A key issue in the turn-of-the-century period, amalgamation had the power to provoke fears of a blurring of racial boundaries and the loss of white supremacy. When propagated by one of their own race, it evoked criticism from African Americans who feared that it would lead to wholesale accommodation and the loss of racial heritage. Arguments for and against amalgamation can be found in Hopkins's usual sources, Delany, Brown, and Perry. But an even broader context is provided by Charles Chesnutt's series "The Future American," an essay by Anna Julia Cooper, and George Washington Williams's history, which are close in time and method to the *Primer*.

Charles Chesnutt's three-part series called "The Future American" was published in the late summer of 1900 in the white *Boston Evening Transcript*.[14] There can be no doubt that Hopkins read it because it provoked quite a controversy locally. In these three articles, Chesnutt advocates miscegenation and intermarriage as the solution to the American race problem. If the races were mixed, he argues, racism would disappear automatically. Believing, much like Hopkins, Brown, Delany, and Perry, that amalgamation between the white and black races already began under slavery, he makes it clear that "the future American race—the future American ethnic type—will be formed of a mingling . . . of the various racial varieties" (97). His model rests on the assumption that in three generations, the white race would have absorbed the black race through mandatory intermarriage. He gives as examples of this ongoing process the many southern families with dark blood in their veins. His priorities are sufficiently clear when he writes: "If it is only by becoming white that colored people and their children are to enjoy the rights and dignities of citizenship, they will have every incentive to 'lighten the breed,' . . . that they might claim the white man's privileges as soon as possible" (106).

Predictably, the series was received with much criticism, especially from contemporary African Americans, who accused Chesnutt of succumbing to the supremacist notion that only the white race possesses the key to wealth, superior intellect, and culture. Although Chesnutt might well have tried to be ironic in much of what he says, the essays must be taken at face value because any possible ironic meaning was not really obvious to his contemporary (and most of his later) audience. The comments by both SallyAnn Ferguson and Arlene Elder on the reprinting of this text in 1988 point out the inconsistency in his argument and trace his "concept of cultural dichotomies popular at his time" back to his own mixed-race ancestry (Elder 123). Elder reads an incongruity in his "advocacy of racial amalgamation as the ultimate solution to America's social ills when such a blending would result in an invisibility guaranteed to strike terror in more hearts than those consciously agreeing with the Reverend Thomas Dixon Jr.'s white supremacist novels or with latter-day Fundamentalist prophecies of Armageddon" (123).[15]

Hopkins certainly referred to Chesnutt when she called the future American the mixed-race American, but she never went so far as to claim that amalgamation would cure all social ills. Her repeated use of the term "future American" in the "Charles Winter Wood" article signed by J. Shirley Shadrach and in the *Primer* shows her concern with this very enticing idea: "For the sake of argument, let us admit that there may be some foundation for the fears of the South that amalgamation may produce a race that will gradually supersede the present dominant factors in the government of this Republic" (*Primer* 28). The "future American," descended from the best white families of the South, would possess the best traits of the two races. Fictional representations of this type are the various light-colored protagonists in her novels and short stories. One of the villains in *Contending Forces* is described, however, as a descendant of slaves and southern crackers, a combination that the narrator calls "a bad mixture—the combination of the worst features of a dominant race with an enslaved race" (*Contending Forces* 91). Thus the tendency in her writing to refer to the weaker race—and to explain a character on the basis of his ancestry, a tendency that puzzles so many readers—can be explained within the larger context of her views on amalgamation. Races must mingle, but only a complementary combination of two races can induce character and intelligence in a mulatto race.

Both Chesnutt and Hopkins professed basically the same opinion, and hence a similar incongruity can be found in them. Anthony Appiah traces the source of this inconsistency in Du Bois's essay "The Conservation of Races" (1897). He points out Du Bois's movement away from a "scientific"—that is, biological and anthropological—conception of race to a sociohistorical

notion (23). He sees as the thesis in this classic dialectic the denial of difference and as the antithesis "the acceptance of difference, along with a claim
that each group has its part to play; that the white race and its racial Other
are related not as superior to inferior but as complementaries; that the Negro
message is, with the white one, part of the message of humankind" (25).
This dialectic is similar to that used by feminism: "on the one hand, a simple
claim to equality, a denial of substantial difference; on the other, a claim to a
special message, revaluing the feminine Other not as the helpmeet of sexism,
but as the New Woman."

A close analysis of Hopkins's treatise and Chesnutt's articles will show
a very similar agenda. Hopkins fervently argues for equality and accepts
the difference between the races only through acknowledgment of the message that the Negro race contains. It is a revaluation of racial difference, yet
neither a denial nor an acceptance of it. Appiah calls this strategy "not the
transcendence of the nineteenth-century scientific conception of race" but "a
revaluation of the Negro race in the face of the sciences of racial inferiority"
(25). Whereas Du Bois cannot consistently identify the "family of common
history" (26), the source of tension in Hopkins is her attempt to emphasize
the ancient greatness, present and past achievements, and future glory of the
African American while she refers at the same time to the supremacy of the
white race. It is a tension that strongly influences her fiction and that must
be seen as nurturing rather than impairing it. As Chesnutt acknowledges in
his acceptance speech for the Spingarn Medal in 1928: "My physical makeup
was such that I knew the psychology of people of mixed blood in so far as
it differed from that of other people, and most of my writings ran along the
color line, the vaguely defined line where the two major races of the country
meet. It has more dramatic possibilities than life within clearly defined and
widely differentiated groups" (qtd. in Elder, "*MELUS* Forum" 126).

Another source for both Hopkins and Chesnutt is Anna Julia Cooper's
essay "Has America a Race Problem; If So, How Can It Best Be Solved?"
which is included in her collection *A Voice from the South*. A short analysis
will illustrate the background common to Hopkins and Chesnutt and show
that their view of history is not extreme but typical. Whereas Hopkins and
Chesnutt contend that a certain mixture of races is necessary to maintain
the artistic vitality of the dominant race, Cooper argues that conflict is necessary to produce healthy races: "Progressive peace in a nation is the result
of conflict; and conflict, such as is healthy, stimulating, and progressive, is
produced through the co-existence of radically opposing or racially different elements" (*Voice* 151). In the westward movement of civilization, the

highest degree of civilization is now reached in the American, but the high status of its civilization is endangered because of its racism and intolerance: "Compromise and concession, liberality and toleration were the conditions of the nation's birth and are the *sine qua non* of its continued existence" (165). Cooper's credo is persuasive: "The God of battles is in the conflicts of history. The evolution of civilization is His care, eternal progress His delight. As the European was higher and grander than the Asiatic, so will American civilization be broader and deeper and closer to the purposes of the Eternal than any the world has yet seen. This the last page is to mark the climax of history, the bright consummate flower unfolding *charity toward all and malice toward none*" (166). Cooper predicts that ultimately no race will be superior forever because races "that are weakest can, *if they so elect*, make themselves felt" (167). And the advantages will be manifold: America will put an end to race prejudice, political tyranny, religious bigotry, intellectual intolerance, caste illiberality, and class exclusiveness (168). Of course, Cooper knows that there is a race problem in America, but her view of it is to see it as a chance for the future, not a curse eternally put on the black people. "We would not deprecate the fact, then, that America has a Race Problem. It is guaranty of the perpetuity and progress of her institutions, and insures the breadth of her culture and the symmetry of her development" (173). She cites spontaneity, instinct for law and order, respect for authority, inaptitude for rioting and anarchy, gentleness and cheerfulness as laborers, and deep Christianity as the positive character traits of the black people that counterpoise the European "anarchy, socialism, communism, and skepticism" that poured in with the other immigrants.

Cooper's basically Ethiopianist argument clearly shows that Hopkins could rely on a belief in the positive force of history, a belief that was common in the circle of educated African Americans. It is a testament to Cooper's and Hopkins's manipulation but not transcendence of racial stereotypes. The familiar essentialist characterization of the former slaves as gentle and meek are reinterpreted to stand in for their need to elevate the potentially positive side of the African American character in times of political strife. It is also a statement of nativism that comes up time and again in many writers of her time. John Higham defines nativism as "every type and level of antipathy toward aliens, their institutions, and their ideas" (3). It manifested itself in anti-immigration laws, literacy tests for immigrants, or fear of foreign radicals. It often included racial nativism, in which "the" American was designated as Anglo-Saxon (see Higham 3–11, 68–105). Writers like Cooper argued for the inclusion of the African American as "native" Americans and their literature as more "typically" American than many other texts and, therefore, sounded antiforeign on occasion, and so did Hopkins. In the story "Bro'r Abr'm Jimson's Wedding," Hopkins has a colored bellboy insult an Irish maid, an incident that triggers all kinds of antiforeign and anti-Irish prejudice.

Another source of Hopkins's treatise must be dealt with in order to show that African American history was a scholarly subject in her time and that Hopkins could, indeed, take much for granted. This is George W. Williams's *History of the Negro Race in America, 1619 to 1880*, a two-volume study numbering more than a thousand pages, published in 1883. Dickson D. Bruce calls this book "the most significant early account of ancient Africa" and claims that it was generally "acknowledged as the first important effort by a black writer to do a *scholarly* general history, based on significant primary and secondary research" (685–86). Williams's book, Bruce claims, had great impact. At the time of its publication, it was reviewed fairly widely, even in the white press. The *Atlantic Monthly* gave it lengthy and positive comment, and it even received favorable notice in the *Westminster Review* of London.[16] William J. Simmons includes George W. Williams in his *Men of Mark: Eminent, Progressive and Rising* of 1887 and numbers him "among the intellectual stars which shine in the zenith of the Negro world" (549), calling his history one of the "standard works" (560).

At that time, most arguments used to establish the inferiority of the Negro were based on the view that either environment had caused it or that inferiority "was the product of innate biological differences" (Bruce 697).[17] Williams's views are based on biblical evidence that seems to prove that all mankind is "of one blood," as in Acts 17:26. Once this point is established with as many quotations from the Bible as possible, Williams, preceding Hopkins, points out how black people have been part of the growth of civilization since the earliest times.

Williams answers the question why the Negro fell from his high state of civilization by stating that it was due to sin, "forgetfulness of God, idolatry" (24), a statement that Hopkins turns into "Ethiopia fell because of her arrogance and her stiff-necked idolatry" (31). Williams may also have influenced the view of the present state of the African people that becomes apparent in Hopkins's *Of One Blood*. He cites numerous examples of atrocities of Negro tribes and argues that "the Negro is but the most degraded and disfigured type of the primeval African" (48). The view that contemporary Africans were a nation somewhat uncivilized, savage, and primitive was typical of Ethiopianism.

Written between 1874 (*The Rising Son*) and 1905 (*A Primer of Facts*) and thus at a time when lynching dominated the African American reality more than political and social gains, these texts document the transition in tone from a note of hope for the future to one of defiance and call to agitation. George W. Williams ends his monumental work on a very optimistic note: "Race prejudice is bound to give way before the potent influences of character, education, and wealth. And these are necessary to the growth of the race" (2:551). Mutual trade and aid will nurture both the American and the African cultures and societies and carry both to progress. "NEVER GIVE UP THE BALLOT," however, is the imperative with which Hopkins chooses to end her treatise. The emphasis is on the call to agitation for full civil rights. Her negotiations in race end with a political message.

It is a concept of the valuable past, collective history, and pride in descent that Hopkins shares with her forerunners and contemporaries. After referring to Psalm 68:31, Martin Delany writes: "We shall boldly advance, singing the sweet songs of redemption, in the regeneration of our race and restoration of our fatherland from the gloom and superstition and ignorance, to the glorious light of a more than pristine brightness—the light of the highest godly civilization" (109). Rufus L. Perry is even more laudatory of the ancient realm of the Cushites:

> Now what the Cushite *was*, certainly has some bearing on an intelligent judg-
> ment of what he is, and is to be. It should inspire him with an ambition to
> emulate his forefathers; for if to the memory of the distinguished Negroes of
> modern times we add the historic facts reaching from Menes to the Christian
> era attesting the greatness of the ancient Cushites, of whom we are lineal
> descendants, it were pusillanimous in us, and dishonoring to our ancestors, to
> be ashamed of either our color or our name. (160–61)

In her *Primer of Facts*, Hopkins engages in this project of using historical memory,[18] a clear profession of race pride, and a call for political and racial activism. Concerned as she was with the many attempts to define race in scientific terms, she could not yet see it as a social category alongside class and gender, as Evelyn B. Higginbotham argues. Still, the fact that a historical survey leads her to an analysis of the contemporary political and economic situation, as well as her constant intermingling of issues of race and gender, shows that she was aware of the power plays working behind all attempts at subjugating a group of people on the basis of race and gender.

As a full publication, *A Primer of Facts* is the last extensive utterance of Hopkins for the coming years. From a biographical standpoint, it is easy to read her bitterness about her treatment at the *Colored American Magazine* when she writes: "Newspapers and magazines have been subsidized or destroyed if the editors fearlessly advocated the cause of humanity" (*Primer* 21). We find a rare statement of her bitterness toward the political and social climate of her time: "We cannot cease from agitation while our wrongs are the sport of those who know how to silence our every complaint and plea for justice" (27). She sees her own fate as symptomatic of that of other African American intellectuals. Taking together *A Primer of Facts* and her series in the *Voice of the Negro*, it is obvious that Hopkins was concerned with the freedom of the press, the power and influence of Booker T. Washington, and the new century's labor problem and race riots. Both the "Dark Races" series and the *Primer* prove her profound insight and deep thinking about race and labor, while they show her disillusionment with her position as an active African American woman in the field of journalism. It is necessary to establish this background before engaging more specifically with her negotiations in literature. Her journalistic background deeply influenced these negotiations, which comprise her views on the matter of race literature and her own practice as a writer of fiction.

Negotiations in Literature
1900-1905

The Values of Race Literature

*P*auline Hopkins opens the preface to her first novel, *Contending Forces: A Romance Illustrative of Negro Life North and South*, by saying: "In giving this little romance expression in print, I am not actuated by a desire for notoriety or for profit, but to do all that I can in an humble way to raise the stigma of degradation from my race" (13). Her tone of female modesty was felt to be appropriate by many women writers of her time and concealed her outspoken and articulate voice. In calling her story a "romance," she grounds herself firmly in a tradition, and neither her undertaking nor her style is new or runs totally against the grain of literature at the turn of the century. Her goal to lift the stigma of degradation from her race serves as an apologia for this "somewhat abrupt and daring venture." The goal, she feels, justifies the means, and her "simple, homely tale, unassumingly told, which cements the bond of brotherhood among all classes and all complexions," will foster tolerance and promote her audience's awareness of color relations in the North and the South.

Hopkins, as this chapter sets out to demonstrate, was not alone in her undertaking. She was part of a generation of like-minded African American women writers. It is my firm belief that Hopkins was one of the guides to the footsteps of a future generation. Viewed against the background of the literary discourse of her own generation, she undertook the task of presenting the hardships, injustices, and wrongs committed against her own race. She chose to write about light-colored heroes and heroines, slavery and Reconstruction, dark-colored laundresses, maids, mothers and daughters, and white villains and their black servants, as well as about connections between Africa, Europe, and America. Her project was inclusive rather than exclusive, and many of her choices of style, genre, narrative voice, plot, and setting may be explained by grounding them firmly in their historical contexts.

Hopkins's preface to *Contending Forces* can best be evaluated when it is put in context with the more general African American literary discourse of her time. This discourse shows that it is the duty of the race woman to

135

engage in literature, that literature has a social function to which the writer must be committed, that race literature is an American record of the past that comprises many possible perspectives.[1] The texts that will be treated here in greater detail are Anna Julia Cooper's essay "One Phase of American Literature," which is included in her *A Voice from the South;* Victoria Earle Matthews's "The Value of Race Literature," a speech that she first gave in Boston in 1895; two essays by Mrs. N. F. Mossell (Gertrude Bustill Mossell) from her collection *The Work of the Afro-American Woman,* which appeared in 1894 and was reprinted in 1908; as well as George M. McClellan's contribution to Donald Culp's anthology *Twentieth Century Negro Literature* (1902). The texts demonstrate the nearly unknown and usually unacknowledged discourse going on among African American men and women of that time about the use and function of literature. They lead to a discussion of the readers of this literature and to questions of genre.

For Hopkins, literature is a means of education and possesses a social and political function. Every writer must be committed to the common cause of teaching a lesson in antiracism while captivating the audience by the mere force of the tale. Hopkins is firmly convinced of the rightfulness of her mission, as she maintains in her preface: *"No one will do this for us; we must ourselves develop the men and women who will faithfully portray the inmost thoughts and feelings of the Negro with all the fire and romance which lie dormant in our history,* and, as yet, unrecognized by writers of the Anglo-Saxon race" (14; emphasis in the original). In this sense, Hopkins's general literary project of writing simple, homely tales with "fire and romance" in them is expanded to include pedagogical material and political content. Long political speeches follow scenes in which the plot is propelled forward, often with the help of coincidence. Although later literary critics tend to detect a stylistic incompatibility between the simple tale and its political teaching, Hopkins and her generation of writers clearly see no contradiction at all. Race literature is written by one of the race about the race and for the benefit of the race.

She was certainly acquainted with the many slave narratives, Paul Laurence Dunbar's and Charles Chesnutt's dialect writings, Chesnutt's, Harper's, and Wells Brown's novels about light-colored heroines and heroes, and the pietistic/religious fiction by Emma Dunham Kelley-Hawkins and Amelia E. Johnson.[2] Their combination of melodramatic with didactic and political elements influenced Hopkins. The occasional depiction of stereotypical characters, such as the tragic mulatto and the comic dark-colored character, imposed a burden of legacy on her, which she sometimes adopted and some-times wrote against. This was the strategy she began when she wrote *Peculiar Sam*, and this is the strategy she will pursue in her fiction.

In "Literary Workers," part of her "Famous Women of the Negro Race," Hopkins professes a firm conviction that it is the duty of the race woman to study and discuss the "race question" despite adversities: "We know that it is not 'popular' for a woman to speak or write in plain terms against political brutalities, that a woman should confine her efforts to woman's work in the home and church" (277). Gender-based role assignments impose restrictions upon all women of her time, and race puts an additional stress on women, all of which, Hopkins argues, must be counterbalanced by extra care and awareness: "The colored woman must have an intimate knowledge of every question that agitates the councils of the world; she must understand the solution of problems that involve the alteration of the boundaries of coun-tries, and which make and unmake governments" ("Some Literary Women" 277). The writers she singles out for special praise are Phillis Wheatley, Frances E. W. Harper, Mary Church Terrell, Ida B. Wells-Barnett, and Mary Ann Shadd Cary.[3] Race literature is, therefore, an integral part of the women's club movement.

Her praise of Frances E. W. Harper, her most famous role model, is espe-cially illuminating. She writes about Harper as a writer but points out her career as a lecturer and activist in more detail. She emphasizes her battle for freedom in the time of slavery and her continuing struggle afterward for equality in education, civil rights, and the rights of women. While she also admires Mary Church Terrell for her intellectual brilliance and high social position and Mary Ann Shadd Cary for her multiple skills as schoolteacher, school superintendent, publisher, editor, and lecturer, her praise of Harper is more pronounced. Hopkins saw herself as following in the footsteps of such famous foremothers as Wheatley and Harper, while at the same time preparing the way for future generations. Hopkins may also have been in-fluenced by Harper's inclusion of material about Canada as a place of refuge and her admiration of John Brown's rebellion, both of which became part of Hopkins's novel *Winona*.

It is no surprise, then, that her two-part "Literary Workers" essay ends with a very optimistic and hopeful statement. It must be remembered that the date is April 1902 and that Hopkins was still safely established at the *Colored American Magazine*. "Why is the present bright? Because, for the first time, we stand face to face, as a race, with life as it is. Because we are at the parting of the ways and must choose true morality, true spirituality and the firm basis of all prosperity in races or nations—honest toil in field and shop, doing away with all superficial assumptions in education and business" ("Literary Workers [Concluded]" 371).

This basically optimistic view was shared by a generation of African American women writers who are now considered part of a tradition of pre–Harlem Renaissance writers. Gertrude Mossell was born in 1855 and died in 1948, her life thus spanning nearly an entire century, and experienced the hardships of slavery, Reconstruction, the end of Reconstruction, woman suffrage, the Harlem Renaissance, and the two world wars. Mossell and Anna Julia Cooper were of nearly the same age; Cooper, having been born in 1858, lived until 1964, while Victoria Earle Matthews was born in 1861 and lived until 1907. With Hopkins and several other prominent writers, such as Ida B. Wells (1862–1931), Fannie Barrier Williams (1855–1944), and Mary Church Terrell (1863–1954), we have an entire generation of African American women intellectuals who shared some educational and career possibilities.[4]

In all these writers there is a decidedly feminist tone, a firm conviction that the African American woman has a role to occupy in the fight against oppression and discrimination, that she has more than sufficient material to write about, and that, above all, over the course of history, she has commanded respect and admiration. Although race literature never meant women's literature with the added aspect of race, and although the differences between male and female writers of African American descent were never larger than the differences between writers of different racial origins, these African American women saw the values of race literature from a woman's point of view. Similar to most women's writing of that period, it had to fight the general neglect of the woman's voice.

In 1895 Victoria Earle Matthews spoke at the First Congress of Colored Women of the United States, in Boston, about "The Value of Race Literature," a text that McHenry calls "the manifesto of the black women's movement" (190). This important congress, organized by Boston's prominent Josephine St. Pierre Ruffin, might well have been the meeting point between Cooper and Matthews, both of whom gave speeches, and Hopkins, who was definitely part of the Boston intelligentsia at that time. The example of Matthews proves that Hopkins was influenced by her peers and that her project was typical rather than extraordinary. Matthews claims the need to write against prejudice and injustice. She proposes "the indubitable evidence of the need of thoughtful, well-defined and intelligently placed efforts on our part, to serve as counter-irritants against all such writing that shall stand, having as an aim the supplying of influential and accurate information, on all subjects

Portrait of
Mrs. Mary Church Terrell.
Source: Culp, *Twentieth
Century Negro Literature*,
172.

relating to the Negro and his environments, to inform the American mind at least, for literary purposes" (136).[5] She defines race literature as "the preserving of all the records of a Race, and thus cherishing the materials saving from destruction and obliteration what is good, helpful and stimulating" (144–45).

In her clear postulations for the content of race literature, Matthews might have influenced the literary undertakings of Hopkins directly. For her, writers must "win a place by the simplicity of the story, thrown into strong relief by the multiplicity of its dramatic situations; the spirit of romance, and even tragedy, shadowy and as yet ill-defined, but from which our race on this continent can never be dissociated" (131). At the same time, race literature must be critical as well: "Race Literature does not mean things uttered in praise, thoughtless praise of ourselves, wherein each goose thinks her gosling a swan" (144). In her opinion, true race literature is based on the educated, well-considered argument: "True culture in Race Literature will enable us to discriminate and not to write hasty thoughts and unjust and ungenerous criticism often of our superiors in knowledge and judgement"

(145). Adhering to the general principles of the African American and the white women's club movement, she sees woman playing an important part in this project: "When living up to her highest development, woman has done much to make lasting history, by her stimulating influence and there can be no greater responsibility than that, and this is the highest privilege granted to her by the Creator of the Universe" (146).

In its deepest sense, Hopkins and others considered race literature typically American. In her essay "One Phase of American Literature" in her collection *A Voice from the South*, Anna Julia Cooper claims that literature, in order to gain the "distinction of individuality" and an "appreciative hearing" (176), must contain something "characteristic and *sui generis*" (175). Cooper firmly believes that only by presenting themes that result from American realities can American literature become distinctive: "And 'twas not till the pen of our writers was dipped in the life blood of their own nation and pictured out its own peculiar heart throbs and agonies that the world cared to listen." Hopkins's undertaking in *Contending Forces* is definitely one example of a story "dipped in the life blood" of her nation. In that sense, one could say that Hopkins does what Cooper says writers should do. Cooper sees the African American as subject, inspiration, and distinguishing topic—or, as she phrases it, the "great *silent* factor" (178)—so long unacknowledged in mainstream American life and literature. She explains the success of Stowe's best-selling *Uncle Tom's Cabin* by its use of the material "indigenous to American soil and characteristic of the country" (181). No doubt, Hopkins saw as the one great subject of race literature the "thrilling incidents and escapes and sufferings of the fugitives, and the perils of their friends" (347), as she calls it in the "Charles Winter Wood" article that she published as J. Shirley Shadrach. The conclusion from both Cooper's article and Hopkins's ideas is that race literature must contain certain topics, foremost among them the history past and present of the African American, in order to be called race literature.

In addition to race literature being defined by the choice of subject and character, another argument puts it firmly into the context of Americanness. Victoria Matthews points out the basic problem of how to see and what to do with what is called "Race Literature" in contrast to American literature in general. The undeniable fact of the different treatment of the American Negro and former slave would lead to a literature that "will of necessity be different in all essential points of greatness, true heroism and real Christianity" from American literature (129). The "separate but equal" doctrine of the *Plessy v. Ferguson* decision of 1896 is foreshadowed here when

Matthews juxtaposes the Negro as the typical American yet a distinctive one: "We are the only people most distinctive from those who have civilized and governed this country, who have become typical Americans, and we rank next to the Indians in originality of soil, and yet remain a distinct people" (130). For her, literature is the vehicle for "the unnaturally suppressed inner lives which our people have been compelled to lead" (131). To this day, the arguments Matthews uses continue to engage generations of critics writing about African American or any other nonmainstream literature. How do we define the difference between white or mainstream American and African American literature? Is there any? How can any race/minority/group call itself more typical than the others?

In order to mark off the term *race literature*, Cooper as well as Matthews try to define it positively by pointing to writers whose portrayal of this subject does not correspond to it. The white author Cooper singles out for criticism is William Dean Howells, the eminent Boston scholar and writer, editor of the prestigious and influential *Atlantic Monthly*. Her verdict is severe. When Howells treats the Negro theme in his novel *An Imperative Duty* (1891), it is clear to Cooper that he "does not know what he is talking about" (201).[6] Cooper is especially appalled at Howells's racial generalizations that allow his "horrified young prig" (202), the heroine Rhoda Aldgate, to describe the people in the colored church, presumably of the best colored society, as possessing "the frog-like countenances and cat-fish mouths, the musky exhalations and the 'bress de Lawd, Honey,' of an uncultivated people" (202–3). Cooper writes indignantly that "it is an insult to humanity and a sin against God to publish any such sweeping generalizations of a race on such meager and superficial information" (203).

All their lifetimes, writers such as Cooper and Hopkins had to suffer under these "sweeping generalizations" of blacks as unchaste, primitive, and immoral.[7] Cooper bitterly remarks that it is the Anglo-Saxon himself who seems to be characterized by "such overweening confidence in his own power of induction that there is no equation which he would acknowledge to be indeterminate, however many unknown quantities it may possess" (203–4). She calls "this obtrusive and offensive vulgarity, this gratuitous sizing up of the Negro and conclusively writing down his equation" the most common and damaging factor in the relationship between the two races (203). Cooper is especially angry at Howells's treatment of the better stratum of black society and points out that there exists "a quiet, self-respecting, dignified class of easy life and manner . . . of cultivated tastes and habits" (207). Rhoda Aldgate in Howells's novel could have easily formed lasting friendships and found loving support if she had cared to look for it. Cooper was not alone in her criticism of Howells. It has been argued that Frances Harper intended her novel *Iola Leroy* as an indirect refutation of Howells.[8]

Cooper concedes that most blunders in Howells's novel result from unintentional ignorance and that even a great novelist such as Howells cannot yet "think himself imaginatively" into a colored person's place (209). Cooper's point is well taken and emphasizes her overall concern, one that is shared by such fellow writers as Hopkins, Matthews, and Mossell: the need for their own voice, an African American voice, to assert itself. At the same time, they point out the undercurrent of African American topics, characters, and plots that influence the writing of their white contemporaries but which usually go unrecognized in critical discourse.[9]

Both Cooper and Hopkins are motivated by a desire to apply certain moral standards to the topics and characters portrayed. Cooper, for example, vehemently opposes a poem by the white writer Maurice Thompson, "A Voodoo Prophecy," because it is too violent and vindictive toward white people. The African American as literary subject may not be portrayed as too vindictive nor as too conciliatory. Cooper laments the fact that "an authentic portrait, at once aesthetic and true to life, presenting the black man as a free American citizen, not the humble slave of *Uncle Tom's Cabin*—but the *man*, divinely struggling and aspiring yet tragically warped and distorted by the adverse winds of circumstance, has not yet been painted" (222–23). Much like Hopkins's effort to "raise the stigma of degradation" from her race (*Contending Forces* 13), this generation of writers does not see the solution to the race problem in war or riot but rather in a change of attitude of white people toward African Americans. By pointing out the inherent worth, the potential for heroism, and the noble characters of their black and mixed-race heroines and heroes, these writers sought to refute stereotypes and improve race conditions. The time to instigate rebellion, hatred, and blunt criticism had not yet come. It must be pointed out that Cooper's treatment of this poem might help explain why such writers and thinkers as Cooper and Hopkins did not survive as influential figures in the Harlem Renaissance. The content of a poem such as Maurice Thompson's, when it came from an African American writer, appealed very much to the more rebellious spirit of the later, younger generation of African American artists. Its rejection by writers like Cooper and Mossell adds to the prevalent, albeit often unjustified, reproach of accommodationism and a too conciliatory attitude of this earlier generation of intellectuals.

Much like Hopkins, Cooper, and Matthews, their contemporary Gertrude Bustill Mossell, writing under her husband's name as Mrs. N. F. Mossell, is convinced that the written word carries the record of their race and their history and that only literature in its various forms demonstrates the lessons of the past. In "A Sketch of Afro-American Literature," published in 1894 as part of *The World of the Afro-American Woman*, Mossell writes: "The intellectual history of a people or nation constitutes to a great degree the very heart of its life. To find this history, we search the fountain-head of its language, its customs, its religion, and its politics expressed by tongue or pen, its folklore and its songs" (48). She already claims "a literature of its own that must be studied by the future historian of the life of the American nation" (49–50). The term *literature*, here as in other instances, comprises the many various forms from folklore and songs to short story and drama.

From the beginning, African American women writers had to compete with the male writers of the race, who often found it easier to publish. The two writers who dominated the fiction of this period were Charles W. Chesnutt and Paul Laurence Dunbar, while an unjustly neglected writer was Sutton E. Griggs. In his overview of African American literature in his contribution to Donald Culp's *Twentieth Century Negro Literature: A Cyclopedia of Thought on the Vital Topics Relating to the American Negro* (1902), Professor George Marion McClellan, poet and journalist, gives an early example of the privileging of the African American male writer over his female contemporary. He singles out Dunbar and Chesnutt as the two great writers of the period. He is generally very enthusiastic about Dunbar and his dialect verse: "But for some pathos and to put the Negro forward at his best in his humorous and good natured characteristics the so-called dialect is the best vehicle, and in these lines, and these lines only, is Mr. Dunbar by far greater than all others" (280). In fiction he singles out Charles W. Chesnutt as the greatest writer of all, "the best delineator of Negro life and character, thought and feeling" (284).[10] If later readers hoped to find a reference to Hopkins in this article, they would be disappointed. McClellan obviously either did not know her or did not regard her as important enough to include her in his list of writers.

Race literature, to summarize, was defined by the choice of the African American as subject and by certain standards in the presentation of this topic, including high moral attitudes and an adherence to the general values of the American nation. It possessed a social function, and every writer had to be committed to it. It was an imaginative record of the past and a true record of the many facets of contemporary African American life. As Matthews puts

Portrait of Professor
G. M. McClellan.
Source: Culp, *Twentieth
Century Negro Literature*,
274.

it, able black women aimed at "shrinking at no lofty theme, shirking no serious duty, aiming at every possible excellence, and determined to do their part in the future uplifting of the race" (145).

All writers of Hopkins's generation had to face an audience divided along racial lines, with allegiances running the gamut from race solidarity to negrophobia. The problematic address to a double audience accompanied African American writers for many years. To Hopkins, writing fiction included treatment of gruesome subjects such as "lynching and concubinage" (*Contending Forces* 15), of which concubinage led to a mingling of the races. The ideal reader she must have had in mind was certainly interested in African American history in general and knowledgeable about contemporary racial problems in particular and shared her outrage at injustice and discrimination and her ingrained belief in the equality of races, the importance of the role of women, and a tolerance toward people of mixed origin. Her fiction set out to persuade the skeptical white reader that colored characters could possess impeccable manners and morals, social refinement, and sophisticated political thought. The ideal reader would recognize her irony and sarcasm when she spoke about social equality. He or she would also be familiar with world literature in general and understand allusions to famous masterworks and allusions to other works of African American literature.

Of course, not all readers met these criteria. Some of them were not at all captivated by the force of Hopkins's first novel, *Contending Forces*, and other fiction included in the *Colored American Magazine*. A letter from the white reader Cornelia Condict remonstrates with Hopkins about her writing of interracial love affairs: "Does that mean that your novelists can imagine no love beautiful and sublime within the range of the colored race, for each other?" ("Editorial," March 1903, 398). Condict's reason for opposing "tragic mixed loves" is that these stories "will not commend themselves to your white readers and will not elevate the colored readers" (399). Based on a concept of literature as social message, this letter may have been reprinted because of the typical complaint it expresses. Hopkins's answer must be taken as a response that focuses not only on her individual contribution to literature but as a comment on black writer–white reader interaction in general. Hopkins first of all attacks the white southern woman for trying to determine the choice of her subject matter: "My stories are definitely planned to show the obstacles persistently placed in our paths by a dominant race to subjugate us spiritually." Her defense of amalgamation as "designed by God for some wise purpose" sounds familiar to her readers and needs no further explanation.[11] Then Hopkins beats Condict on her own grounds when she refutes her argument that Charles Dickens would have written in defense of the neglected colored people of America: "If [Dickens] had been an American, and with his trenchant pen had exposed the abuses practiced by the Southern whites upon the blacks—had told the true story of how wealth, intelligence and femininity has stooped to choose for a partner in sin, the degraded (?) Negro whom they affect to despise, Dickens would have been advised to shut up or get out." Condict's criticism shows Hopkins that white people simply do not understand *"what pleases Negroes."* Hopkins, therefore, sees herself between the Scylla and Charybdis: "If you please the author of this letter and your white clientele, you will lose your Negro patronage. If you cater to the *demands* of the Negro trade, away goes Mrs. ——" (400).

An earlier announcement for *Contending Forces* predicted this kind of white criticism: "The book will certainly create a sensation among a certain class of 'whites' at the South, as well as awaken a general interest among our race" ("Editorial," Sept. 1900, 262). The differing reactions to the book are also apparent in the response from the black Chicago clubwoman Mrs. Albreta Moore, who writes: "It is all absorbing from the first page to the last.

The only disappointment to me was to read 'Finis.' In point of composition, plot and style of writing it cannot be excelled. This book should be classed as one of the standard works of the day" ("Announcements," Oct. 1901, 479). Hopkins had no easy task, it seems, to negotiate the various demands and restrictions upon her fiction. Later criticism of her by African American writers took as their starting point exactly the same accusation as Mrs. Condict. Her concentration on interracial love and her emphasis on genteel values would no longer be accepted. Significantly, however, the source of these attacks would change: now the offended party was the African American audience, whereas before it was the white reading audience. Here we find the same ambiguity that pervades her entire life: caught between accommodation and rebellion, between race pride and her belief in the American civilization as superior, between her sense of woman's mission and the overall male-dominated society, she sometimes strove to take a middle course and sometimes opted for rebellion, but she could not always negotiate such a course to the satisfaction of everybody.

In an essay published in 1928, James Weldon Johnson adequately captures the dilemma of Hopkins when he writes about the double audience of the African American writer. This writer must stick to the "conventions and limitations" of the white audience ("Dilemma" 250), while at the same time his themes have been appropriated by white writers (Johnson here refers to the stage in particular). The writer's relationship to his black audience is equally difficult: "He has no more absolute freedom to speak as he pleases addressing black America than he has in addressing white America. There are certain phases of life that he dare not touch, certain subjects that he dare not critically discuss, certain manners of treatment that he dare not use—except at the risk of rousing bitter resentment." He calls the taboos of black America as "real and binding as the conventions of white America" and argues that in "past years they have discouraged in Negro authors the production of everything but *nice* literature; they have operated to hold their work down to literature of the defensive, exculpatory sort. They have a restraining effect at the present time which Negro writers are compelled to reckon with." In essence, this is another version of the argument between Hopkins and Mrs. Condict in the *Colored American Magazine* of two decades earlier. Johnson seems to understand the black writer's quandary: "I judge there is not a single Negro writer who is not, at least secondarily, impelled by the desire to make his work have some effect on the white world for the good of his race" (251). Johnson (1871–1938), roughly twenty years younger than Hopkins, belonged to a slightly older generation in comparison to the "new" Negro generation of Langston Hughes, Claude McKay, Countee Cullen, and Walter White, who were all born in the last decade of the nineteenth century or in the early twentieth century. Yet he was one of the few writers who bridged these two generations and became an important figure in the Harlem Renaissance as literary critic, writer, and field secretary of the NAACP.[12]

Johnson's argument also occurs in W.E.B. Du Bois's influential essay "Criteria of Negro Art" (1926), in which, among other topics, he explores the dilemma of the double audience. He argues that "the white public today demands from its artists, literary and pictorial, racial pre-judgment which deliberately distorts Truth and Justice, as far as colored races are concerned, and it will pay for no other" (95). Like Hopkins and Johnson, he adequately recognizes the market situation of the black artist. But what he says about the black audience can be taken as an indirect criticism of the preceding generation: "On the other hand, the young and slowly growing black public still wants its prophets almost equally unfree. We are bound by all sorts of customs that have come down as second-hand soul clothes of white patrons. We are ashamed of sex and we lower our eyes when people will talk of it. Our religion holds us in superstition. Our worst side has been so shamelessly emphasized that we are denying we have or ever had a worst side. In all sorts of ways we are hemmed in and our new young artists have got to fight their way to freedom." The key terms in this paragraph—*unfree, bound, ashamed, superstition, denying, hemmed in*—all speak of a view of the past as limiting and limited as to freedom of artistic expression. It can be easily assumed that he regarded such a character as Sappho Clark in *Contending Forces* or Jewel in *Hagar's Daughter* or Reuel Briggs in *Of One Blood* as sexually inhibited, ashamed of their Negro descent, and generally hemmed in.

Hopkins's fate at the hands of critics and fellow writers did not alter significantly when a post–Harlem Renaissance generation began to write. A few examples show that a disregard for turn-of-the-century race literature was still grounded in the same perceptions. Although one cannot accuse, for example, Richard Wright for the neglect of a writer whom he probably did not even know, his statement in "Blueprint for Negro Writing" might stand as typical: "Generally speaking, Negro writing in the past has been confined to humble novels, poems, and plays, prim and decorous ambassadors who went a-begging to white America. They entered the Court of American Public Opinion dressed in the knee-pants of servility, curtsying to show that the Negro was not inferior, that he was human, and that he had a life comparable to that of other people. For the most part these artistic ambassadors were received as though they were French poodles who do clever tricks" (315). Wright probably alluded to such writers as Nella Larsen, Jessie Fauset, and perhaps Du Bois, but it can be assumed that he would have included Hopkins if he had known of her. Wright then writes about the importance of the Negro church and folklore, hardly a new aspect in African American literary criticism. The concept of the kind of race literature Matthews, Mossell, Cooper, and Hopkins propagated was obviously sadly out of fashion, resulting in a sense of rootlessness and isolation that later writers (like Alice Walker) lamented. For generations, possible role models were lost, left unread, and undervalued.

In "Everybody's Protest Novel" (1955), James Baldwin writes about Eliza and George Harris of Harriet Beecher Stowe's *Uncle Tom's Cabin*, among others, dismissing them because "we have only the author's word that they are Negro and they are, in all other respects, as white as she can make them" (16). He characterizes Eliza as "the beautiful, pious hybrid, light enough to pass . . . differing from the genteel mistress who has overseered her education only in the respect that she is a servant." The "badly written and wildly improbable" earlier American protest novels were "a mirror of our confusion, dishonesty, panic, trapped and immobilized in the sunlit prison of the American dream. They are fantasies, connecting nowhere with reality, sentimental" (18, 19).

In his *Negro Voices in American Fiction* (1948), Hugh Gloster includes a short discussion of Hopkins's *Contending Forces* in his chapter "Negro Fiction to World War I." It is not altogether unsympathetic, but it contains an evaluation of her effort as "unsuccessful": "Perhaps the best comment that may be made about the book is that it provides interesting sidelights on the struggles of a middle-class Negro family for education, employment, and social adjustment in post-bellum Boston" (34). Yet when he opens the next part of this chapter, on Charles Chesnutt, he writes: "To move from Mrs. Harper, J. McHenry Jones, and Mrs. Hopkins to Charles W. Chesnutt is to proceed from untalented narrators to a gifted novelist, for Chesnutt is one of the significant figures in American Negro literature." This statement shows not only the continuing prominence of Chesnutt, who was one of the few writers of this period who enjoyed repute without much interruption, but also shows that earlier fiction was lumped together as lacking artistic excellence and interesting subject matter. Even as late as 1991, male critics occasionally professed a similar kind of disdain for the generation of Hopkins. Houston A. Baker, for example, in *Workings of the Spirit*, still argues that the authors of this period "were unable to produce more than a preacherly shadow text of the nadir." The reason for this is the absence of a "black women's vernacular southern culture" (30), which produces a "kind of detached wonder" in, for example, Harper's *Iola Leroy*, with its "endless pages of exposition and lofty sentiment—its creakingly mechanical and entirely predictable plot" (31). After a critical reading of Addison Gayle's similarly caustic critique of William Wells Brown's *Clotel*, Ann DuCille calls this attitude the "bogeyman that haunts not only *Clotel* but a great deal of nineteenth-century African-American literature" ("Where in the World" 453). It is "a prescriptive sense of 'the right direction,' a tendency on the part of contemporary critics to privilege a particular notion of black identity and 'the black experience' and to fault early writers for, in essence, not being 100 years ahead of their time."

The situation remained basically the same through the more radical period before and after World War II, during the Black Aesthetic movement, and into the 1970s. With an increasing emphasis on protest literature based on the black vernacular and a politics directed toward the urban black working class, writing that evolved out of a black middle class, like Hopkins's, became associated, as William J. Harris puts it, "with false values, the desire to be white and therefore inauthentic" ("Black Aesthetic" 68). Hopkins's works were out of print. There was no possible contemporary of hers anymore who had known her. There was hardly any writer, professor, or literary critic who knew her work or cared enough about her to include it in an anthology.[13]

This short discussion of the intended audience of race literature and its critics naturally leads to the aesthetic criteria contingent upon questions of genre. In her *Reading for Realism*, Nancy Glazener speaks of a romantic revival of the 1890s that combines the dominant realistic mode with romantic content. She reads Hopkins's preface to *Contending Forces* against the background of the realism propagated by the *Atlantic Monthly* and related magazines. Glazener argues that her " 'daring venture' creates a connection between her work and the adventure fiction privileged by the late nineteenth-century romantic revival" and that Hopkins's "simple, homely tale, unassumingly told" echoes "the rhetoric used in the *Atlantic* group to praise realism's stylistic spareness and democratic social mission, except for the reference to 'complexions' " (10). Romance, Glazener points out, was the name of the genre Hopkins had to use because "her narrative dealt with whipping, rape, and lynching—events relatively typical within the history of any family descended from slaves, but events that challenged the aesthetic and emotional muting required by high realist connoisseurship" (119). She puts Hopkins's undertaking on a more general level and thereby questions the fundamental assumption of realism as an objective term:

> The density of Hopkins's generic markers attest to how thoroughly a network of generic possibilities filtered authors' public presentations of their own work, and probably their private understandings of it as well, but the oscillation that Hopkins makes between late-century versions of realism and romance is more revealing yet. Events such as the whippings, public rapes, and lynchings that occur in *Contending Forces* were distinctly at odds with the construction of "simple, homely" realism by the *Atlantic* group and may have demanded, in her estimation, a shift into romance, even though their real place in the experience and history of many black families aligned such events with realism. (10–11)

The tricky question here is the combination of genres: the adventure tale, the detective story, the realistic story, the historical novel, and the romance. Elements of the romantic and sentimental and melodramatic plot were needed to present the grim historical past and portray the present. The chapter about Hagar's beautiful daughters will prove this point more fully. Elements of the adventure and detective stories were needed to make the tale palatable to the reading public. As Giulia Fabi argues in *Passing*, elements of the utopian novel validated the various moves between fictitious plot and a dystopian reality.

In her preface, Hopkins stresses the fact that the "incidents portrayed in the early chapters of the book actually occurred" (14). In the second part of the book, she quotes from a southern newspaper to establish the background of the lynching incident. In this, as Jerry H. Bryant argues, Hopkins joins the claim to verisimilitude that he finds in nearly all the African American novels of racial violence of the period between 1892 and 1922 that he discusses. Whereas before Hopkins's time the authors and publishers of slave narratives strove to establish the authenticity of their tales, these writers claim verisimilitude to "emphasize that the atrocities they describe are not inventions sensationalized for commercial appeal" (Bryant 98).[14] The fire and romance that so appealed to her readers were taken from actual occurrences. And still, although Hopkins emphasizes that her fiction is based on facts, she cannot be put simply in the realist school of writing, when we apply Joseph McElrath's argument about Chesnutt to Hopkins. McElrath says that Chesnutt was a "remarkable romancer, insightful 'moral realist,' and . . . historically significant social critic" (92). The textual evidence he cites of Chesnutt's deviance from the tradition of realistic concerns is his use of the intrusive narrator and of plot constructions that include coincidences. Both of these apply to Hopkins as well. McElrath further cites Chesnutt's letters to Howells, George Washington Cable, and Albion Tourgée, which show his discounting of the worth of the realist approach. In a letter to Tourgée in 1889 and in his "The Negro in Art" of 1926, Chesnutt is revealed as a writer who "could not resist the lure of the Romantic" (99), as McElrath puts it, and as a writer who thinks that "it is the highest privilege of art to depict the ideal" (qtd. on 105).

While many critics up to the present moment see in this combination of genres, for example, "an uncertainty of form" that ultimately leads to the artistic failure of these works in which "the novel, the romantic melodrama, and the tract compete for dominance" (Bryant 100), other perspectives see in Hopkins "a radical experimenter whose work will be read in the next century as a model of early modernist innovation and revolution in the United States" (Ammons, "Afterword" 211). Hopkins's experimentation with form, content, and political message contains the argument that implicitly runs through most of the writing of this turn-of-the-century generation. Literature is propaganda, and racial questions are included in writing for the sake of race and not only for the sake of art.[15]

Elizabeth Ammons and Claudia Tate are among a group of recent critics who see the uncertainty of form as significant and not as an accidental result of bad craftsmanship. For Tate, the multiple generic markers reflect the contradictions of Hopkins's time. She points out that in *Winona*, Hopkins "relied on the popularity of the formula novels to entertain her readers with adventure and intrigue, while she manipulated the plot to incite the reader's sympathy for the virtuous mulatta heroine and scorn for those harboring racist viewpoints who threaten the heroine's happiness" (*Domestic* 200). The "simple, homely tale, unassumingly told, which cements the bond of brotherhood among all classes and all complexions" is used once more as a reminder to white America that heroism is not restricted to Anglo-Saxons and that injustice must be avenged no matter the guise under which it appears (*Contending Forces* 13). Ammons treats the many ambivalences in the text that a reader must contend with and that result mainly from the fusion of genres: "The multivocality of the text is immediately obvious—and by no means totally under control. Generically the novel combines the western, fugitive slave narrative, romance, potboiler/soap opera, political novel, and traditional allegory to tell the story of the paradisiacal possibility but real life destruction of a truly mixed-race North American family" ("Afterword"

214). Ammons calls upon the polyvocality of the novel as analyzed by Bakhtin in order to write about the contradictoriness inherent in much of Hopkins's writing and her life (217).

All this theoretical debate is part of the general background to Hopkins's fiction. *Contending Forces: A Romance Illustrative of Negro Life North and South* was first registered in 1899 and published in 1900. What she intended as a "humble tribute written by one of a proscribed race" (*Contending Forces*, title page) has turned out to be a fascinating account of a writer's imagination. It is her most topical novel, a document of the black woman's club movement. Negotiating between private and public spaces, it steers an uneven course between protest and a positive view of the future. Hazel V. Carby argues that Hopkins wrote an "alternative fictional history of close blood ties through miscegenation" (*Reconstructing* 128). Susan Gillman treats her novels as "race melodramas" ("The Mulatto"). Lois Brown calls *Contending Forces* a "racialized sentimental narrative" ("To Allow No Tragic End" 69). And many other critics and readers have read their own concerns into the novels and the short stories and thus prove that even if the creative writing of Pauline Hopkins was nearly lost in the annals of history, its resurrection has led to an appreciation of her efforts and to a reappraisal of the literature of her time.[16]

Hagar's Daughter: A Story of Southern Caste Prejudice is the first of the three serial novels that Pauline Hopkins published in the *Colored American Magazine*. Between March 1901 and March 1902 the story appeared in twelve installments under her pen name Sarah A. Allen. By setting the novel in decidedly white surroundings, and by introducing all three of her heroines as white women before it is found out that they possess some black blood, Hopkins contrives to "write a 'black' story that unravels in the heart of elite Washington society" (Carby, "Introduction" xxxviii).[17]

Winona: A Tale of Negro Life in the South and Southwest was published in six installments from May until October 1902. In contrast to the preceding serial novel, Hopkins published it under her own name. It was advertised, in March 1902, in the same column that identified Sarah A. Allen as Pauline Elizabeth Hopkins, as "a dramatic tale" ("Editorial," March 1902, 335). The first installment gives 1891 as the copyright year, which might be proof that Hopkins wrote this part earlier but could not publish it. The Hopkins Papers at Fisk contain some scenes from an early drama that was registered as "Winona" in 1878 (see L. Brown, "Essential Histories" 31). The second installment cites the year 1901 as the copyright year. This means that there either was an earlier version of part of the novel or that she began to write it earlier and then changed her plan and added other material. The short advertisement says that Winona, "a free child of mixed blood," became a slave and was rescued heroically: "Her rescue and restoration to her rightful home and fortune by a brave young Negro gives a thrilling story, filled with incidents of heroism for which many Negroes have been noted in our past history" (335). Interestingly, this advertisement identifies Judah as the hero and does not mention the English aristocrat Warren Maxwell or the setting and background of John Brown's Kansas mission. Hopkins must have changed her intent when she resumed her writing of the story for publication in the *Colored American Magazine*. She must have decided to question the heroism of Judah and emphasize the central role of Warren Maxwell.

Of all the serial novels, *Of One Blood; or, The Hidden Self* is the most forceful and has captured especially the interest of the contemporary reader.[18] Its intricately woven plot that combines American scenery with contemporary and ancient Africa in the form of a tangled family story is invested with elements of spiritualism and mesmerism as well as the well-known story of miscegenation resulting from slavery. It was published between November 1902 and November 1903 in eleven installments.

The following discussion will concentrate on moments of transition. In *Contending Forces*, it will be the transition from the slave past to contemporary Boston, which entails a treatment of the legacy of the past that can be exemplified in the life story of Sappho Clark. This novel also demonstrates that the domestic space, the home, is closely interrelated with national and international spaces. In *Hagar's Daughter*, it is the transition in various forms between the identities of the protagonists, a transition between races and even between genders. The emphasis will be on the fate of the beautiful woman who stands between the races and on questions of genre. In *Winona*, the transition takes place at an earlier time and treats the close interaction between England, the United States, and Canada. It also concerns the changing forms of manhood between the dark-colored African American Judah and the white Englishman Warren Maxwell. In *Of One Blood*, the predominant transition is the one between America and Africa in terms of history, values, family connections, male and female roles, and between a glorification of ancient Africa and the exceptional quality of the African American man.

The courtroom scene from *Hagar's Daughter*, with the triumphant performance of old Aunt Henny, a former slave and later cleaning woman, leads to another chapter that concentrates on the subplots that introduce folk characters, former slaves, servants, or the common people. Most often family stories are resolved through their help, and in general they play important roles and are lovingly drawn. Their stories speak of class differences between various groups of African Americans. Their strategies for survival in Hopkins's Boston or the Washington of 1882 allow the author to extend the romantic content of the novels into a discussion of a less exclusive part of society and negotiate the transition from the past into the present of her time. Hopkins's careful balance between the uses of black dialect and standard English shows her concern that the portrayal of the African American experience not be restricted to one part of society only. It also shows that the tradition of dialect writing and the slave narrative could be easily transported into the Boston of the beginning of the twentieth century.

Originally, only *Contending Forces* survived the test of literary history and market demands, with occasional references to it in histories of literature and a reprint in 1978. But the continuing interest in Hopkins today is based on all four novels and the short stories. Seven stories were published in the *Colored American Magazine* from 1900 to 1903, and one later story appeared in the *New Era Magazine* in 1916. During the time of the magazine's existence, some fifty short stories were published altogether, enough to warrant the claim that there was a kind of *Colored American Magazine* school of short-story writing, which was decidedly influenced by Hopkins. Christmas stories, stories about spiritual phenomena, dialect stories, and stories about passing constitute an organic whole. Hopkins contributed to all these topics and most probably initiated or encouraged the publication of many of the other stories. An evaluation of her short fiction in the context of the general *Colored American Magazine* canon is long overdue.

The republication of the three serial novels opened the eyes of many critics to the potential in Pauline Hopkins. The thrilling romance plots, sensational details, occasional veiled references to famous men and women of her time, and the very astute analysis of the political situation prompted the interest of her contemporary readership. A good hundred years later, Hopkins's fiction can be placed into a larger cultural context, and her innovative spirit, her deviation from tradition, and her place in this tradition can be adequately evaluated.

Contending Forces of the Slave Past

he engraving of the whipping scene at the beginning of *Contending Forces* (1900) offers an excellent opening for a discussion of Pauline Hopkins's fiction. In addition to the contrast between the female victim and the two male torturers, there is a subtle play of colors in this black-and-white engraving. The whiteness of the woman on the floor stands out in contrast to the dark attire of the man looking down upon her, while the white shirt and trousers of the man occupied with the whip are repeated by the white color of the whipping post and the trunks of the trees in the background. The only horizontal figure in the picture is that of the woman, and this horizontal line is also reflected in the snakelike curling of the whip. The scene reveals, literally in black and white, Hopkins's concern with the contending forces—political and social—of the slave past.

The whipping of Grace Montfort—and her powerlessness as a victim— must be seen as representing slavery in all its cruelty, and it forcefully refutes any historiography of the plantation past as an idyll of benevolent master and contented slave. According to Richard Brodhead's study of corporal punishment in antebellum America, whipping is *the* central image of slavery. Brodhead points out the "embodiedness of whipping" and "the perfect asymmetry of power expressed in the whipping scenario" (14). Depictions of scenes of lynching take up the role of whipping in the period after the Civil War. Jerry Bryant calls lynching the "synecdochal image of the post-Reconstruction condition of the freedperson" (76). Hopkins was clearly aware of the power such images had in the popular mind. In her preface to *Contending Forces*, she contends: "The atrocity of the acts committed one hundred years ago are duplicated today, when slavery is supposed no longer to exist" (15).

More than any of the other novels, *Contending Forces* shows the continuing concern with the past in a respectable middle-class African American family representative of Hopkins's Boston. The choice of character, setting, and political content reflects the author's deeply felt need to explain the present, especially the terror of mob violence, as a product of the past. The decidedly middle-class home, the role of women combining homemaking with race work, and the emphasis on the political speeches of the main male characters reflect Hopkins's general passion for negotiations in gender, race, and class that is also evident in her journalism.

The novel's opening in 1790 on the island of Bermuda illuminates the international dimension of slavery. The well-meaning but naïve slaveholder Charles Montfort decides to transfer his entire estate with family and slaves to the United States to escape the imminent abolition of slavery on the island. Although the narrative voice does not condone slavery in the West Indies, it puts it into perspective by comparing it to the exceptionally cruel and harsh form of slavery in America. On the day that Charles Montfort lands on Pamlico Sound near Newbern, North Carolina, this side of slavery is personified in the novel's archvillain, Anson Pollock, and the two scoundrels, the burly Bill Sampson and the cruel Hank Davis. They are jealous of the wealth of the family and spread the rumor that Grace Montfort, Charles's beautiful wife, possesses black blood. Throughout the novel, however, the real racial background of Grace and Charles is never revealed. It is the rumor that matters, not the real drop of black blood. Both Bill and Hank are poor whites working as overseers and slave traders. They are uneducated and possess no ameliorating character traits. Yet the system of slavery gives them the power to satisfy their vile intentions, while all the refinement and gentle instincts of the Montfort family do not save them from their tragic end. Anson Pollock, who has sold his land to Montfort, is suave, educated, and handsome but thoroughly evil. Being the widower of a wife who died under mysterious circumstances, he develops an "unlawful love" for the beautiful Grace (45). He masterminds the burning down of the Montfort house and the killing of Charles Montfort and enslaves their young sons, Charles and Jesse.

When the tragic events take their inevitable course, we see that the system of slavery has engendered corruption, greed, unlawful passion, cruelty, and inhumanity. The "Committee," a Ku Klux Klan–like association, is presented as the cruel result of an immoral environment. The chapter entitled "The Tragedy" denounces a commercial system that disregards the values of humanity: "Nature avenges herself upon us for every law violated in the mad rush for wealth or position or personal comfort where the rights of others of the human family are not respected" (65).

The most heartrending scene is the treatment of the refined and beautiful Grace, the southern plantation mistress who is accused of having some black blood. Bill Sampson and Hank Davis get hold of her and tie her to the whipping post. The ensuing scene is described in full detail, with wild cries, shrieks, the flowing of blood, the consciousness of torture, and the contentment of the two men who inflict the pain. The picture at the opening of the book is now explained. The two men are identified as Bill and Hank, the woman lying in her blood is Grace Montfort. "When Hank Davis had satiated his vengeful thirst he cut the ropes which bound her, and she sank upon the ground again—unconscious, bleeding, friendless, alone" (69–70). When Hazel Carby reads this scene as a metaphorical rape, she may be right. The utter degradation of a woman and her helplessness in the face of brute manhood imply violence analogous to rape, even if it is not mentioned explicitly here.

Grace's doom is lived out by Lucy, her beautiful and light-colored slave foster sister. After Grace's suicide by drowning soon after the whipping, Lucy is taken as mistress by Anson Pollock. Her lack of choice at his hands is not narrated in detail, but it does not take much imagination to presume that she did not have an easy life.[1] The fates of both white and black women are intricately interwoven. It is one of the main messages of this first part of the novel: wrongs committed against one member of the human family are crimes committed against all.

The sensational details and thrilling incidents put the novel into the genre of sentimental fiction. Hopkins's African American readers, however, certainly recognized the bitter historical reality behind the story that was set in the recent past. When the connection of the past with the present is worked out in later chapters, history becomes the experienced family past and helps explain the present state of affairs. *Contending Forces* is thus part of the historical project that Hopkins also carries out in her biographical sketches and *A Primer of Facts*. Fictionalizing the past allows her the passionate commitment that she, herself one of the "proscribed race," deems necessary to condemn past wrongs.

Around the year 1900 and three generations later, the outdoor paradise of Bermuda is replaced by an indoor shelter in Boston. The scene is as idyllic as the earlier island scene, but the time and circumstances are radically different. The boarding house at 500 D Street, a respectable part of the South End of Boston, is the home of the Smith family. The mother, called "Ma" Smith by all her friends and boarders, is the widow of Henry Smith, a freeborn Negro from Virginia who had been a seaman until he settled in Boston, saved enough money to make the first payment on a house, and continued to struggle and work hard to meet the payments. He married the "Mulattress from New Hampshire" and they had two children, William Jesse Montfort and Dora Grace Montfort (83). The reader will immediately recognize the connections with the story that precedes the main part of the novel and identify Ma Smith as Jesse Montfort's and Elizabeth Whitfield's daughter and William and Dora as their grandchildren.

"The simple, homely tale" the author promises the reader in the preface describes the family on a cold winter evening, after a day of cleaning in preparation for Sappho Clark, their expected lodger, when Dora joins her mother in the "cosy kitchen" (80). The atmosphere of latent violence that dominated the earlier part of the novel is replaced by one of harmony. Dora's "graceful figure," her dark-brown hair, and her "delicate brown face" set the tone for this loving and happy northern home. More than once the house is called a "nest" (88), a description that agrees with the atmosphere of coziness, loving care, and sheltering surroundings. Today some readers will value this part of the book for its sociological information about this time; at Hopkins's time it served as proof of respectability, achievement, and progress, all of which are virtues that needed to be defined and defended rather than taken for granted.

The Smith home is decidedly middle class: "The table was carefully spread with a nicely ironed cloth of spotless white, red-bordered napkins lay at each plate, a good quality of plated silverware mingled with the plain, inexpensive white ware in which the meal was to be served" (88). For a later evening reception, Dora and Ma Smith provide "plenty of good home-made cake, sandwiches, hot chocolate, and . . . ice cream or sherbet" (103). The parlor has a piano in the corner, obviously a symbol of an educated household at that time, and the handsome piano lamp throws "a soft, warm glow over the neat woolen carpet, the modest furniture and few ornaments."

The narrator, who intrudes on the narrative from time to time with comments and background information, emphasizes the importance of this middle-class standard. The narrator refers to the surprise of white people that so many colored families manage to live so well when nearly "every avenue for business" is closed to them (86), and that these families manage to educate their children and give them a refinement that equals that of white children. They are described as ambitious, intelligent, open-minded, and cultivated. As the narrator says, "With this people it is a common occurrence to find a genius in a profession, trade, or invention, evolved from the rude nurturing received at the hands of a poor father and mother engaged in the lowliest of service, who see not the nobility of their sacrifices in the delight afforded them in watching the unfolding of the bud of promise in their offspring." A poor and humble beginning, it is implied by the intrusive narrative voice, serves as the ideal ground for nurturing genius, and this truth applies to the colored race "when we see the steady advance of a race overriding the barriers set by prejudice and injustice" (87). In this long and descriptive chapter, Hopkins wants to counter the common prejudice against the poverty, lack of education, dirt, ignorance, and bad character of the stereotypical Negro of her time.

The room in the boardinghouse that is described in great detail is Sappho Clark's. "The iron bedstead and the washing utensils were completely hidden by drapery curtains of dark-blue denim, beautifully embroidered in white floss; a cover of the same material was thrown over the small table between the windows; plain white muslin draperies hid the unsightly but serviceable yellow shades at the windows; her desk and typewriter occupied the center of the room, and a couch had been improvised from two packing-cases and a spring, covered with denim and piled high with cushions; two good steel engravings completed a very inviting interior" (98). Sometime later, this beautiful, artistic setting provides the right kind of atmosphere for Dora and Sappho to spend a stormy, cold afternoon. The room has a good stove, a rocking chair, a small round table. Sappho serves lunch in dainty china dishes, and Dora is made comfortable with cushions, a hassock, and a scarlet afghan over her knees. There is even a refrigerator, a "box ingeniously nailed to the window seat outside, and filled with shelves" (119).

This description is evidence of the fact that "decorating tables and hanging draperies becomes an expression of freedom" (1), as Amy Wolf states in an article that interprets the control over the domestic sphere as a necessary step in the advancement of the African American woman after slavery. Dora and Sappho's "shared pleasure in the domestic" highlights their "shared virtue" (Wolf 4). When this space is invaded, usually violently, virtue is endangered. Grace Montfort is brutally removed from her home and whipped; Sappho is threatened later by the unwelcome entry of John Langley into her room. Debra Bernardi argues that the invasion of the private usually speaks of a more public agenda, a conflict between "public and private, personal and political, national and international, and male and female spheres of concern" (203). Even a less aggressive "invasion of influence" (211)—attempts at changing white American attitudes and improving African American lives—shows a power play that has its roots in violent invasions on both the domestic and national levels.

Much attention is given to the details of furniture and decoration that speak of an eye and mind oriented toward the sense of comfort of women at that time. Will's room, by contrast, is not described in detail; it is only said that he needs a certain untidiness to feel comfortable. Significant conversations and meaningful encounters take place in the kitchen, parlor, and Sappho's room. This sort of local color that is part of Hopkins's undertaking must have appealed greatly to her audience. It served as a reminder to her white readers that African Americans could live in as much comfort as white people and that young women like Dora and Sappho enjoyed and deserved these comforts as much as their white counterparts. The "comparative barrenness" that the narrator had foreseen for Charles Montfort when he decided to move to the United States has given way to cultured refinement (30).

The "respectable" part of colored society that the Smith family belongs to sees it as their duty to "uplift the race" by contributing to the education of the disadvantaged and setting a good example. When Ma Smith finds out that most of her lodgers are "respectable though unlettered people" with "kindly hearts and honesty of purpose" (102), she decides to offer occasional musical evenings or reception nights so that they may get acquainted with each other, have the opportunity to discuss topics of interest, and learn by example: "She argued, logically enough, that those who were inclined to stray from right paths would be influenced either in favor of upright conduct or else shamed into an acceptance of the right" (102). This reflects a general desire in the better-educated and relatively wealthy part of colored society to impose their regulations of good behavior and proper conduct on as many of their fellow African Americans as possible so that they might do credit to them and not shame them in public. In this sense, *Contending Forces* is a document of the women's club movement, presenting exemplary characters and settings that show off the achievements of a generation whose parents and grandparents were still born in times of slavery.

The Smith family is descended from the white Jesse Montfort and, therefore, is a family of mixed racial origin. Dora is described as "brown," and Will is "tall and finely formed, with features almost perfectly chiseled, and a complexion the color of an almond shell" (90). Sappho Clark, the story's heroine, is tall and "fair, with hair of a golden cast, aquiline nose, rosebud mouth, soft brown eyes veiled by long, dark lashes" (107). It is no surprise then that, much like other notable colored families, the Smiths take pride in their "significant family history," as Gatewood calls it (9), and their relatively light skin color. The first part of the boardinghouse chapters has Ma Smith tell stories about her father, who was practically white because the black blood of his parents was never an established fact.

The social set of the Smith family and their friends demonstrates a class consciousness as much as a race consciousness. Questions of family background, living conditions, and morals and manners are as important as in any other society. Skin color must be added as a further distinguishing marker between the so-called upper four hundred and other African Americans employed in less respectable professions. Once the narrator even drops remarks about the "highly cultured Caucasian" and "the inferior black race" and remarks about the best white blood flowing in the veins of many African Americans (87). Prospective boarders, for example, are told they must be "pretty nice" or, "You've got to be high-toned to get in there" (103). This color consciousness, an unwitting acceptance of white standards of beauty and deportment, is all-pervasive at Hopkins's time and does not contradict a basic sense of race consciousness and race pride.[2] Similar to what she writes in her essays, this shows Hopkins's transcendence of racial stereotypes but not their complete abandonment.

Much care is taken to set the tone, describe the setting, and establish an atmosphere of culture, general good intentions, hard work, and delightful enjoyments for Boston's African American population. The overall realistic setting in this section of the narrative is deliberately nonsensationalizing. African American middle-class life revolves around family, work, and the church in the same way that mainstream American middle-class life does. Sensational details are brought in after it has been established that this part of society has as much a right to their lifestyle as any other part. Lynching, discrimination, and injustice, which are the essential elements of the plot, serve the purpose of pointing out a deeply ingrained system of race prejudice that threatens to undermine the welfare of the entire nation.

To propel the action forward, therefore, the central conflict, the unraveling of Sappho's tragic past, must take center stage. At the age of fourteen, Mabelle Beaubean, as the beautiful daughter of a colored planter in New Orleans was called then, was abducted and raped by her father's white half-brother, a state senator and very wealthy man, and was rescued from a brothel a few weeks later. After her father had been killed by a mob and his house set on fire, the family's faithful servant, Luke Sawyer, took her to a convent. In this convent she gave birth to a son and then disappeared from public and was deemed dead by her friends. Luke Sawyer, himself a victim of earlier violence when his own family was killed by a white mob because of his father's success in business, remained the only witness of the cruelty. Grace Montfort's earlier fate is lived out by Mabelle Beaubean and threatens to destroy the future happiness of Sappho Clark. The whipping has become rape. In essence, both Sappho's and Luke's fates repeat tragic occurrences from the time of slavery, although they occur years later. There is definitely no improvement over slavery, a fact that is reinforced by the references to mob violence and economic injustice. Sappho must change her name and her identity, disown her son, and is made to bear the fear of detection of her past. Apart from the personal trauma she suffered at the hands of her relative and despite a tragedy she could neither foresee nor avoid, she must live with the consequences: she bears the stigma of the fallen woman, the woman who has borne a child out of wedlock and so has little hope of finding a husband who would ignore this shame.

Her past becomes the measuring rod for a test of character. Dora Smith, the typical Yankee girl, for example, is characterized by her goodwill and gaiety, her thrift, her pragmatic frame of mind, and her capacity for Christian charity, loyalty, and loving care. Her mother sees in her a "happy, healthy, active girl, with a kindly disposition" (179). From the very beginning, the conversation between Dora and Sappho in Sappho's room touches upon the most important topic of the novel, which is Sappho's fall, although the subject is not mentioned directly. Dora's creed is simple: "My religion is short, and to the point—feed the starving thief and make him an honest man; cover your friend's faults with the mantle of charity and keep her in the path of virtue" (100). Dora does not condemn the male thief or female sinner if the circumstances justify the deeds. She addresses Sappho's problem directly, and, without knowing it herself, she sounds reassuring: "I believe that we would hang our heads in shame at having the temerity to judge a fallen sister, could we but know the circumstances attending many such cases" (101). Yet Sappho is not ready to accept the offer and rid herself once and forever of the burdens of the past.

In all four novels, the fate of the mulatta woman, her beauty, and her potential for tragedy take up much space. In *Contending Forces*, the discussion of the mulatta and her role in contemporary society is instigated mainly by Mrs. Willis, the clubwoman and organizer invited to direct the educational part of the meeting of the sewing circle, a typical Saturday afternoon entertainment to prepare for the annual fair of their church. While the girls are sewing, they are getting an educational lecture by Mrs. Willis. Hers is a moral, judicious voice preaching the message of self-confidence, moral virtue, and character-building. Her talk of the day is "The place which the virtuous woman occupies in upbuilding a race" (148). She addresses the issue of the black woman's putative immorality and lack of virtue, one of the most pressing topics of the day. With many of the women present being of mixed-race origin, Mrs. Willis needs to negotiate her terrain by steering the middle course between condemning interracial unions and blaming the daughters of these unions for their origins. One young woman raises the issue of mixed blood and the common accusation of many white people that the mulatto race is "a mongrel mixture" combining "the worst elements of two races" (150). Mrs. Willis adds a remark about "the burden which is popularly supposed to rest upon the unhappy mulattoes of a despised race" (152). Dora now vehemently denies being unhappy because she is a mulatta. Her common sense and pragmatism have helped her come to terms with her position in society as a mixed-race woman.

Sappho is drawn to Mrs. Willis as a woman of authority and public standing. She dares open the same issue that she talked about with Dora earlier in the privacy of her room. Sappho asks her about the problem of illegitimacy in black society, and Mrs. Willis gives a very pragmatic and commonsense answer, one that does not differ in substance from Dora's: "I believe that we shall not be held responsible for wrongs which we have *unconsciously* committed, or which we have committed under *compulsion*. We are virtuous or non-virtuous only when we have a *choice* under temptation" (149). She opts for a clear break with the past in favor of working for the future: "Let us cultivate, while we go about our daily tasks, no matter how inferior they may seem to us, beauty of the soul and mind, which being transmitted to our children by the law of heredity, shall improve the race by eliminating *immorality* from our midst and raising *morality* and virtue to their true place" (153).

What Mrs. Willis argues for in her conversation with Dora is that past history should not totally influence the present and that a new beginning should be granted to all those who suffered some wrong against their wills. In its fundamentally practical consideration, her attitude is pragmatic and very justifiable and is certainly the path many African American women took who left their past, usually in the South, and started a new life in the North. In essence it repeats Booker T. Washington's view of the past as a preparation for present progress, not as a wrong that needs to be righted. What Mrs. Willis (and Booker T. Washington) cannot take into consideration is that the past was still not far enough removed to be entirely forgotten in this first generation after slavery, in this time when lynching and other forms of violence perpetuated discrimination and violated the rights of so many African Americans. She also does not understand the inner drive in a woman such as Sappho to come to terms with what happened to her, her feeling of shame and even sin for which she wants to atone. It is interesting to notice that Will Smith later repeats this same sentiment when Sappho wants to confess to him and he cries out: "I do not care for the past" (312). Both Mrs. Willis and Will miss the central point in their Yankee pragmatism: history will repeat itself, and only a full acceptance of this history will form Sappho into a woman capable of great love.

For a long time in the narrative, it seems that Sappho is destined to end
tragically like so many heroines of mixed race before her. In the end, she is
rescued through the love and manly conduct of Will Smith, who discovers her
whereabouts and reunites with her. This movement of the plot is made during
a visit to New Orleans, where Dora lives with her family. Although most of
the novel's setting is the North, the South is the site of the decisive reunion
of Will and Sappho. Significantly, the southern environment contributes to
the resolution of all narrative loose ends. The site where Sappho was raped
and disinherited becomes the beginning of a new generation. Dora and Dr.
Lewis and her family decide to build their future there in working for the
race. The subtle message is that pragmatic young northern women like Dora
should go south in order to help "uplift the race" and promulgate race work.
However, intellectuals like Will and Sappho are envisioned as moving to
Europe as a utopian, race-free place. Following the argument of Giulia Fabi
about Harper's *Iola Leroy* (1892), the ending must be seen as self-consciously
utopian when it "open[s] a space beyond contemporary social realities" in
opposition to the "dystopian post-Reconstruction reality of segregation and
violence" (*Passing* 59, 63). Will Smith wants to found a school "which should
embrace every known department of science, where the Negro youth of
ability and genius could enter without money and without price" (386). He
envisions this school as being situated abroad, where equality is possible.

Throughout the novel, it is obvious that Hopkins applies the ideals of race
literature to her own fiction. *Contending Forces* is deeply committed to presenting a record of the past and correcting injustice and discrimination in
contemporary America. Whereas many chapters move forward through the
mere force of the tale, other chapters take more time in establishing the
political and social climate of the time.

Parallel to the chapters concentrating on the sewing circle and church fair
and the circle of women, chapters 12 through 15, "A Colored Politician,"
"The American Colored League," "Luke Sawyer Speaks to the League," "Will
Smith's Defense of His Race," and chapter 17, "The Canterbury Club Dinner,"
provide the reader with speeches, public sentiment, background information
about politicians, and recent acts of cruelty. Typical of the times, the speakers
are all male, although the women are not only part of the interested audience
but also a substantial target of the speeches.

The Boston meeting of the Colored League is originally brought about
by the report of another cruel lynching in the South following another case
of a black man allegedly raping a white woman.[3] It is a "public indignation

meeting" instigated by the call to action of the more radical race leaders and an attempt by moderates and white politicians to calm them down (225). The extensive record of the meeting was certainly recognized at Hopkins's time as thinly disguised criticism of the style of race leadership and the double moral-ity of white politics. Will Smith, John Langley, and Arthur Lewis are seen in their respective public roles as young intellectual thinker, ambitious but corrupt politician, and southern educator. In the chapters revolving around the Colored League and the Canterbury Club dinner, the political content of the novel predominates.

Arthur Lewis embodies the Washingtonian educator, motivated by a de-sire to train his people in industrial crafts and to refrain as much as possible from political agitation. His school in Louisiana is a replica of Washington's Tuskegee, down to the fact that the students build it all themselves. The narrator, clearly voicing the opinion of Pauline Hopkins, disapproves of the accommodationist attitude that goes along with an emphasis on education without the necessary political power. The narrator talks about the hope that through education the race question might be forgotten in a general surge toward prosperity, and then adds: "Delusive hope that grasps at shadows!" (243). In contrast to Lewis, Will Smith believes in philosophical and clas-sical education. While his career and his studies at Harvard and Heidelberg resemble those of the young W.E.B. Du Bois, his Boston education and early training provide him with the exemplary models of such earlier abolitionist crusaders as Frederick Douglass and inspire in him their belief in political agitation.[4]

Shortly before the meeting, John Langley, Will Smith's light-colored friend and local politician, is addressed by the white politician Herbert Clapp, whom Hopkins identifies in her preface as the "ex-Governor Northen of Georgia, in his memorable address before the Congregational Club at Tremont Temple, Boston, Mass., May 22, 1899" (16).[5] In this private meeting with Herbert Clapp, John Langley comes off as a rather outspoken advocate for the rights of colored citizens and against the lack of elbowroom for the African Ameri-can politician, but he is induced by Clapp into public restraint when he bribes him with the remunerative public job of city solicitor. In this atmosphere of mutual distrust and competition, the job offer tempts John Langley and shows the general potential for political corruption of the time. His shrewd and bitter observation, the ill-treatment of the African American politician, is the fictional subject of a number of Hopkins's contemporaries.[6] John Lang-ley's public speech then excuses the South for its practice of lynching and calls for confidence in the government: "It is discretion to act coolly, calmly and deliberately; to look at all sides of a question before we jump at conclusions" (252–53). Langley even says: "We thoroughly understand the attitude of the whites. Let us not offend the class upon whom we depend for employment and assistance in times of emergencies" (253). His speech reflects a personality that has been corrupted by personal greed and political unscrupulousness.

At the meeting of the American Colored League, the white politician Herbert Clapp's speech centers upon the stereotypical image of the brutal black man raping the white woman. Clapp says, "I am absolutely opposed to mob law. But there is an unwritten law, . . . which demands the quickest execution, in the quickest way, of the fiend who robs a virtuous woman of her honor to gratify his hellish diabolism" (248). His speech repeats the most devastating sentiment of the time. The denigration of the black man as a rapist and the white woman as his unfortunate victim has led to more lynchings than any other accusation. Although the audience knew or felt that the charge was unjustified in most cases, they were distraught and put on the defensive.

The second speaker is Dr. Arthur Lewis. As an educator who lives and works in the South, Lewis is also interested in playing down the danger of a riot. He calls to mind the fact that these northern meetings often do the influential and educated people in the South great harm and "retard [them] greatly in the accomplishment of [their] designs" (249). Lewis agrees with Clapp that "politics is the bane of the Negro's existence" and assures the South that they do not want social equality (250). "If we are patient, docile, harmless, we may expect to see that prosperity for which we long." His speech is received with some dissatisfaction. Arthur Lewis takes a different stand in a later private meeting, the Canterbury Club dinner. He openly rejects the common belief that all the cases of lynching were a result of black men raping white women. In comparison to his public speech, his statement is quite strong, especially when he says: "We invite investigation in this direction, and you will then find that it is *not* a characteristic of the black man, although *it is* of the white man of the South" (298). This dichotomy between public speech and private opinion reveals Hopkins's analysis of Booker T. Washington's sometimes contradictory attitudes toward race questions, depending on where and to whom he was speaking.

The speeches by Clapp, Langley, and Lewis are received quietly, without much applause, and even with evident disfavor. Coming five years after Washington's famous Atlanta Exposition speech, a repetition of Washington's accommodationist attitude, Hopkins contends, cannot be accepted at a time of continued lynching and violence. Although Washington's speech met with much public acclaim and Governor Bullock even shook his hand, none of the three speeches in *Contending Forces* arouses much enthusiasm. Boston, the historical site of much antislavery agitation, is not the proper place for leniency toward the race question. Hopkins reproduces three speeches, all of them of some length, and shows the audience's disapproval as a sign of her own political convictions and as a message to her people that this is how such arguments should be received. It is, therefore, understandable that her narrator presents these three speeches and has them followed by the kind of reception she would have wished for similar speeches, but that she gives much more space to the following story of Luke Sawyer and the long speech by Will Smith.

The next speaker after Clapp, Langley, and Lewis is Luke Sawyer, who reduces the general political discussion to a single family story. A topic that for most northerners is abstract and remote is illustrated by the case of an interracial family that the reader later finds out is the tragedy of Mabelle Beaubean and Sappho Clark. Sawyer accuses the speakers before him of "conservatism, lack of brotherly affiliation, lack of energy for the right" and exposes the "power of the almighty dollar which deadens men's hearts to the sufferings of their brothers" (256). Here he explicitly confronts his audience with the dire consequences of an American economy that favors the rich and suppresses the poor, the colored, the uneducated. Luke Sawyer voices an opinion that is familiar to readers of Hopkins's journalism, which is emphasized when he utters the line that gives the book its title: *"These are the contending forces that are dooming this race to despair!"* (256). The family story he tells underlines the political message and connects the various parts of the plot by giving us information about the heroine's past. Luke Sawyer's speech decidedly changes the tone of the meeting. When, at the beginning of his speech, he speaks about his own terrible family past, the meeting turns emotional: women cry and confusion reigns. When he adds to his own tale the tragic story of Mabelle Beaubean, one woman, Sappho Clark, must be carried out. This part of the narrative proves the applicability of Sandra Gunning's argument with reference to Chesnutt's *The Marrow of Tradition*, namely that "the domestic sphere is the real battleground over race and rights" (65–66).

In *Contending Forces*, the reader's sympathies are now directed toward Will Smith, whose speech is given a full chapter and is met with much approval. He brings the meeting to a conclusion and represents most closely Hopkins's ideal race leader. To readers of her time, the equation between Lewis and Washington was certainly only a dimly veiled one. Her praise of the character of Will Smith, whose career resembled that of Du Bois and referred to the activism of Frederick Douglass, was recognized by her readers as containing the political message and social criticism she intended by it. These allusions contributed to the prominence of the novel and its author and to a large degree constituted her early fame. The tone of latent violence that dominates the novel from the moment that Sappho's tragic past is revealed was also interpreted by her readers as a warning that race relations were fragile at best and endangered at worst. Will Smith's concluding words may be taken as a political cry for agitation and unity in the face of violence and injustice:

> My friends, it is going to take time to straighten out this problem; it will only be done by the formation of public opinion. Brute force will not accomplish any-thing. We must *agitate*. As the anti-slavery apostles went everywhere, preaching the word fifty years before emancipation, *so must we do to-day*. Appeal for the justice of our cause to every civilized nation under the heavens. Lift ourselves upward and forward in this great march of life until "Ethiopia shall indeed stretch forth her hand, and princes shall come out of Egypt." (272)

Hopkins's having him include one of her favorite Bible passages and her call for agitation, both of which also appear in her journalism and her *Primer of Facts*, clearly show that she identifies with his views.

When writers of Pauline Hopkins's generation are accused of favoring light-colored heroes and heroines over dark-colored ones, this novel testifies to the complexity of this charge. John Langley is a thoroughly unlikable and evil character. He is unheroic, and the reader is made to feel that he deserves a miserable end. This is exemplified in his denigrating attitude toward women, his lust after their bodies without regard for their minds and sentiments. Instead of Will Smith's lofty ideals and protective urge toward Sappho, John Langley puts her into the category of the promiscuous and immoral woman:

> Her beauty intoxicated him; her friendlessness did not appeal to his manliness, because, as we have intimated, *that* was an unknown quality in the makeup of this man. Her coldness urged him on; and Jealousy, the argus-eyed attendant of Love, and its counterfeit—Infatuation—warned him that Will's love was returned, and made him impatient to force upon her an acceptance of his own devotion, at whatever cost. (226–27)

John Langley is denied manliness, the supreme ingredient of the desirable man. The explanation for this lack of virtue in him is his descent from the same Anson Pollock who ruined Grace Montfort's life. The grandmother, Grace's slave Lucy, was forced into a union without mutual consent. Therefore, John Langley was "a descendant of slaves and Southern 'crackers.' We might call this a bad mixture—the combination of the worst features of a dominant race with an enslaved race" (90–91). Since this statement is attributed to the voice of the intrusive narrator, which so often resembles that of the author Hopkins, it shows her concern in fiction with the question of amalgamation.[7] It must be stressed here that the bad legacy of John Langley comes from his white father, the early separation from his mother, his poor childhood as an abandoned and half-starved beggar, and his drive for education without a corresponding development of his moral faculties. As the narrator says, "With him, might was right. This man was what he was through the faults of others" (336). There is hope for his redemption at the end, however, when he waits for death looking at the field of ice in the Arctic cold where he is mining for gold. He realizes the mistakes he has made, and his death, therefore, is interpreted in conciliatory words: "That undisciplined soul went forth to wander in celestial spheres, there to continue the salutary lessons begun on earth, under the guidance of God's angels, who minister to the needs of the immortal soul" (401).[8]

The whipping scene, the account of Sappho Clark's past and John Langley's attitude toward her, and the reaction of the public to lynching and injustice largely form Hopkins's concern with the repetition of history in her first novel. The legacy of the past is present everywhere in the Boston of her time and elsewhere in the United States. In the novels that follow *Contending Forces*, her preoccupation with this part of the collective American past is taken up, proof of the fact that she had found her subject in writing. Slavery is the common ground that leads to violence and demands its victims among white and colored families. The system of slavery, as depicted in *Hagar's Daughter* and *Winona*, breeds human cruelty. The burden of the past reveals itself even over the distance of a generation removed from actual enslavement, as shown in *Hagar's Daughter* and *Of One Blood*. Hopkins presents families contending with this past, repeating acts of violence, and prolonging a victimization that had its sources in this past.

Hagar's Beautiful Daughters

*I*n the March 1903 issue of the *Colored American Magazine*, when Cornelia Condict criticized Pauline Hopkins for writing about interracial love rather than intraracial love, her reproach was basically aimed at the figure of the mulatta, the beautiful light-colored woman who may pass for white and who occasionally marries a white man without letting him know of her ancestry.[1] In a country where interracial marriage was legally forbidden—in the case of Alabama even up to the election of the year 2000—the position of the mulatto was and continues to be of special and conspicuous significance. It is not surprising, then, that when African American writers are looking for a subject "dipped in the life blood of their nation" (Cooper, *Voice* 175), a subject that allows them to treat both the African American and white American side of race relations, they choose to include mixed-race characters. For many, the most enticing subject is the nearly white woman whose trace of black blood leads to tragedy, becomes a test of character, and allows bitter, ironic attacks against a system of double morality. Beauty and virtue, when they are combined with color, highlight a nation's concern with race, class, and the role of women. This chapter will demonstrate that the treatment of the mixed-race character may be seen in close connection with such aspects of genre as the sentimental or melodramatic mode, the detective story, tales of adventure and local color, or political and social tracts. Pauline Hopkins recognized the possibilities inherent in the fictional negotiations of color in combination with beauty and virtue, although this way of writing did not always meet the expectations of her audience.

Like the Smith family in *Contending Forces*, many light-colored African Americans formed their own "blue vein societies" or "upper 400" reserved for African Americans of light color, good education, wealth, or prominent family background. Although they usually measured their success against that of the white society and although many of them chose to pass for white, most would define themselves as African American despite any visible blackness. As many recent studies have shown, the fundamental issue at stake here is that of race itself, including whiteness as a supposedly superior and unquestionable category. To challenge the boundaries of race, as people of mixed-race origin usually do, includes contesting the established nature of progress, civilization, manhood, and virtue as privileges of the so-called dominant race or hegemonic group. The case of light-colored heroines who pass between the races, as is the case with the women in *Hagar's Daughter*, is an especially good example of what Mary V. Dearborn writes about in *Pocahontas's Daughters:* "Miscegenation, or intermarriage, functions in the American cultural imagination and in ethnic fiction as a locus for the ambivalence of author and readers to questions of gender, ethnicity, inheritance, and identity" (132). The subject of miscegenation and its result, the mulatto, attracts the ethnic woman writer because of its aptness and promise and because it allows her, as Dearborn says, "to explore her own ambivalence and that of her culture to female sexuality and ethnicity, to protest against the ways in which intermarriage has assumed oppressive meanings and has expressed an oppressive actuality, and to displace into fiction complex social and economic problems" (132–33).

In the fiction of the pre–Harlem Renaissance period, the issue of voluntary, involuntary, temporary, or permanent passing takes up much fictional space. The exchange of babies and mistaken identities are the stock ingredients of this literature, beginning with William Wells Brown's several treatments of the theme in the various versions of *Clotel*. The topic appeals to both black and white writers, as shown by the novels of Frances E. W. Harper, Jessie Redmon Fauset, Nella Larsen, Charles W. Chesnutt, Sutton E. Griggs, Paul Laurence Dunbar, Walter White, Harriet Beecher Stowe, Mark Twain, and William Dean Howells.[2] Often they illustrate what Giulia Fabi calls the "profoundly different literary traditions" of novels of passing in African American and white-authored representations (*Passing* 3). Recently, Janet Gabler-Hover has presented a comprehensive analysis of *Hagar's Daughter* in the context of a number of white-authored Hagar novels.

The crossing of color lines has the power to arouse interest and public controversy. While it stirs fear in the white population about the colored son- or daughter-in-law who would bring disgrace and taint the family color forever, it excites antagonism in the African American population about a disloyalty to the race and acceptance of the superiority of the white race. From a much later point of view, Claudia Tate writes about the disapproval by many readers of this color discrimination: "Whereas Hopkins saw mulattoes as the racial stock of a new people, we have viewed this group not as representative of but antagonistic to the black population" (*Domestic Allegories* 146–47).

There are many figures but few reliable sources for defining the exact amount of passing. Werner Sollors enumerates the "dramatically heteroge-neous" figures (*Neither Black* 280–84), and Samira Kawash emphasizes the secrecy surrounding real-life acts of passing, to the extent that most evidence can only be found in literature (127). *Hagar's Daughter* is a fine example of an African American novel imposing its own criteria on the acceptance and nonacceptance of passing as a viable movement in African American society.

The opening of *Hagar's Daughter* (1901–2) focuses on Charleston, South Carolina, where on the memorable date of December 20, 1860, secession from the northern United States was declared. The historical setting at a crucial moment in American history sets the scene for the subsequent ac-tion. The first chapter discusses the political background from the opinion of a narrator clearly opposed to slavery and war and adequately portrays the "spirit of unrest and uncertainty" of the time (4). The second chapter, however, opens with part of the general setup of the period that is much more specific and graphic: the slave market with the ignoble treatment of women, men, and children, reminiscent of all the slave narratives that in-clude scenes of misery taking place there. There is no chapter break between the slave-market scene and the convention at the St. Charles Hotel where the leading southern politicians gather to discuss the election of Lincoln. By putting them next to each other, they are both presented on a similar level, hypocritical, cruel, heartless, and unjust. When Jefferson Davis says out loud, "The principle of slavery is in itself right, and does not depend upon difference of complexion" (15), he not only voices the opinion of the political delegates but also that of the numerous slave traders. His talking about the irrelevant color of the skin, the complexion, foreshadows future action in which a person does not have to be black in order to become a slave. Hopkins clearly expects her readers to understand her sarcasm in the juxtaposition of these two scenes.

The pandemonium reigning in the great hall is the proper setting for the appearance of the villain of the book, St. Clair Enson, second son of a wealthy plantation owner, a gambler and reckless womanizer who turned politician.[3] Soon after the nomination of Jefferson Davis as first president of the Confederate States of America, St. Clair receives the message that his brother has a daughter who will become his heiress and thus replace him in the line of heritage. What is seen by the narrator as a tragedy on the national scale is coupled here with a personal tragedy for the second son of a planter, born and bred in affluence, but with no inclination toward honest income. St. Clair's friend, the slave trader Walker, introduced as "the vile dealer in human flesh" (18), becomes the devil's advocate when he promises Enson that he will help him get rid of the wife and heiress. The story then continues with a view of a happy family, matrimonial bliss, and contented slaves, a harmonious surrounding that is soon and tragically invaded by St. Clair, who was first seen in a significant public surrounding.

The description of the title heroine in *Hagar's Daughter* is a good illustration of the typical beautiful woman of mixed-race origin. From the beginning her beauty predestines her for a heroic role: "the pure creamy skin, the curved crimson lips ready to smile—lips sweet and firm,—the broad, low brow, and great, lustrous, long-lashed eyes of brilliant black—soft as velvet, and full of light with the earnest, cloudless gaze of childhood; and there was heart and soul and mind in this countenance of a mere girl" (35). Hagar Sergeant fascinates her considerably older neighbor and owner of the plantation, Ellis Enson, because of this combination of beauty and innocence and promising womanhood. Their marriage and the birth of a daughter fulfill all their desires for happiness. But since the year is 1860, and the location a slaveholding state, and since the birth of a child replaces Ellis Enson's brother St. Clair in the line of heritage, St. Clair and Walker accuse Hagar of being a foundling with black blood in her veins. St. Clair's mean motif of economic covetousness is successful because it is based on some old records that are hard to prove false.

When Hagar faints after the revelation of her racial background, she is confronted with the ghosts that threaten the existence of her life as wife and mother and those that threaten her existence as a white woman. What follows should be called the first scene of revelation because it is succeeded by later ones that echo and revise it. Hagar asks herself, "Was she, indeed, a descendant of naked black savages of the horrible African jungles?" (57). Lacking the visible outward signs, the "black skin, crinkled hair, flat nose and protruding lips" commonly associated with the African (56), Hagar cannot identify herself with the black race. Educated and brought up as a white woman, she voices as much prejudice against this race as the average white woman. And since slave status does not depend solely on complexion, as she sees when she looks at her own white skin, Hagar is forced to search for reasons elsewhere:

> Here was a woman raised as one of a superior race, refined, cultured, possessed of all the Christian virtues, who would have remained in this social sphere all her life, beloved and respected by her descendants, her blood mingling with

the best blood of the country if untoward circumstances had not exposed her ancestry. But the one drop of black blood neutralized all her virtues, and she became, from the moment of exposure, an unclean thing. (62)

The two sides of the juxtaposition are clearly defined and accepted: the superior race is refined, cultured, Christian, and virtuous, which leads to love and respect for the white woman and her descendants, whereas black blood stigmatizes woman as unclean and without virtue. The best blood of the country is white; a black woman who is both virtuous and respectable is a contradiction in terms. Hagar does not succumb, however, to total self-loathing because she remembers in this moment of trial, as Gabler-Hover notes, the history of the biblical Hagar as the "powerful archetypal pattern of female pride and survival" (131).[4] She then remembers and quotes from a poem of "intense Egyptian nationalism."[5]

Within the novel, this traumatic experience of crisis, this "brief symbolic death," as Judith Berzon calls this moment in the typical tragic mulatta's life (123), has far-reaching consequences. Hagar knows that her enslavement, however unjustified, must have practical, irreversible, and terrible effects. While she struggles with the idea that a drop of black blood mars her beauty and virtue, she is sundered with fear about a subsequent loss of love, protection, and social standing. Her marriage is legally invalid, so her child is illegitimate and will also be enslaved.[6] This moment, therefore, stands for the decisive turning point in the life of the romantic heroine and the test of character of the male figures around her, placing Hagar in the tradition of the tragic character of mixed-race origin destined for death. It is due to Hopkins's remarkable vision and power of insight that *Hagar's Daughter* refers back to but does not entirely adhere to this accepted model.

From a slave's point of view, the cruelty of the slave system lies in hard and exploitative labor as much as in the insecurity to which family life is exposed. The most distressing scenes in slave narratives are always the separation of husbands and wives, of mothers and children. This separation is enacted in *Hagar's Daughter* for both sides of the slave household. The white brother violates the rights of his brother, and the white father fears losing his wife and child. Slavery strikes home with a vengeance, and the drama is no less tragic when it affects the white members of the slave-holding family. In the course of the action it will lead to the separation of two brothers, to an uncle courting the hand of his own niece, and to a father and mother who fail to recognize their own child. "Amalgamation," as Ellis Enson says later in the novel, "has taken place; it will continue, and no finite power can stop it" (270). He thus echoes Hopkins's answer to the charge directed against her by Cornelia Condict, in which she says: "Amalgamation is an institution designed by God for some wise purpose, and mixed bloods have always exercised a great influence on the progress of human affairs" (399). Of course, as Hopkins has clearly indicated in her "Furnace Blasts II" essay, however, intermarriage presupposes the consent of the couple, and only the power of love justifies this union (350–52). Family ties cannot be severed with impunity, even if the family members concerned are of mixed-race origin.

All the intricate plot movements culminate in a scene that stands out for its evocative power in a way similar to the whipping scene in *Contending Forces*. Hagar's desperate leap from Long Bridge within sight of the nation's capitol demonstrates more than anything else the heartrending cruelty of a system in which a mother chooses to kill herself and her child rather than live in slavery. The scene in William Wells Brown's *Clotel* that serves as a model for Hopkins speaks of a preoccupation of the African American imagination with the deep and bitter irony in this act. A nation that is proud of "Life, Liberty and the pursuit of Happiness" for everyone, created equally, as unanimously declared in its Declaration of Independence, must witness within the boundaries of its very capital the act of despair of a slave mother with her child. Since this leap and similar acts of mothers who would rather kill their children than have them grow up as slaves were most certainly familiar to her readers, Hopkins's repetition of such a well-known scene not only points out the longevity of the African American memory but also reminds the reader of the legacy of a past that will haunt the national memory.

A painting by J. Alexander Skeete illustrates the leap from the bridge.[7] Hagar and her infant daughter are painted in white colors, and something like a halo is around Hagar's head. Her leap from the bridge is the act of despair of a woman and mother who sees the future in dark colors. Having to choose between the "profane, inhuman monsters into whose hands she must inevitably fall" and death (74), she chooses the latter: "Then she raised her tearful, imploring eyes to heaven as if seeking for mercy and compassion, and with one bound sprang over the railing of the bridge, and sank beneath the waters of the Potomac river" (75). To all evidence, Hagar dies fulfilling the fate of the tragic mulatta. Judged by a view of literature as a series of interrelated texts,[8] Hopkins's forceful narrative can therefore be interpreted as reflecting the literary tastes of her time, as building upon earlier scenes of revelation in which the racial background of a character plays a major role, and as foreshadowing later texts that revise the melodramatic content of such a revelation.

This scene is rife with dramatic and emotional force, a force that certainly appealed to the readers of her time but repelled many later readers. The leap from the bridge and Hagar's first scene of revelation are usually seen as melodramatic, a term most often used to imply literary incompetence and trivial content. Among the many literary critics who have set out to rethink the function of melodrama in literature, Peter Brooks has written: "Melodrama is indeed, typically, not only a moralistic drama but the drama of morality; it strives to find, to articulate, to demonstrate, to 'prove' the existence of a moral universe which, though put into question, masked by villainy and perversions of judgment, does exist and can be made to assert its presence and its categorical force among men" (20). Paying attention to the genre of the melodrama in combination with race, Susan Gillman tries to refute the "mistaken assumption that melodrama, as an aesthetic form, has a trivial or simplistic relation to social context" ("The Mulatto" 224). She argues that "race melodrama responds formally with varying imaginary resolutions to an array of social contradictions generated in the post-Reconstruction era by the conflicting demands of racial, sexual, and national identities" (225). A melodramatic content combined with powerfully melodramatic or pathetic scenes allows Hopkins to combine the fast-moving plot in *Contending Forces* with long discussions of the political background. In *Hagar's Daughter*, these scenes can be judged as a sort of mask for the "conflicting demands of racial, sexual, and national identities" to which Gillman refers. No doubt, Hopkins can be seen as the kind of moralist bent upon pointing out and enhancing the principles of right and wrong Brooks has in mind. To many people in her time, this must have been a contradiction in terms. As an African American woman, she was either assigned to a position in society as a minor member of the workforce or relegated to the category of the loose woman. Morality was usually not associated with the character of an African American woman. As my previous chapters about the woman's era and race literature have argued, Hopkins and the women of her generation took great pains to prove themselves capable of judging behavior and social movements in terms of right and wrong. It was no wonder then that the genre of melodrama held a great attraction for them. There is a moral universe, and African American women had to raise their voices to propagate it.

In a recent study, Linda Williams reexamines the many negative assumptions associated with the sensationalist and pathetic content of melodrama in light of its usefulness for nonwhite and nonmainstream writers: "American racial melodrama deploys the paradoxical location of strength in weakness—

Illustration for *Hagar's Daughter* in the *Colored American Magazine*, May 1901. The caption reads: "With one bound she sprang over the railing of the bridge."

the process by which suffering subjects take what Nietzsche calls *ressenti-ment*, a moralizing revenge upon the powerful achieved through a triumph of the weak in their very weakness" (43). As if Hopkins had wanted to predict her role as a model for a later generation—a "literary foremother," as Claudia Tate calls her—Hopkins lets the weak triumph. Hagar reemerges as one of the strongest female characters in her fiction. Hopkins's heroines, Hagar, Sappho Clark, Winona, and Dianthe Luske, are rewarded with moments of triumph that defy their status of weakness. Theirs is the moral victory, however ambiguous it might be. Melodramatic elements are linked to a reversal of the tragic mulatta model, which could also be called the decentering of the plot of the tragic mulatta, as will be shown below.

The meeting of all the major characters in disguise is often treated as coincidence and considered a major flaw in the development of plot. Faced with the common assumption that coincidence and melodramatic elements prove the "lowness" of this form over other reputedly more sophisticated narrative devices, Jane Gaines reinterprets coincidence as a "highly economical solution for the storyteller" and asks the contemporary reader to consider "how coincidence is really a secular version of divine intervention, the only intervention that can rescue the powerless in the unjust world of social fiction" (58). Her argument about the disregard of melodrama because of a system of rewards that is not given because of "work-world values" but due to the "motives of the heart" rings more than true in the context of Hopkins's fiction (59). In a society where African Americans had little access to power and wealth, such other motivations as happiness, family values, and requited love had to be used as substitutes for economic rewards.

Critics of the generation immediately following Hopkins's usually accused her, as Benjamin Brawley does, of writing "traditional tales, political tracts, and lurid melodramas" ("The Negro in American Fiction" 186). Underlying this summary dismissal of much writing of this period is the devastating repudiation of their artistic competence in combination with a treatment of the racial situation as too accommodating. Brawley and other later readers did not realize that the mixing of genres was designed to reinterpret the melodramatic as a realistic rendering of a reality that was not easy to explain or interpret nor easy to live with as a collective memory. While it evoked questions of identity and power, melodrama concealed these concerns in sentimental rhetoric and pathetic scenes. To move beyond the dismissal of a whole generation of writers, such critics as Gillman, Brooks, Jane Gaines, Linda Williams (in the field of melodrama) and such scholars as Tate,

Ammons, Carby (in the field of African American women's studies) achieved a thorough reevaluation of the merits of melodramatic elements in fiction. The emphasis on morality, social context, and questions of power resolved the critical dilemma.

Hopkins chooses Washington, D.C., as the setting for the second part of the novel and has one part of the action take place within a government building. She does not go so far as to claim, as William Wells Brown does, that one of the founding fathers, Thomas Jefferson, fathered slave children, one of whom leaped from the Potomac bridge with his grandchild in her arms, but her setting in the political society of Washington must be taken as a comment on the intricate relationship between the government and the legacy of the slave system.

When the story resumes in Washington, D.C., in 1882, there is no immediate correspondence between the principal actors and the former characters. The focus is on the fickle nature of identity where race and social status are concerned. As in *Contending Forces*, the protagonists are carefully set out to form couples, alter egos, and foils. The two Ensons are now General Benson, a public officeholder, and Chief Henson of the Secret Service. As before, General Benson, as St. Clair Enson is called now, intends to harm a family that Henson, originally Ellis Enson, later finds out to be his own once more. Benson, together with his accomplice Major Madison, the former slave trader Walker, was involved in the murder of Abraham Lincoln, and both assumed new identities in order to escape their death sentences. Hagar has become Estelle Bowen, the second wife of millionaire Senator Zenas Bowen of San Francisco. Bowen's daughter Jewel is later discovered to be Hagar's and Ellis Enson's own daughter. And Walker has turned into the cunning mine-owner Major Madison and appears now with a beautiful daughter, Aurelia, whose racial background as a quadroon is concealed. In the white set of characters, only Cuthbert Sumner, a wealthy New Englander who is engaged to Jewel Bowen, does not appear in the earlier action. The pairing of the two brothers and of Benson and Madison is repeated in Benson's affiliation with his former slave Isaac, who, in the meantime, has married Aunt Henny's daughter Martha. While all the white and seemingly white characters have taken on new identities, the former slaves are still recognizable and will eventually help reveal the identities of all the white characters.

In contrast to the male cast, the three principal women all seem to be white but possess some black blood. In education and manners, they are not distinct

from upper-class ladies. They pass because their physical appearance is more
white than black (Hagar and Aurelia) or because they have no knowledge of
their origin (Jewel).

Zenas Bowen meets Estelle in San Francisco and is struck by her great
beauty. They get married within a short time, and she becomes a loving and
honest wife who always has his good fortune in mind and even encourages
him in his political life: "Thanks to her cleverness, he made no mistakes and
many hits which no one thought of tracing to his wife's rare talents" (82).
Zenas Bowen himself is not a fool, but Mrs. Bowen has contributed decisively
to his career without ever intruding in public. "Mrs. Bowen simply fulfilled
woman's mission in making her husband's career successful by the exercise
of her own intuitive powers." And yet it is Estelle who voices the deeply felt
belief that a "woman's life is hard, hard, from the cradle to the grave" (136).
She utters these words to herself at a moment when she tries to comfort
her beautiful daughter because she was heartbroken over Cuthbert Sumner.
From her own experience (at that time in the plot, the reader guesses at her
real identity), she knows that beauty alone does not guarantee happiness.

As the wife of millionaire Zenas Bowen, she is called upon once more to
defend herself, her interests, and the interests of Jewel, whom she considers
to be Bowen's daughter. When a lawyer confronts her with the will that
Zenas Bowen made in which he allegedly named the two villains of the
story as trustees, she does not acquiesce easily. "The expression of her face
was intense, even fierce; her mouth was tightly closed, her eyes strained as
though striving to pierce the veil which hides from us the unseen" (201–2).
The lawyer admires her as a "fearless woman" (202). When General Benson
reveals to her what he thinks is her real past, she does not faint immediately,
nor does she shrink from him. In what must be considered a second scene
of revelation, the narrative shows that the twenty intervening years have
made a decisive difference. Mrs. Bowen defends herself as well as she can.
"She moved toward him with disheveled hair, foaming lips and one arm
outstretched in menace" (207). There is no trace of despair; in contrast,
there is aggression and menace: " 'I admit nothing; I deny nothing. Prove it
if you can,' she muttered in a strained tone." She does not give in as easily
as before and demonstrates that if a villain tries to repeat history, he will be
faced with bitter opposition.

Within the chronology of the fiction of Hopkins, this signals a definite
development in her power as a writer of visionary insights. Whereas in *Contending Forces* Sappho is stricken when John Langley threatens to reveal her
past to Will Smith, Mrs. Bowen has grown beyond the Hagar of the past in

force and stamina. The argument that she is now strong because she has been passing as white for many years is not conclusive. She was raised a white woman when she first heard about the drop of black blood in her. Her initial despair then was caused by the very realistic threats to her status as a married woman and that of her child as legitimate and white. In this scene twenty years later, she has grown in age and experience, and there is hardly anything St. Clair Enson can still take from her, especially because she thinks her daughter has not survived the leap from the bridge. Although the fate of her daughter Jewel repeats more or less closely the fates of many other tragic mulattas in contemporary novels, there are deviances, and Jewel cannot be classified as tragic merely because of her race. Hopkins's next novel, *Winona*, will show that there is a total reversal of the force of the tragic content of the mixed-race heroine.

Much like her mother, Jewel Bowen can be seen as a typical heroine. "Her hair was fair, with streaks of copper in it; her eyes, gray with thick short lashes, at times iridescent. Her nose superbly Grecian" (82). Her beauty is "of the Saxon type, dazzling fair, with creamy roseate skin." She accepts all the flattery and attention as her rightful due, setting her outward appearance and her character on an equal plane: "She was proud with the pride of conscious worth that demanded homage as a tribute to her beauty—to herself." Very often there is a reference to her white skin, the plaits of bright hair, the sweetness of her voice, the earnestness of her first love, the innocence of the young girl. Sumner calls her his "Blossom" and "white angel of purity" (102, 103).

The beauty of Sappho Clark, Hagar and Jewel, Winona, and, in *Of One Blood*, Dianthe Luske and Queen Candace is startling. Often the classical beauty of their creamy skin, dark eyes, and Grecian noses alerts the attentive reader to their possible African origin. This is especially prominent when Queen Candace is described as "a Venus, a superb statue of bronze, moulded by a great sculptor; but an animated statue, in which one saw the blood circulate, and from which life flowed" (*Of One Blood* 568). One answer to the question of why so many of the early African American heroines are similar in beauty and type is that it made identification with them easier. At Hopkins's time, the standard of beauty was the Anglo-Saxon roseate skin, beautiful hair, and sparkling eyes. This description would be immediately familiar to the reader from the numerous heroines in sentimental fiction. DuCille points out that it "was a strategy of the times, this attempt to argue for equality by establishing resemblance, by collapsing difference into sameness, by pointing out the mutability of race and the absurdity of white society's color codes through the trope of the mulatto, tragic and heroic" ("Where in the World" 454). Her choice of light-colored heroines, typical of her time, is clearly motivated by her continuing emphasis that character is more important than color.

The fascination for Hopkins's readers arose from this combination of beauty and race and from the innocence of a virtuous woman who ends in tragedy because of an invisible drop of black blood. As Hazel Carby writes, mulatto characters serve "as a vehicle for an exploration of the relationship between the races and, at the same time, an expression for the relationship between the races. The figure of the mulatto should be understood and analyzed as a narrative device of mediation" (*Reconstructing* 89; see also Kristina Brooks 124). Sean McCann argues that "the golden-skinned Sappho gave Hopkins a vehicle for illustrating the way an image of racial identity could be developed over and above the facts of biological descent" (799). For a writer like Hopkins, who thought that race distinctions did not predetermine character, the beautiful mixed-race heroines, all the possible daughters of Hagar, provided the perfect means to probe race relations.

The beauty of Jewel must be compared to the description of her foil, Aurelia Madison, Walker's daughter by a slave, who originally met Jewel in school in Canada, where she passed as white. Aurelia is first described as a "voluptuous beauty with great dusky eyes and wonderful red-gold hair" (90). At the Bowen ball, where the two beauties can be observed side by side, their different types are highlighted. Aurelia makes her entrance and all the guests are captivated: "This woman was quite the loveliest thing they had ever seen, startling and somewhat bizarre, perhaps, but still marvellously, undeniably lovely. Her gown was a splendid creation of scarlet and gold. It was a magnificent and daring combination. Her hair was piled high and crowned with diamonds. A single row of the same precious stones encircled her slim throat. She looked superbly, wondrously beautiful" (115). At that same ball, Jewel wears a white robe and pearls around her neck. There can be no greater contrast between the two types of women, the innocent and pure heroine versus the femme fatale with her luring sexual charms. The description and character of Aurelia can be seen as a sign of the writer exploring her own and her culture's ambivalence toward female sexuality (see Dearborn 132–33). Cuthbert Sumner sees in Aurelia a "gorgeous tropical flower" and in Jewel "a fair fragrant lily" (103). And although he is engaged to the latter, the former "caused his blood to flow faster, it gave new zest to living." As the fascinating, strong, and sexually attractive woman, the depiction of Aurelia foreshadows later developments of the heroines in African American fiction in the works of Zora Neale Hurston, Nella Larsen, and Jessie Fauset.[9]

In contrast to Jewel, Aurelia is strong enough to withstand her fate. When she is confronted with Sumner's repulsion at her being a quadroon, she confronts him bravely, even savagely: "I will not fly—I will brave you to the last! If the world is to condemn me as the descendant of a race that I abhor, it shall never condemn me as a coward!" (238). The narrator interprets this third scene of revelation for the reader: "Terrible though her sins might be—terrible her nature, she was but another type of the products of the accursed system of slavery—a victim of 'man's inhumanity to man' that has made 'countless millions mourn.' There was something, too, that compelled admiration in this resolute standing to her guns with the determination to face the worst that fate might have in store for her. Something of all this Sumner felt, but beyond a certain point his New England philanthropy could not reach." Aurelia is a victim, but she is definitely not the type of tragic mulatta that Jewel partly embodies. In all her scheming, Aurelia is motivated by a real love for Sumner and a decided longing for respectability that is denied her only because of her racial background and not because of her refinement and culture. "Once his wife, she told herself, she would shake off all her hideous past and become an honest matron" (92). One cannot blame Aurelia for trying to achieve this goal, although her lack of race solidarity does not gain her the narrator's or the reader's sympathy.

It is Elise Bradford, the young white secretary of General Benson, who reveals Aurelia's racial background to Sumner. In a rare moment in African American literature, the white and southern Elise talks openly and with empathy about the fate of women such as Aurelia. There is a potential for sisterhood between women of all races that was rarely realized in the age of Pauline Hopkins:

> Yet Aurelia in a measure deserves our pity. The loveliness of Negro women of mixed blood is very often marvellous, and their condition deplorable. Beautiful almost beyond description, many of them educated and refined, with the best white blood of the South in their veins, they refuse to mate themselves with the ignorant of their own race. Socially, they are not recognized by the whites; they are often without money enough to but the barest necessities of life; honorable, they cannot produce sufficient means to gratify their luxurious tastes; their mothers were like themselves; their fathers they never knew; debauched white men are ever ready to take advantage of their destitution, and after living a short life of shame, they sink into early graves. Living, they were despised by whites and blacks alike; dead, they are mourned by none. (159)

Elise, the southern woman who herself fell into the trap of General Benson and has borne a son out of wedlock, sees the larger perspective of the quadroon and octoroon woman: "But black blood is everywhere—in society and out, and in our families even; we cannot feel assured that is has not filtered into the most exclusive families. We try to stem the tide but I believe it is a hopeless task" (160).[10]

In her very shrewd and perspicuous considerations, Elise links the question of color with that of class. There is something like "high" or "better" society in the white world, but the African American is seen as always the same: illiterate, ill-bred, immoral. The many educated African Americans who do not fit into this mold do not have an acknowledged place in society. Elise also addresses the fates of the many light-colored women who die early after their short lives as mistresses of some white man. She is the only white woman in the novel who feels pity and not repulsion. Only a character who must be seen as a "fallen" woman herself, however, can muster up enough courage to admit this. There is an element of revengefulness in her act, because it is she who gives Aurelia away and thus instigates much of the action following upon this.[11]

After the courtroom scene in which her identity is made public, Aurelia disappears from public view, alone and desperate, but she does not die from shame or a broken heart, as Jewel does later on. Her fate is very similar to that of Hagar. Hagar also disappeared twenty years before and started a new identity as a white woman and became the honest matron that Aurelia wanted to be. It is implied that Aurelia will continue her life somewhere else, possibly as a white woman. The life stories of both Aurelia and Hagar strongly argue against the tragic mulatta plot. They are self-reliant and do not suffer self-doubt because of their racial identity but because of social prejudice. Both lead adventuresome and thrilling lives although, of course, Hagar is much more virtuous and admirable than Aurelia. Hopkins does not collapse the moral categories between them.[12] Instead, her case serves to prove that even virtue and courage do not protect a black woman from prejudice and accusations. One cannot say that they are portrayed in correlation with the usual concept of heroines, despite their color. They are heroines because of their color. And there can be no better argument to vindicate the rights of mixed-race women than this. Hopkins subtly manipulates her audience into accepting this argument.

When Jewel, who had married Cuthbert Sumner while he was still imprisoned for murder, learns that the woman whom she considers her stepmother is a colored woman, she feels as much love toward her as before. But Sumner is upset and reveals his relief over the fact that Hagar is only Jewel's stepmother. When Hagar finally discovers that her infant was saved from the waters of the Potomac by Zenas Bowen and adopted as his child, she and Ellis Enson shed many tears out of relief about the survival of their daughter, who had been Hagar's stepdaughter for such a long time. This is the fourth scene of revelation in the novel; again, it has the power to disrupt love and separate families.

Jewel now must face the fact that she herself is colored. Hagar's fate is repeated twenty years later, a fact that shows that the dismal treatment of the African American woman, not limited to the system of slavery, reveals a permanent and deeply ingrained disdain of her positive character and potential for true womanly traits. In the decisive moment of revelation, however, Jewel is not so much aghast at the color in her veins as at the possible reaction of society toward her being of mixed blood. "It was horrible—a living nightmare, that she, the petted darling of society, should be banned because of her origin. She shrank as from a blow as she pictured herself the astonishment, disgust and contempt of her former associates when they learned her story" (280–81). She faints also because she knows that Sumner will not accept her origin. Indeed, Cuthbert Sumner sadly fails this test of manhood, and Jewel eventually dies of a broken heart.

Of all the characters in the novel, it is Cuthbert Sumner who is made to represent the typical reaction of a northern man to the woman of mixed race. The process going on in his mind after he learns that Jewel's stepmother is Hagar is worth quoting in full:

> Cuthbert Sumner was born with a noble nature; his faults were those caused by environment and tradition. Chivalrous, generous-hearted—a manly man in the fullest meaning of the term—yet born and bred in an atmosphere which approved of freedom and qualified equality for the Negro, he had never considered for one moment the remote contingency of actual social contact with this unfortunate people.
>
> He had heard the Negro question discussed in all its phases during his student life at "Fair Harvard," and had even contributed a paper to a local weekly in which he had warmly championed their cause; but so had he championed the cause of the dumb and helpless creatures in the animal world about him. He gave large sums to Negro colleges and on the same principle gave liberally to the Society for the Prevention of Cruelty to Animals, and endowed a refuge for homeless cats. Horses, dogs, cats, and Negroes were classed together in his mind as of the brute creation whose sufferings it was his duty to help alleviate. (265–66)

There is hardly a more ironic and bitter condemnation of the so-called liberal attitude of the northern man than this. It must be taken as a brave and courageous move on the part of the real-life Hopkins that she dared criticize a man who is made to stand for the liberal spirit of the North. Certainly real-life experiences motivated her to do so. It all comes down to the question of how liberal-minded a person is when the racial question becomes more than a simple abstract problem. The narrator and Hopkins condemn the attitude of northern philanthropy that throws together animals and negroes much as the southern slaveholders had seen the Negro as a piece of property. The "brute creation" that Sumner had been told to mind is not considered human. Of course, the reader is prepared for this attitude of Sumner's and compares it to the reaction of Ellis Enson when he found out about Hagar. This connects a line that can be drawn between the South and the North. Although Ellis Enson at first rejects Hagar out of a feeling of shock, he later decides to stay with her and take care of her. Sumner, however, is offered the easy way out by Jewel when she sets him free.

When Jewel is abducted by General Benson and when Sumner is thrown into prison because of an indictment for murder, the novel develops into adventure and detective fiction, with multiple layers of identity that will be disentangled with the help of Detective Henson and the black maid. In conventional detective fiction, the ending marks the resolution of the mystery and the restoring of order because the evil forces are removed and the good ones dominate. This is definitely not the case in *Hagar's Daughter*, and most critics have pointed this out.[13] As Carby remarks, "St. Clair and Walker represented immorality and rampant greed, but their imprisonment did not return society to happiness. Neither were the heroes and heroines secured in their social positions when what appeared to be the prime threat was removed. Ultimately, the political forces that Hopkins wanted to indict could not be embodied in individually good or bad characters" (*Reconstructing* 151). By removing St. Clair and Walker from the public, the story resolves individual tragedy but does not remedy evil in general. These two characters embody vice, but the vice, as Sumner sees it—the pollution of the soul, the deadening of the moral senses, and the refusal of the true doctrines of Divinity (284)—is seen as too encompassing to be removed with two single persons.

Together with her appropriation of melodrama as a viable fictional genre, *Hagar's Daughter* thus also makes use of elements of the adventure and detective genres. There are many elements of detective fiction: the lone detective hero, the clever interpretation of evidence, disguise and risky action, and, above all, the grand courtroom scene are part of a book that condemns racism and injustice on a grand scale. In *The Blues Detective*, Stephen Soitos finds in *Hagar's Daughter* "the earliest known use of African American detective tropes in a work written by a black American containing a black detective," by which fact Soitos recognizes that this novel has "broken ground by illustrating how detective conventions could be signified on by African American writers" (61). By extensively analyzing elements of passing, disguise, coincidence, the role of voodoo prophecy, and the double-conscious detective abilities of Venus, Soitos emphasizes the new use of this form as a "vehicle for social criticism" (59).

In the end, the sentimental content of what appears to be a typical tragic mulatta plot dominates over the more prominent adventure story. Hagar and Ellis Enson are reunited, but Jewel dies offstage, somewhere in Europe of something like the "Roman fever" that affected the heroines of Edith Wharton and Henry James. Jewel, however, is only one of the heroines in this story. Her death gives rise to a more general discussion of the outcome of all events. Cuthbert Sumner hastens toward Enson Hall, finally sure that he will not give up Jewel and that their union is God's will. When he finds her grave, he is in despair: "Then it was borne in upon him: the sin is the nation's. It must be washed out. The plans of the Father are not changed in the nineteenth century; they are shown us in different forms. The idolatry of the Moloch of Slavery must be purged from the land and his actual sinlessness was but a meet offering to appease the wrath of a righteous God" (283–84). Cuthbert's realization of the Christian doctrine of charity and the equality of humankind prompts the narrator to claim: "Cursed be the practices which pollute the soil, and deaden all our moral senses to the reception of the true doctrines of Divinity" (284). By grounding the ending of her novel in Christian doctrine, Hopkins may have hoped to guide her readers to a better understanding. It is strange to have her narrator talk about Sumner's "actual sinlessness," considering the fact that he repeatedly professes some strong prejudice and even repulsion toward the Negro race. Sometime earlier he talked about a possible union with Aurelia after he had learned about her racial background: "The mere thought of the grinning, toothless black hag that was her foreparent would forever rise between us. I am willing to allow the Negroes education, to see them acquire business, money, and social status within a certain environment. I am not averse even to their attaining political power. Farther than this, I am not prepared to go" (271).[14] To this, Ellis Enson, the older and wiser of the two, replies with the evocation of some "higher law" that Cuthbert must find and then follow, whereby he would ennoble his nature. Ellis Enson also quotes to him William Wordsworth's "A boy's will is the wind's will, And the thoughts of youth are long, long thoughts" (271). He thus puts the development of unprejudiced thinking on a level with growing up. The immature boy is linked with prejudice; the grownup develops a moral capacity and a Christian understanding. To see this from the nation's perspective, Ellis Enson here also criticizes the nation's general immaturity and unwillingness to grow and, in the jargon of nation-building, to become great. It is once mentioned about Sumner that he was destined to become a manly man through education (265), and it is now implied that he will only grow out of his childish ways when he understands the lessons taught by Jewel's death: namely, that the degradation of the legacy of slavery must be ended once and for all.

Jewel dies because of the loss of love, not because she considers her ancestry to be tragic. It is interesting to note that Hagar's marriage with Enson is not questioned at all. The reader feels that they deserve each other after so many trials. Race is not part of the problem anymore. It is for these reasons that one can say that the tragic mulatta plot is decentered in this novel. Not only does this precede an even more forceful deviance from a potential model in Hopkins's next novel, *Winona*, it also foreshadows the treatment of the mixed-race character in later works by African American women writers.

Winona, Manhood, and Heroism

*I*n Hopkins's fiction, the female protagonists correspond to the image of the beautiful heroines under duress who either must be rescued or rescue themselves through memorable deeds. The roles available to her male figures also correspond in part to accepted positions of heroes and villains, with race added to their noble or ignoble character traits. There is always an underlying argument about the validity of racial inheritance that puts black and white men at opposite ends of the scale of development. Often the test of manhood involves the position they take toward the woman of mixed blood. More than any other set of characters, the rivalry between dark-colored Judah and white Englishman Warren Maxwell in *Winona* reflects the debate surrounding the nature of manhood and heroism in a race-conscious environment. In essence, the description of them as opposite types of men highlights the differences underlying the rivalry between manly Will Smith and cowardly John Langley or between John Langley and accommodationist Arthur Lewis in *Contending Forces*, between Ellis and St. Clair Enson in *Hagar's Daughter*, or between Charlie Vance and the servant Jim Titus in *Of One Blood*.

There is no doubt who will win the love of the heroine or who will be rescued in the end. Reward is based on exceptional bravery, faithfulness, and manhood. The concept of manhood in the nineteenth century, as Gail Bederman has shown in *Manliness and Civilization*, was based on the Victorian middle-class ideals that "a man was self-reliant, strong, resolute, courageous, honest" (qtd. in Bederman 6). A real man would lay claim to a male body, male identity, and male power (10). When this claim was challenged through immigrants, working-class men, women, and nonwhite people, the familiar structure of power was endangered and had to be defended.[1]

While the intellectual heroism of Reuel Briggs is the subject of the next chapter, this part of Hopkins's negotiations in gender treats the male characters in *Winona*, the white cast of male characters in *Hagar's Daughter*, and

Charlie Vance's experiences in Africa. The concepts of manhood and heroism are called into question when they are at odds with racial identity.

Hopkins's third novel, *Winona* (1902), the only novel set exclusively before the Civil War, begins on an idyllic island in Lake Erie, near Buffalo on the Canadian border, a wilderness, untamed but not savage anymore: "The green world still in its primal existence in this forgotten spot brought back the golden period unknown to the world living now in anxiety and toil" (291). The happy family in this golden period consists of a white father of English descent, the mixed-race daughter, the adopted black son, and an old Indian woman as housekeeper. Elizabeth Ammons calls this family the trope for the truly human North American family: "multicultural, multiracial, anti-imperialist, unnational, antimaterialistic, environmentally attuned" ("Afterword" 214).

The first sight the reader has of Judah, the young, courageous, and brave Negro who grew up as an Indian, is in a canoe rowing with Winona to their secluded island, surrounded by the primeval forest. The curly hair and dark skin color identify him as a Negro. His origin is rather odd. He is the son of a fugitive slave who died during her escape. He was then adopted by another fugitive slave who later married a white man, the rightful heir to a large English estate, who became known as "White Eagle," an honorary Indian. Winona is the daughter of the white man and this light-colored fugitive slave. Both Judah and Winona are captured under the Fugitive Slave Act by Colonel Titus, the owner of a plantation in Kansas, and his overseer Bill Thomson. Judah's mother was Bill Thomson's property and Winona's mother was Colonel Titus's. After these two villains have killed "White Eagle," they enslave Judah and Winona.

Colonel Titus's plantation is situated near Kansas City, and the year is 1856. The historical background is the debate over admitting Kansas as a slave state or free state. The border ruffians, here the gang of Colonel Titus's overseer and his accomplice Bill Thomson, try to intimidate the antislavery settlers, who are supported by a militia led by the fanatic John Brown. In 1856 a gang of border ruffians rode into the antislavery town of Lawrence, Kansas, set it afire and killed several people. This act was answered in retaliation by John Brown's ritual murder of five proslavery men from Kansas at Pottawatomie Creek. By concentrating on John Brown's murder of these men rather than on his much more prominent and heroic later attack at Harper's Ferry, Hopkins chooses to question the morality of violence in itself, while she refrains from advocating any overt call for agitation or slave rebellion.

Apart from Judah, the followers of John Brown and the fighters in his camp are white, and thus the agency and responsibility for what happens is placed on them.

This is the historical setting for the appearance of the dark-colored Judah, a "lion of a man" (320), whose physical strength makes him "a noble figure," the "living statue of a mighty Vulcan" (323). Raised in freedom and educated in the spirit of Indian nobility, he is unfit for slavery and unwilling to accept the cruelty of his master. The climactic scene of his being "broken in" in terms of slavery is preceded by what is called a dramatic "battle-royal" (325), during which he tames a wild horse. He uses the hypnotic eye of the Indian and shows the most daring horsemanship ever seen by the spectators. But this proud and brave act serves him ill in the eyes of his owner, Bill Thomson. Judah is sent to be whipped and withstands the cruel beating stoically. "But every stroke of the merciless lash was engraved on his heart in bleeding stripes that called for vengeance" (327–28). There is no doubt that Judah lays claim to his male body and male identity. However, he is denied access to power because of his race. Moreover, he is whipped because his owner feels threatened by one of the so-called inferior race being physically stronger and more daring. Bill Thomson is a good example of the white man in power challenged in his status, identity, and position of power by the strong African American male.

Judah's stoic endurance of the hardships of slavery is his way of surviving as a slave on a plantation that is pervaded by an atmosphere of violence and ill-feeling. Bill Thomson's wife, for example, whips her maid at random, depending on her mood. His and Winona's only friend is Warren Maxwell, a young English aristocrat, who travels through the United States in search of the heir of the English Carlingford estate. Without her knowing it, White Eagle was the rightful heir and was killed by Colonel Titus, his own cousin, after he had been recognized by him.

Judah's majestic physical frame is described by Warren Maxwell, who admires his strength: "In him was the true expression of the innate nature of the Negro when given an opportunity equal with the white man" (335). It is clear that only the foreigner, the Englishman, can make this observation. There is something like an "innate nature" of the Negro, but this nature is not shiftlessness, cowardice, or malice; it is courage, strength, and intellectual curiosity. Later, these qualities in Judah are furthered through the helpful counsel and guidance of the benevolent patriarch John Brown. In his camp, Judah learns "the sweetness of requited toil together with the manliness of self-defence" (374). Through the depiction of both Bill Thomson and

Colonel Titus as cruel, mean, dishonest, and, in the end, cowardly, the white American slaveholder is presented as breeding violence and ill-feeling, not advancement of civilization and progress. With the introduction of Warren as an Englishman and Colonel Titus's and White Eagle's background in the English aristocracy, the issue of slavery is furthermore treated as international rather than national.

The romantic background of the story is the love relationship between the light-colored, mixed-race Winona, the Englishman Warren Maxwell, and the very dark-colored Judah. When Winona first appears in the story as a young girl of about fourteen years, she is compared to a fragile flower with her "beautifully chiselled features, the olive complexion with a hint of pink" (292). Much like the young Mabelle Beaubean and Hagar, she leads a happy and contented life. Two years later, a slave on Colonel Titus's plantation, Winona has grown into "a womanhood blessed with glorious beauty that lent a melancholy charm to her fairness when one remembered the future before such as she" (320). She is educated in order to increase her value on the slave market, but Winona's fate is different. With the help of Warren, she and Judah escape from the plantation and find shelter among the well-meaning community of John Brown's followers.

She falls in love with Warren Maxwell, who, as an Englishman, does not regard her racial background as a dramatic impediment to their union. In what I consider a decentering of the plot of the tragic mulatta, Winona is not really the main character in the story. She does not have to die, and her tragedy is avoided; the political action of antislavery agitation is seen to be more important. When she discusses her future fate with Warren, Winona says that she would rather go into a convent than marry a man who knew nothing about her past. There is not even the slightest hint that she is in despair because of her color or that she would not be able to cope with life. It is Warren who sees in her a "young goddess" and a "childwoman" (404). These contradictory views of her reflect Warren's inconsistency toward Winona, not Winona's own self-conception. She talks about the degradation of the two years she had to spend as a slave (406), not about the degradation of herself because of her mulatto mother. Her early training as an Indian accounts for this remarkable absence of any feeling of shame or worthlessness: "In the primal life she had led there had entered not a thought of racial or social barriers" (376). Instead of being crushed by her experiences, Winona is made stronger through them, even if it means that she becomes knowledgeable beyond her years: "This poor child had learned things from which the doting mother guards the tender maidenhood of her treasure with rigid care" (356).

Whatever the "things" may have been, Winona becomes wiser and more mature than she has been before. Some of her self-assurance can be traced to her youth and some ignorance, but most of it comes out of her liberal upbringing and early training. There is an innate feeling of nobility in her when she says, for example: "I cannot marry out of the class of my father" (406). The home she thinks is rightfully hers is that of her father's English family. The nobility of this heritage is certainly seen as stronger than that of her mulatto mother.

One can hardly argue that Winona is a passive agent only. She disguises herself as a boy, blackens her face, and risks her recapture as a slave when she is thrown into the same prison that contains Warren Maxwell's cell and a lockup for runaways. Much like Venus Johnson in *Hagar's Daughter*, she is an active participant in the action. In the Brown camp, she discovers the cave that will later serve as a place of refuge for the women and children during the fight. When the men depart, Winona, rifle in hand, is left in charge of the homestead. And on their hard trip back up north to Buffalo, Winona complains as little as the others. A truly western girl, she has learned to cope with hardships.

At the same time, Judah feels deep love for her and jealousy when he sees her affection for Warren Maxwell. His bitterness at the sight of the loving relationship between Warren and Winona causes him to ponder the question of race relations and social equality: "Was it for this he had suffered and toiled to escape from his bonds? If they had remained together in slavery, she would have been not one whit above him, but the freedom for which he had sighed had already brought its cares, its duties, its self-abnegation. He had hoped to work for her and a home in Canada; it had been the dream that had buoyed his heart with hope for weary days; the dream was shattered now" (357). Of course, Judah realizes that his dreams are selfish, and slavery would not have been a solution at all. It is to Hopkins's credit that she discharges a utopian solution to the plot, in which Winona and Judah would marry after successfully escaping to Canada. This was the subject of *Peculiar Sam*, but she cannot tell the same story again.

Still, the tricky problem remains to be solved. Why is Judah not allowed to love and marry Winona? Is it solely the difference in skin color that prevents this union? Both were reared in the same surroundings, and both are described as noble and heroic. One part of the answer lies in the "chemistry of the spirit" that draws Winona and Warren to each other in love (357). Judah and Winona were raised as brother and sister. Winona, as she tells him, has no love to give to Judah. Hopkins knew too well that such white readers as Cornelia Condict would have wanted a happy ending in marriage between Judah and Winona. Yet, in Hopkins's eyes, the happiness of this union would have been grounded in race rather than love. Hopkins always demanded the same rights for African American as for white American women. A marriage based on love would lead to understanding and mutual respect. It is also important to note that throughout the novel, the problem is mainly Judah's, not Winona's. Winona does not love Judah, and the fact that she not only dares to fall in love with the white Englishman but also fights for him and rescues him in the end, proves that Hopkins goes beyond the oversimplistic dichotomies of white and black upon which heroism and love are based.

Moreover, this is only part of the question involved. Winona appeals to Judah's generosity and true-heartedness after he complains bitterly that the white man gets it all. Winona reminds him that not all white men are the same. Judah replies, "You are right—you are right! But how is a man to distinguish between right and wrong? What moral responsibility rests upon him from whom all good things are taken? Answer me that" (379). As in other instances, Hopkins's writing here bears a resemblance to William Wells Brown's ideas in *Clotel*, in which Clotel, after she has been sold to Mr. French, muses: "What social virtues are possible in a society of which injustice is the primary characteristic? in a society which is divided into two classes, masters and slaves?" (92). Winona cannot answer this question except with tears, nor can a narrator now take over and impose some authorial comment on the justification of these questions, because there simply is no answer.

What are, indeed, the moral responsibilities of a suppressed people, deprived of self-defense, self-assertion, and the development of virtues? To ask this question in the language of a different context: How can the colonized subject be made responsible for good and evil? It can all be reduced to questions of power. If the possibility of moral development is taken from the subjected people, they cannot be expected to know the right answers. Judah—and with him Hopkins and many of her contemporary African American intellectuals, at some point or other in their lives—had to find a solution to this. Much in keeping with Hopkins's general journalistic practice, her implicit answer is that it is not through violence that race strife can be solved. She poses the question and hints at the possibility that must have preoccupied most of her contemporaries. Race riots are much in the public limelight at the beginning of the twentieth century and remind white Americans forcefully of the fact that lynch law and the Ku Klux Klan cannot be fed to the public without possible retaliation. Hopkins must be given credit for asking the question; it cannot be put at her door that she does not solve the race problem in her fiction when there is no solution to it in real life.

In the context of the fictional world of *Winona*, the problem can be resolved with the help of clear-cut perspectives. The antislavery men under John Brown are good, heroic, faithful; the proslavery men under the leadership of Jim Titus and Bill Thomson are bad. At the beginning of the battle between John Brown and his followers against the rangers, this polarization is stated directly and unequivocally: "It was a terrible struggle between the two great forces—Right and Wrong. Drunken with vile passions, the Rangers fought madly but in vain against the almost supernatural prowess of their oponents [sic]" (412). Rage and violence is their rightful case, but in the case of dark-colored Judah, the question cannot be solved easily because race predominates over heroism and manliness.

Whereas John Brown, Parson Steward, Ebenezer Maybee, and Warren Maxwell are allowed "ungovernable rage," Judah is denied this privilege. When they are about to rescue Warren Maxwell, Judah is at the point of shooting his former tormentor Bill Thomson. He is held back by John Brown because of the pressing need of time but promised he will be allowed to take revenge later. In a dramatic scene during the decisive battle, Judah finally corners Bill Thomson and regards him as his prey. Thomson, now a coward, fears his rage. "Judah smiled. It was a terrible smile, and carried in it all the pent-up suffering of two years of bodily torture and a century of lacerated manhood" (414). His rage is justifiable, and after he has made Thomson jump off the ledge, Hopkins ends this installment leaving the image in the reader's mind. The fierce and dominant African American triumphs at the death of his enemy.

The next and final installment reinforces this image: "A superb, masterful smile played over the ebon visage of the now solitary figure upon the mountainside. In his face shone a glitter of the untamable torrid ferocity of his tribe not pleasing to see" (417). In contrast to the other men, who all commit murder and atrocities, Judah's act of killing is characterized by a ferocity that is untamable, a notion that implies savage, primal instinct. To Judah, as he now contemplates his brave fight, it is, however, a just retribution for wrongs committed: "To him his recent act was one of simple justice. Hate, impotent hate, had consumed his young heart for two years. An eye for an eye was a doctrine that commended itself more and more to him as he viewed the Negro's condition in life, and beheld the horrors of the system under which he lived" (417). His recalling of Old Testament justice is in accord with his earlier depiction as a lion of a man, a Vulcan, a majestic figure. Modern justice is not sufficient for his purposes. This dramatic scene now demands an interpretation that comes from an authorial narrator, a voice that can put the deed in a general context and comment upon it: "Judged by the ordinary eye Judah's nature was horrible, but it was the natural outcome or growth of the 'system' as practiced upon the black race. He felt neither remorse nor commiseration for the deed just committed. To him it was the only chance of redress for the personal wrongs inflicted upon Winona and himself by the strong, aggressive race holding them in unlawful bondage" (417–18). These comments are the direct counterpart of an earlier view of the same system of slavery by Colonel Titus, when he utters the common justification of slavery and its improving effect upon the slaves: "But see what we've done for the Africans, given them the advantages of Christian training, and a chance to mingle, although but servants, in the best circles of the country. The niggers have decidedly the best of it" (332). It is emphasized now that what the Negroes learn is suffering, rage, and hatred. "Unlawful bondage" cannot be justified and must, by necessity, lead to retaliation.

It is remarkable that Hopkins feels the need to explain the act of violence by a black man at all. The image of the brutal African American man obviously prompts her to justify an act that otherwise is unremarkable in a battle situation. To her credit, Hopkins does not shy away from using stereotypes, but she always adapts them to her own purposes, undermines their validity, and questions their trueness. In the character of Judah she reconciles both his savagery and his nobility, without posing them at opposite ends of the racial spectrum. Judah does not strike a heroic pose only, he is allowed to be both noble and savage at the same time. The complexity of his character is understood by the reader to be an inevitable result of his upbringing and past experiences.

Judah, standing on the cliffside, ponders "queries and propositions and possibilities" (418). The thought of freedom, the thought that he paid back the cruelties inflicted on his body and soul, fills him with exhilaration. One must add that John Brown and Parson Steward both witness this scene and do not restrain him. They even cheer him loudly, rejoicing over winning the battle and Judah's act of retribution.

Shortly afterward, Judah is drawn to the sight of the fallen man and finds Winona at the side of the severely wounded and dying man. This final showdown between Winona and Judah clarifies their positions. Judah wants to shoot the man, but Winona, in the name of Christian mercy, keeps him back. In this scene, the gentle and compassionate nature of the woman is set against the harsher male nature. The outcome is a battle of the sexes as much as a battle between dark black and lighter black. Winona catches the "ferocious light that still glimmered in his eyes" and argues with him for the life of Thomson. Judah defends himself: "He is the hater of my race. He is of those who enslave both body and soul and damn us with ignorance and vice and take our manhood" (422). The indictment of the southern slaveholder opens the much more general question of how to cope with national guilt and wrong. The answer given in *Winona* is that retribution by the wronged can only be prevented when people like Winona are guided well and instructed in Christian mercy. It turns out that the justification of Judah's restraint also lies in Thomson's deathbed confession and his atonement. This development of the plot is only one aspect of the great moral question, however. As regards the relationship between Judah and Winona, Judah is clearly seen as too fierce and savage for her civilized and refined mind and manners.

There are two discourses going on at the same time, one about the nature of manhood and manliness, the other about the so-called innate nature of the Negro, which is usually taken to be animalistic. Both discourses, as Bederman has shown, depend upon each other. Writing about the educational theories of G. Stanley Hall, Bederman links the temporary and necessary acts of savagery of a young boy to his later development into full manhood. On the level of nation-building, the white race can only become superior when these acts of savagery are encouraged: "Civilized, manly man had achieved his self-restrained evolutionary eminence precisely because, in the past, he had shown his capacity for savage, passionate, violent masculinity" (116). The argument does not apply to the young male of any other color, because black children as adolescents "stopped developing, because their ancestors had never gone on to evolve a higher intelligence" (93). For this reason, Warren's uncontrolled passion serves him as a necessary act of growing up, in order to overcome these instincts and develop true superiority, while Judah's emotion only reinforces the savagery already inherent in him as a black man and hinders the development of higher capacities.

At the same time that Bill Thomson lies dying in the tent, John Brown gives orders to shoot the captured rangers. This highly important killing does not need any extra justification in the novel. It is seen as part of the "holy war" (419), the decisive battle between "Right and Wrong." So how can John Brown and the Parson justify this killing while Judah must be kept back from committing the same deed? Although Ebenezer Maybee joins John Brown out of a spirit of rightful antislavery sentiment and the thrill of the adventure that this campaign promises, Parson Steward's fighting spirit results from the Old Testament concept of an eye for an eye. Yet it is a "kin' o' rough

jestice fer a parson" (350), as Maybee says. Parson Steward justifies himself
with the biblical mandate that the unbelieving must be thrown out of the
temple. When some ruffians threaten to disrupt his Sunday service, he tells
the listeners: "I girded up my loins and taking a pistol in each hand, I led forth
my elders and members against the Philistines." The fact that later he is shot
at, left for dead, and then nursed back to health is more than sufficient proof
that God looks upon their cause benevolently. "Oppression is oppression"
is the Parson's answer to the doubting mind (351). Any kind of oppression
must be abolished, be it slavery or the denial of one's civil liberties. The actual
battle scene is, therefore, the battle between right and wrong, the Christian
soldier versus the barbarian intruder. "Like the old Spartans who braided
their hair and advanced with songs and dancing to meet the enemy, the
anti-slavery men advanced singing hymns and praising God" (412).

Hopkins clearly tries to justify the act of John Brown, which was not
met with much public acclaim at the time. For her, John Brown became a
decidedly heroic figure even before his attack on Harper's Ferry. She certainly
knew Frank Sanborn's The Life and Letters of John Brown, Liberator of Kansas,
and Martyr of Virginia (1885) and shared his admiration for this historical
fighter for the causes of antislavery.[2] She also relied upon George Washington
Williams's assessment of the importance of John Brown in his History of the
Negro Race. In 1883, not even a generation removed from "Bleeding Kansas,"
Williams praises John Brown's active fight against slavery that did not restrict
itself to mere oratory. At Osawatomie, Williams argues, Brown "denounced
slavery as the curse of the ages; affirmed the manhood of the slave; dealt
'middle men' terrible blows; and said he 'could see no use in talking' " (215).
His rhetoric reminds us of the justification of violence used by John Brown
in Winona: "His ideas of duty were far different; the slaves, in his eyes, were
prisoners of war; their tyrants, as he held, had taken up the sword, and
must perish by it." Hopkins certainly shared Williams's judgment of John
Brown: "John Brown is rapidly settling down to his proper place in history,
and 'the madman' has been transformed into a 'saint.' When Brown struck
his first blow for freedom, at the head of his little band of liberators, it was
the almost universal judgment of both Americans and foreigners that he was
a 'fanatic.' . . . But many of the most important and historically trustwor-
thy truths bearing upon the motive, object, and import of that 'bold move,'
have been hidden from the public view, either by prejudice or fear" (222).
John Brown's death by hanging is seen as martyrdom. Judah's heroic fight,
in contrast, risks being judged as the outcome of base instincts and a primitive legacy. Hopkins thus writes about double standards in the evaluation

of heroism that also anger her when she discusses, for example, the heroic feats of Toussaint L'Ouverture or Robert Morris. She clearly sees Judah as the example in her fiction of the noble Negroes who are "tongues of living flame speaking in the powerful silence of example, and sent to baptize the race with heaven's holy fire into the noble heritage of perfected manhood" ("Robert Morris" 337). Judah eventually leaves the United States with Winona and Warren Maxwell. In England he reaps the benefits of his boldness when he enters the service of the queen: "His daring bravery and matchless courage brought its own reward; he was knighted; had honors and wealth heaped upon him, and finally married into one of the best families of the realm" (435).

In contrast to Judah, Warren Maxwell, his foil and rival for the love of Winona, needs more manly courage and rage. An English aristocrat, Maxwell undertakes the most improbable adventures in any of Hopkins's fiction. He is the fourth son of a noble family and has taken up the law in order to finance his own life. His "frank, good-looking boyish face and honest, manly bearing" identify him as the conventional hero who will rescue the heroine after numerous adventures (342). But the contradiction in this description between the "boyish" face and his "manly" bearing speaks of a deeper dichotomy in his nature. At the beginning he is naïve and ignorant. After White Eagle's death, he wants to do some good and take care of Winona and Judah regardless of the fact that they are "only niggers and Injuns" (303). Real manhood must be earned through endurance, however. Warren's fate at the hands of Bill Thomson's gang may seem much too exaggerated and improbable. After all, he is already near the point of being literally set afire when Colonel Titus rescues him, subjects him to a pro forma trial, and has him sent to prison for a year before he is to be hanged. But his escape from the stake is not more far-fetched than other white men's near killing in Indian camps. In African American fiction, his fate is even surpassed in a work such as *Imperium in Imperio* (1899), by Sutton E. Griggs, in which one of the two heroes disguises himself as a colored maid and works in a white household, is shot at, nearly hanged, and just barely escapes being slashed up. The hairbreadth escapes must be seen as concessions to the reading public and, secondarily, as devices that enhance the inherent nobility and power of endurance of the heroes.

Warren's observations when he suffers his own near-burning give the intrusive narrator the occasion to expose the lynch mob as the brutal beast it really is: "It was not the voices of human beings, but more like the cries of wild animals, the screaming of enraged hyenas, the snarling of tigers, the angry, inarticulate cries of thousands of wild beasts in infuriated pursuit of their prey, yet with a something in it more sinister and blood curdling, for they were men, and added a human ferocity" (367). The phrase "for they were men" plainly denounces the claim to humanity of the white man who is capable of such barbarous action and thus inverts the stereotype of the ferocious nature of the Negro. His feeling of pity for the infants who are brought to witness the torture reminds contemporary readers of later stories about lynching, especially the famous "Going to Meet the Man" by James Baldwin, which depicts the harm done to a child's mind through the witnessing of such a scene.

Implicitly, Warren's denial of humanity to white people of the American South challenges the great foundational myth of the United States, such as propagated in the ten-volume *History of the United States* that George Bancroft wrote between 1834 and 1876. This history reflected the great American epic, the discovery and settlement of a new world, which was nearly empty, and the struggle against the wilderness and subsequent creation of a nation. It celebrated the victory of liberty-loving peoples over authoritarianism, the United States becoming the model state to which all civilizations should aspire.[3] As an outsider, Warren's view of the institution of slavery in the United States allows for a harsh condemnation of its barbarism, cruelty, and injustice. Intolerance, class discrimination, and decadence are usually associated with the old-world experience, but in *Winona* they are assigned to the American South. As a prisoner, Warren fears that he must live in a hostile country instead of in the America that is "supposed to advocate and champion the most advanced ideas of liberty and human rights" (381).

Warren's experiences in the prison where his cell is connected by a small hole with a lockup for slaves lead the narrator to declare: "Unhappily we tell no tale of fiction. We have long felt that the mere arm of restraint is but a temporary expedient for the remedy, but not the prevention, of cruelty and crime. If Christianity, Mohammedanism, or even Buddhism, did exercise the gentle and humanizing influence that is claimed for them, these horrors would cease now that actual slavery has been banished from our land; because, as religion is the most universal and potent source of influence upon a nation's action, so it must mould to some extent its general characteristics and individual opinions" (385). This long aside draws a parallel between the system of slavery and the system of discrimination and oppression at the time of the writing of this story. As in *Contending Forces* and *Hagar's Daughter*, Hopkins strongly believes that the lesson of history must be learned so that future wars can be prevented. Although Hopkins does not openly criticize the present government for the deterioration of race relations and the church for its lack of influence, she does so indirectly. Claudia Tate calls this strategy of hers "discursive displacements" (*Domestic Allegories* 200). For Hopkins and many of her contemporaries, slavery is not a school that educates its pupils (i.e., slaves) to full responsibility, nor is the church the great beneficial power that brings enlightenment to the former African heathen. But given the power of Washingtonian philosophy and the influence of church leaders, it is safer for her to concentrate on a real historical figure and battle than to write more openly about the present time. Discursive displacement is, therefore, a very useful term for describing Hopkins's writing strategy, which invests an existing story with a second meaning not explicitly stated but well understood by her contemporary readers. Along the lines of my discussion concerning melodrama, coincidence, and the sentimental mode in my earlier chapter about *Hagar's Daughter*, it becomes obvious that Hopkins makes use of existing modes and generic conventions and subverts them to prove the existence of a moral universe (P. Brooks 20), introduce the social context (Gillman, "The Mulatto" 224), and have the weak triumph over the powerful (Linda Williams 43).

Warren compares himself to Christ, and this experience teaches him a deeper understanding of the nature of Christianity than all his previous religious training. He is depicted as the figure of the Christian martyr that Jerry Bryant finds in earlier heroes of African American fiction (57–69), with the decisive difference that he is white and does not have to die in the end.[4] Even in the eyes of Judah, who carries him out of the prison after his long sickness, he has gained some respect. "He felt all his passionate jealousy die a sudden death as pity and compassion stirred his heart for the sufferings of his rival" (396). Warren gains manhood and earns respect through these hard experiences. His firsthand view of the dark side of slavery motivates his later fight, and he is now allowed uncontrollable rage: "At last he had caught the full spirit of the fiercest; the blood mounted to his brain, and with ungovernable rage, thinking only of the sufferings he had endured in the dreadful time of imprisonment, he continued his rain of blows upon his prostrate foe until the very limpness of the inert body beneath him stayed his hand" (412). In contrast to Judah, there is no justification needed for his destructive force. "Ungovernable rage" is a sign of his manhood that becomes him well. Hopkins's decision to assign the type of Christian martyr turned heroic warrior to a white man shows her evaluation of this role. Warren Maxwell's potential for endurance, his willingness to understand the mechanism of racism, and his sometimes naïve belief in a perfect world cannot be repeated in any of the black male characters. African Americans have endured far too long, they have learned about the mechanism of racism through hard experience, and they cannot be naïve about a perfect world for all races.

At the same time, Hopkins could not possibly show and openly approve of an act of physical violence of a black man against a white man. She was forced to negotiate her way between the two opposing depictions of violence as coming from men of different races. Although it is known that Hopkins thought about the subject of *Winona* in the early part of her career in the 1890s, the serial was finally published from May to October 1902. This date coincides with the publication date of Thomas Dixon's *The Leopard's Spots*, one of his racist novels instigating race prejudice and strife.[5] It is conceivable that she meant it to be a corrective to the overbearing depiction of the primitive and savage nature of the Negro propagated in this novel. The characters of John Brown and his followers and the forbearing and liberal character of Warren Maxwell were certainly meant to provide role models that white American men were to emulate.

Considerations of manliness also pervade much of Hopkins's other writing. In her novels, Judah is the only noble and brave African American of dark complexion who is allowed center stage. Only Madison Washington, whose role in "A Dash for Liberty" will be discussed later, and Luke Sawyer in *Contending Forces*, are similarly dark and brave characters. Luke is described as a very dark man "of majestic frame, rugged physique and immense muscular development." He is definitely a heroic figure: "His face was kindly, but withal bore the marks of superior intelligence, shrewdness and great strength of character. He might have been a Cromwell, a Robespierre, a Lincoln. Men of his physiological development—when white—mould humanity, and leave their own characteristics engraved upon the pages of the history of their times" (255). He is, however, not the same type of warrior as Judah and Madison Washington because he is never given the chance to defend his rights with a weapon in his hands. He is the faithful servant of the Beaubean family, the son of a proud black businessman, and the victim himself of a violent disruption of both the Beaubean and the Sawyer families. His role is that of recorder of the past and missing link between two periods of time.

Most white male characters in Hopkins's fiction are subjected to the test of manhood by way of examining their positions on the race problem. Although Warren Maxwell in *Winona*, for example, passes the test bravely, Cuthbert Sumner, St. Clair Enson, and, to some extent, Ellis Enson in *Hagar's*

Daughter fail. Compared to the heroic set of white men in *Winona*, most white characters in *Hagar's Daughter* are not allowed heroic status. In contrast to the sympathetic portrayal of John Brown and Warren Maxwell, in *Hagar's Daughter* Hopkins included only the redeeming figure of the western hero, Zenas Bowen, whereas General Benson, Major Madison, Detective Henson, and Cuthbert Sumner confront various personalities of post-Reconstruction politics and rich Washington society. None of them is a real hero figure, manly, selfless, courageous, and tolerant, whose behavior and thoughts would enlist all the reader's sympathy. Her decision to thus portray these white men may easily be taken as Hopkins's decision to prove that a white man has no more potential to be heroic than a black man.

Zenas Bowen is presented as the shrewd but honest self-made westerner whose career began as a mate on a Mississippi steamboat. He joined the Federal forces and fought bravely. After the war he invested in mining property and became fabulously rich. In appearance he is described as of middle height, lank, and graceless: "He had the hair and skin of an Indian, but his eyes were a shrewd and steely gray, wherein one saw the spirit of the man of the world, experienced in business and having that courage, when aroused, which is common to genial men of deadly disposition" (80). He is the only character in Hopkins's fiction who is described as slightly dark without the later revelation that he has black ancestry. His origin as a self-made western man, a well-known type in the literature at this time, allows the combination of a weatherbeaten and swarthy exterior with the stamina of a western hero. He loves his family and is described as possessing a "strong intellect and staunch integrity" (275). His only fault turns out to be some gambling. But even if Zenas Bowen proved himself to be an exceptionally tolerant and loving husband to his wife, about whose past he knew practically nothing, he never had to stand the test of real manhood. He never had to learn that his beloved daughter Jewel and his wife were colored.

General Benson has not lost any of his social charm since the reader last met him as St. Clair Enson. He has a "lavish expenditure and luxurious style of living at Willard's Hotel" (93). His charming voice still pleases the women and makes him a favorite in society. As head of a department in the treasury, he has access to the best part of Washington society. When he meets Hagar as the wife of Senator Bowen, he seems to recognize her, but apparently, although Estelle/Hagar has grown whiter, she cannot immediately place him as her former husband's evil brother. Although this scene may be taken as an example of plot inconsistency, it shows that the corrupt, evil, and mean trait in him is intuitively felt by Estelle/Hagar and even young Jewel, who asks herself why she should "shrink from him with a loathing she could not repress" (139).

Major Henry Clay Madison, president of the Arrow-Head Mining Company of Colorado, is described as "short, stout, more than fifty, with gray hair and ferret-like eyes, close-set, and a greenish-gray of peculiar ugliness" (95). The former slave trader with the infamous name of Walker has assumed names reminiscent of Henry Clay (1777–1852), a statesman famous for supporting federal financing of internal improvements in the opening of the West and as the "Great Compromiser" in the nullification crisis,[6] and of James Madison, one of the Founding Fathers of the republic and instrumental in the drafting of the Bill of Rights, Jefferson's secretary of state, and president from 1809 to 1817. Both were slaveholders, a fact in which Hopkins might have found sufficient justification to assign their names to one of the arch-villains of her novel.

Henson appears on the stage only much later in the novel. He is "a well-preserved man of sixty odd years, middle height, and rather broad, but not fleshy. His thick iron-gray hair covered his head fully and curled in masses over a broad forehead" (187). His expressive eyes and pleasant face are marred by a long scar that crosses his face diagonally and thus serves as a sign of recognition for the reader. He is the chief of the secret service and has earned fame as detective. He gains the redeeming quality of wisdom earned through years of suffering and pain. His profession as a detective also signals his capacity for insight, however late it might come.

Hopkins uses all her white male characters to criticize society. Except for Zenas Bowen, they are not manly men. What *Hagar's Daughter* shows more than the other novels is that manhood cannot be a race-neutral term. Assigning manhood and heroism to an African American man, the race question naturally forms an integral part of his personality. But by also applying it to the characterization of white men, Hopkins demonstrates that men can only be manly and heroic when their attitudes toward nonwhite people are liberal, based on mutual understanding and tolerance. The question then arises: What is needed to turn a white man into some sort of manly man? This is not the main concern in Hopkins's writing, but an interesting answer is given in *Of One Blood* with the character of Charlie Vance.

In this novel, it is not only Reuel who will profit from his voyage into the heart of Africa. In *The Africa That Never Was*, Hammond and Jablow argue that in his Indian stories "Kipling developed the idea that the colonies were the most admirable school for character building of young Englishmen" and that the heroes of the popular colonial novels of such writers as John Buchan or Henry Rider Haggard "all emerge from their African ordeals strengthened and ennobled, ready to face the responsibilities of manhood" (103).[7] Without a doubt, Reuel can be used to prove this point. This character-building force of experience under hardship is also obvious in Charlie Vance, one of the minor characters in *Of One Blood*, the happy-go-lucky, carefree, joking, and extremely good-looking brother of Aubrey Livingston's fiancée, Molly. As a tourist, the rich, young, and very typical American youth accompanies the expedition "for the sake of the advantages of such a trip" (498), and he soon becomes Reuel's best friend. He takes the traditional tour that usually leads the young English or American gentleman to the European continent in order to round off his education. Here this effect is achieved in Africa, the continent that was rarely acknowledged in literature as suitable for this purpose.

Far away from home, "Adonis" Charlie Vance retains a lot of his American lifestyle, opinion, and prejudices. When Professor Stone tells them about the ancient African civilization in Ethiopia, Charlie cries out, "You don't mean to tell me that all this was done by *niggers*?" (532). Later he is dumbstruck at these novel ideas about the order of history: "He had suffered so many shocks from the shattering of cherished idols since entering the country of mysteries that the power of expression had left him" (534). In this sense, Charlie Vance, a partly comic figure, reflects the naïve American's perplexity in the face of new facts and revolutionary ideas.

Charlie changes, however, after he hears about his sister's death by drowning and Dianthe's supposed death. After Reuel has disappeared, Charlie is determined to find him and turns into a "serious-minded man of taciturn disposition" (580). He is "learning many needed lessons in bitterness of spirit out in these African wilds" (581). After he and Jim Titus have been captured by representatives of the Cushite civilization, and when he, as a representative white American, is accused of the bad treatment of black people in America, he begins to feel a touch of embarrassment about the racial situation at home. John Gruesser sees his stammering response to the provoking questions of the Cushite dignitary Ai as "one of the novel's most memorable moments" ("Hopkins' *Of One Blood*" 77).

His time as a prisoner teaches him a firmness and responsibility of mind he had not known before. He and Jim Titus manage to flee and happen to discover the treasures that were the goal of the expedition. The sight of the precious stones, however, does not bring happiness. They are without value in this non-American surrounding. He finally realizes that he and the black servant are closely bound to each other: "Where was the color line now? Jim was a brother; the nearness of their desolation in this uncanny land, left nothing but a feeling of brotherhood" (590). In a way, he finds the answer to the question about social equality that Judah had asked himself in *Winona*. Although Hopkins knew that at her time real social equality, "the affinity of souls, congenial spirits, and good fellowship" among people regardless of race and class was utopian (*Winona* 377), she still envisioned it as an ideal. It is her way of writing against the real barriers cemented by Jim Crow laws and regulations.

Charlie Vance thus reflects Pauline Hopkins's vision that, removed from the narrow confines of American society and seen from a distance, the typical American youth will realize the irrelevance of racial distinction and that only race tolerance turns an average youth into a manly man. In contrast to him, Cuthbert Sumner never reaches this state because he never leaves the United States. This vision may have been Hopkins's motivation when she set her fourth novel in the heart of Africa, choosing as its hero a mulatto passing for white who undergoes a profound pan-African experience that proves his manliness and the high order of African American civilization.

"Of One Blood" and
the Future African American

*O*f *One Blood* (1902–3) is the only one of the four novels by Pauline
Hopkins that features a mixed-race male character who passes
for white. It is the only novel by Hopkins and one of the few African
American novels of the period that combine an American with an African
setting. The guiding thought of this chapter, therefore, is movement and
transition in various forms. In *Contending Forces*, there is movement in time
and space between the Bermuda of the late eighteenth and the Boston of the
early twentieth centuries. *Hagar's Daughter* is dominated by metaphorical
transition, the passing between black and white identities, and the movement
in time from the beginning of the Civil War to the Washington of the 1880s.
In *Winona*, the transition is from freedom into slavery and back into freedom,
with all the changes of identity and self-understanding this involves, and the
movement in space from Canada to the slaveholding South, to Kentucky,
back to the Canadian border, with a final reference to England. *Of One Blood*
includes even more transitions, physical ones from the United States to Africa
and back again, and psychological ones affecting the passing of identities,
the search for knowledge and enlightenment. It also contains a temporal
and spatial movement into a utopian realm and the mythic African past,
which includes the central dichotomy of the novel between this past and the
realistic African present. Although much of the action takes place in Africa, it
is really about America, another example of Hopkins's strategy of discursive
displacement referred to earlier (Tate, *Domestic Allegories* 200).

Reuel Briggs, the protagonist, is depicted as possessing the moral and
intellectual capacity to fulfill the function of the ideal American race leader,
intelligent, courageous, brave, and manly. He chooses to pass for white in
order to gain a good education and leaves America for Africa because of
financial reasons. Some of his movements and some of his attitudes are pervaded by ambiguities that make his portrayal realistic and credible. In the

following discussion, his movements between America and Africa structure my analysis.

The first part of the novel, set in Boston, is introduced with a view of the student of medicine, Reuel Briggs, in his bare and desolate study room. Reuel is in despair and thinks of suicide. He has studied too long and too hard, his room is cold, and his mood is aggravated by his having read a book about spiritual phenomena called *The Unclassified Residuum*. The readers who have pursued Hopkins's career at the *Colored American Magazine* will have been reminded of the opening of her very first short story in the first issue of the magazine, "The Mystery Within Us," which presents a similar situation. The study of spiritual phenomena leads Reuel to consider some lines in this book taken from William James's essay "The Hidden Self," an essay that obviously influenced Hopkins. Reuel, her protagonist, quotes from the book: "The phenomena are there, lying broadcast over the surface of history" (442). It is said that these were words of haunting significance: "No matter where you open its pages, you find things recorded under the name of divinations, inspirations, demoniacal possessions, apparitions, trances, ecstasies, miraculous healing and productions of disease, and occult powers possessed by peculiar individuals over persons and things in their neighborhood" (442–43). Over the course of the novel, all these phenomena will be seen to come true in connection with one or another of the three protagonists. Reuel has "the power" (443), as he says here, which includes the power to awake the seemingly dead from their stupor. Dianthe Luske, his female counterpart, reveals the faculty of clairvoyance, trances, ecstasies, and miraculous healing and is made subject to someone else's demoniacal will. Aubrey Livingston clearly possesses the powers of a demon; he is the evil force whose knowledge serves egoistical purposes rather than love and art (Dianthe) or selfless exploitation of scientific facts (Reuel). All the evidence is there; it takes an open mind, intelligence, perseverance, and obstinacy to unearth it. Thomas J. Otten calls his article about *Of One Blood* "Pauline Hopkins and the Hidden Self of Race" because, he argues, race and mind must be seen as "each other's doubles" (229). He concludes from his analysis of the text in combination with the William James articles that "race is here construed as an interior element, as a secret buried within the personality, as a 'submerged' side of the self: in James's terms, an aspect of the self that is 'fully conscious' yet sealed off from normal consciousness, that preserves and represses memories of guilt and trauma." It makes sense to accept Otten's conclusive arguments for this novel, which features a virtual journey into an underground ideal state, and to see it as a metaphorical exploration of the racial self.

Read from the perspective of Pauline Hopkins, the novel sheds new light on the philosophical thoughts of William James. It must be seen that the sentence which fascinates Reuel—"Phenomena unclassifiable within the system are therefore paradoxical absurdities, and must be held untrue" (James 247)—had a special meaning for a writer who most probably saw herself as not classifiable within a system. It can be imagined that she wanted to prove with her hero Reuel that paradoxical absurdities—read black intellectuals—did exist and that she had a mission for Africa and America. Reuel, the guiding spiritual leader in the Harvard hospital and of the expedition, and Hopkins, the imaginative writer, are really one and the same. They both discover hidden treasures, decipher concealed messages, and read the chart that leads to them. The hidden self that William James identifies as the supernatural is, for them, racial. After Dianthe, for example, discovers that Reuel and Aubrey are her siblings, there is a comment from the narrator: "The slogan of the hour is 'Keep the Negro down!' but who is clear enough in vision to decide who hath black blood and who hath it not? Can any one tell? No, not one; for in His own mysterious way He has united the white race and the black race in this new continent" (607). The concealed part of the American identity is racial. Reuel, more than any other protagonist in the Hopkins canon, tries to overcome race as a limitation upon his possibilities. His longing and his dream vision at the beginning of the novel include the idea that he will conquer "by strength of brain and will-power" (445); race, however, is not part of this vision. But as soon as he has "the lovely vision of Venus" (446), the view of a beautiful woman who appears to him and later materializes as Dianthe, it is clear that there is something missing in him, that his hidden self includes an awareness of his racial family.

Reuel Briggs is acknowledged by his friends as "a genius in his scientific studies" (444); his origin is thought to be either Italian or Japanese. In outward appearance, Briggs is blessed with "superior physical endowments," which include "the vast breadth of shoulder, the strong throat that upheld a plain face, the long limbs, the sinewy hands," an athlete's head "covered with an abundance of black hair, straight and closely cut, thick and smooth," and an aristocratic nose "although nearly spoiled by broad nostrils" (443). And, possibly to alert the reader to his racial background, his skin is described as white "but of a tint suggesting olive, an almost sallow color which is a mark of strong, melancholic temperaments" (444). Reuel Briggs is clearly meant to engage the reader's sympathy. His Grecian type of beauty foreshadows the later description of the Cushite Queen Candace and points to the theory that the Egyptian and later the Greek civilization grew out of the Ethiopian negroid civilization around Meroe from the Cushite reign.[1] As in earlier descriptions of heroes and heroines in Hopkins, outward appearance reflects inner virtue and history in general. The intent of this description is to establish him as a strong personality, a natural leader of men. In most respects, Reuel Briggs moves around with the freedom of the average white man; he has been trained in a scientific world dominated by white men and has appropriated the bearing and worldview of a white man. At the same time, it is also obvious that his double heritage will provide the novel with a basis for conflict and dramatic action.

For a long time in African American history, the term *black intellectual* was considered an oxymoron, a contradiction in terms because African Americans were usually assigned minor intellectual capacities. In his conclusive study *Color and Culture: Black Writers and the Making of the Modern Intellectual*, Ross Posnock analyzes the inherent ambiguity of the character that Hopkins invents: "What Hopkins's opening tableau suggests, then, is that *black intellectual*, legislated by science as outside the realm of normal existence, is an alien life form. Thus to represent such 'absurdities' is to create science fiction fantasy" (65). To Posnock, Reuel Briggs is the black intellectual, a "hero who is a composite, and not only racially" (67). Like William James, whose work he is reading, Briggs is a "charismatic Harvard scholar whose fondness for the wayward and the marginal cuts against the grain of scientific orthodoxy," and like W.E.B. Du Bois, he is "a Harvard-educated 'Afro-American' [Hopkins's phrase] genius who, in theorizing about double consciousness, wishes neither his American nor his African self to be lost." Again, in the context of Hopkins's life, the likeness between Reuel and Du Bois is an indirect criticism of the position of Booker T. Washington in his aversion toward the higher education of African Americans.

Reuel Briggs has taken the decision to pass for white in order to benefit from the better educational advantages the nation offers. While the narrative point of view is remarkably free from obviously criticizing him for this, some critics see this implicitly as a sign of weakness and a lack of manliness. In the context of the "new psychology" that Reuel is interested in, Reuel can be seen, especially in his suicidal mood at the beginning of the novel, as suffering from neurasthenia, "that peculiarly American 'nervousness' that George M. Beard made famous in 1881" (Schrager 185), which became epidemic especially among middle-class and upper-class intellectuals. By applying the symptoms of this disease—nervous excitement, suicidal thoughts, a tendency to despair—to Reuel, critic Cynthia Schrager sees neurasthenia as "a trope for the situation of the African American who is 'passing' " and argues: "Reuel's 'horror' at the so-called 'Negro problem' and his characterization of himself as an 'unfortunate' link his morbid psychological state to his social condition as a black man passing as white" (188, 187). Although the argument that Reuel's act of passing shows his "moral bankruptcy" makes some sense from a late-twentieth-century perspective (Schrager 203 n.9), and although it is mentioned that Reuel is later made to feel ashamed of his passing, he cannot be seen as betraying his race. Despite some negative and weak aspects attached to the act of passing, Reuel's passing for white is not the main subject of the novel; he is seen as the Ethiopianist hero who will redeem his race by connecting it with its glorious past. Logically, therefore, the partly escapist and utopian ingredient of his experience in the hidden city of ancient Africa must be taken as a necessary step in the development of his identity as an African American. The vision of him as actively taking part in the shaping of Africa in the future must be seen as the final phase of his learning process, which leads him to assume the logical role of leadership as an educated African American.

Reuel Briggs discovers that "in the heart of Africa was a knowledge of science that all the wealth and learning of modern times could not emulate" (576); this statement surely stirred the interest of the late-nineteenth-century reader who was trained to regard Africa as uncivilized and savage. It was startling because it spoke of a racial pride that the average colored American was not then used to hearing. Although Africa was widely unknown in terms of personal experience, Africa as a literary topos was well known to most black Americans and much discussed.[2] British colonialists—who, as Dorothy Hammond and Alta Jablow argue in *The Africa That Never Was*, brought forth a "tidal wave of literary production" (76), including voluminous descriptions of flora, fauna, scenic wonders, numerous travelogues, and innumerable scientific and literary tales—provided information to a reading public interested in exotic surroundings, a reading public that certainly was not restricted to the European continent.

Africa, the "dark continent," was usually associated with the negative side of what Abdul R. JanMohamed calls the central trope of colonialist discourse, namely the "manichean allegory," which is "a field of diverse yet interchangeable oppositions between white and black, good and evil, superiority and inferiority, civilization and savagery, intelligence and emotion,

rationality and sensuality, self and Other, subject and object" (82). As a minority group, colored Americans were not at all exempt from sharing the
belief in this oppositional discourse. Quoting the Italian Marxist Antonio
Gramsci, Jackson Lears calls this period of American culture one of cultural
hegemony in which "dominant social groups maintain power not through
force alone but through sustaining their cultural hegemony—that is, winning
the 'spontaneous' loyalty of subordinate groups to a common set of values
and attitudes" (Lears xvii). Nancy Leys Stepan and Sander L. Gilman speak
of "internalization" as a strategy employed by minority groups to respond to
racist ideology. By "internalization," they refer to "the very profound psychological and social introjection of negative images and meanings contained in
the stereotypes, in the construction and understanding of one's self-identity"
(89). Reuel himself, when he travels to the inner city of his empire, feels
he is "at variance with the European idea respecting Central Africa, which
brands these regions as howling wildernesses or an uninhabitable country"
(565). The "singularly grand, romantically wild and picturesquely beautiful" scenery he discovers solicits his admiration and respect for the people
inhabiting it.

Hammond and Jablow claim that the colonists were attracted to life in
Africa because it "held out the possibilities of freedom of movement and a
general independence from the constraints of life in Great Britain" (78).[3] In
Hopkins's case, it must be added that it offered her narrator the freedom to
think a thought barely possible in the American context: that all races are
equal and that race distinctions are not traceable to behavior or innate values
and virtues. Africa as the archetypal "other" of the European and also the
American imperialist mind become in *Of One Blood* the place of encounter,
in a positive sense, with one's past. The Africa of the British explorers—
it is no coincidence that the archaeological expedition is led by Professor
Stone, a British scientist—the country of cannibals and savages, becomes
the cradle of civilization in which this early African American hero finds
his roots. Hopkins enwraps her central Christian argument—"Of one blood
have I made all races of men" (590)—in the formulaic garb of the adventure
story and the ghost story. This message is conveyed in a very conclusive,
convincing way to late-nineteenth-century readers used to plot intricacies,
supernatural occurrences, tales of adventure, love, and sentiment, and tales
about Africa, the "dark continent."

Reuel's admiration of the ancient African empire comes rather late in the
novel. When he lands in Tripoli, his and Charlie Vance's views are more
typical of the average American's attitude toward contemporary Africa. The

tenth chapter (out of a total of twenty-four)—or the fourth installment in the original serial novel—recounts the move of the archaeological expedition from America to Africa. Upon approaching Tripoli, Reuel views "a landscape strange in form," a portion of Africa "whose nudity is only covered by the fallow mantle of the desert," a view that leads him to the conclusion that "the race who dwelt here must be different from those of the rest of the world" (509). Seen through Reuel's eyes (his attitude is assumed to be identical with that of the rest of the party), the expedition's first view of Africa combines the average Anglo Saxon–American fascination with exotic surroundings and an awareness of difference in the form of an immediate remark pertaining to its "uncivilized" status:

> In the distance one could indeed make out upon the deep blue of the sky the profile of Djema el Gomgi, the great mosque on the shores of the Mediterranean. At a few cable lengths away the city smiles at them with all the fascination of a modern Cleopatra, circled with an oasis of palms studded with hundreds of domes and minarets. Against a sky of amethyst the city stands forth with a penetrating charm. It is the eternal enchantment of the cities of the Orient seen at a distance; but, alas! set foot within them, the illusion vanishes and disgust seizes you. Like beautiful bodies they have the appearance of life, but within the worm of decay and death eats ceaselessly. (509)

This first scene in Africa, from the deck of their transatlantic ship, on the eve of their first disembarkation, shows Reuel and Charlie Vance surveying the city from a distance, from an elevated position. At this moment they have no practical knowledge of the country at all; their only theoretical background is the famous exhibition of Egyptian relics by P. T. Barnum that toured the United States in the latter part of the nineteenth century (see Gillman, "Occult" 67), to which Charlie Vance refers. Mary Louise Pratt analyzes the typical moment in the approach of a party of explorers or travelers aboard a ship in which they see Africa for the first time. She calls this an instance of the "monarch-of-all-I-survey" (201), a kind of verbal painting producing "the peak moments at which geographical 'discoveries' were 'won'" for the home country. Similar to the traditional travel writing of the nineteenth century, such as Richard Burton's *Lake Regions of Central Africa* (1860), which Pratt uses as her example, Hopkins makes use of aestheticized landscape painting. The sight is seen as a painting with background and foreground; the great mosque in the background, domes and minarets and palms in the foreground. There is a rich density of meaning. The reference to the figure of Cleopatra with its allusion to cunning but "penetrating" charm; the juxtaposition of a view from a distance ("eternal enchantment") versus the view from inside ("the worm of decay and death"); the eternal enchantment versus the vanishing illusion—all these descriptive passages in *Of One Blood* characterize the view of Africa from a Western, decidedly Christian position, and foreshadow later comments about the non-Western state of civilization of modern Africa.

Reuel Briggs displays mastery over what he sees. He is in a position to evaluate and judge. He approaches the oriental city from the outside, from a ship that transports an expedition whose intent it is to explore ancient treasures. Exploring in this sense means locating and then possessing the treasures. The expedition is partly composed of businessmen, and it is later said that some of the treasures were transported back to England for display (540). Taking all this together, Reuel's position is that of explorer/conqueror; he is more American than African American. This can also be taken as a political position in which the author chooses to refute charges that Africa is the natural homeland of all African Americans. There is no difference in perspective between Reuel and Charlie Vance at this point in the narrative. This is the position that Reuel learns to revise when he later discovers his royal ancestry. It is part of the development of his character that he experiences shame at his initial attitude.

Their first encounter with Africa's people is with "a horde of dirty rascals" (511). This description conforms to JanMohamed's definition of colonialist literature as "an exploration and a representation of a world at the boundaries of 'civilization,' a world that has not (yet) been domesticated by European signification or codified in detail by its ideology" (83). So, while the group of explorers recoil at the jostling, noise, and general uproar, they are simultaneously drawn to the exotic scenario: "Under the Sultan's rule Tripoli has remained the capital of a truly barbaric state, virgin of improvements, with just enough dilapidated abandon, dirt and picturesqueness to make the delight of the artists. Arabs were everywhere; veiled women looked at the Christians with melting eyes above their wrappings" (512). The narrative then proceeds in the manner of a travelogue, with the expedition setting out across the desert: "The soft blue sky was cloudless, the caravan seemed to be the only living creature larger than a gazelle in the great solitude" (515). And the drivers' song reminded them of "Venetian gondoliers, possessing as it did the plaintive sweetness of the most exquisite European airs." The most impressive moment of this part of their journey is when Reuel Briggs strolls into a royal ruin and finds himself face to face with a leopard. It is a moment of high tension, of man versus wild beast, in which Reuel, in keeping with his description as a heroic character, ultimately wins, although he needs the help of his friend Charlie Vance. Structurally, this incident finds its counterpart in Reuel Briggs's even more heroic later encounter with a lion. It also serves to highlight the supernatural strength of his personality under peril.[4]

When the expedition finally reaches its destination, the island of Meroe, Charlie Vance, whose perspective is taken to stand for that of the rest of the expedition,[5] sees a "dirty Arab town" (526). He suffers from despair and a loss of heart when he is confronted with "a pile of old ruins that promised nothing of interest to him after all." This is what the "real" Africa is like: "the desolation of an African desert, and the companionship of human fossils and savage beasts of prey." It is significant that at exactly the moment when the expedition reaches its aim, Charlie, like the other men, is disappointed and does not feel the kind of elation he had expected. In a scene similar to that of his first view of Tripoli from aboard the ship, he once more looks at the landscape. Now his position is from inside a tent, but his glance is only very cursory: "Clouds of dust swept over the sandy plains; when they disappeared the heated air began its dance again, and he was glad to re-enter the tent and stretch himself at full length in his hammock." The gaze is averted because the sight is too overpowering for him to bear. Charlie clearly holds a view of Africa here that offers nothing for the future, no sign of a bustling, developing, or even progressive life: "It was a desolation that doubled desolateness, because his healthy American organization missed the march of progress attested by the sound of hammers on unfinished buildings that told of a busy future and cosy modern homeliness. Here there was no future. No railroads, no churches, no saloons, no schoolhouses to echo the voices of merry children, no promise of the life that produces within the range of his vision. Nothing but the monotony of past centuries dead and forgotten save by a few learned savants." No other description reflects in such a succinct way the novel's ambiguity. America represents progress, the future, modern life, industry, religion/Christianity, companionship, and education, while Africa lacks all these qualities. Sometime later, roaming around the ruins of the once beautiful Meroe, an ancient center of learning and the arts, the narrator muses: "Now, however, her schools are closed forever; not a vestige remaining. Of the houses of her philosophers, not a stone rests upon another; and where civilization and learning once reigned, ignorance and barbarism have reassumed their sway" (538).[6] Reuel later echoes this sentiment when he marvels at the beauty of the hidden part of the empire but bewails with "an American's practical common sense" this "waste of material" because access to this beauty is impeded through the stretches of desert (565).

A similar ambiguity lies in the description of the Indians and the frontiers-man in *Winona*. The Indians, as Ammons points out, behave in a stereotypical way: they glide around, move noiselessly, display stoicism, and profess advanced knowledge of plants and animals ("Afterword" 216). Winona is once even called "a pretty squaw" (*Winona* 375). As Ammons continues, "Drawing on stereotypes, positive and negative, Hopkins's novel is not about Indians. It is about Hopkins's fantasy of non-Western cultural affinity and solidarity among people of color on the North American continent" (217). In the same sense, one could conclude that *Of One Blood* is not about Africa as a real place on the contemporary map. Although Hopkins's view of it is well informed, it is the type of Africa that Hopkins and her set of characters imagine as useful for their agenda of correcting the view of African Americans as an inferior, good-for-nothing, ignorant people born to be enslaved. This is another example of discursive displacement, Hopkins's strategy to move action in time and space away from contemporary America in order to criticize prejudice and injustice.

After these rather typical remarks about the present-day situation of Africa, the focus of the novel, the display of the glorious African past, takes center position. Professor Stone, the British leader of the expedition, produces a mysterious chart that holds "the key to immense wealth" and the promise of finding a hidden treasure (528). The history of ancient Ethiopia that Professor Stone elaborates upon now replaces any concern for the present state of Africa. This part of the novel most closely resembles Hopkins's historical treatise, *A Primer of Facts*, with its references to the greatness of the Cushite civilization and Meroe, to biblical passages justifying this view, and to linguistic research. Hopkins's strategy here centers on the reversal of predominantly negative into positive images. The "cursed" sons of Ham, for example, become the "blessed" founders of an ancient empire (533). Although the discourse is still based on scientific notions prevalent at her time (see Stepan and Gilman 92), the science of racial distinctions is profoundly questioned in the end, and the potential of the African heritage for improving the status of the American Negro is emphasized.

The movement into the heart of Africa entails for Reuel a movement into his own self, intricately linked with his own racial awakening. The point of contact between himself and his past is the power of second sight. In his Cushite mentor Ai he finds this power developed to perfection. So it comes as no surprise that the one achievement that Reuel admires most in African civilization is the science of occultism. When he says that "in the heart of Africa was a knowledge of science that all the wealth and learning of modern times could not emulate" (576), "science" here means occultism, mesmerism, and supernatural powers. Although the nineteenth century developed a concept of science as "the dominant mode of cognition of industrial society," as "apolitical, nontheological, universal, empirical, and uniquely objective" (Stepan and Gilman 77), Hopkins's identification of supernaturalism with science was not at all extraordinary at the turn of the century, when "notions about clairvoyance, curative elixirs and mesmerism" circulated (Otten 237). The supernatural becomes the African heritage per se; it is the connecting link between the American present and the African past. As such it serves Hopkins as a positive reminder of the richness of African culture—a richness that when appropriated by an American colored man can imbue him with racial pride and lead to personal fulfillment. Otten argues that by writing these tales about supernatural occurrences, the writers "make available alternative strategies for thinking about bodies and minds"; they "widen the controlled ambiguities of racist discourse" and thus "perform a crucial sort of cultural work" (236). It must be added that supernaturalism here also serves the function of displacing scientific theories classifying races into superior and inferior ones with alternative ones that allow the main protagonist to combine his white exterior and his superior intellectual capacity with an African past. In this sense, the hidden city of Telassar, in which Reuel Briggs is confronted with his familial past and racial heritage, becomes the side of the American Negro hidden from public view. The voyage into the heart of Africa is used to reveal a splendid richness and superior intellect that make the Negro people the equal of white people.

In one of the central scenes, Reuel Briggs, the hero-scientist, is solemnly crowned King Ergamenes, thus fulfilling a prophecy that a king will come who "shall restore to the Ethiopian race its ancient glory" (547). The setting for the ceremony is one of splendor in a luxurious marble hall with fragrances, silken curtains, statues, sculptures, and colosses guarding it. Reuel's crown is "set with gems priceless in value," and the central gem is "the black diamond of Senechus's crown" (553).

Before this scene, when Reuel awakens from unconsciousness and tries to solve the mystery of why he was transported to this underground palace, he is, above all, bewildered at the beauty and luxury surrounding him. He is lying on "a couch composed of silken cushions, in a room of vast dimensions, formed of fluted columns of pure white marble upholding a domed ceiling where the light poured in through rose-colored glass in soft prismatic shades which gave a touch of fairyland to the scene" (545). The men surrounding him are dark in complexion, yet they "ranged in complexion from a creamy tint to purest ebony" and their faces are "perfect in the cut and outline of every feature," their forms are "Grecian in effect" and "athletic and beautifully moulded." Ai, the man he learns to respect as the prime minister of this people, is of "kingly countenance, combining force, sweetness and dignity in every feature" (546). Reuel recognizes in him a model leader: "The grace of a perfect life invested him like a royal robe." The luxurious and highly artistic surroundings and the noble and dignified people around him all speak of a view of Africa hitherto hidden from Reuel and his group of British and American explorers who have come to explore ancient treasures for mainly economic reasons. The men of various shades of color point to the utopian setting that is the goal of what Giulia Fabi calls Reuel's "race travel" (*Passing* 47).[7]

The solemn act of crowning is clearly designed with images that point to the utopian setting: the underground city, the mysterious entrance, the people who seem to emerge from an earlier time. It is the culmination in a development of the plot that has been hinting at Reuel's royal bearing from the beginning. When Reuel is instructed about the past history of the empire, the historical explanation for the downfall of the Cushite empire from past glory is given in the form of a recitative in the language of the Old Testament alluding to God's punishment of the overly materialistic and unbelieving people. The reference to the predominant financial goals of contemporary America cannot have been missed by the readers of the novel. This is certainly the main target of this part of the narrative. The materialism that is manifest in the novel—in the figure of Charlie Vance, for example, in the part of the expedition made up of businessmen interested only in the alleged treasure hunt, and in the haughty, sensual, and unbelieving character that caused the downfall of the ancient Cushite empire—finds its counterpart in the typical American. History repeats itself, as Hopkins says in her *Primer of Facts*. If this ancient and rich civilization had to succumb, then the modern but also corrupt American civilization can fall. The biblical example of God destroying the earth through the flood speaks of the fall of empires that may be repeated anytime.

In the novel's predominantly Christian argument, however, it is the African civilization that supposedly will benefit from the contact with America. "O Ergamenes, your belief shall be ours; we have no will but yours. Deign to teach your subjects" (563). This plea by Ai comes after he has explained to Reuel the governing principles of their state. In rudimentary form, Ai here presents an alternative ideology based upon strict social rules, an elaborate hierarchical social and political structure, and a belief in an Old Testament

"Supreme Being" (562). All this must be contrasted with the common view of Africans as childlike and primitive. Reuel is fascinated by Ai's explanations, but he immediately laments the lack of fundamental New Testament beliefs: "What of the Son of Man? Do you not know the necessity of belief in the Holy Trinity? Have not your Sages brought you the need of belief in God's Son?" (562–63). In this sense, Reuel is very much the colonizer/missionary who brings religion to the heathen race.

In correspondence to the dreamlike and visionary nature of Reuel's adventure, the emphasis of the Telassar sections is on atmosphere and a lush and luxurious civilization. It is here that Reuel finds elements of a flourishing life: fertile fields, vineyards, moving crowds, and great buildings, all of which stand in vivid contrast to the Africa he knew before.

Of One Blood offers a blending of nearly all of Hopkins's main thematic concerns: history; the roles of mixed-race men and women; the revelation of one's racial past, manliness, and heroism; and the future role of race leadership. The sphinx, which dominates the square through which Reuel was led before the crowning ceremony, bears the inscription that may stand as a motto for Hopkins's writing: "That which hath been, is now; and that which is to be, hath already been; and God requireth that which is past" (552). The past of ancient Africa and American slavery influences the present, foreshadows the future, and demands attention under the scrutiny of Christianity. At the same time, *Of One Blood* also invites the reader to ask questions about the future role of the African American race leader. In Reuel Briggs, Hopkins envisions an intellectual and manly African American hero, but she cannot paint an altogether flattering portrait; she also points out his shortcomings and the burdens he must carry.

One of Reuel's shortcomings is his paternalistic attitude toward women. Queen Candace is described as a classical beauty, so beautiful that she can appear only in an unrealistic setting. She is perfect in body and mind, serious, intelligent, and chaste—in short, the ideal representation of womanhood. In accordance with the novel's concept of male-centered civilization and the male-female power situation, on their first meeting, Queen Candace appropriately lowers herself to Reuel/Ergamenes: "Grave, tranquil and majestic, surrounded by her virgin guard, she advanced gracefully, bending her haughty head; then, gradually her sinuous body bent and swayed down, down, until she, too, had prostrated herself, and half-knelt, half-lay, upon the marble floor at Reuel's feet" (567–68). The relationship of power is instantly made clear: the beautiful, civilized African woman lowering herself to the powerful, nearly white African American man and explorer. But Hopkins is not content to rest with this obvious, too simplistic polarization. It will be a reciprocal relationship: Reuel will learn from this ancient civilization and will eventually find his ideal companion and "give to the world a dynasty of dark-skinned rulers" (570). In turn, he will teach the Cushite people about modern culture. Hopkins thus envisions a cross-cultural, pan-African, and cross-continental fertilization.

Before Reuel can delight in this ideal relationship, however, he is sent back home to solve the mystery of his family background and the fate of Dianthe. From the beginning of his relationship with her, he is seen as the dominating male who is fascinated by her beauty and sees himself in a position of shaping her identity. After Dianthe is reanimated from her deathlike rigor, Reuel decides to conceal her background as one of the stars of the Fisk Jubilee Singers, whose singing had fascinated audiences. With the consent of Aubrey Livingston, her identity is reconstructed as that of poor white Felice Adams, who had an accident and lost her memory. Several critics discuss the role of Dianthe as that of the artist who has lost her voice and has been denied artistic expression (Horvitz 252; Schrager 191; Kassanoff 171). These critics also question Reuel's ulterior motive in his efforts to shield Dianthe from her past: "I will give her life and love and wifehood and maternity and perfect health" (479). Although his concern for Dianthe is devoid of the malevolence that Aubrey shows her, he does not acknowledge her right to determine her fate herself.

When, in the absence of Reuel and thinking him dead, Dianthe/Felice recaptures her voice as a singer and with this her past, this moment of revelation shows clearly that the past, her real self, is always near her as a shadow. It is literally a double voice that is being heard when Felice starts to sing: "A weird contralto, veiled as it were, rising and falling upon every wave of the great soprano, and reaching the ear as from some strange distance. The singer sang on, her voice dropping sweet and low, the echo following it, and at the closing word, she fell back in a dead faint" (502). As before, Dianthe/Felice sings, "Go down, Moses, way down in Egypt's land, / Tell ol' Pharaoh, let my people go," a song that not only stands for the experience of the slave longing for freedom but can also be taken as a calling out to the absent husband, Reuel, to let him go from ancient Egypt in a literal sense. Dianthe/Felice is so overwhelmed by regaining her consciousness that she faints once more. When she wakes up again and finds herself in the menacing presence of Aubrey, who threatens to reveal her identity as an African American, she is rendered powerless once again. "In vain the girl sought to throw off the numbing influence of the man's presence. In desperation she tried to defy him, but she knew that she had lost her will-power and was but a puppet in the hands of this false friend" (504).

The predominant image of Dianthe as a victim at the hands of powerful men is only corrected after she has met old Aunt Hannah, a former slave renowned for her powers of voodooism and witchcraft. Aunt Hannah reveals to Dianthe her true origin as her granddaughter and the daughter of Mira. The name of Mira is first mentioned in a story that Aubrey tells a spellbound audience about his father evoking the power of clairvoyance in Mira, his slave mistress. Mira is sold after she tells her master's guests about the imminent danger of the Civil War that will leave all the women at the dinner table widows. Mira had three children by her former master: Dianthe, Reuel, and Aubrey. Aubrey was exchanged for the master's legitimate child and was raised as the white son and heir. Both of Dianthe's marriages are thus incestuous. More than that: Aunt Hannah also reveals that Mira was the daughter of old master Livingston and the mistress of his son. To all evidence, Mira had to be his half-sister, although this relationship is assumed rather than stated explicitly. For that reason, Reuel, Dianthe, and Aubrey are siblings as well as first cousins. As a critic says, "Here, the monogenist 'kinship' of all people engenders an incestuous nightmare. The shared blood of oppressor and oppressed breeds a generation of mulatto children who cannot recognize their siblings and thus, as Mary Dearborn observes, always risk violating the incest taboo" (Kassanoff 171).

Reuel's royal bearing, apparent, for example, in the role of leadership that comes natural to him, is derived from his direct descendance from Ethiopian royalty. His faculty of clairvoyance, however, comes from both sides of his inheritance: from Ethiopian royal powers and the mesmeric power of his father, Dr. Livingston, who frequently hypnotizes Mira. The African royalty in him singles him out from the average African American. But it is the American new-world experience of slavery that sets the drama rolling. Only one of the three siblings is excluded from the royal line. Aubrey's education as a white man makes him unsuitable for heroic or royal or more than average behavior. His cunning, his greed, his unlawful and ungovernable passion set him in line with the white father, the slave master, who discarded his slave wife when he married a white woman. The white part of his inheritance and his upbringing as a white southern gentleman have corrupted him and led to his cruelty.

After this revelation, Dianthe takes on a more active role. She prepares a poisonous drink for Aubrey, who forces her to drink it herself. For one short moment, the three siblings meet in a kind of family reunion that brings the melodramatic content to a conclusion. Dianthe has already taken the poison that is slowly killing her. She is only waiting for Reuel before she can die. "Strains of delicious music" announce him (614): "It was the welcome of ancient Ethiopia to her dying daughter of the royal line" (615). In a pathetic cross-cultural and cross-national scene, Dianthe hears the music of her African and European ancestors. It is clearly a moment destined to be of superior import that strikes the modern reader as beautifully ironic: "Welcome, great masters of the world's first birth! All hail, my royal ancestors—Candace, Semiramis, Dido, Solomon, David and the great kings of early days, and the great masters of the world of song. . . . O, let me kneel to thee! And to thee, Beethoven, Mozart, thou sons of song." Dianthe dies in the arms of Reuel, and Aubrey soon after takes his own life by drowning. The family reunion is not a happy one. Justice is done, but the great work of God cannot be judged: "Caste, prejudice, race pride, boundless wealth, scintillating intellects refined by all the arts of the intellectual world, are but puppets in His hand, for His promises stand, and He will prove His words, 'Of one blood have I made all races of men'" (621).

Of One Blood is dominated by the vision of a blooming, well-ordered, civilized African culture and society. Hopkins's central argument about the common and unifying bond between all human races allows her to criticize American racist tendencies, to express racial pride, and to call for a revision of history. By giving her African heroine the name of the historical Queen Candace, whereas her American, light-colored heroine must die, the novel hints at the life-giving force and future potential that Hopkins envisions in the heart of Africa.

There are controversial opinions about who is the ideal type of the African American race leader, and the scales would balance between Will Smith in *Contending Forces* and Reuel Briggs, the two characters in the two novels that most fully represent Hopkins's criticism of contemporary race relations. Will Smith, reunited with his beloved Sappho, leaves for England to work for an improvement of race conditions outside the United States. Reuel Briggs, in contrast, returns to Africa to guide his people into the future. It is implied that he might be the one prince of Ethiopia who will emerge and save the modern world. The work ahead of him is hard and demanding, and Reuel is described as being burdened with memories of the past and past sins. Although he looks into the future, he is not seen as shaping its course to his full satisfaction. At the end of *Of One Blood*, the narrator assumes the superior power of an almighty God who will solve the race problem over all questions of class, racial inheritance, materialism, and science. While this may seem an escapist longing on the part of Reuel Briggs upon his return to Africa, where he witnesses the slow conquest of the continent, it shows Reuel taking up an active role and working for his race in the continent of its origin.

Folk Characters and Dialect Writing

*I*n all of Hopkins's fiction, folk characters are an integral part of the world of her heroines and heroes. Hopkins clearly tries to reconcile her own and her characters' aspirations to middle-class respectability with a need to demonstrate race solidarity. Former slaves often form the connection between the earlier and later lives of the main characters; they are allowed humorous remarks; their life stories often speak of the thrift and expediency of their strategies for survival in a racist surrounding; their loyalty speaks of their positive moral abilities, while their evil ways usually reflect bad passions in their masters or employers. When a representation of them invokes the comic minstrel stereotypes that Hopkins was familiar with from her early stage career, they are never ridiculed or exploited as stereotypes only. Rather, they pass judgment on the manipulations of the white characters and condemn misbehavior in their own ranks.

The inclusion of a character such as Aunt Henny in *Hagar's Daughter* shows Hopkins's concern with African Americans of all colors and professions as likable and worthy characters in her fiction. When, in her preface to *Contending Forces*, she writes that "I have introduced enough of the exquisitely droll humor peculiar to the Negro (a work like this would not be complete without it) to give a bright touch to an otherwise gruesome subject" (16), she acknowledges the demands upon African American authors of her time to include comic relief and dialect writing, one of the most forceful traditions in American writing. The folk tales of George Washington Cable, Thomas Nelson Page, and Joel Chandler Harris found a large audience, and such African American writers as Paul Laurence Dunbar and Charles W. Chesnutt attracted more readers through their dialect than their nondialect writing. And Hopkins herself well knew from her past that comic scenes on the stage helped to establish a bond with her African American audience.

In an analysis of Charles Chesnutt's ambiguous attitude toward the use of dialect and folk characters in his fiction, Eric J. Sundquist points out the ambivalence between Chesnutt's "clear aspirations to middle-class professional respectability" and his occasional detachment "from the irrationality of conjure" (295). Chesnutt's attitude can be taken as representative of that of Hopkins and her generation of women writers. Sundquist says that the "black middle class often ignored or ridiculed the folk culture that survived in trickster stories and plantation tales, in minstrelsy, and on the black stage, or that was preserved in the spirituals and was beginning to flourish in jazz" (298). Therefore, dialect was never used by the characters destined to be heroes or heroines. Often they are portrayed as being interested in the tales of the folk characters, such as Sappho in *Contending Forces*, but they refuse to believe in superstition themselves. Theirs is an attitude of detached, benevolent observation, anxious to demonstrate the progress achieved through their superior education and culture. But given the fact that the African American middle class formed only a small percentage of the population and reading public, and adding to this the fact that most of the predominantly white readers expected certain stereotypes, authors like Hopkins felt obliged to include both sides, the African American middle class as their predominant concern as well as descriptions of comic characters. The tension, as Sundquist calls it, "between capitulation to stereotypes and the desire to find an audience for African American literature" affects the use of dialect and folk characters in Chesnutt's and Hopkins's fiction (304). As will be shown, however, Hopkins never compromised her sincere effort to portray them as likable, true-to-life, and even exemplary characters.

The implications of Chesnutt's writing, such as in his well-known story "The Wife of His Youth" (1899), as Sundquist sees it, are clearly "to join with the lower classes in the struggle for rights; to put the good of the community before the advances of the few who are able to enter directly into the white social and cultural mainstream; and to take control of the popular conceptions of 'the old plantation life' that are being generated by racist commentary and unscrupulous artistry" (300). At the same time, dialect, similar to black music, lent itself to a deliberate signification upon stereotypes and the liberation of a language dominated by the white masters (see Sundquist 304, 306). In this sense, black dialect can be seen as "both an assault on the authoritative diction of the master's language and a means of generating a secretive language in which linguistic and musical traces of African heritage survive" (323).

Bethany Johnson sees in dialect writing and the controversial critical debate about it a sign of the most contradictory issues of the time: "the tensions between protest and accommodation, racial solidarity and studied elitism, disavowal and celebration of the past, ridicule and empowerment, appropriation and reappropriation of cultural stereotypes, superficial acceptance and internal subversion" (65). By using the poetry of Silas X. Floyd, a contributor to the *Voice of the Negro*, Johnson traces his use of dialect back to the same tensions that informed Hopkins's writing: "The flexibility of the dialect format enabled African Americans to express contentious interpretations of the past within the paradigm of romanticization to promote social change and cultural criticism" (68). This is a very apt description of the literary agenda of Hopkins and her generation.

The opinions and studies of these critics demonstrate that in recent years the use of dialect in African American fiction has been reevaluated to include aspects of flexibility, social criticism, and style, all of which replace former charges against dialect writing as capitulation to stereotype. The many excellent studies by such scholars as Sundquist, Bethany Johnson, Martin J. Favor, and Gavin Jones, to name only a few, show this recent development in African American literary criticism.

Hagar's Daughter is set largely in the white society of Washington, D.C. Although a thrilling murder and detective story dominate the plot and determine its largely white setting, a group of colored characters plays an important role. Most former slaves have become servants. Although the white characters conceal their identities from each other, the colored characters remain the same and to a certain degree are aware of the white characters' disguises. Carby says that the colored characters "gained their own community space and no longer had to live in the midst of the white community that Hopkins created" (*Reconstructing* 149). Martha Johnson, Aunt Henny's daughter, is married to St. Clair Enson's/Benson's former slave Isaac, and they have two children: Oliver, who is still in school, and Venus, who gave up her desire to become a teacher in order to help Oliver through school. She is now Jewel Bowen's competent maid. Martha takes in washing to help pay the mortgage on their house, and Aunt Henny has a government job as cleaning woman in General Benson's department.

From the beginning Isaac is seen as St. Clair Enson's alter ego in devilry. His character exemplifies the movement from slavery to freedom, from dependency to responsibility, negotiating the difficult terrain between self-directed lives and persistent economic need. More than in any other character, the close relationship between master and slave, their mutual dependency, and their inextricable lives are brought to the fore. They were raised together and have more of a close relationship than the two brothers. When St. Clair loses Isaac at the gambling table, Isaac soon turns up again at Enson Hall. He is a reliable and trusted slave and later valet, even though the trust is based more in mischief and crime than in honorable deeds. After his marriage to Martha and their move to Washington, Isaac is not a very good husband and father and often does not bring home money to support the family. Isaac's loyalty to his former master remains extremely strong: "Lawse, de times me an' young massa had t'gedder, bar hunts, an' gamblin' 'bouts, an' shootin' and ridin'. He goin' so fas' I skacely cud keep up tuh him. We bin like brudders. All his clo's fits me *puffick*! Our size is jes' de same as ever" (177). There is never the insinuation that they were real half-brothers, but the idea of it cannot be denied. Like master like slave, Martha muses (174). The only instance in which Isaac openly disobeys his master is when he does not kill Aunt Henny, his own mother-in-law, after she witnessed St. Clair's murder of Elise Bradford. Isaac is, indeed, proud of his son and daughter and remains loyal to his family. In contrast to his master, he refrains from crime when it affects his own family. He is shiftless to a certain degree but not evil and mean.

Looking at the novel from both a late-nineteenth-century and a late-twentieth-century point of view, Kristina Brooks argues that Hopkins's early readers would "view her racially objectified characters within the context of the minstrel tradition," while late-twentieth-century readers would regard Hopkins's portrayals of what she calls a mammy, a buck, and a wench "as racial pornography, figures objectified and denigrated solely on the basis of their racial identity" (120). While I agree with Brooks that the minstrel tradition must be seen as a necessary background and that the black characters are objectified on the basis of their racial identity, I disagree with her conclusion that this leads to denigration. Isaac and his family are capable of development; cunning and tricksterism are his survival strategies so that he can contribute to the income of his family.

No doubt, Isaac is meant to represent a type character, the former slave badly influenced by his master, the partly dishonest, partly responsible later freedman still loyal to his former master. Another example of the servant doing his master's bidding is Jim Titus in *Of One Blood*. Once more, a servant is sent out to murder the man his master, Aubrey Livingston, considers his rival and enemy. Ironically, Jim Titus bears the same name as Colonel Titus, the plantation owner in *Winona*, a play on names that signifies that evil can take on many disguises and colors. Jim Titus partly fails in his attempts to involve Reuel Briggs in dangerous situations. When he dies in the underground vault of Telassar that conceals the treasure, he dies out of greed, but he repents his sins. He tells Reuel about Aubrey's evil schemes and reveals his knowledge about the fact that Aubrey, Reuel, and Dianthe are siblings. His reason for committing wrong is simple: "Aubrey Livingston was my foster brother, and I could deny him nothing" (593). Again, it is the infamous connection between an unprincipled master and a loyal slave that leads to the destruction and moral corruption of both.

In *Contending Forces*, there is another character exemplifying the move from slavery to freedom. Dr. Abraham Peters, a former slave, tells Sappho that he gained a rather prominent position when he was still a slave because he was said to possess the evil eye and has used this power to his own profit ever since. Similar to Chesnutt's Uncle Julius stories in *The Conjure Woman* (1899), Peters has learned to profit from a sort of superstition that fascinates white and black people alike. Superstition becomes intricately linked with religion. Peters sees no contradiction between his Christian belief and his power of magnifying. When he becomes janitor in a house of Christian Scientists, he has enough practical sense to combine the faith-cure and his own powers and to make good money out of them. His common sense tells him that the best faith-cure cannot work when it is an unreasonable cure that is demanded or, as he puts it, " 'cause we ain't got horse sense nuff to use *discreetion* in puttin' our faith on subjects that is approvin' to the Lord, an' will fit in with his own idees 'bout runnin' the business of the universe" (139). He also says, "Faith-cure won't operate on any man where it was *pre*ordinated that a *pre*tickler man was to die with a *pre*tickler complaint." Through his considerable common sense and by being able to profit from the white man's love for a good joke, he uses both his wit and ingenuity to make people respect him. The role of the trickster he assumes teaches the lesson of how a slave could survive slavery, how a poor man could win the heart of the beloved woman, and how an uneducated and poor worker could survive in the cold North.

In most of Hopkins's fiction, gender is negotiated along with class and race because most folk characters are women. In *Contending Forces*, the sewing-circle afternoon, the Colored League meeting, and the Canterbury Club dinner provide several prominent men and a few women with public voices that reflect the pressing debates of their time and impose a political tone on the love story. At some points in the story, it seems that the political message is predominant and that the love story only serves as the means to carry this message. This same feeling comes through in the parts of the novel where the various folk characters appear. There can be no doubt that these parts interested the contemporary reader at least as much as the love story and that the author put a lot of energy and care into the drawing of these characters and the development of their stories. While the political topics aim at the education of the readers, the folk sections aim at entertainment.

The stories told by and about Dr. Abraham Peters, Mrs. Ophelia Davis and Mrs. Sarah Ann White, the young reverend Mr. James, and Sister Mary Jane Robinson serve several purposes. They bring in the bright touch, representing the large part of colored society that is not well educated but ambitious, economical, and of simple nobility. These characters are not ridiculed, and the narrative voice usually remains nonjudgmental or gently ironic. They also treat the issues nearest the hearts of readers: job opportunities, color prejudice, public behavior, church politics, and matters of the colored women's club movement. In the overall concern of the novel, to cement "the bond of brotherhood among all classes and all complexions" (13), the lower-class types play an important role. "Uplifting the race" is not an empty slogan; when it is invested with concrete fates and characters, it is presented as a sensible and commendable project.

Two chapters of *Contending Forces* are devoted to the fair, a major social event of colored society. The income from the fair is destined to pay off the mortgage on the building of this most prominent Boston colored church, and each of the formidable churchwomen competes to bring in more money than the others. The two parties are headed by Mrs. Davis, who is associated with the organizer Ma Smith and Mrs. Willis, and by Sister Mary Jane Robinson, a former cook who is herself aspiring to some higher position in society after her husband had been left a legacy of five hundred dollars. Robinson is heard to voice prejudices against the other party, which she calls the colored four hundred, "them high-toned colored folks" (186). She accuses these "white-folksey colored ladies" of not having to work hard while her own "old-fashioned busy-bees" were cooks, servants, and laundry ladies (186, 195). The resentment of this group toward the better educated and more affluent part of society is quite bitter. Robinson, for example, holds it against their pastor that he married a light-colored woman: "Can't tell what *is* the matter with these colored men; a good wholesome-lookin' colored woman with kinkey hair don't stan' no livin' chance ter git a decen'-lookin' man fer a husban', an' I fer one am a-settin' my face agin them men" (187). Class differences here go hand in hand with color prejudice, and Mrs. Robinson voices a complaint that is very common and widespread among the less affluent segment of the black population of that time. The objects of desire of both parties are a piano, a silver set, a gold watch and chain, and a diamond pin, all of them of considerable value and prestige. The piano would go to the woman who has sold the most tickets, possessed the most receipts for food consumed, and had the most votes in her favor.

The humorous tone connected with these simple, uneducated, but busy and tremendously efficient women is gentle and well-meaning. They tell stories of their present and former employers and thus shed light on the white society from the servants' point of view. In most cases, such as Mrs. Davis's account of her part in the Mason wedding, the colored servant sees herself as performing some important work and takes pride in the appreciation and affection extended to her by her white employers. Both Mrs. Robinson and Mrs. Davis boast of the white families who support them and try to imitate their lifestyles to some degree. Thus Hopkins holds up a mirror, gentle yet unflattering, to a society that does not recognize its own hypocrisy. Sister Robinson criticizes the pastor for marrying a near-white woman at the same time that Sister Davis reveals pride in her white family's activities.

While the gentle officiousness of Mrs. Willis is resented to a certain degree by the highly cultivated Sappho, the busy churchwomen and organizers are presented as indispensable members of the colored community. It turns out that in the end, after a week of extreme work, the church can pay off the entire mortgage. And when the pastor asks the community to "dwell together in brotherly love," Sister Sarah Ann White says, "the *brothers* had nuthin' to do with it, it was Ophelia Davis an' nobody else" (218).

Job discrimination, color prejudice, poor living conditions, and large families are the problems that dominate the lives of the folk characters. But love and marriage also occupy them as much as the richer members of their society. In particular, there is the affair between Mrs. Davis, who must be more than fifty years old, although she only confesses to being thirty-five, and the young reverend Mr. James. The two come in contact at the musical reception given at the beginning of the story to introduce Sappho to the boarding house. From then onward, Mr. James has set his eyes on Mrs. Davis and her fortune. Mrs. Davis and Mrs. White jointly own a laundry business and have become successful in this line of work. Despite their difference in age and fortune, Mrs. Davis is quite happy with the prospect of marriage and naïvely believes in his superior motives, although her good friend Sarah Ann White warns her against him. The most hilarious story surrounding the courtship is her bicycle ride with Mr. James. This relatively recent new sport attracts the attention of passers-by, who happen to see the two of them sailing down the street right into a heap of sand. Courtship and love and marriage are here seen from the lighter side. There is definitely no tragedy in it, and no sense of ridicule. The young reverend's motive in marrying the older woman may not be simply love, but since it seems to make both parties happy, it proves much common sense in a young man without means. The tradition behind this love story between the servants, as we might say, is classical and certainly serves the purpose of offsetting the more lofty ideals of the hero and heroine. At the same time, it shows that love does not have to be complicated and that more roads than sacrifice and despair lead to happiness.

In *Contending Forces*, folk characters play important roles, but in *Hagar's Daughter* they occasionally dominate the plot. Aunt Henny, Martha, and Venus represent three generations of women spanning the time from slavery to freedom, from the plantation to the big city. Aunt Henny was Hagar's nurse and later became cook in Enson Hall. From the beginning she has been a witness to the crime of St. Clair Enson and points to him as the origin of all the evil that befalls Hagar and the Enson family. In the main part of the novel, she is a cleaning woman who gains her steady job by having bravely guarded a lot of government money. One can easily see this reward of a lifetime of hard work as bitter irony, illustrative of the official attitude of the government toward the former slaves. But it affords her, with forty dollars a month, the sort of reliable income that contributes to the education of both her grandchildren. A government appointment, even as a cleaning lady, is worth more than any other reward.

Aunt Henny has her great day when she is called as a witness in the trial of Sumner. Seventy years old, she presents a quaint figure in the witness box: "The old negress rocked herself to and fro in her chair. She made a weird picture, her large eyes peering out from behind the silver-bowed glasses, her turbaned head and large, gold-hoop earrings, and a spotless white hand-kerchief crossed on her breast over the neat gingham dress" (255). In this crucial scene, Hopkins's narrative must complete a tour de force. Shortly before Aunt Henny's testimony, Aurelia was discredited as a witness because it became known that she is a colored woman. Now Aunt Henny's evidence is the important piece that will bring all the loose ends together. Again, a colored woman's word must be defended against overwhelming white witnesses. Now, however, our sympathies are clearly engaged by Aunt Henny.

Hopkins solves this situation by putting Aunt Henny in a setting that reminds the reader today of a stage arrangement similar to what we envision *Peculiar Sam* to have been like. Humor is used to disguise harsh reality, and the use of dialect helps to enforce the stereotype of the comic African American, guileless and credible. A good example is the mutual misunderstanding between Aunt Henny and the judge, her self-assured use of language and employment of fit metaphor in the following exchange, which is taken from her telling the judge that she worked later hours than usual in General Benson's offices:

> "After I'd been in 'bout an hour, I hearn people talkin' in one ob de rooms— the private office—an' I goes 'cross de entry an' peeks roun' de corner ob de po'ter—"
>
> "The what?" interrupted the judge.
>
> "Po'ter, massa jedge; don' yer kno' what a po'ter am?"
>
> "She means, portière, your honor," explained Gov. Lowe, with a smile. "Go on, aunty."
>
> "I peeked 'roun' de corner ob de po'ter, an' I seed Miss Bradford an' de Gin'ral settin' talkin' as budge as two buzzards. He jes was makin' time sparkin' her like eny young fellar, an' fer a mon as ol' as I kno' *he* is, I tell you, gemmen, he was jes' makin' dat po' gal b'lieve de moon was made o' green cheese an' he'd got the fus' slice."
>
> A suppressed laugh rippled through the room. (254)

This is a perfect example of what Eric Lott sees as the "distorted mirror, reflecting displacements and condensations and discontinuities between which and the social field there exist lags, unevennesses, multiple determinations" (8), referred to earlier in the analysis of *Peculiar Sam*. Aunt Henny serves as the reflection through which white people learn the truth about their own depravity. The court, the core of law and order as most Americans conceive it, must learn to understand not only the language of this African American woman but also its implications. As with *Peculiar Sam*, certain traditional minstrel roles are reversed: the judge is made to look foolish, and although the audience may laugh at Aunt Henny, she carries her point.

Only after her statement turns out to be actually ruining the lives of two white men, General Benson and Major Madison, does the attorney general fiercely attack her claim to the truth. The attorney general calls for lynch-law to prevent anyone in believing "an ignorant nigger" rather than the word of a "brilliant soldier" (257). In this white man's country, it is implied, a Negro's word has no validity. Chief Henson is needed to give credibility to her story, and only then can the real criminal be put on trial. Despite this, Aunt Henny's speech remains the memorable moment in the trial.

In contrast to Isaac, Martha makes the move from slavery to freedom effortlessly, recognizing well that effort and industry will eventually pay off for her and her family. She is a hardworking woman who loves her children, educates them as well as possible, and still laughs a lot. She is especially proud of her son Oliver, who is clever enough that the family saves money to send him to college. His "gay and fearless bearing" makes Martha proud (170), since it is not accompanied by the recklessness of his father. There is a decided improvement in the nature of the Negro in this first generation born after slavery. Reminiscent of Will and Dora Smith, the two younger Johnsons are determined to make their ways.

Apart from being a good mother and hard worker, the grown-up Martha has become a wise woman with a realistic grasp on reality as it concerns colored women, now that slavery no longer separates families. When she says, "Yer mammy 'spec' to wurk 'tell she draps inter the grave. Colored women wasn't made to take their comfit lak white ladies. They wasn't born fer nuthin' but ter wurk lak hosses or mules. Jes' seems lak we mus' wurk 'tell we draps into the grave" (171), she becomes an early model for Janie Crawford's grandmother in Zora Neale Hurston's *Their Eyes Were Watching God*. She is relieved to find out that Venus is seen with Sumner's servant John Williams, whom she trusts as a perfect gentleman because, as she says to Venus, "gittin' jined to a man's a turrible 'spons'bility" (219). When she lovingly chides her son Oliver to do her bidding and put schoolwork aside for the more important task of finding his grandmother, she proves herself a very capable educator, placing family values above education and thus preparing her son for the hard facts of life. If he is not able to find some adequate job after college, he can always rely on his family. She is well aware of the different classes in African American society and the difference between the well-educated and the less-educated people. This is why she says to her son: "I don't want ter feel that a chile o' min's too biggotty to do anything hones' fer a livin'. Don' you turn up yer nose at washin', an' yer may jes' thank God ef you gits a 'ooman when you git jined that'll help you out in that business when college learnin' ain't payin'" (171). She knows all too well that brown skin color will make it difficult for Oliver to find his way in the world. Her goal in education—"to bring you an' yer sister to a realisin' sense of the sin in the wurl" (172)—touches upon the age-old concept of mothers that education is not only book learning and scientific facts but also a preparation for the necessities of life and the evil of the world. The deeply Christian background is part of this, too, while her belief in superstition still speaks of a former condition in slavery in which even Christianity was no guaranteed source of salvation: "There is some things in this wurl that college education won't 'splain, an' you can't argify an' condispute with 'em,

neither" (172). It is a belief in a superior power that cannot be explained
and that leads the colored population to an acceptance of fate that would be
unbearable otherwise.

One must see Aunt Henny as an effort by Hopkins to revise the typical
cliché of the cleaning woman, while her granddaughter Venus presents a
new interpretation of the role of maid. Whereas most critics point out and
admire Venus's courage as an early detective figure,[1] she begins her career as
a capable and trusted maid. She cleverly uses her position to find the most
important clues that will eventually lead to the unraveling of the puzzle. Even
before Chief Henson sees in her "a young colored girl who had an extremely
intelligent, wide-awake expression" (223), she has done some important
detective work and has drawn some conclusions herself. It is especially her
position as maid that has opened these possibilities to her. When General
Benson visits Mrs. Bowen after her husband's death, he threatens her before he
whispers something into her ear, obviously recognizing her former identity.
Venus is outside and overhears Benson threatening Mrs. Bowen. She is not
at all ashamed that she must confess to Chief Henson that she had been
listening: "I reckon I was, and a good job, too, or I wouldn't have this to
tell you" (225). Eavesdropping is a delicate subject that potentially betrayed
the confidence between mistress and servant or, as was the case in the times
of slavery, between mistress and slave. Aunt Henny, even then, warned her
daughter Martha about telling the family secrets. The same applies to Venus:
there is never the feeling that she would tell family secrets unless they are of
a nature that threatens her mistress's own interests. The servants know more
about their employers than the latter would care to acknowledge.

When Venus finally takes over as a detective in the disguise of a boy,
she turns out to be unusually competent, brave, and resourceful. Kristina
Brooks sees her as the African American woman "who can think, speak, and
act as a full subject" and interprets her function as a bridge "between the
(slave) ancestors and the (free) descendants, and between the southern and
northern cultures where these characters are located" (147). John Cullen
Gruesser writes about Venus: "Knowing how to operate in both the black
and white worlds, the doubly-conscious Venus has the uncanny ability to
slip into and out of different roles, dialects, and even genders in pursuit
of truth" (*"Hagar's Daughter"* 2). She is "part of a new African American
generation, one aware of but largely untainted by the past and with great
potential." Her involvement in the plot became an important role model for
later fiction, as Gruesser argues: "Subsequent black crime writers, including
those who have achieved great commercial success in the 1990s, follow the

pattern established by *Hagar's Daughter*" (4). It must be added that Hopkins's revision of the role of maid also inspired some followers. In the *Colored American Magazine* of 1906, there is a long story (or novella) by Gertrude Dorsey Brown[e] that made use of another clever and plucky maid. Ora Williams in "A Case of Measure for Measure" is a college-educated and very competent maid to a southern beauty who must be rescued from her own folly. In Hopkins's novel, Venus is clearly devoted to her young mistress, and her motivation for taking action comes out of a genuine liking for a mistress who is gentle and polite. Ora Williams becomes involved because her young employer is foolish, naïve, and prejudiced. Both maids, however, regard their positions as dignified and good sources of income when other avenues of profession are closed to them. They both teach their mistresses a lesson and offer a role model for maids and servants that is devoid of the usual demeaning and comic undertones.[2]

The plot of *Winona* includes fewer black folk characters than the other novels, although it is the only novel that features a set of white characters speaking dialect. Only the very ending is given to a group of neighbors around Aunt Vinnie, the colored housekeeper at the Maybee Hotel. Surrounded by her friends, a group of black and white people, she tells the story of Winona and ends it with a moral: "Glory to God, we's boun' to be free. Dar's dat gal, she's got black blood nuff in her to put her on de block in this fersaken country, but over dar she's a lady with the top crus' of de crus'. Somethin's gwine happen" (436). The colored girl who is a slave in the United States and a lady in England is a hopeful sign for a better future. Many more signs prophesy the near delivery from bondage, because, as Aunt Vinnie sings, "Dis is de year of Jubilee": "Ole Satan's mad, an' I am glad, / Send de angels down. / He missed the soul he thought he had, / O, send dem angels down" (437). The religious interpretation of the tale at the end takes up the great theme of "Right and Wrong," the battle between the forces of the devil and the army of God.[3]

My discussion of the women folk characters in Hopkins has deliberately been grouped around publication dates to show the development in her writing. She moved from *Contending Forces* and its clearly secondary plot of the women around the fair to assigning a major role to Venus and Aunt Henny in the solving of the detective plot in *Hagar's Daughter*. By going back in time in *Winona*, Hopkins did not need this division in class between characters of black color, instead making some of the white characters speak in dialect. *Of One Blood*, to round out this discussion, only includes the characters of Mira and Aunt Hannah, both of them former slaves, as folk characters. Although they provide crucial information, the African setting of the major part of the novel offered little opportunity for dialect and folk characters.

In the context of all of Hopkins's fiction, some additional stories that she published in the *Colored American Magazine* must be mentioned. "General Washington: A Christmas Story" (Dec. 1900) and "Bro'r Abr'm Jimson's Wedding: A Christmas Story" (Dec. 1901) are two out of seven existing stories that use dialect and black folk characters. Together with Georgia F. Stewart's "Aunt 'Ria's Ten Dollars" and "The Wooing of Pastor Cummings" and Gertrude Mossell's "Mizeriah Johnson," they form a small but interesting number of stories in the first two years of the magazine's existence that document the lives of African Americans who are not at the center of power, such as street urchins, maids, servants, the women in the neighborhood who mean well and struggle hard to find a position in society, and the men who have money but no education (Brother Jimson) or who are getting an education but have no money (the young reverend Mr. James in *Contending Forces*). Charles Chesnutt said to an interviewer who questioned him about his dialect stories that "those dialect stories, while written primarily to amuse, have each of them a moral, which, while not forced upon the reader, is none the less apparent to those who read thoughtfully" (qtd. in Andrews, *Literary Career* 39).

In Hopkins's first Christmas story, the title character, ironically called General Washington, is a street urchin living in the capital. After the disappearance of his father and the death of his mother, he survives by selling chitlins and dancing the intricate steps of the hoedown or the Juba. Streetwise as a result of his practical education, he also takes care of a stray kitten and forms lasting friendships with the other poor children. The narrator does not attempt to conceal the poverty, dirt, and precariousness of his existence. At the same time, the young boy's ingenious way of selling chitlins places him in the long line of trickster figures that were well known to the reading public. When he meets the fair granddaughter of Senator Tallman, she tells him about God and heaven and touches some innate longing in him for someplace that is warm, offers clothes and food in abundance, and is even available to black people. While this conversation emphasizes his innate goodness, it is also the cause for his tragic end. General Washington later hears some people talk about breaking into the senator's house, warns him about it, and is shot at by the burglars. In a pathetic scene, the young boy regains consciousness in a warm and soft bed in the senator's house and moves the old man to tears and instills in him a greater faith in the good intentions of the Negro. His conversion of the senator is seen as justifying his death. The use of dialect in this story functions as a means of characterization, not stigmatization. There is humor in the description of his playing tricks to sell chitlins, but the child is never ridiculed. The harsh reality that the boy's fate reflects is presented to challenge the white man's ingrained prejudice about the worthless Negro.

The second Christmas story is the more intricately woven "Bro'r Abr'm Jimson's Wedding." The basic idea of it resembles that of Chesnutt's "The Wife of His Youth," but its treatment by Hopkins is quite different. Mr. Ryder in Chesnutt's story belongs to the "Blue Vein Society," the upper-class club that grants admittance only to those of light color, good education, good family background, and, if possible, business success. He is about to become engaged to a young and, in fact, much younger lady of his acquaintance with whom he shares an interest in poetry and art. With this schoolteacher of nearly white skin color and much better education, he sees a bright future ahead of him. But on the day he organizes a ball for the occasion, an old, poor, and very dark woman visits him and tells him about her long and faithful search for her slave husband. When Mr. Ryder tells this story to his guests at the ball, he asks if they would accept this woman as his wife if the husband had developed into a successful businessman. His near-fiancée nods, and in a dignified and noble move he presents to the guests the wife of his youth.

Hopkins treats the same story in a very different way. From the beginning, the "Blue Vein Society" in this New England city is characterized in terms of the intricate connection between money and social position: "The Afro-Americans of that city are well-to-do, being of a frugal nature, and considering it a lasting disgrace for any man among them, desirous of social standing in the community, not to make himself comfortable in this world's goods against the coming time, when old age creeps on apace and renders him unfit for active business" (107). These "small Vanderbilts and Astors," as they are ironically called, have their own rules regulating social behavior and especially engagements, their own scale of professional dignity, and their own classification according to property that differs in quality but not in essence from that of the real Vanderbilts and Astors. When the neat and pretty Sister Chocolate Caramel Johnson joins the church, not only her old acquaintance, Widow Nash's son Andy, has his eyes on her, but also the older and rather wealthy Brother Abraham Jimson falls in love with her head over heels. He thus crushes the hopes Widow Nash had for him prior to the arrival of Caramel. Caramel falls in love with his money more than with old rheumatic Brother Jimson himself, as she tells Andy: "Andy Nash, you always was a fool, an' as ignerunt as a wil' Injun. I mean to have a sure nuff brick house an' plenty of money. That makes people respec' you. Why don' you quit bein' so shifless and save your money. You ain't worth your salt" (114).

Soon after this conversation, Andy, who works as a bellboy, incidentally slips on a wet floor and begins to quarrel with the Irish cleaning girl, whom he also strikes on the mouth. After this quarrel, which is symptomatic of the antagonism between the Irish and African American part of New England's society, Andy is put into jail and his bail is set at twenty dollars. Instead of helping him, however, Brother Jimson speaks badly about him to the judge. When he next talks to the Widow Nash, she gives him a scourging of the tongue that takes him down considerably. She eloquently accuses him, the "ol' rhinoceros-hided hypercrite" (120), of his lack of solidarity with people of his own race, of his lack of Christian mercy, and of his mean spirit. Widow Nash's speech is the climax in this story: "A nigger's boun' to be a nigger 'tell the trump of doom. You kin skin him, but he's a nigger still. Broadcloth, biled shirts an' money won' make him more or less, no, sir" (119–20). She demonstrates the power women held in this society and reminds Brother Jimson and her audience of the need for race solidarity that goes beyond personal ambition. This is also the real lesson of the story: an African American is bound to his race and not to class or personal preference. In this sense, "Bro'r Abr'm Jimson's Wedding" takes up a topic from *Contending Forces*, the color consciousness of the Smith family and their boarders, and assumes a position of sympathy with the large part of the African American population that could not make it into the "Blue Vein Society." Hopkins clearly saw both sides of the story, the precarious move up into middle-class status through thrift, education, and strict social behavior, and the struggling of the majority of people against discrimination, poverty, and lack of opportunity.

A short time later, on Christmas Day, the wedding between Caramel and Brother Jimson is about to take place. After a description of the many and costly presents and the bride's lovely dress, the ceremony begins and is duly interrupted by the appearance of Brother Jimson's lawful wife and six sons. There is no evidence of quiet dignity, neither on the part of the wife nor on the part of the guests. Brother Jimson is evicted from the city, and poor Caramel gets married to her faithful Andy. In the tradition of Chesnutt, the story is written to amuse the audience, but the moral is always evident, namely that character is still more important than money or position.

Hopkins clearly tries to reconcile her aspirations as a serious writer and the drive to middle-class respectability of her colored characters with a race solidarity that extends to colored people of all parts of society. Some of the stories she includes about folk characters, such as Abraham Peters or Ophelia Davis, read like vignettes on their own introduced for comic relief. Like Charles Chesnutt and Paul Laurence Dunbar, she finds this a pleasure and a burden at the same time. She realizes very well that folk stories are a genuine part of her writing and that they can be used to comment upon white society and the political situation in general. Aunt Henny's discourse with the judge shows the satiric potential that lies in the language of a seemingly comic old black mammy. Venus's behavior proves that courage and intelligence are not character traits restricted to the heroines and heroes speaking standard English. Still, Hopkins knows about the restricting forces of writing exclusively in dialect and thus catering to prevalent cultural stereotypes. By combining both standard English and dialect as well as middle-class and folk characters, Hopkins resolves the tensions between her readers' expectations and cultural criticism as well as social aspirations and solidarity.

Short Stories in the "Colored American Magazine"

*I*n the nine years of its existence, the *Colored American Magazine* published some fifty short stories, the majority of them by women. Thirty of them have been collected by Elizabeth Ammons in *Short Fiction by Black Women, 1900–1920*, a collection that includes a number of stories from *Crisis* (from 1912 to 1920) as well.[1] A closer analysis reveals a range of subjects, from dialect stories to treatments of the tragic mulatto, from brief sketches to fully developed novellas, with a concurrent panoply of characters ranging from street urchin to colored high society. There is something like a *Colored American Magazine* school of story writing. As literary editor up to 1904, Hopkins was in a position to encourage writers and include stories she herself chose. As a writer herself, she also influenced the subject matter of some of the stories and thus has to be seen as participating in an ongoing dialogue among African American women fiction writers. Gabler-Hover calls them "empowering tales of women" that emphasized the bonding between women (124). There were certainly younger writers who imitated her example, although the dearth of biographical material about many of them makes it impossible to pursue their careers outside the *Colored American Magazine*. There are definitely some trends (e.g., stories about supernatural phenomena, dialect stories, stories about miscegenation and interracial love), which speak of a school, albeit local and limited, of contributors to the *Colored American Magazine*.

Some of the names attached to the stories are clearly pseudonyms. Hopkins published six stories as Pauline Elizabeth Hopkins and one, "The Test of Manhood," as Sarah A. Allen, her known alias. It is less obvious that M. L. [Maitland Leroy] Osborne, author of "A Wild Mountain Rose" in the first issue of the magazine, other stories, and the serial *The Stress of Impulse* (Aug. 1900–Jan. 1901), was probably also O. S. Borne of the story "The Doctor's Great Discovery" (May 1900; see also Otten 252–53 n.18). Additional

240

pseudonyms are "A. Gude Deekun" (A Good Deacon?), who published six stories/sketches between May 1901 and January 1903; and "Deesha," who published two sketches in June and July of 1905. In many cases, there is a conspicuous absence of biographical information about the short-story writers: Anne Bethel Scales, O. S. Borne/Maitland Leroy Osborne, Charles Steward, Georgia F. Stewart, Ruth D. Todd, Kate D. Sweetser, Lelia Plummer, Frances Nordstrom, Edith Estelle Bulkley, Gertrude Dorsey Brown[e], Grace Ellsworth Tompkins, Maude K. Griffin, T. H. Malone, and Osceola Madden. In some cases, it cannot even be determined if the writer is female or male. In her collection of thirty stories by black women in the *Colored American Magazine*, Elizabeth Ammons identifies two of the authors who contributed several stories. Ruth D. Todd is a "black servant working in the home of George M. Cooper in Philadelphia," and Gertrude Dorsey Brown[e] is a sales agent of the magazine in Newark, Ohio ("Introduction" 9–10). Even R. S. Elliott, in his rather comprehensive "Story of Our Magazine" of May 1901, which includes numerous biographical sketches of editors, contributors, and agents, does not identify M. L. Osborne, who had just finished his long serial *A Stress of Impulse*. The same article also does not mention Sarah A. Allen, whose *Hagar's Daughter* had just begun and who would be identified as Hopkins only much later, or give a clue to the identity of "A. Gude Deekun." It can be assumed that some of these writers only published a few stories, but the intriguing hypothesis remains that some of these names may have been pseudonyms. Among the short-story writers published in the *Colored American Magazine*, only Angelina W. Grimke ("Black Is, as Black Does," August 1900); Gertrude Mossell ("Mizeriah Johnson: Her Arisings and Shinings," Jan.–Feb. 1902); Fannie Barrier Williams ("After Many Days: A Christmas Story," Dec. 1902), and Marie Louise Burgess-Ware ("Bernice, the Octoroon," Sept.–Oct. 1903) can be easily identified today. Grimke became a famous writer in the Harlem Renaissance, and the others were well-known clubwomen.

Some of the stories are grouped together through related topics, like the Christmas stories of December 1902. Hopkins's "The Test of Manhood" and Fannie Barrier Williams's "After Many Days" ask for a comparative reading. Some of the stories treat the theme of such spiritual phenomena as clairvoyance and mesmerism: O. S. Borne, "The Doctor's Great Discovery"; M. L. Osborne, "The God of Terror"; Hopkins, "The Mystery Within Us"; Grimke, "Black Is, as Black Does"; and Anne Bethel Scales, "Beth's Triumph." Another group, as has been shown already, can be described as dialect stories. Beginning with Hopkins's "Talma Gordon" (Oct. 1900), a total of eight stories can be loosely linked together through their topics of passing and interracial love.

It is important to note that not all these stories treat African American characters and topics. This phenomenon is especially noticeable in the stories included in some early numbers of the magazine, the stories by Borne and Osborne, Hopkins's "A Mystery Within Us," and the Anne Bethel Scales story, all of which were published between May and September 1900. There are some later stories in which the reference to race is not obvious, although it can be assumed that the characters are African American. It must be pointed out, however, that with Hopkins's growing influence as editor, the stories were usually more outspoken on matters of race.

As with all good collections of short stories, there are some that stick out as remarkable beyond the immediate context of their place of publication. "A Mystery Within Us" is remarkable because it comes first in the new magazine and has a singularly interesting situation at its center. "Talma Gordon" is another such story that easily reaches the narrative power and density of argument of Hopkins's long fiction. "The Test of Manhood" sticks out because it is in such close connection with another story and thus reflects the possibilities of intertextual criticism. "A Dash for Liberty" stands out as well because of its treatment of a historical topic and the use of the type of the heroic slave.

The first story by Hopkins published in the first issue of the *Colored American Magazine* is "The Mystery Within Us." It introduces one of the topics that Hopkins wrote about throughout her career. In a conversation between two friends, Jack, the first-person narrator, and Tom Underwood, a poor physician, it is revealed that Tom Underwood received certain scientific insights and knowledge in his sleep through the person of a deceased eminent physician. This dream or vision or supernatural inspiration prevented Tom from committing suicide and led him to scientific fame and worldly wealth, due to the discovery of some formula for the preservation of life. His Hamlet-like discovery that "there are more things in heaven and earth than are dreamt of in *our* philosophy" goes hand in hand with the ghost's admonishment to "develop the latent faculties with which you have been most generously endowed" (21, 24). Based on a biblical sense of God's will that must be followed, which will be revealed to anyone in times of need, Tom Underwood acts upon the deceased Dr. Thorn's advice. He tells the story to his trusted friend Jack and thus to us, the readers. This narrative device is a common one that was used by Hopkins quite often.

Cynthia D. Schrager argues that "The Mystery Within Us" "intriguingly combines the secular rags-to-riches narrative with a version of its religious antecedent—the spiritual autobiography of sin and redemption" (186). In her analysis, this story "presents material success as a dividend in the more important business of spiritual uplift. Moreover, it substitutes a spiritual and collectivist ethos for the values of materialism and individualism typically associated with dominant American culture." The elements of the poor struggling physician, suicidal despair, and spiritistic visitation resemble the opening of Hopkins's novel *Of One Blood*, in which Reuel Briggs, much like Tom Underwood, will find his way to a mission of altruism that is larger than mere material success (see Schrager 186). Thomas J. Otten points out that, apart from the many sketches about notable African Americans, the *Colored American Magazine* also featured stories about supernatural phenomena that might well have been included because of Hopkins's editorial influence: "These sketches, all of which are at least vaguely supernatural, all of which tell stories of altered states like dreams and mesmeric trances or of secret potions and elixirs or of clairvoyant communications and messages from the dead, seem to have nothing to say about racial difference; their characters usually are not even racially marked. Indeed, one could plausibly argue that in such sketches their authors studiously ignore the ways in which African-American identity had been displaced, constricted and warped" (234). Otten argues that these stories that echo the works of Poe and Hawthorne are not escapist stories, "which merely entertain," but rather stories that "challenge racist politics and reclaim racial heritage." By undermining concepts of identity and questioning its racial structures, Otten writes, "such tales are part of a larger effort in black letters at the turn of the century, one that culminates in Hopkins's *Of One Blood* and DuBois's *Souls of Black Folk*" (234).

"The Mystery Within Us" in the first volume of a new magazine can be read as a plea for action to colored people despite the fact that the characters are not racially marked. Develop your mental faculties and you will achieve great things, it seems to admonish. Coming as it does in the early part of a new century, it certainly speaks of great optimism, a faith in God and in some benevolent force outside the known world, and also a faith in the great benefit of friendship that makes the telling of the story possible. Jack, the listener, functions as the prototype of the ideal audience, curious, benevolent, keen to listen and hear, ready to accept whatever will be told. In that sense, this short story can be seen as a kind of signal to the prospective audience: stay here and listen, you will hear wonderful things.

In addition to M. L. Osborne's "A Wild Mountain Rose" and Hopkins's

"The Mystery Within Us," the opening number of the magazine contains "The Doctor's Great Discovery," which is signed by O. S. Borne. The parallels to Hopkins's story are rather obvious. Again, it is the search for the elixir of life and eternal youth that is the great discovery here. But while this discovery leads to the death of the original inventor and to the wealth and fame of his reincarnation in the Hopkins story, it takes a stranger course in Borne's story. Told from the perspective of the doctor's friend Robert, we learn about his invention of an elixir of eternal youth and the effect it has on him, like the blackening of his gray hair and his youthful appearance. When Robert visits the doctor three years later, the story is continued by the doctor's young wife, who leads him into a nursery and shows him a baby that is revealed to be the doctor. The doctor's self-experiment is certainly successful, but, reduced to an infant state, he is deprived of the power to tell it. The wife, triumphant now that she can prevent his further experimentation and relieved of the care of the old doctor, smiles and proudly presents the baby to the visitor.

There can be no doubt that as early as the first issue of the magazine, stories are arranged on purpose. With "The Mystery Within Us" and "The Doctor's Great Discovery," the purpose was most likely one of ironic comparison. When in "The Mystery" the young scholar develops the latent faculties in him and listens to some kind of otherworldly guidance, he grows into a mature and responsible human being. Much like Reuel Briggs in *Of One Blood*, he is open to experiences that lie outside common forms of knowledge. The doctor in the second story, however, embodies the corruption of egoistical pursuit of knowledge. The elixir of life, so long the object of desire of scientists, is here literally reduced to the elixir of eternal youth. The parody of self-centered research is the ironic counterpart of the discovery of mysterious forces within oneself. Although race is not part of the content here and the mystery within Tom Underwood is not his racial self, as is the case with Reuel Briggs, race can be inserted as a hidden message when the identity of Hopkins and the context of the publication are taken into consideration.

The August 1900 issue features part 1 of the two-part "Beth's Triumph," by Anne Bethel Scales, which in subject matter and style very much resembles the writing of Hopkins. It starts with a description of the loving friendship between two college girls, Louise and Beth, which reminds the reader familiar with Hopkins's previous fiction of the intimacy between Dora and Sappho in *Contending Forces*. Louise, a "tall, beautiful, strong-minded girl, with two soft peach-blooms upon her cheeks, and a complexion like the richest of Jersey cream" (33), asks Beth, the story's first-person narrator, for help because she feels magnetically drawn to a man whose threatening presence she fears but cannot resist. In a dream, Beth has a vision that shows her the man's sinister intent; she has a good friend find out the truth of his background and thus saves Louise from him. Some of the aspects of this story show a close proximity to Hopkins's writing: the friendship between the two girls; the vision that reads like a shortened version of Reuel Briggs's experiences with dreamlike states; the presence of a villain with a magnetic force on the heroine reminiscent of Aubrey Livingston's hold on Dianthe in *Of One Blood*; and especially the way Beth justifies her belief in supernatural powers. She says, "The day of Jacobs, Josephs, and seers, whose dreaming has foretold great good or evil, has passed, 'tis true, but since all admit that history repeats itself,—why allow it to be robbed of its repetitous [sic] power in this instance alone?" (42).

Three possible conclusions may be drawn from these similarities: Anne Bethel Scales is a pseudonym for Hopkins and she wrote the story herself, leaving something like a signature in the phrase that she used so often, namely that history repeats itself. It is tempting to take "Beth's Story" as another Hopkins story, especially since biographical research did not yield anything about Scales. Hopkins may have chosen to write under a pseudonym in order to test how the audience would reply to her prose, to camouflage her real involvement in the *Colored American Magazine* and thus enable her to publish more. Alternatively, the topic was so common and obvious to writers of their time that both Scales and Hopkins might have used it. The third conclusion is to say that even at that early stage of her involvement with the magazine, Hopkins had large editorial powers and could choose the stories she liked best and which most resembled her own style of writing.

The second, considerably longer story Hopkins published under her own name in the *Colored American Magazine* was "Talma Gordon," by far the most interesting and provocative tale not only in the context of Hopkins's short fiction but also in the context of the many other stories in the magazine. It appeared as one long story or short novella in October 1900. The story is laid out in multiple layers, and a clever control of the narrative voice removes it from its original setting only to lead back to it in a triumphant closure. Dr. William Thornton entertains his friends from the Canterbury Club of Boston, familiar to the readers of *Contending Forces*, at his palatial Beacon Street residence. The topic of the day is "Expansion; Its Effect upon the Future Development of the Anglo-Saxon throughout the World." Dr. Thornton, an eminent physician who has become famous because of some miraculous cure of a chronic or malignant disease (reminiscent of the doctor in "The Mystery Within Us"), astonishes them all by his emphatic avowal that he believes in intermarriage with other races when "they possess decent moral development and physical perfection" (51). He adds what can be taken as one of the most liberal statements of any character in a Hopkins story: "Given a man, propinquity, opportunity, fascinating femininity, and there you are. Black, white, green, yellow—nothing will prevent intermarriage. Position, wealth, family, friends—all sink into insignificance before the God-implanted instinct that made Adam, awakening from a deep sleep and finding the woman beside him, accept Eve as bone of his bone; he cared not nor questioned whence she came" (51–52). The frame story is now interrupted by the doctor's story, which is later interrupted by Jeanette Gordon's story that is itself then interrupted by the words of Captain Gordon himself.

The story treats the fate of the Gordon family. Captain Gordon is a retired sea captain who was engaged in the East India trade. He has two daughters, Talma and Jeanette, by his first wife, who brought into the marriage the money that solved the financial problems of the Gordons. It is rumored that the two daughters do not get on well with their stepmother, the captain's second wife, with whom he has a son. The young and gifted Talma is sent to Italy to develop her artistic talents. Upon her return, the family organizes a great welcome party. Talma is described as "a fairylike blonde in floating white draperies, her face a study in delicate changing tints, like the heart of a flower, sparkling in smiles about the mouth to end in merry laughter in the clear blue eyes" (53). Jeanette, in contrast, seems to have inherited her father's stern austerity. At this party, Dr. Thornton is present as the family physician and trusted friend.

After the party, during a terrible thunderstorm, the left tower of the house where Captain Gordon, his wife, and their young son live burns down, and soon after their bodies are carried outside. Their deaths, however, were caused by the slitting of their throats and not by fire. Suspense increases when the two daughters are indicted because of some quarrel between Talma and her father about her suitor and because it is revealed that Captain Gordon meant to leave his daughters only a small annuity while the fortune would go to his son after his death. No will, however, can be found. Talma's case is put to trial, but because of a lack of legal evidence, she is found not guilty. All the while strange and terrible stories about Captain Gordon's methods as a sea captain come to the surface. And although there is no proof, this certainly helps to give Talma the benefit of the doubt. Talma is "like one stricken with death," her mouth drawn and pinched, her eyes full of passion and despair, while Jeanette shows signs of a beginning disease: "hollow cheeks, tottering steps, eyes blazing with fever" (58). Both girls leave the country to live in Italy, where Jeanette soon after dies and Talma disappears from public view.

The tale later continues in Dr. Thornton's sanitarium, where one Simon Cameron, coming from the California gold fields, engaged his professional services because of an advanced stage of tuberculosis. Talma Gordon also places herself in his care. She appears overtired and listless, presenting "the sight of a human soul tortured beyond the point of endurance; suffering all things, enduring all things, in the silent agony of despair" (61). With this reunion of the main characters of the story and the introduction of a person who is presented as someone sinister with a mysterious past, the story can now take a decisive turn. Talma reads to Dr. Thornton a letter from her sister, Jeanette, in which Jeanette tells her that she once overheard a conversation between her father and her stepmother about the will that would grant only a small annuity to the two girls. When Jeanette confronted her father about this, Captain Gordon told her about the birth of his first son, the girls' brother. The boy showed clear signs of a dark skin color. After accusing the mother first of adultery, it turns out that in fact the mother was an octoroon and thus possessed some negro blood. Jeanette then knew why she and Talma were often treated without respect and why the mother was repudiated and eventually died of grief. The "cold cruelty of relentless caste prejudice" worked against them, even if it concerned children far removed from their African American ancestry (65). Jeanette then tells her sister that she meant to kill her father, stepmother, and half-brother, but that someone had already killed them when she entered the room that night.

While Talma tells these facts to the doctor, her lover, the young painter Edward Turner, is present in what is another scene of revelation. He instantly recoils from her: "I could stand the stigma of murder, but add to that the pollution of Negro blood! No man is brave enough to face such a situation" (66). Similar to Ellis Enson and Cuthbert Sumner in *Hagar's Daughter*, with downcast eyes, he bows before Talma and leaves her sad and resigned. His act proves the deep-seated prejudice rooted in some unconscious fear of atavism, the belief that some obscure and dark ancestral strain would eventually affect Talma's offspring. He is indeed not brave enough to stand this situation; he does not pass the test of manhood and thus deserves the minor role he has in the story.

In *Neither Black nor White Yet Both*, Werner Sollors defines atavism accord- ing to Aristotle as " 'great-grandfather-ism,' a descendant's surprising 'resem- blance to grandparents or more remote ancestors rather than to parents' "

(49). In his chapter "Natus Aethiopus/Natus Albus," he traces the historical development of this theme from Aristotle, through Pushkin, to some modern versions as found in Kate Chopin, Pauline Hopkins, and George Schuyler. While earlier reactions to the dark child led to expressions of wonder from his white parents, it later led to accusations of adultery on the side of the mother and then to reactions of horror, even "the white horror of horrors" when a grandparent or parent cannot recognize himself or herself in the child (66). In "Talma Gordon," all these elements are present. When Captain Gordon's first wife gives birth to a dark son, he accuses her of adultery, and then the true story is revealed by her adoptive parents. The horror Edward Turner expresses after hearing Talma's story is prototypical.

Immediately afterward, Simon Cameron confesses that he murdered the Gordons. Captain Gordon is now revealed as a vengeful, evil, greedy, and extremely cruel man who murdered Cameron's father after they buried the treasure he had seized in a piratical manner. Cameron's murders were the result of economic exploitation in the East India trade. Cameron, an East Indian himself, avenged his father's death. As in *Winona*, "Talma Gordon" here highlights the international dimension of exploitation and the legacy of the slavery past. Both lead to moral corruption, pain, and murder. In addition, the intermingling of races perpetuates history in the present time.

Back at the Canterbury Club, Dr. Thornton presents to his friends the wife about whom all those present have been curious for a long time because of her rumored beauty and the romance surrounding their marriage. He had married Talma Gordon and thus triumphed over prejudice and shown the true spirit of New England liberalism. By comparing the story to Kate Chopin's "Désirée's Baby," Sollors argues that Hopkins "may thus be said to have redirected the emotional energies of the modern racialist contexts of the *Natus Aethiopus* motif toward normalizing an interracial marriage plot" (74). Of course, there is no mentioning of the reactions of the audience to the doctor's revelation. But it can be safely assumed that, whatever they may have been, the doctor's love would not have been diminished.

The most remarkable fact about this story is Hopkins's conscious decision to present Talma's fate as untragic. One must keep in mind that the story was published in October 1900, a time when Hopkins may have been thinking about *Hagar's Daughter*, whose first installment came in March 1901. The prototypical life of a woman whose invisible portion of black blood leads to a tragic end is still present, however, in this story, as it is in all the other stories about light-colored women included in the *Colored American Magazine*— if not directly as subject matter, at least indirectly as some kind of master narrative. Jeanette Gordon, the older and the more mature of the two Gordon sisters, feels an inner drive to revenge herself on her father and stepmother, but she cannot stand the subsequent stress and social ostracism that results from the unjustified accusation of murder. Talma's health deteriorates after she receives the letter. But her reading of the letter to both Dr. Thornton and her lover reveals a strength of character that does not allow her to keep her identity a secret, which would potentially threaten any future relationship unless revealed from the start.

Dr. Thornton's telling of the story, in turn, shows a presumably enlightened personality that moves beyond limits of race. It has the aim of proving his wife's superior upbringing and "decent moral development and physical perfection" (51). While the story in itself proves the "existence of a moral universe" (P. Brooks 20), and while it has a very complex relationship to social context (Gillman, "The Mulatto" 224), it subtly demonstrates the real system of power relationships. Without a doubt, it is still Dr. Thornton's story. His presence throughout the tale he narrates gives him the authority to shape it into a thrilling story of mistaken identities, wrongs committed, revenge, and adventure. Talma Gordon does not tell her own story, she waits to be presented to the doctor's friends and the readers as some kind of curiosity, pitied yet still exotic. Although their marriage and the declaration of its racial background must have been more than courageous on the part of Hopkins and shows her close affinity to and deviance from the expected standards of the tragic mulatta story, "Talma Gordon" must be taken as one step in the development of Hopkins as a writer. It demonstrates her mastery of plot and narrative density and reflects the intricacy, multiplicity, and unforeseeable complications in the American multiracial family. *Hagar's Daughter* can definitely be seen as a continuation beyond this model, giving more space to the heroines and assigning more varied roles to them.

An evaluation that does justice to the outstanding quality of "Talma Gordon" must include a discussion of "The Test of Manhood" in context with Fannie Barrier Williams's "After Many Days," both of which appeared in the December 1902 issue of the *Colored American Magazine*. These two stories and a few more will be analyzed in order to point out the many possibilities for treating the subject of passing, their melodramatic content, the social criticism behind the tragedy, and the questioning of the system of power inherent in them. "The Octoroon's Revenge" (March 1902) and "Florence Grey," by Ruth D. Todd (Aug.–Oct. 1902); "Bernice, the Octoroon," by M. Louise Burgess-Ware (Sept.–Oct. 1903); and "Scrambled Eggs" (Jan.–Feb. 1905) and "A Case of

Measure for Measure," by Gertrude Dorsey Brown[e] (six installments in 1906), show the many possible ways of treating the subject, combining humor and tragedy.

Pauline Hopkins published her short story "The Test of Manhood" under her pen name Sarah A. Allen. She could be confident that its topic of passing would be familiar to her readers and rouse their interest, while its potential for a fairy-tale ending would appeal to the Christmas spirit. In this story, the crossing from one color into the other arouses a deep-seated fear of what a white character calls "the wholesale pollution of our race" (206). It is the conversation between a southerner and his more liberal northern friend that puts the notion of passing into the head of the central character, Mark Myers. The northerner, whose conversation he overhears, suggests that the color problem will solve itself if the many light-colored African Americans would simply decide to "disappear and turn up again" as white people (205).

Mark Myers is an eighteen-year-old southerner with "soft dark curls, big dark eyes, and the peach-like complexion of a girl" (205), by which description readers would immediately recognize him as a light-colored mulatto. His "peach-like complexion" also hints at the feminine quality that was often attributed to this type. The test he will have to pass plays on the common notion that mulattoes lack the virtues and strengths of real manhood. Mark decides to leave his beloved and caring mother and try his fortune in the North. His educational background is indicated by his speaking a carefully modulated dialect in contrast to the southern dialect of an uneducated character such as his mother. When Mark arrives in the great northern metropolis, he introduces himself immediately by proving his honesty. He picks up the well-filled purse of the lawyer John E. Brown and returns it to him with only a moment of hesitation. He not only prepares his own successful future in this way—Lawyer Brown offers him a job—but also disproves the common belief that the migrant Negro from the South is shiftless and good-for-nothing.

Mark Myers now passes as a white man, a move that turns out to be a financial gain but, predictably, entails a psychological loss. He thinks with regret of his mother, whom he will never see again: "From now on she should no more exist—*as his mother*—for he had buried his old self that morning, and packed the earth hard above the coffin" (209). Passing is a form of dying when it demands the complete abandonment of a former life.[2] His new life must be a masquerade in which one part of him lies concealed. Frequently he invokes images of a peaceful, idyllic, and happy South, replete with the scent of magnolias and the music of the Virginia reel, but education, being called to the bar, and ten thousand dollars in his pocket offer adequate substitutes.

Mark's reminiscences of the Edenic South are contrasted with the view of the snowy cold of the North as it affects his mother, Aunt Cloty, who has come into the same city to search for her son. She is befriended by Lawyer Brown's daughter Katherine, who is to be Mark's fiancée. The narrator takes his time to depict Katherine as a "petted favorite of fortune" (212), whose charity is rewarded with the quaint stories of this typical southern mammy type. Aunt Cloty is a real folk character, and her deep affection renders her likeable to both Katherine and the reader. In an inevitable turn of the plot, Katherine invites Aunt Cloty to spend Christmas Eve with her family, where Mark is expected to be present also. Mark declares his love to Katherine, and then they all meet in a Christmas reunion. The interesting moment comes when Mark is confronted with his mother, who screams when she recognizes him: "After that scream came a deathly silence, Mark stood as if carved into stone, in an instant he saw his life in ruins, Katherine lost to him, chaos about the social fabric of his life" (217). The images of petrifaction, ruin, and chaos speak of a divided inner state of being that is lifeless and stonelike while chaos reigns. The real test of manhood is now Mark's acceptance of his mother. The story ends: "Another instant his arms were about his fond old mother, while she sobbed her heart out on his breast" (217). In making the decision to embrace his mother rather than reject her, Mark resembles Mr. Ryder of Chesnutt's "The Wife of His Youth." The decision is a moral one, not primarily a racial one, as William L. Andrews points out in his analysis of the Chesnutt story (*Literary Career* 114). Mark proves himself to be superior to the lure of the North, which accepts an equality between the races when the African American part of the equation is unknown or silently ignored. The "real test of manhood" is not marriage to a white woman but an acknowledgment of past obligations. The story ends here; the reaction of the Brown family is left out. The reader may construct his or her own sequel.

It can be assumed that Hopkins's readers, whom she assumed to be well-versed in the literature of the time, were aware of Thomas Dixon's *The Leopard's Spots*, published in that same year (1902). In one scene, the Klan visits the African American population of the county to warn them away from voting. Major Dameron interprets the turnout at the voting booth: "All cowards will stay at home. Any man, black or white, who can be scared out of his ballot is not fit to have one. Back of every ballot is the red blood of the man that votes. The ballot is force. This is simply a test of manhood. It will be enough to show who is fit to rule the state" (163). This use of the concept of

manhood to denote the violent exercise of white power shows the obstacles
that writers of Hopkins's generation had to overcome in order to find some
positive self-image.

Hopkins's story appears in the same issue with one by Fannie Barrier
Williams, who was Hopkins's fellow activist and clubwoman from Chicago.
She was the wife of attorney S. Laing Williams, a loyal supporter of Booker T.
Washington in Chicago. Williams published in the *Colored American Maga-
zine* and also, like Hopkins, in the *Voice of the Negro*. Both women criticized
Washington's emphasis on industrial education. The affiliation with or antag-
onism toward this prominent race leader runs as a kind of red thread through
much of the writing and the lives of women as prominent as Williams and
Hopkins. Williams attended the New England Conservatory of Music, the
School of Fine Arts in Washington, D.C., and taught school until her marriage
(Loewenberg and Bogin 263–64).

By reversing the gender of the person who is found out to pass involun-
tarily, Williams's "After Many Days" treats the tragic subject, the woman who
looks white but is found out to possess a small quantity of black blood. It is
the more commonly found form of the passing story. "After Many Days" is
set on the stately Edwards plantation in Virginia during the Christmas season
some twenty years after the Civil War. It is the story of young and beautiful
Gladys Winne meeting old Aunt Linda, a trusted and privileged servant at
the Edwards plantation where Gladys pays a Christmas visit. It turns out that
Aunt Linda is Gladys's grandmother, because her equally beautiful and light-
colored daughter had a tragic love affair with the master's son. As a character,
Aunt Linda recalls Aunt Hannah's strength of character and long-suffering
in *Of One Blood*.

Gladys Winne is horror-stricken by what she hears, but now that she
knows, she cannot go back to ignorance.[3] There is hardly a more memorable
moment in the story than when Aunt Linda urges her granddaughter to keep
this a secret, and Gladys says: "Ah, but I know, my God, what have I done to
deserve this?" (229). Even Aunt Linda, relieved about the great secret finally
told, realizes the "awful possibilities of her divulged secrets" (228). In a
strangely contorted sentence, the narrator renders the ambiguity between
the need to tell a secret and the need to keep it and connects the horrors of
slavery with race prejudices after the war: "Aunt Linda had felt and known
the horrors of slavery, but could she have known that after twenty years of
freedom, nothing in the whole range of social disgraces could work such
terrible disinheritance to man or woman as the presence of Negro blood,
seen or unseen, she would have given almost life itself rather than to have

condemned this darling of her love and prayers to so dire a fate." The dire fates of white women and men who were discovered to be colored were well known to the readers of the *Colored American Magazine:* they range from divorce, disinheritance, financial losses, loss of social status, and loss of moral rights to loss of family. Gladys now decides to confide in her hostess, Mrs. Edwards, who cautiously confirms Aunt Linda's story. Mrs. Edwards is a gentle and understanding white southern woman; her capacity for tolerance is great but limited. Although she knows of two colored girls who are supposedly the daughters of her own husband and pities them, she can only move within a restricted social realm. She voices a "covert threat" (231): Gladys must not reveal her secret. It becomes a question of keeping knowledge to oneself or revealing it. Gladys has seen the desperate and overpowering urge in Aunt Linda to reveal her secret, and she cannot live with the silence herself.

Gladys's fiancé Paul Westlake is a young man with a liberal worldview who has spoken with "fervid eloquence" about the "Negro problem" (233). In this he resembles the characters of Ellis Enson and Cuthbert Sumner in *Hagar's Daughter*, Warren Maxwell in *Winona*, and Edward Turner in "Talma Gordon." His views are now put to the test, as an abstract problem becomes invested with a deeply personal element. When Gladys tells him her secret after a short while, he gives her outer appearance a careful scrutiny, as if race could be detected by some mark, some flaw, nearly invisible, but still there. "You, my flower," he says, "is it possible that there can be concealed in this flawless skin, these dear violet eyes, these finely chiseled features, a trace of lineage or blood, without a single characteristic to vindicate its presence? I will not believe it; it cannot be true" (236). The striking opposition between the visible, which is white, and some other secret behind it, which is black, takes hold of him. The horror of it all comes home to him when he thinks of heredity, the fear that the black blood may assert itself on some offspring.

Gladys gives him some time for consideration, and on their second meeting she is rewarded with a demonstration of "his love, his protection, his tenderest sympathy" (238). Again, the story does not move beyond this ending: the conflict is not really resolved, perhaps because it is unsolvable. A Christmas carol sung by a trained voice and the plaintive melody sung by a "group of dusky singers beneath the windows" adequately closes the story with a mingling of the two voices, the black and white ones, in something of a "singular harmony" (238). Still, the "dusky singers" know their place outside the realm of the southern mansion.

Taken together, these two stories combine a variety of elements commonly found in fiction about mixed-race characters. There is voluntary

(Mark) and involuntary passing (Gladys); passing for economic motives and the subsequent loss of family ties (Mark); the secrecy surrounding a possible discovery in "After Many Days"; the figure of the old mammy or faithful, albeit bitter servant and former slavewoman; and above all, there is the test that this interracial love must go through before a true relationship is possible. Although both stories make use of plot contrivances, which should not be judged from outside the accepted conventions of the time, and standardized characters, both stories use suspense, surprise, and conflict successfully. Much like in "Talma Gordon," the mulatto characters, both a man and a woman, are presented as genteel, well bred, and morally superior. In both stories, however, direct mention of miscegenation through marriage is avoided.

In March 1902 Ruth D. Todd published "The Octoroon's Revenge." Reminiscent of the basic situation in *Clotel*, in which the young slave girl is set up as a mistress by Horatio Greene and then abandoned by him because he must make a more advantageous marriage, this situation is repeated in substance although with a decisive change: the time is now 1875, ten years after the war. The young, beautiful, and light-colored servant girl is seduced by the son of her employer and then, when she is pregnant, abandoned for a white wife. The wife later dies while giving birth to a girl, and the servant exchanges the two babies when the white daughter dies. About twenty years later, Lillian Westland, the daughter who has been reared as the heiress but educated in a spirit of tolerance by her real mother, elopes with the mulatto coachman of her father. Only shortly later, old Mr. Westland dies after the servant has told him the story about the exchange of the baby girls. The ending is triumphant. Lillian inherits her father's money and moves with her beloved mulatto husband and her mother to Europe. Above all, this story attests to the adaptability of a theme that started in the time of slavery but can easily be carried over into turn-of-the-century America.

In the three-part story "Florence Grey," by Ruth D. Todd, published between August and October 1902, the character of the beautiful mixed-race heroine is brought to perfection. Florence Grey is the daughter of an extremely wealthy colored family; she is beautiful, refined, well educated, and possesses the bearing of a lady. She is also the admired and recognized leader of the upper strata of colored society. When the reckless and immoral white Dick Vanbrugh makes advances toward her, he is received with as much ill-favor and discouragement as possible. He is, however, passionately fixed upon possessing this "colored damsel" and abducts her (160). He imprisons her in his house, which is run by his trusted old mammy. The two young colored housemaids, the nieces of his mammy, however, recognize from newspaper reports the face of the heroine as that of Florence Grey and eventually rescue her so that she can be reunited with Jack Warrington, the upwardly mobile and promising young college graduate.

In the time frame of Hopkins's serial novels, "Florence Grey" came after the publication of *Hagar's Daughter* from March 1901 to March 1902 and toward the end of *Winona*, which ran from May to October of 1902. In this context, it can be seen as proof of Hopkins's influence on her fellow writers in terms of character and subject matter. Dick Vanbrugh's passion for Florence is presented as being as immoral and evil as that of St. Clair Enson toward Hagar and later Jewel in *Hagar's Daughter*, and that of Anson Pollock for Grace Montfort and John Langley toward Sappho in *Contending Forces*. The fact that Hagar, Jewel, Sappho, and Florence resemble each other in beauty, education, and refinement reflects the contemporary stereotypical standards of beauty for heroic female figures. It is remarkable, moreover, that Dick Vanbrugh is helped by a devilish type of Negro who resembles Isaac in *Hagar's Daughter*. In both *Hagar's Daughter* and "Florence Grey," the heroines are abducted and rescued with the help of some colored maids. Of all these stories, "Florence Grey" bears the most outspoken message about the growing self-confidence of the African American heroine and her decided opinions about the undesirability of an interracial relationship based on some notions of white male superiority that are clearly seen as unfortunate remnants of the slave past.

A story that demonstrates that not all light-colored heroines must end tragically is "Bernice, the Octoroon," by M. Louise Burgess-Ware. Looking beyond the stereotypical melodramatic tone of the story, one finds an interesting treatment of the theme of passing. In more senses than one, this story offers the acceptable way out of the dilemma of miscegenation from which the other three stories shy away. It also shows that the treatment of the topic as it was begun in "Talma Gordon" motivated other writers to look at the subject in novel ways. After Bernice has learned about her colored ancestry, she makes the best of it, works with poor colored people in the South, and is finally rewarded with the love of a man truly worthy of her.

The obvious conclusion from a comparative reading of these stories is that the tragic mulatta stereotype is a model that needed to be revised. Talma Gordon and Bernice and Lillian Westland, cutting across color lines, are rewarded with true love, and the future for Mark Myers and Gladys Winne looks bright. In still another story, even the white father, married to a colored woman without his knowing it, is willing to cast his gaze beyond the racial lens to learn to appreciate how the other half of society lives. Gertrude Dorsey Brown[e]'s "Scrambled Eggs," which was published in January and February 1905, sees the humorous side of passing and the many transformations this entails. The ingredients of the scrambled eggs, the mixture of yellow and white that serves as the motif in this story, are two baby girls who are exchanged. In the course of time this exchange becomes the skeleton in the closet that leads to blackmail and much dramatic action, including the eventual conversion of the racist father into a tolerant man. The young heroine, having recuperated from a disrupted wedding ceremony, finally says: "I think we all have been very silly to spend so much time weeping and mourning over the fact that we are of Negro extraction. Are we not as good as we were before we found this out? . . . Have we changed in our love for each other? Have our feet become longer or our lips thicker or have horns begun to grow on our heads?" (352). Dora's gain from a thorough lesson in how the other half lives is the message to white people that humanity is more basic than race. It is not tragic, the story wants to say, to be colored.

One of the few examples of the reverse process, the voluntary and involuntary passing of white people for colored, is Gertrude Dorsey Brown[e]'s "A Case of Measure for Measure," included in six installments in the *Colored American Magazine* of 1906. The passing scheme works on a number of levels, its comic implications are manifold, and the "perplexing question" of the interplay between race, class, and gender turns into a real lesson for more than one of the white characters (408). Although this story was published after Hopkins's time as literary editor of the *Colored American Magazine*, it clearly showed her influence through the character of the colored maid, the detective plot, and the lesson taught of moral decency and intellectual worth of the colored characters.

As soon as passing is made to work in the opposite direction, from white to black, the absurdity of seeing color as determining character is laid bare. The common denominator of all these stories, however, is that color does test character in a substantial way. Edward Turner's and Mr. Westland's characters are reflected in their reaction to Talma's and Lillian's racial background ("Talma Gordon" and "The Octoroon's Revenge"). Dr. Thornton ("Talma Gordon"), Mark Myers ("The Test of Manhood"), Gladys Winne and Paul Westlake ("After Many Days"), Bernice and her fiancé Garrett ("Bernice, the Octoroon"), the entire Grey family, including the white father and his colored wife and children ("Scrambled Eggs")—all of them prove their manhood and true womanhood and show noble traits and commendable behavior in their reactions to mixed-race origins, while the multiple exchanges and cross-racial behavior lead to more awareness and tolerance in "A Case of Measure for Measure."

In addition to these stories about passing, Hopkins wrote two stories about heroic male figures with dark skin. "A Dash for Liberty" was published in August 1901 as her fourth story in the *Colored American Magazine*. This issue included the chapter of *Contending Forces* that appeared as a story and the sixth installment of *Hagar's Daughter* that Hopkins published as Sarah A. Allen. Its theme is a slave rebellion on board the *Creole* instigated by Madison Monroe, a slave who had escaped to Canada and returned to free his wife, Susan. He is captured and taken onboard ship, together with 134 other slaves, in order to be sold in New Orleans. A beautiful octoroon slavewoman is assaulted by the captain, and Madison, who has been working on his liberation all along, casts off the iron bar around his ankles, frees the slavewoman, kills the captain, and captures the ship. The next day, Madison finds out that the beautiful slave whose face he could not see before is Susan, his beloved wife. After landing in Nassau, the slaves are offered hospitality and protection.

The historical background is the 1841 slave rebellion on board the *Creole* with Washington Madison as leader. Hopkins's rewriting of this "significant moment in African American history" recalls the earlier treatments of this rebellion by Frederick Douglass, William Wells Brown, and Lydia Maria Child (Gruesser, "Taking Liberties" 99).[4] Gruesser argues that Hopkins's story can be read as her "declaration of independence from both the white historical record and earlier writing by African American and white abolitionist authors" (99). In the following analysis, "A Dash for Liberty" will be seen as part of the Hopkins canon, and the connection to her novels will be explained.

The links to both *Hagar's Daughter* and *Winona* are manifold. Madison Monroe bears the same name as the villain slave dealer Walker, who later turns into Major Henry Clay Madison. *Hagar's Daughter* and "A Dash for Liberty" were published at the same time, and thus any repetition of names must be seen as significant. The significance of this must be judged from a modern point of view, because Hopkins's contemporaries could not identify her as the Sarah A. Allen of *Hagar's Daughter*. Walker/Madison is a decidedly evil character, responsible for the enslavement of Hagar and her daughter. He took the name after he had to conceal his true identity because of his involvement in the assassination of President Lincoln. Many southerners, however, would argue that this assassination was a brave act and made him a hero. By contrast, Madison Monroe is an African American hero. His freeing of the slaves on board the *Creole* must be judged as heroic for African Americans, but it certainly would have meant the death sentence under other than British jurisdiction.

John Gruesser deals with the change of names from Washington Madison to Madison Monroe. The name-givers George Washington and James Monroe were presidents from Virginia and slaveholders. The name Monroe might have been kept because of President James Monroe's support of emigration to Liberia, while the dropping of the name Washington implied criticism of Booker T. Washington, which makes this story one more stone in the mosaic of Hopkins's feeling toward the race leader (see "Taking Liberties" 104–5). In addition, it must be added that Monroe was also the middle name of James Monroe Trotter, one of the influential and radical leaders of the African American community in Boston. Hopkins admired this outspoken activist for the rights of African Americans.

Madison Monroe, the African American hero bearing the name of two American presidents, is also reminiscent of the brave young fighter Judah in *Winona*. Madison is described as "an unmixed African, of grand physique, and one of the handsomest of his race. His dignified, calm and unaffected bearing marked him as a leader among his fellows. His features bore the stamp of genius. His firm step and piercing eye attracted the attention of all who met him" (90). Like Judah, he is one of the few heroes in early African American fiction who is not light-colored and does not belong to some middle-class setting. His strength and endurance are the result of his African and not his American background. Judah's source of strength is his early upbringing in the free northern and Indian surroundings. Madison's source of strength and determination is a love that defies the boundaries of slavery.

Like Judah, he is in love with a light-colored woman, the beautiful octoroon Susan. The description of her is similar to that of Winona: her dazzling beauty, her superb figure, and "the long black ringlets, finely-chiselled mouth and well-rounded chin, upon the marbled skin veined by her master's blood" (96). Susan's beauty and refinement—it is mentioned that she is a lady's maid and can sing and dance, all of which will bring more money on the slave market—are, however, the result of her dominant white ancestry. Her grandfather had served in the Revolutionary War and in both houses of Congress. The blood of the proudest families of Virginia is mingled with that of the slaves. This leads the narrator to remark: "Who wonders that Virginia has produced great men of color from among the exbondmen, or, that illustrious black men proudly point to Virginia as a birthplace? Posterity rises to the plane that their ancestors bequeath, and the most refined, the wealthiest and the most intellectual whites of that proud State have not hesitated to amalgamate with the Negro" (94). Susan's case serves as an example, often repeated in fiction and journalism, that amalgamation is a fact and cannot be denied. The descendants of these white families cannot be neglected and kept in the state of bondage. Gruesser argues that Hopkins "decries white America's insane and impossible pursuit of racial purity, often used as a justification for acts as contradictory as lynchings and the sexual exploitation of black women by 'chivalrous' southern men, the very group responsible for widespread amalgamation in the first place" ("Taking Liberties" 111–12).

Susan is not very active in the story. She motivates Madison's action but would not have been able to defend herself against the captain's attack. Without the help of Madison, she would have gone overboard. Death by drowning seems to her preferable to rape. This movement repeats the moment in *Hagar's Daughter* in which Hagar flees with her infant daughter from the slave pen in Washington, D.C., and jumps off the bridge to escape enslavement. Unlike Hagar, Susan is rescued by Madison, whom she does not recognize immediately as her husband, another similarity to the serial novel in which relatives often do not recognize each other.

The most interesting fact about the relationship between Susan and Madison is that a union between this light-colored woman and a very dark African American is taken for granted and not questioned at all. What Judah says in his jealousy after seeing Winona and Warren Maxwell is right, after all. Slavery puts them on an equal level. There is no difference between them because they are both slaves. But as in *Winona*, slavery is an insufficient answer. Slavery has brought them together, but the master would have sold them separately. It is their common love of liberty that brings Susan and Madison together in the end. It is a lack of love, however, that prevents a coupling of Judah and Winona. From a modern point of view, knowing that Allen and Hopkins are one and the same person, it appears that "A Dash for Liberty" serves as a kind of corrective for *Winona* in the envisioning of a union between the very dark man and the light-colored female and as a corrective to *Hagar's Daughter*, in which all the mulatta heroines fall in love with white men. The love story in "A Dash for Liberty" is decidedly not tragic, the union between Madison and Susan presented as ideal.

Madison addresses the issue of the effects of spiritual and physical subjugation when he tries to justify and explain his mission to Virginia to his

Canadian employer. Mr. Dickson wants to keep him back and persuade him that one or two more years would help them free Susan anyway. Madison, however, cannot agree: "Imagine yourself in my place; how would you feel? The relentless heel of oppression in the States will have ground my rights as a husband into the dust, and have driven Susan to despair in that time. A white man may take up arms to defend a bit of property; but a black man has no right to his wife, his liberty or his life against his master!" (89). There is an indirect reference to the master's privileges with a slavewoman that is the core of so much fear, antagonism, and action in most fiction about slavewomen. The main problem, as Madison sees it, is the lack of any civil rights: he cannot defend himself or his family against the slaveholder. This leads to a veiled threat of some kind of slave rebellion, ever-present in the relationship between master and slave. Mr. Dickson recognizes this "desperate blood" in Madison and tries to exact the promise from him that he will be "discreet, and not begin an attack" (90). Madison cannot promise him nonviolence; he can only say: "I promise not to be indiscreet," whatever that means.

The tricky question of right and wrong, addressed more fully in *Winona*, is not a problem in this story. Madison is seen as acting rightfully when he begins a mutiny on the *Creole*. As the narrator says, "Every act of oppression is a weapon for the oppressed. Right is a dangerous instrument; woe to us if our enemy wields it" (98). The story leaves out the view of the white man, except for the mean-spirited captain who approaches the helpless slavewoman.

In the context of the other short fiction included in the *Colored American Magazine*, "A Dash for Liberty" stands out in its tone of despair, veiled threats, and violence. There is only one other story that equals it in tone, although not in depth and narrative consistency. "As the Lord Lives, He Is One of Our Mother's Children" appeared in November 1903 and is, together with the final installment of *Of One Blood*, the last known and identified piece of fiction by Hopkins in the magazine. It begins with the dreaded scenario of African Americans living around the turn of the century, when lynching and bestial brutality were horrifying signs of the ongoing antagonism between the races. In a large western town, the Reverend Septimus Stevens witnesses the lynching of a black man who is accused of killing a white man, while his companion manages to flee. The unfortunate victim is described in noble terms: "He was a grand man—physically—black as ebony, tall, straight, deep-chested, every fibre full of that life so soon to be quenched. Lucifer, just about to be cast out of heaven, could not have thrown around a glance of more scornful pride. What might not such a man have been, if—but it was too late. 'Run fair, boys,' said the prisoner, calmly, 'run fair! You keep up your end of the rope and I'll keep up mine' " (277–78). The dramatic scene, from which the witness shrinks, ends in a "thousand-voiced cry of brutal triumph" when the work is done. The reverend soon learns the real background of this alleged murder after he takes in a sick man, who looks white and behaves in a gentle and well-educated way. The story he hears is one of black enterprise and business sense that is ruined during the race riot of Wilmington, North Carolina, in which the man's family was burned and he and his friend, the one who was later lynched, were forced to leave the town. The Wilmington race riot was an infamous chapter in history that Hopkins's reading public was familiar with because it had just occurred in 1898. Charles Chesnutt's novel *The Marrow of Tradition* treats the riot in all the complex historical and personal conflicts that caused it and that resulted from it. In the Hopkins story, the two men moved west to work in the mountains, but a fellow from Wilmington began to torment and threaten them. When he was found dead, the two friends were accused of murder, although there was no direct proof.

One part of "As the Lord Lives" concerns the reverend's inner conflict of whether to report the man who worked for him or to conceal his identity. As a liberal and deeply Christian man, he firmly believes in the possibility of fair treatment for the so-called Negro problem and, therefore, lets him go. The man later finds a way of repaying him by removing a large tree from the tracks of the train on which he knows the reverend and his young son would be riding. He dies but saves the reverend and his son through this heroic act. The reverend later finds the true murderer, and the two African Americans are publicly exonerated by "a repentant community" (286).

The strength of the story lies in the depiction of the two men as heroic and brave. The dark man dies with dignity and the light man heroically. Their deaths reinforce the liberal spirit of the reverend and contribute to a change of attitude in this community. In this sense, they are not in vain. But the story does not go beyond the rather far-fetched and improbable act of Gentleman Jim at the end. There is no sense that the reverend would have done so much without the sacrifice of the mulatto. The Christian spirit of love, mercy, and an equality between all men that pervades the story is consistent with Hopkins's overall concern in her fiction. "As the Lord lives, he is one of our mother's children"—the line that the preacher keeps repeating is another version of her "Of one blood have I made all kinds on earth," which motivates so much of her writing.

With these two stories and *Winona*, all pure rebels in Hopkins's fiction are dark colored. Men who are described as physically violent are dark; men who are race-leaders in a more intellectual way (Will Smith, Arthur Lewis,

Reuel Briggs) are light-colored. Many readers have criticized Hopkins for this essentializing of the common racial stereotyping of her time. But Hopkins's vision was never narrow and included many facets of the racial spectrum. Luke Sawyer, Judah, and Madison Monroe can be depicted as behaving nobly in violent scenes without any obvious break in narrative voice or major plot inconsistency. And the more gentle and light-colored Will, Arthur, Reuel, and Mark Myers do not come off entirely without criticism. Reuel and Mark pass for white at some point in their lives, Will is depicted as helpless when Sappho disappears, and Arthur's patronizing attitude toward women is criticized. The scope of her characters in many shades of color proves that Hopkins moved beyond the limits of stereotypes.

Within the context of the short stories included in *Colored American Magazine*, Hopkins's stories stand out for several reasons. They are well crafted and include a variety of characters and topics, such as supernatural phenomena, miscegenation, and the connections between gender, race, and class. Some of her stories are directly related to each other and to her longer fiction; some of them open a discussion about the topics of passing, mixed-blood heroes and heroines, and the nature of heroism. Although Hopkins did not publish it as a separate volume, her short fiction can thus be evaluated as a consistent body of writing. Her influence as an editor can be felt in the inclusion and arrangement of several other stories. Her influence on Anne Bethel Scales (who is most closely identifiable with Hopkins) and Gertrude Dorsey Brown[e] proves the outstanding impact she had as editor. The dialogue between her and Brown[e] and Ruth Todd goes beyond her time as literary editor. Brown[e]'s "A Case of Measure for Measure" shows an enduring debt to the model offered by Hopkins. Above all, this discussion of a set of stories highlights the importance of the *Colored American Magazine* as a medium of publication for diverse, often controversial, high-standing literature, as a medium for opening up intertextual relations as well as social criticism. As a publishing venture, it initiated a reversal of stereotypes and began a process of revising master narratives much earlier than commonly acknowledged. Hopkins's role as a formative influence can no longer be disregarded.

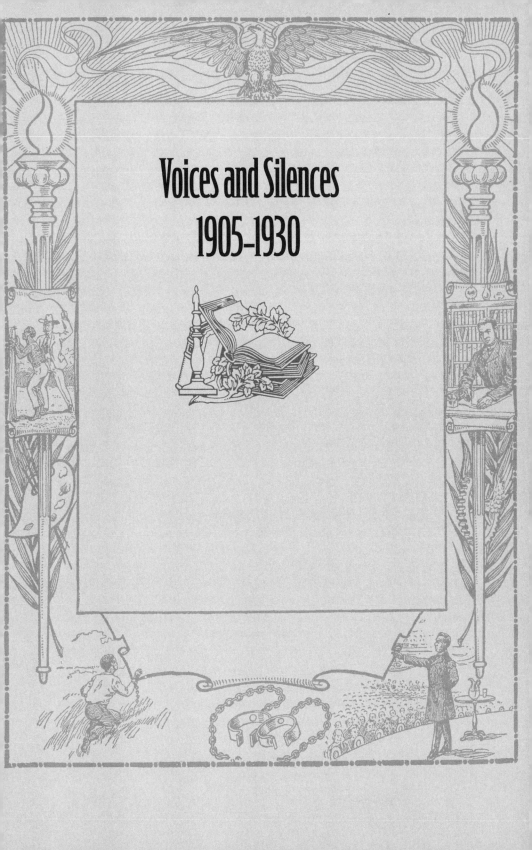

Voices and Silences
1905-1930

On the Platform with Prominent Speakers

*H*opkins's prolific years were dominated by her journalism and her own writing. She was engaged in editorial work and the day-to-day business of publishing a magazine much of the time. Some of her time, however, was always devoted to community work in the women's club movement and public lecturing. Two speeches in 1905 and 1911, respectively, demonstrate her consistent concern with racial issues, politics, and the role of the African American woman.

There are records of six public lectures by Hopkins between March 1903 and November 1905. Two of them were for the Boston Literary and Historical Association, two for the St. Mark Musical and Literary Union.[1] In *The Other Brahmins: Boston's Black Upper Class, 1750–1950*, Adelaide Cromwell reprints a program of the St. Mark Musical and Literary Union, which lists a presentation by Miss Pauline Hopkins on November 19, 1905 (82). The president of the union at that time was Maude A. Trotter, the wife of William Monroe Trotter. Lois Brown argues that Hopkins's "appearances at the union meetings symbolize her inclusion in a formal group of outspoken anti-Bookerites and followers of Du Bois" ("Essential Histories" 53). Her relationship with the Trotter family is confirmed when she appears on the organizing committee for the William Lloyd Garrison Centennial that was initiated by William M. Trotter. William Lloyd Garrison (1805–79) was one of the earliest and best-known abolitionists, whose dedication to the cause included even imprisonment and near tar-and-feathering. As founder of the *Liberator*, he printed fiery antislavery articles. He was an influential member of the New England Anti-Slavery Society (founded in 1831) and the radical president (for twenty-two terms) of the American Anti-Slavery Society (*Dictionary of American Biography* 168–72).

Trotter's *Guardian* of December 16, 1905, quotes from her speech delivered during this meeting at Faneuil Hall and thus provides a good record of her oratory. Her participation in the Garrison celebration and the printing of her speech in the *Guardian* clarify two facts about Hopkins. She was seated on the platform with a number of prominent speakers, white and black. She was part of a meeting that included notable mainstream American and African American speakers: Moorfield Storey (once secretary to Charles Sumner and the future president of the NAACP), Albert E. Pillsbury (a nephew of the abolitionist Parker Pillsbury), Frank Sanborn (one of the last living abolitionists), and others.[2] Even after her dismissal from the *Colored American Magazine*, she was one of Boston's leading African Americans. In addition to this, she was also part of the more radical and activist segment of the colored population. Trotter, the notable, renowned radical, allotted a prominent place to her speech in the celebration and even printed a picture of her on the first page of the *Guardian*, next to the pictures of William Lloyd Garrison and other prominent speakers at the centennial.

Some of the presentations were singled out by Trotter for publication in the *Guardian* because they corresponded most closely with his own political views. Hopkins's speech comes after a much-applauded address by Albert E. Pillsbury, in which he said, for example: "The work that Garrison began is not yet done. (Applause.) It must be done by agitation, with fire kindled at the same altar. (Applause.) It must be done by the black man himself. (Applause.)" (4). Hopkins's own speech is interrupted by applause several times. In great rhetorical manner, she compares Garrison with Martin Luther: "Side by side with Martin Luther's 'Here I take my stand,' is the 'I will be heard' of William Lloyd Garrison." After pointing out the individual responsibility to incite reform, she stresses woman's role in the drive for reform and emancipation and calls herself a black daughter of the revolution. This gives her speech a very feminist tone. Lois Brown calls this part of the speech "one of her most combative statements—one which reveals her belief that American racial injustice has been perpetrated since its very beginnings and serves notice that she is preparing to challenge its very foundations" ("Essential Histories" 56). Hopkins draws more applause when she indicts the South for its disfranchisement and emphasizes the black man's fitness for the ballot. When she cries out, "Let us vow . . . to keep alive the sacred flame of universal liberty in the Republic for all races and classes, . . . and let the voice of the agent and lecturer be constantly heard" (4), her speech becomes a proof of her rhetorical power, her outspoken views on political agitation, and her deeply humanitarian concern. She ends her speech with the biblical quotation about all people being of one blood that comes up in her writing so often. At the end of 1905 and at the age of forty-six, Hopkins certainly possessed such a prominent position in Boston that she was seated in this celebration, and the ensuing lack of information about her in the following years is all the more disconcerting and difficult to understand.

Hopkins also delivered an address at the Boston centenary celebrating the one hundredth birthday of Charles Sumner on January 5–6, 1911. This celebration was recorded by William Monroe Trotter in a volume, *The Two Days Observance of the One Hundredth Anniversary of the Birth of Charles Sumner.* Charles Sumner (1811–74) was elected to the U.S. Senate from Massachusetts in 1851 as a Free Soil Democrat. He was outspoken about the wrongs of the Fugitive Slave Bill and slavery. After a speech in 1852 that branded the barbarous system of slavery, he was attacked by Representative Preston Brooks of South Carolina with a cane and nearly died of the wounds inflicted (*Dictionary of American Biography* 208–14).

The celebration was organized by the New England Suffrage League, whose corresponding secretary Trotter was, and the National Independent Political League, assisted by a Citizens Auxiliary Committee. Pauline Hopkins's name appears on the list of this committee. The celebration is remarkable for the mass of people it drew into its audience, the number of distinguished speakers, and the political content of many addresses. There was, for example, open criticism of the leadership of Booker T. Washington and of the Senate candidacy of Henry Cabot Lodge. Lodge (1850–1924) was elected congressman in 1886 and advocated the "Force Bill," which was designed to establish federal supervision over all polling places during national elections and thus to prevent the exclusion of colored voters in the southern states. The bill was defeated, and Lodge never crusaded for the rights of African Americans again. From 1893 to the end of his life he represented Massachusetts in the U.S. Senate (*Dictionary of American Biography* 346–49; Schneider 29–54).

In a speech to those present, Mrs. M. Cravath Simpson, president of the Anti-Lynching Society of Afro-American Women, said: "This American nation, whilst it can boast of attaining in learning and ingenuity the highest heights of man, must hide its face with shame for its lack of conscience, its treachery and injustice, which envelops it like a pall" (31). In one of the many comparisons between the time of Sumner's engagement for the abolition of slavery and the commitment of 1911 to equal rights, Mr. E. H. Clement, writer and former editor in chief of the *Boston Transcript*, said: "Had a different attitude and habit of thought been bred in the American masses during the past thirty years, as Lincoln and Sumner desired; had the influence of the civil rights bill been at work, we should not have seen the race problem in the perilously inflamed state of the present hour" (51). Frequent complaints were raised against Jim Crow laws, intolerance, disfranchisement, labor injustice, mob law, etc. The keynote of the entire celebration was Sumner's "prophetic sentence uttered after the ratification of the Fifteenth Amendment to the Constitution": "Liberty has been won, the battle for equality is still pending" (Trotter, "Preface"). All this proves that Hopkins's concerns with still-prevalent race prejudices and a worsening of race relations was shared by other African Americans involved in public work.

Hopkins spoke on Friday afternoon on a platform with a number of prominent speakers. Some of the speakers were Trotter himself; Rabbi Charles Fleischer of the National Anti-imperial League; Mrs. Florence Howe Hall, daughter of Julia Ward Howe; Frank Sanborn of Concord, the oldest original abolitionist still active at that time and whose book about John Brown, Hopkins had certainly read; Dr. Horace Bumstead, former president of Atlanta University; and E. H. Clement, a famous Boston editor (see Trotter 37–55). After praising Sumner as an "intellectual and moral giant" (48), Hopkins attributes his failure and the antagonism he met in his lifetime to the forces of conservatism. In this indirect reference to the conservative race leader of her time, Hopkins says that conservatism "protects conditions and perpetuates them, and dreads and resists the innovations of the reformer." In her usual rhetorical device of generalizing upon the particular, Hopkins says: "We believe that now is the psychological moment for the forward movement of the dark races upon the world's arena. . . . Were Senator Sumner with us today, he would be in the forefront leading the forces engaged in the uplift of all humanity." Drawing upon her powers as orator, Hopkins then uses metaphor to emphasize her message:

> Life today is the Negro question. Socialism, the Labor question, Woman Suffrage, New Nationalism, Child Labor, White Slavery, the New Thought, Christian Science—life is the loom, mind the weaver, thought the thread, our good and evil deeds the warp and woof, and the web is the character to posterity as Mr. Sumner bequeathed his to us. Call us then, no longer Negroes, that name so fraught with blood and tears and bitter memories of contemptuous tolerance—but call us Men, mighty factors in the solving of human problems.
>
> The secret of evolution is profound. This American Republic was founded by the Almighty Economist who governs the great seas of progression and retrogression, tossing them hither and thither at his will by unexpected countercurrents. Here all races have found a refuge from persecution; here all races

were represented among the Abolitionists; here all races are to be participants in the new order of things slowly evolving out of the present unrest. (48–49)

In this only document of Hopkins's political stand between 1905 and 1916, it comes out clearly that she belonged to the radical camp around Trotter and was as outspoken against racial discrimination as before. Her hope in the power of the United States to draw together all different races and her belief in the power of men, with no racial qualifier attached to them, is unbroken. She does not call herself a black daughter of the revolution, as she did in 1905, but the list of causes that occupy her life at the time comprises an astonishing array of subjects, from socialism to suffrage, child labor, and white slavery. Hopkins was never narrow-minded in the sense that she saw the Negro problem as surpassing any other in importance and impact. Her commiseration went out to all races of the world and to all downtrodden people. Her lifelong activism took another turn when she undertook a new publishing venture, the editing of the *New Era Magazine*.

The "New Era Magazine"

*H*opkins made a brief comeback as editor of the Boston-based *New Era Magazine* in 1916, together with Walter Wallace, her former colleague at the *Colored American Magazine*. The magazine attempted to recreate and revitalize the goals of the former publication, with a series on "Men of Vision" and the fragment of a novel, *Topsy Templeton*. Hopkins also planned a column entitled "Helps for Young Artists," which showed her continuing concern for the advancement of young artists. *New Era Magazine* ceased publication after two issues and received hardly any comment, not even by Du Bois, who had commented on the changes of the *Colored American Magazine* earlier. Johnson and Johnson speculate that he might have seen the *New Era Magazine* as a potential rival to his own *Crisis* (*Propaganda* 68).

The *New Era Magazine* is subtitled "An Illustrated Monthly Devoted to the World-Wide Interests of the Colored Race." Its flyleaf advertises that it is "devoted exclusively to the best interests of the colored race, not alone in this country, but throughout the world. The rapid progress made by the race in this country during the past twenty to twenty-five years, as well as present-day progress will be fully and accurately shown. The magazine will deal fully and frankly with all questions affecting the real progress of the race, and will do its utmost to assist in developing the literature, science, music, art, religion, facts, fiction and tradition of the race throughout the world" (March 1916).

Articles that were being prepared included essays about Africa, Puerto Rico, Haiti, color prejudice, mechanical arts, colored masonry, women of color and the suffrage movement, Negro artists in Europe, reforms in Liberia, education, music, practical help for young men in business, hints to young artists, reminiscences of early days, and business. The international and national concerns clearly distinguish it from the *Colored American Magazine* under Fred R. Moore. The overall design of the magazine also documents

Front cover of the *New Era Magazine*, February 1916. Courtesy of Black Print Culture collection, Special Collections and Archives, Robert W. Woodruff Library, Emory University.

Hopkins's continuing concern with matters of race, politics, and literature well beyond her more famous years at the *Colored American Magazine*.

Hopkins can be credited with two articles about "Men of Vision," which continue the earlier "Famous Men of the Negro Race" series. The articles treat Mark René Demortie and Reverend Leonard Andrew Grimes, while an essay announced for the Easter number was to be about Henry Highland Garnet. Hopkins began to publish a serial novel, *Topsy Templeton*, of which two installments still exist. One short story, "Converting Fanny," is signed Sarah A. Allen and shows a considerable development in subject matter and narrative technique. It is likely that she wrote the sketch about Crispus Attucks that opened the second number of the magazine. The prospectus also mentions a series called "Facts Pertaining to the Early Greatness of the African Race," planned for future issues. The title and contents were directly taken from Hopkins's *Primer of Facts*.

Looking back with the title of her magazine to Josephine St. Pierre Ruffin's club publication *Woman's Era* (1894–97) and with an editorial statement similar to that of the *Colored American Magazine*, Hopkins was forward-looking in her attempt to exercise control over a race publication. She had prepared the necessary conditions for herself as editor and main contributor. Thus she is one of the few women journalists brave enough to venture into the full-scale publication of a journal. It is not clear why the magazine failed after only two issues, especially since the third number had been well planned and organized.

Hopkins made free use of Harriet Beecher Stowe in the novel she meant to publish in the *New Era Magazine*. The two installments of *Topsy Templeton* show not only in the title that the subject matter of *Uncle Tom's Cabin* was still in her mind. Miss Ophelia is the role model for Miss Sophronia Newbury, "tall, spare, white-haired, and thirty-five, with shrewd eyes and a friendly smile" (1:11). Miss Newbury and her sister Betty, whose full name is Mrs. Elizabeth Hopkins-Templeton, live in well-to-do circumstances in Boston. Miss Newbury is a spinster while Betty is married to a man, a noted intellectual, who suffers from a severe neurological disorder. They decide to adopt the mulatto child of their servant, who has left her in their care.

This Cindy is a very pretty young black woman. Her child is considerably lighter than she is, and Betty immediately interprets this fact: "Mrs. Templeton groaned in spirit, but made no outward sign, for, to the fortunate in life, depravity seems the natural state of the lowly and wretched" (1:18). Cindy takes advantage of the soft hearts of the two sisters, lies to them about her being abused by employers, and then leaves the child. The child is adopted by the family, christened Topsy Templeton, and given into the care of their trusted servant David Davis and his wife.

Motivated by a similar desire as Miss Ophelia, Sophronia explains her intentions to her friend and family lawyer Asa Day: "The idea is for us to *personally* superintend the education and rearing of the child as an example of what may be done by environment and moral uplift" (1:12). Her ideas are centered around what she calls "our Negroes" (1:13). While she has a loathing of the recent immigrants who live in slums, she thinks that the Negroes "may become our bulwarks if we deal rightly with them." Sophronia sees the undertaking as a kind of adventure that will increase her stock of "eccentricities" that she is collecting for a study. These "eccentricities" are, for example, unusual crimes or eccentric characters noted down by her and her secretaries in an attempt that she calls "patriotic" rather then "philanthropic." Her well-meaning intentions do not have their origin in pity for this particular destitute child but come from her general interest in anything queer and unusual. Asa Day understands her motivation but does not question it.

The characters Hopkins introduces in this fragment are familiar to readers of her fiction. The two sisters are the benevolent northern philanthropists, the descendants of the earlier abolitionist activists. They mean well but are not always efficient. Their self-righteousness rests upon their ingrained belief in the superiority of the Anglo-Saxon race ("we pure Americans" [1:13]), which is also the source of their racism. Asa Day, the good-humored lawyer, is less idealistic and shows a considerable degree of race and class prejudice, but as an old friend of the family supports the sisters (perhaps out of love for Sophronia). The invalid husband is very similar to Reuel Briggs. He is a divinity student, a descendant of Dr. Samuel Hopkins, dedicated to his studies: "The divine element within him prompted him to a life of unselfish devotion to his work, regardless of the push and pull of desire" (1:15). There is, however, some weakness in his character. He discovered that "he was God and brute crossed." He committed some sins of the flesh, not detailed in this part of the narration. One may assume that they are the source of some plot elements that would be revealed later.

An interesting sidelight is shed on two minor characters, the cook and the chambermaid. They are both jealous of Cindy's good standing with the two sisters. Before the sisters see her true character, they understand that she is going to exploit their goodwill. When she leaves the child behind, their anger and concern are understandable. They fear that the misbehavior of this one servant could affect all of them and endanger their positions in the household.

This action makes up three chapters of the novel and is dominated by the genteel atmosphere of the Newbury-Templeton household. The next chapter brings a change in scene and time. It is ten years later, on a cold winter afternoon, when the schoolchildren leave the school building. Several boys chase a small colored girl, Topsy, whose "frail figure breathed defiance in every curve" (1:20). She fights the group of boys wildly, like a little devil, but is knocked unconscious. The boys all leave her in a hurry and her friend, Pick-Axe Davis, tries to help her. This is the conclusion of the first installment.

In the second installment, Topsy's teacher takes her to the hospital, where the surgeons pronounce that they cannot help her. Dr. Alwyn is called in to exert his extraordinary powers. Like Reuel Briggs, he possesses "a strange power in some cases" (2:76), the power of reanimation from apparent death that readers remember well from *Of One Blood*. In contrast to Reuel, Dr. Alwyn is, however, a rather ambiguous character: "His form was spare and his features delicately cut and emotionless, wavy chestnut hair was thrown well back from an intellectual forehead. A man of wonderful intellect, but one shrank from the piercing eye—large and with dilating pupils of changing colors, now blue—now gray, with the straight eyebrows uncommonly thick and nearly meeting the eye at the outer corner." His type is similar to that of Aubrey Livingston, and the conflict, which is prepared by this description, may be assumed to arise in various ways. It is said later that he is a deeply prejudiced man and holds the idea that Negroes and monkeys are of the same species. He has some scheme in mind, some kind of experiment, which is unspecified at this moment in the narrative but which seems to involve Topsy and does not forebode anything good for her.

He has a very beautiful wife who remains mysterious. She is not known to Sophronia and Betty, although Dr. Alwyn is the cousin of Betty's husband. There is only one glimpse of the wife when she meets her husband at the hospital: "The woman was beautiful with a singular beauty that defied the placing of her nationality" (2:84). Whether she is really colored or whether even both of them are colored or whether Samuel Hopkins-Templeton is Topsy's father is open to assumption.

Dr. Alwyn successfully reanimates Topsy. In the ensuing bedside conversations between Topsy, Betty, and Asa Day, Betty is determined "to improve the child's neglected personality in earnest" (2:78). Reminiscent of the Topsy of *Uncle Tom's Cabin*, the child reasons with Asa and Betty about why she had to begin this fight: "I just *had* to get Joe fixed," and "A colored person has just got to fight her way along in this world, Mrs. Templeton" (2:79, 80). Race relations in the North are seen from a child's perspective. Her foster mother has instructed her to defend herself when she is attacked. Topsy is naïve, but she is also streetwise and has a cunning understanding of the real racism and hatred behind the attitudes of most white people. She says to Betty, for example: "I mean *onery* white folks—cops and them kind. You are the real thing. Pick-Axe says there's no skimmed milk about you; you're cream all right. But these common white folks—take 'em away" (2:79).

When Asa Day roars with delight at her manner of reasoning, he displays the same kind of spirit that saw entertainment in the lives of colored people that to them was bitter reality. To be fair, he is well-meaning and honest, and probably even sees the real-life background in Topsy's wise and true words, which the idealism in Mrs. Templeton prevents her from seeing. Nevertheless, he exploits her for his own amusement as a specimen of the comic Negro stereotype.

Much like the original Topsy, this Topsy moves even such a hard-boiled racist as Dr. Alwyn to empathy. When she says, "I only wisht I was white; I believe I'd bear to be skinned!" (2:81), he is as touched as the others. Asa Day then tells Topsy a long story about the little pigs and the alligator that is supposed to teach her the lesson that the young ones should heed the advice of their elders "but are taught only by the hard and bitter lessons of Experience" (2:84). This may be a foreshadowing of later events in which Topsy is subject to harsh lessons. It is assumed that Dr. Alwyn is part of this when he mysteriously says to his wife, who had taken a look at the child and wants him to leave her alone, "Such a chance has never come to me before—never." The second installment ends on this note of suspense.

This fragment of *Topsy Templeton* proves several facts about Hopkins. It shows that she was still active as a writer even after an interval of several years. It also shows that at this time of her life, she decided to develop material she had used before rather than go off into entirely new territory. The northern setting, the gentle and genteel sisters, the mysteries surrounding Dr. Alwyn and his wife, and a child character who is modeled and named after a well-known book remind the reader of elements in her earlier fiction. Does Hopkins want to say that race relations have not changed substantially? Topsy's fight with the group of boys and their earlier hassling with her are signs of racial strife, and the unreconstructed racism of Dr. Alwyn shows that prejudice is as prevalent as before.

It is appropriate that Hopkins should have left a fragment as her last publication. There are so many fragments in her own life, so many questions left open. The suspense intimated at the end of the second installment is the same kind of suspense about her life that motivates the present-day critic.

Hopkins's last known short story is "Converting Fanny," published under her pen name Sarah A. Allen in the *New Era Magazine* in February 1916. This story stands out because of its narrative technique and subtly humorous and feminist tone. It is another dialect story in which a black father complains over the telephone about the bad conduct of his daughter Fanny. The Reverend Johnson Brown has called Brother Sam Mingo, the father, to question him about his behavior toward his daughter. Although Brown's participation in the conversation is left out, enough is learned about him through Sam Mingo's reaction. The father readily admits having beaten his daughter in an effort to convert her to an old-time religion and proper conduct. There seems to have been a long history of growing alienation between this old-fashioned father and his young and self-confident daughter. While he can still accept her dancing the cakewalk and the tango and her appropriating new table manners, he cannot accept that she wants to go to college. And he absolutely draws the line when her behavior in church changes because she claims she has converted from Methodism to Episcopalianism and insists on reading her prayers out of the book. The father cannot tolerate this instance of misbehavior and whips her severely. The reverend's cautious voice, received indirectly, keeps warning him that he must accept the new manners and morals and that he cannot whip her into religion. The humor results from the father's stubborn insistence that his was the right behavior, while the reverend takes him down step by step. In the end, he tells the father that his daughter has taken out a warrant against him.

The story is different from the earlier stories in that it does not tell a conventional tale with a developed plot, several characters, and an omniscient narrator. It foregrounds the voice of the father and thus highlights his stubbornness and old-fashioned ideals. The reverend clearly represents the community in general. He threatens to bring the father's behavior to the board of church stewards and openly advocates the cause of the daughter. The reader's indirect knowledge of the daughter is that she is a thoroughly modern and self-confident young woman who wants to improve her manners and her education. The story thus contains a much more feminist view of the rights of women than any of her earlier stories. "Converting Fanny" stands, therefore, in contrast to the fragment of *Topsy Templeton*, which picks up topics and characters that Hopkins had used before.

The Late Years

*I*n her study of Boston's black upper class, Adelaide Hill Cromwell calls the period between 1830 and about 1910 or 1915 "the period of integration" (197). This time can be divided into a "stage of protest," which began with the leadership of William Lloyd Garrison in 1831 and lasted till the end of the Civil War. It was followed by a "stage of florescence," during which the African American community "realized sufficient political and economic achievement to have justified the fondest hopes of Garrison, Phillips, Douglass, Hayden, Sumner, and other liberals." It furthered the development of an upper class, which "measured up to standards of the prevailing community, regional, or national upper class." A subsequent "period of decline," however, set in at about 1910 for two reasons: "the lack of supporting interest in the Negro within the larger society and the Negro community's inability to resolve its own problems." The African American upper class, Cromwell argues, were "unable to meet directly the challenges in their own structure produced by the sudden invasion of foreign-born and southern-born Negroes and were further confused by observing a different and unfamiliar alignment of forces within the majority structure" (198).

Hopkins's late years can be dated from about 1916, when she failed with the *New Era Magazine*, to her death in 1930. It is the period in which growing age, financial problems, and probably physical ailment made it difficult for her to be as active as before. It corresponds with the period of decline that Cromwell locates on the local level in Boston and with a number of international agendas that did not further a climate of tolerance between the races, classes, and sexes in the United States.

John Hope Franklin writes about the year before the United States formally joined the First World War: "Lynchings and other forms of violence increased, to add to the concern of Negroes. In 1916 Jesse Washington was publicly burned in Waco, Texas, before a cheering mob of thousands of men, women, and children. In South Carolina a well-to-do Negro farmer, Anthony Crawford, was mobbed and killed for 'impudence' in refusing to agree to a price for his cottonseed. In Mexico twenty-two Negroes of the Tenth Cavalry were killed while on a mission pursuing a deserter" (335). Tulsa also witnessed a devastating race riot, the aftermath of which Franklin observed firsthand, in 1921. While service in the armed forces did not solve the problems of discrimination and segregation, the economic situation on the home front came to depend on African American labor (see Franklin 333–53). An increasingly large number of southerners moved to the industrial regions of the North. And yet the return of African American troops to the United States did not lead to a "wholesale distribution of the blessings of liberty" (355). The Red Summer of 1919 told of growing unrest and disappointment. The defeat of the Dyer antilynching bill, close investigations into the causes of mob violence, the Garvey movement, and the beginning of a recession in the middle of the twenties certainly influenced the lives of African Americans all over the country. Franklin calls this part of his history book "Democracy Escapes" (354–71).

Passionately committed as she was to racial uplift, black history, and the concerns of colored women, Hopkins's life lost its momentum after the failure of the *New Era Magazine*. The years of relative silence about her between 1905 and 1916, and the years of absolute silence from 1916 to 1930, cannot be reconstructed. The only references are to the lives of her contemporaries, especially to those of Trotter and Chesnutt, whose careers can be compared with hers to some extent. Further sidelights on the lives of Sutton E. Griggs, Paul Laurence Dunbar, Alice Dunbar-Nelson, and Anna Julia Cooper illuminate indirectly the creativity and silence of Hopkins. In addition, this chapter will also investigate the possible developments in literature that led to a negative evaluation of this period and this generation. The answer that evolves most clearly can be found in the assessment of a number of critics and in a combination of a shift in paradigms, the rise of the "New Negro," the central role of Harlem, and a prejudice toward gender and an older generation.

The "independent racial militant" William Monroe Trotter was especially renowned for his participation in the Boston riot in July 1903 (Fox 281). Trotter and some of his friends disrupted a meeting of the Boston Negro Business League that featured Booker T. Washington as one of its prominent speakers. Trotter, his sister, and some friends were arrested, and Trotter was later sentenced to jail for thirty days. This incident was the most prominent public uprising against the leadership of Washington. Was Hopkins in the audience of two thousand people on that fateful night? Is the fact that there is not one single reference to her in Fox's biography symptomatic of the fact that women simply did not count in Trotter's mind? Throughout his life, as Fox argues, Trotter remained antifeminist, combining an attitude of chivalry toward women with a strong belief that their proper place was the home. In this attitude, Trotter was typical of his times. Although there exists one letter from Hopkins to Trotter, and although they must have known each other, the exact nature of their relationship cannot be established.

Reading the account of Trotter's life by Stephen R. Fox, it is remarkable to find out that his career, after 1914, began a long decline in national reputation. In 1914 he had a much publicized interview with President Woodrow Wilson (Fox 175), but he did not find a place in the newly formed National Association for the Advancement of Colored People or any other more national than local organization. His silence was broken only when he protested the showing of the film *The Birth of a Nation* in Boston in 1915, and when he made an adventurous trip to France for the peace conference at Versailles in 1918. He continued, however, to write and publish his thoughts about presidential campaigns, race riots, the integration of a hospital, or the banning of freshman housing for colored students at Harvard. Since he was Hopkins's contemporary and fellow Bostonian for most of his life, it would be interesting to check her involvement in these matters that affected her as much as Trotter. She must have been, for example, part of the crowd of colored citizens who opposed the showing of *The Birth of a Nation* and threatened to demonstrate against it (see Fox 196). The prospectus of the *New Era Magazine* in March 1916 announced that she was planning a series on "Color Prejudice—Its Abuses and Uses" with a symposium of three white writers and three leading colored writers on the recent controversy around the showing of *The Birth of a Nation* (3). What was her attitude toward Garvey and his Negro Improvement Association? How did she react to the development of the NAACP and Du Bois's involvement in it? More important still, why did she not publish in *Crisis*, a journal that surely agreed with her general political and social position? Was it Du Bois who banned her from publication? Did she also suffer, as Trotter did, under Du Bois's rather poignant self-righteousness that made him, for example, try to neglect as much as possible Trotter's role as a race leader and his work for the Negro-American Political League?[1]

Another analogy can be drawn to the career of prominent fellow writer Charles W. Chesnutt. Chesnutt was born in 1858 and died in 1932; their lifespans thus nearly correspond. Unlike Hopkins, Chesnutt had the good fortune of placing a short story with the influential *Atlantic Monthly*, Boston's famous quality journal, as early as 1887. Two collections of short stories, *The*

Conjure Woman and Other Tales and *The Wife of His Youth and Other Tales of the Color Line*, were both accepted by Houghton Mifflin, a renowned Boston publishing house. As his journal and his correspondence show, this early good luck had its drawbacks, because it subjected him to the mercy of publishers who would rather see him continue his conjure-tale stories than plunge into more delicate subjects, such as the race riots in Wilmington, North Carolina. These riots were the subject matter of his second novel, *The Marrow of Tradition*, which was published in 1901. His first novel, which saw publication after years of rewriting as *The House Behind the Cedars* in 1901, had sold considerably well. But neither the second novel nor *The Colonel's Dream* of 1905 could afford him the lifestyle he wanted for himself and his family. Chesnutt eventually gave up writing for his very successful career as court stenographer and published only a few short stories in the last twenty-five years of his life.

Both Chesnutt's and Hopkins's productive years ended after about 1905. Both decided to concentrate on stenography for their living. Although Chesnutt did not give up writing, he could not publish much of what he wrote in his later years. Outside pressure, publishing policies, and an overall climate hostile to writers whose style and subject matter were considered old-fashioned led to the silence of nearly an entire generation.

There is, however, one major difference between the later years of Hopkins and Chesnutt. In 1928 Chesnutt was awarded the Spingarn Medal by the NAACP for outstanding contributions by an African American. This late recognition not only gave him the satisfaction he had been craving but also shows that his writing continued to survive.[2] Hopkins never received any such gratification. In the 1920s her writing was all but forgotten. The scarce notice it received usually accused her of what critics then tended to see negatively as a middle-class view, overattention to the concerns of light-colored heroes and heroines, and a sentimental writing style.

A similar fate befell the other two male fiction writers who are usually named as Chesnutt's peers. Sutton E. Griggs (1872–1933), a Texas Baptist minister, published thirty-three books, among them five novels, and was more widely read than Chesnutt and Dunbar. His novels are concerned with establishing counter-stereotypical images of the African American. His characters are often committed to overt or subversive revolutionary action. Like Hopkins, he tried to publish his works himself, but he was much more successful at this undertaking. His Orion Publishing Company in Nashville, Tennessee, promoted the sale of his books from 1908 to 1911 (Elder, "Griggs" 328). But even Griggs did not make a successful career in the 1920s, and today his novels are usually only treated at scholarly conferences.[3]

The third contemporary is Paul Laurence Dunbar (1872–1906). Sixteen books of poetry, three novels, and numerous short stories attest to his wide range of interest and his writing skills. He became famous through his dialect poetry and was praised, like Chesnutt, by William Dean Howells, the dean of American letters and influential editor at the *Atlantic Monthly*. Like Chesnutt, however, he was also under considerable pressure to continue writing in dialect and to perpetuate a plantation school of writing that was often replete with images of the contented and happy Negro. Dunbar could not cope with the role of representative Negro writer that he was tempted to fulfill. He died of consumption in 1906. His dialect poetry received much adverse criticism in the Harlem Renaissance but was rediscovered in the second half of the twentieth century.[4]

With Hopkins, an entire generation of women writers failed to make it through the Harlem Renaissance. Some of the novels that have recently been resurrected by the Schomburg Library are by authors whose biographical data are difficult to locate. There is, for example, not even a minimal knowledge of the biography of Emma Dunham Kelley-Hawkins, whose two novels, *Megda* and *Four Girls at Cottage City*, have received considerable attention since their republication. Claudia Tate could not pursue the biography of Katherine Tillman, whose novellas, plays, essays, and poems were published in the *A.M.E. Church Review*, beyond the year 1902 (see Tate, "Introduction" 11). There is also some, but not very substantial, knowledge of the life of Mrs. A. E. Johnson, author of *The Hazeley Family* and *Clarence and Corinne; or, God's Way*. The evangelical message, the light-colored heroines, the contrived plots, and the domestic idealization of woman were soon regarded as outdated, old-fashioned, not racial enough, and too much concerned with middle-class values. Like Hopkins, these writers could not survive in the 1920s with its more radical and racialized literature.[5]

The fate of Dunbar's wife, Alice Dunbar-Nelson (1875–1935), can be cited as an example of the lack of encouragement and opportunity of publication that ruined a promising writing career and led to bitterness and despair. Sixteen years younger than Hopkins, her two collections of short stories, *Violets and Other Tales* and *The Goodness of St. Rocque and Other Stories*, were published in 1895 and 1899. Her stormy marriage to Paul Laurence Dunbar lasted only from 1898 to 1902, when the couple separated, although she kept her husband's name despite two later marriages. Dunbar-Nelson settled upon teaching to earn her living because writing did not afford her the necessary financial means. Despite the many articles and stories she wrote for various magazines, the co-editing of her husband's journal, and her work at the Interracial Peace Committee, she never achieved an adequate kind of public recognition. Her efforts to "produce literature," as she herself calls her writing in her diary, never led to subsequent publications that repeated the success of her early volumes of poetry and short fiction. Like Hopkins, Dunbar-Nelson did not correspond to accepted notions of the writer in her time. She was very light-colored, she was outspoken, there were hints at her lesbianism, and she refused to produce the literature her audience wanted to have. She faded into obscurity and was rediscovered only when Gloria T. Hull promoted the publication of her diary and her works.[6]

Anna Julia Cooper was another contemporary of Hopkins. Born in 1858 in North Carolina, Cooper (then Anna Julia Hayward) strove for a classical education that was usually open only to male divinity students. After a brief marriage that left her a widow, Cooper studied at Oberlin College. She was a teacher, later the principal, at the M Street High School for black youth in Washington, D.C. (later named Dunbar High School). In 1906 Cooper was dismissed from her post as principal of M Street High School. The reasons for this dismissal, which destroyed her career to a large degree, may have been, as Mary Helen Washington argues, that she lacked loyalty to Booker T. Washington (*Invented Lives* xxxv). To all evidence, Cooper was caught in the general controversy over the respective values of training and college education for black youth instigated by the clashing opinions of Du Bois and Washington. Cooper, herself well read in the classics, always took pride in sending a number of her M Street graduates to prestigious universities. Being accused of a lack of the "proper spirit of unity and loyalty" meant at that time that she was not conforming to the more powerful "Tuskegee Machine" and was eventually replaced by a Tuskegee man. In a questionnaire, Cooper wrote many years later about this instance of insubordination: "For which unpardonable 'sin' against racial supremacy said principal suffers to this day the punishment of the damned from both the white masters and the colored understrappers" (Cooper, "Survey," question 46). Like Hopkins and other black female intellectuals, she endorsed the Du Bois side in the controversy, obviously with an enthusiasm that put her own career at risk. Although she was called back to M Street, she never became principal again and later even had to fight, unsuccessfully, for a better professional rating that would bring her an increase in wages.[7]

After nearly a lifetime as teacher, scholar, and public spokeswoman, Cooper began to study in Paris for her Ph.D. in 1924 at the age of sixty-six. While on sick leave from M Street High School, she completed her residency requirement in Paris and had to rush home so that she would not lose her job and retirement benefits. At that time Cooper had to cope with her teaching, extensive research, and her role as mother to five adopted grandnieces and grandnephews. In the spring of 1925 she defended her thesis in French in Paris—quite an excruciating experience, as she wrote in her fragmentary, unpublished autobiographical essay.[8] At the same time, this was certainly her moment of triumph in which she could prove to the world the black woman's intellectual worth. Leona Gabel interprets her efforts in the following way: "The Sorbonne experience was at once a triumph and an ordeal; her doctorate was the dream of a lifetime achieved after many years and in the face of great odds. It may have compensated somewhat for the humiliation inflicted upon her as a principal in 1906." Gabel also mentions "the unyielding, unsympathetic attitude of the school authorities and certain of her colleagues regarding her leave of absence" (65–66). All this attests to the fact that education for an intelligent black woman could be achieved only against the greatest odds and was fraught with much heartache.

The time between the 1880s and the 1920s is frequently called a period of transition, one without real significance of its own, rather a preparatory stage for the flowering of the Harlem Renaissance. Only recently have literary historians begun to revise the idea of the Harlem Renaissance as a glorious and innovative movement: "The Harlem Renaissance was not a blip on the flat line of black culture. It was a flowering for which the seeds had been planted decades and even centuries before" (Hine and Thompson 233).

One of the early influential critics is Benjamin Brawley (1882–1939), author of "The Negro in American Fiction" (1916), "The Negro in American Literature" (1922), "The Negro Literary Renaissance" (1927), "The Negro in Contemporary Fiction" (1929), *The Negro in Literature and Art in the United States* (1930), and *The Negro Genius: A New Appraisal of the American Negro in Literature and the Fine Arts* (1937). As Kenny Jackson Williams points out, Brawley stands for a rather conservative and bourgeois view of literature, and " 'Brawleyism' came to signify a type of genteel spirit in life and scholarship that some members of the Harlem Renaissance found objectionable" (96).[9] In his *Negro in Literature and Art in the United States*, he singles out for praise Douglass and Washington as orators, Dunbar as writer of dialect poems, Chesnutt as writer of the color line, Du Bois as writer of *The Souls of Black Folk* ("the most important work in classic English yet written by a Negro" [85]), Braithwaite as an "American" and not necessarily a "Negro" writer (89), and James Weldon Johnson as "one of the most prominent men of the race in the United States" (97). He mentions a few women writers in his chapter entitled "Other Writers" but does not refer to Hopkins under this category. If he had thought of her, it is probable that he would have classified what she wrote about the great theme at hand, namely "the Negro in his problems and strivings," as "traditional tales, political tracts, and lurid melodramas" ("The Negro in American Fiction" 185–86). These are the epithets with which he summarily dismissed a group of writers about whom he wrote in 1916: "Here was opportunity for tragedy, for comedy, for the subtle portrayal of all the relations of man with his fellow man, for faith and hope and love and sorrow. And yet, with the Civil War fifty years in the distance, not one novel or one short story of the first rank has found its inspiration in this great theme. Instead of such work we have consistently had traditional tales, political tracts, and lurid melodramas" (186).

Although Brawley was clearly critical of the new technique and themes in the African American literature of the 1920s, he also found fault with the earlier writers of Hopkins's generation, in whom he found an absence of "distinctly literary or artistic achievement" and a "lack of racial significance" (*The Negro in Literature and Art* 105, 111), a term he used to classify Alice Dunbar-Nelson's poetry.

Charles S. Johnson is the second exemplary critic writing at Hopkins's time who seems to support the typical view of the literature that preceded the Harlem Renaissance. Differing greatly from Brawley, he writes in his introduction to the anthology *Ebony and Topaz* (1927), a collection of art, literature, and essays aiming at interracial understanding and shedding light on African American folk life, history, racial problems and attitudes, and self-definition:

> The Negro writers, removed by two generations from slavery, are now much less self-conscious, less interested in proving that they are just like white people, and, in their excursions into the fields of letters and art, seem to care less about what white people think, or are likely to think about the race. Relief from the stifling consciousness of being a problem has brought a certain superiority to it. . . . The taboos and racial rituals are less strict; there is more overt self-criticism, less of bitterness and appeals to sympathy. The sensitiveness, which a brief decade ago, denied the existence of any but educated Negroes, bitterly opposing Negro dialect, and folk songs, and anything that revived the memory of slavery, is shading off into a sensitiveness to the hidden beauties of this life and a frank joy and pride in it. The return of the Negro writers to folk materials has proved a new emancipation. (10)

Although Hopkins had included folk characters and Negro dialect and had portrayed them more sympathetically and prominently than she has been given credit for by critics and readers, her clear distinction between superior characters who speak standard English and folk characters who speak dialect seems to have found no critical acclaim in the late 1920s. Johnson writes that in his collection *Ebony and Topaz*, he finds "a life full of strong colors, of passions, deep and fierce, of struggle, disillusion,—the whole gamut of life free from the wrappings of intricate sophistication" (11). In "The Negro Enters Literature" of the same year (1927), Johnson calls the time after the Civil War until the beginning of the Harlem Renaissance a "dark period":

> Except for the fading light of a few brilliant survivors of the crisis, nothing of any consequence was produced until Dunbar. Coming at that dark period, when, with the release of the working classes, the independent struggle for existence had become more severe, he caught the concept of the more tolerable Negro in his pathetic and contagiously humorous moods, accepted him without apology and without his miserable baggage of a problem, and invested him with a new humanity. More, he made him likable,—this simple, kindly, joyous creature, with his softly musical dialect and infectious rhythm. (Wintz, *Politics and Aesthetics* 274–75)

Johnson is not so conservative as Brawley, but he also speaks of Chesnutt as the "one novelist of competence" (275). Without giving specific names, he calls the years between 1900 and 1915 "years of restlessness, uncertainty and transition," in which "Negro writers struck a note of frank discontent ranging in temper from bitter resentment to Christian forebearance."

In a similar vein, William Stanley Braithwaite, Hopkins's Boston contemporary and a writer who was published in the *Colored American Magazine* under Hopkins's editorship, writes: "All that was accomplished between Phyllis Wheatley and Paul Laurence Dunbar, considered by critical standards, is negligible, and of historical interest only" ("The Negro in American Literature" 36). Like Johnson, he calls this time a "transitional period" (37). After referring to Dunbar's pathos and humor, he writes that the moods of these writers "reflect chiefly those of the era of Reconstruction and just a little beyond,—the limited experience of a transitional period, the rather helpless and subservient era of testing freedom and reaching out through the difficulties of life to the emotional compensations of laughter and tears." Even Chesnutt, to his mind, is "a story-teller of genius transformed by racial earnestness into the novelist of talent" (43). With the possible exception of Du Bois's *The Quest of the Silver Fleece* (1911), Braithwaite sees no important novels published between 1905, when Chesnutt fell silent, and 1924, when he wrote this essay.

Johnson's "wrappings of intricate sophistication" proved detrimental to the reputation of Hopkins's fiction (*Ebony and Topaz* 11), because it added to Brawley's criticism of her melodramatic tales and their lack of artistic excellence and Charles S. Johnson's and William Braithwaite's condemnation of her absence of artistic power and folk content and her inclusion of too many light-colored and well-educated characters. Her narrative technique and choice of plot and characters did not fare well with either the conservative and older generation or with the younger and more progressive critics.

When Alain Locke, who was professor at Howard University, published the influential *New Negro* anthology in 1925, the interested audience encountered the product of what was meant to be a cultural revolution in African American writing (see Rampersad, "Introduction"). Although Locke writes in his essay "The New Negro" about the emergence of this new generation of artists, his article may be seen as an indirect comment on the preceding generation. In his attempt to characterize the New Negro and define his artistic and intellectual excellence, Locke must have sounded more than disparaging of the earlier generation. It may well be imagined that the older writers still alive at that time—Hopkins, Cooper, Griggs, Chesnutt, even James Weldon Johnson—were offended by his tone. When Locke uses words such as "dynamic," "buoyancy from within," "shaking off the psychology of intimidation and implied inferiority" (4), he implies that the earlier generations lacked these qualities. Harper, Brown, Hopkins, Chesnutt, Griggs, Johnson, and Dunham Kelley-Hawkins, who were intent on portraying noble characters, who were convinced of the spirit of Christianity, the mission of the clubs, and the achievement of the noble men and women of the race, suddenly heard that in art and letters, the African American "instead of being wholly caricatured, . . . is being seriously portrayed and painted," as Locke put it (9). They heard that their minds were "protectively closed portals" and that they were in need of a "fuller, truer self-expression," as if they had all been narrow-minded, cramped, closed-in, restricted, and stilted artists and writers. Locke challenges the young generation to break with "the old epoch of philanthropic guidance, sentimental appeal and protest" (7).

The New Negro's "inner objectives" were defined by Locke as an attempt to "repair a damaged group psychology and reshape a warped social perspective" (10). He called upon him to develop a "more positive self-respect and self-reliance" and to repudiate "social dependence." Imagine a personality like Hopkins, who was active in the women's club movement, who wrote numerous articles about and for the race, who was involved in one of the foremost race journals of her time, when she read the following lines: "Each generation . . . will have its creed, and that of the present is the belief in the efficacy of collective effort, in race co-operation. This deep feeling of race is at present the mainspring of Negro life" (11). She would have agreed whole-heartedly to this creed but would have longed for a bit of recognition for the generation who prepared the path. Locke continues that this creed is "the outcome of the reaction to proscription and prejudice." Hopkins had, in fact, endorsed this idea in her preface to *Contending Forces*, in which she calls herself one of the "proscribed race" and names as her main objective "to raise the stigma of degradation" from her race (13).

The positions the critics and writers took were diverse, although most of them agreed on the aspect of newness and youth in opposition to the older and more conservative generation. Langston Hughes, in his influential "The Negro Artist and the Racial Mountain" (1926), puts it this way: "But this is the mountain standing in the way of any true Negro art in America—this urge within the race toward whiteness, the desire to pour racial individuality into the mold of American standardization, and to be as little Negro and as much American as possible" (166). His emphasis on folk roots, spirituals, jazz, and the blues make Hughes ask of Negro writers to be themselves: "We build our temples for tomorrow, strong as we know how, and we stand on top of the mountain, free within ourselves" (168).

At the same time, Hughes was capable of bitter and satiric comment about earlier writers. In his story "Who's Passing for Who?" he makes fun of passing for white. The first-person narrator advises a white couple about what to read in order to get an impression of passing from a black perspective. The narrator directs them to the work of Nella Larsen and *The Autobiography of an Ex-colored Man* and adds: "Not that we had read it ourselves—because we paid but little attention to the older colored writers—we knew it was about passing for white" (32). Taking into account the fact that James W. Johnson was born in 1871 and Nella Larsen was born as late as 1891, Hughes's remark, however much removed it may have been via a narrative perspective that is meant to be ironic rather than serious, reflected a general disregard for earlier writers that was unfair to Johnson and Larsen but must have been devastating to writers who came from further back in the nineteenth century. Even Alice Dunbar-Nelson felt that she could not be part of the Harlem in-group. Dunbar-Nelson was fifty-four years old in 1929, when she notes in her diary after attending a ball given by the NAACP: "Find a curious selfishness on the part of the Jim Johnsons and the Walter Whites and have my usual loneliness in the crowd. Oh, so pitiful!" (*Give Us* 313).

Brawley, Braithwaite, James Weldon Johnson, and Charles S. Johnson, as well as W.E.B. Du Bois in his 1913 essay "The Negro in Literature and Art," betray, as Giulia Fabi puts it, "the masculinist bias" in their attempts at formulating a canon ("Criticism" 186). Du Bois gives a long list of writers and artists but includes hardly any women at all. Arthur A. Schomburg's "Select List of Negro-Americana and Africana," an appendix to the *New Negro* anthology, supplies a long list of writers and artists clearly designed to establish a canon. The inclusion of texts by women can be easily enumerated: two volumes of poetry by Mrs. Harper, Jarena Lee's *Religious Experience*, and Phillis Wheatley's "Elegiac Poem on the Death of the Reverend and Learned George Whitefield" (423–26). Hopkins is also excluded from the list of "American Fiction Before 1910" (427–28).

Hopkins lived through the Harlem Renaissance, the decade that brought much public recognition to and success for African American artists. This movement was centered largely in Harlem, and young artists from Boston, such as Helene Johnson and her cousin Dorothy West, moved to New York in order to be geographically near the major circles of African American artists. It is safe to assume that Hopkins felt left out and bitter that no recognition came to her. It is remarkable that she set out on a career as editor and full-time writer in 1900, when she was forty years old. It is remarkable because her role models for this were few. Perhaps with the exception of her Boston compatriot Josephine St. Pierre Ruffin, editor of the *New Era*, a club magazine, her choice at this time was unprecedented. It is even more remarkable that she did not give up sixteen years later after many failures and disappointments. Like many women before and after her and like many male African American writers of her generation, she persisted against many odds. It is not, however, uncommon that she had little success after this publication and that she fell silent like so many others writers of this time.[10] Her fate is not at all exceptional, but it is tragic nonetheless, perhaps because it was repeated in so many other lives.

Hopkins died in 1930 after a terrible accident because the flannel bandages she wore to relieve her neuritis caught fire. Dorothy Porter researched the circumstances of her death and writes: "Living in obscurity after 1916, she died on Aug. 13, 1930, at the Cambridge Relief Hospital after suffering on the previous day burns on her entire body when her dress caught fire. She was buried on Aug. 17 in the Hopkins family plot on Lilac Path, in the Garden Cemetery, Chelsea, Mass." (326). So far only three notices of her death have been found. Ann Allen Shockley came across notices in the *Chicago Defender* and the *Baltimore Afro-American*, and Lois Brown located a short reference to her death in the *Crisis* (Shockley, "Biographical Excursion" 26; L. Brown, "Essential Histories" 59).

The silence enveloping Hopkins in her later years is a frustrating one. Her early career as a singer, playwright, and performer and her later career as a writer and journalist were both dependent upon the presence of an audience. It must have demanded a high price on her part when she could not publish any longer. The hopes she had for the future and the efforts she put into her writing and publishing were shattered after she discontinued the *New Era Magazine* in 1916. The fact that she managed to put out at least two issues speaks of her passionate commitment. The quality of the journal attests to her highly developed intellect and a restlessness that made it all possible. Her failure, however, if we can see it as one, speaks of the relentless world of business, where success is measured in financial, not ideological figures. If it is said that Hopkins failed in putting out more issues of the magazine or more of her own writing, this line of thinking can be reversed: she succeeded against great odds in doing what she did—editing two journals and publishing four novels, several short stories, one play, and numerous articles.

The end, of course, belongs to Hopkins herself. She opens her *Primer of Facts*, the text that is reprinted along with this study, with a poem:

> Cities are not great except as men may make them;
> Men are not great except they do and dare;
> Yet cities like men, have destinies that take them—
> That bear them on, not knowing why nor where.[11]

If Hopkins had known that her writing would survive into the twenty-first century, she would have felt that it only proved her thesis that history repeated itself and that excellence would prevail regardless of age, gender, and race. According to this belief, two words must be added to the epigraph to *A Primer of Facts* that she prints after this poem: "The standing of any race is determined by its mighty works and its men *and women* of genius."

Appendix

"A Primer of Facts," by Pauline E. Hopkins

PRELIMINARY REMARKS

Hopkins's treatment of the topic in *A Primer of Facts: Pertaining to the Early Greatness of the African Race and the Possibility of Restoration by Its Descendants—with Epilogue Compiled and Arranged from the Works of the Best Known Ethnologists and Historians* (1905) is not new, as she says in the subtitle of her study. It is compiled from the arguments of early black nationalists and Ethiopianists, while much of the Christian explanation of the development of different races or scientific explanations of race distinctions rests on much-used sources. The Bible, of course, takes pride of place and manifests itself in numerous passages of biblical interpretation and quotation. Hopkins also quotes directly from at least three books: William Wells Brown's *The Rising Son* (1874), Martin R. Delany's *Principia of Ethnology: The Origin of Races and Color* (1879), and Rufus L. Perry's *The Cushite; or, The Descendants of Ham* (1893). She also knew George Washington Williams's *History of the Negro Race in America, 1619 to 1880* (1883). These are the texts Hopkins quotes from directly. All of them, however, reflect thoughts and scientific ideas prevalent in many other texts. Hopkins's major message in *A Primer of Facts* is her insistence upon the position of the black race as a major and active participant in and shaper of the history of humanity.

In my annotations I will identify the passages of Brown, Delany, Perry, and Williams that correspond most closely with passages in *A Primer of Facts*. For the sake of clarity, I will repeat in them some of the information given in the chapter "The Voices of the Dark Races" in the main body of this study. The text has been reset for this publication, and minor spelling and punctuation errors have been corrected on the assumption that Hopkins would have made them had she known about them prior to publication.

A Primer of Facts

Pertaining to the Early Greatness of the African Race
and
The Possibility of Restoration by Its Descendants—with EPILOGUE
Compiled and Arranged from the Works of the Best Known
Ethnologists and Historians

by

PAULINE E. HOPKINS,

Author of "Contending Forces," "Hagar's Daughter," "Winona,"
"Talma Gordon," "Famous Men of the Negro Race," "Famous
Women of the Negro Race," Etc.

PREFACE

Facts Versus Theory:

> "Cities are not great except as men may make them;
> Men are not great except they do and dare;
> Yet cities like men, have destinies that take them—
> That bear them on, not knowing why nor where."

The standing of any race is determined by its mighty works and its men of
genius.

CHAPTER I.

Original Man.

THE CREATION OF MAN.—Man began his existence in the creation of
Adam, therefore all races of mankind were once united and descended from
one parentage.[*]

[*] The common origin of all mankind was the basic tenet of nearly all African American
writers determined to refute the polygenist theories prevalent throughout the eighteenth and nineteenth centuries. See Gossett, esp. chap. 1, "Early Race Theories,"

WHO BUILT THE FIRST CITY?—Cain built the first city in the land of Nod, and called it after his first born, Enoch.[*]

HOW WAS THE GOVERNMENT ADMINISTERED?—Probably there was no established government, and the head of the family ruled his own household according to traditional customs.

WHAT WAS THE ORIGINAL MAN?—Until the entry of Noah's family into the ark, all people were of the one race and complexion.

WHAT WAS THE COMPLEXION?—The Hebrew word Adam signifies red. Adam was so called from the color of his skin. His complexion must have been clay color or yellow, resembling that of the North American Indian.[†]

WHAT WAS GOD'S PURPOSE IN THE CREATION OF MAN?—The promotion of his own glory through man's development and improvement in a higher civilization. The progress of civilization was required of man by God.[‡]

WHAT AGENCIES PROMOTE CIVILIZATION?—Revolution, conquest and emigration. Of these three, emigration is the most effective.[§] From the Garden of Eden to the building of the Tower, there was but one race of people known as such: "And the Lord said, Behold, the people is one and they have all one language."

CHAPTER II.

Division of Mankind into Races.[‖]

WHEN AND HOW DID THE ORIGIN OF RACES BEGIN?—The sons of Noah were three in number: Shem, Ham and Japheth. These were the directors and leaders of the people. They all differed in complexion, and a proportionate number of the people differed in complexion as did the three sons. Shem was the color of Noah, Ham was swarthy, as it is conceded by scholars that Ham means "dark," "swarthy," "sable." Japheth was white.

---

and chap. 3, "Eighteenth-Century Anthropology." See also Delany, chap. 2, "The Creation of Man," 10–11. For more background information on Ethiopianism, early race theories, and ethnology, see Bruce, Fredrickson, Moses, Stanton, and Young.

[*] Gen. 4:16–17.

[†] Delany 12; Brown 44.

[‡] Delany: "The progress of civilization was God's requirement at the hands of man" (16).

[§] Delany: "Civilization is promoted by three agencies—revolution, conquest, and emigration; the last the most effective, because voluntary, and thereby the more select and choice of the promoters" (16).

[‖] Many passages verbatim from Delany, chap. 5, "The Origin of Races," 19–22.

After the confusion of tongues at Babel, each of the three sons of Noah went in different directions, followed by a proportionate number of the people who spoke the same language as the leader. Shem settled in Asia, Ham went southwest, and Japheth to the northwest, the three grand divisions of the Eastern Hemisphere: Asia, Africa and Europe. Therefore, the confusion of tongues and the scattering abroad of the people, were the beginning and origin of races. All this was according to the authority of the Bible (Gen. chapter xi, v. 6). "And the Lord said, Behold, the people is one, and they all have one language; and this they began to do (the building of the Tower of Babel): and now nothing will be restrained from them which they have imagined to do." "So the Lord scattered them abroad from thence, upon the face of all the earth."

Thus God's design in the creation of races was accomplished, because it roused in the people a desire for race affinity, and also to people the remotest parts of the earth.

CHAPTER III.

The Brotherhood of Man or the Origin of Color.

CAN ALL RACES HAVE SPRUNG FROM THE SAME PARENT STOCK?— The answer to this question solves the mystery of the brotherhood of man, showing it is possible for persons of three distinct complexions, as was the case in Noah's family—Yellow, Black and White—to be born of the same father and mother of one race and color. It is an easily understood law of God's all-wise providence.

The human skin[*] consists of three structures: the cuticle or external surface, the middle structure and true skin. The cuticle is a thin, transparent, colorless structure easily rubbed off by abrasion. The second is a jelly-like, colorless substance which throws out clear drops of liquid when the cuticle is rubbed off. The third is the true skin, also colorless or white, naturally. That which gives all races the complexion peculiar to each, lies in the middle skin. It is cellular and each cell is capable of holding whatever enters it in a liquid state. In the white race these cells are empty or partially filled with a colorless substance, clear like water. When color like a flush or blush is seen, it is caused by the red matter entering into the cells of the middle skin.

Elaboration and selection is the first process in the chemistry of all things,

---

[*] Many passages from Delany, chap. 6, "How Color Originates," 22–31, esp. from 25.

animate and inanimate—animal and vegetable and mineral. The coloring matter which enters the cells of the middle skin of the African race is the same red matter, concentrated, which flushes the cheek of the white man under strong emotion. In short, all coloring matter in the human system is pigment; that in a fair face being red, in the tawny being yellow in appearance, the red being modified by elaboration according to the economy of the system of each race.

WHY SHOULD THE SELECTION OF THE SAME COLORING MATTER OPERATE SO DIFFERENTLY IN THE BLACK RACE FROM THAT OF THE OTHER TWO RACES?—or why in the yellow race so differently from the white, if in reality descended from the same common origin of parent stock?—Simply because it is in accordance with the economy of the Creator to give an unerring reproductive system to each race whereby it should always be known by its own peculiar characteristics; the same is true of individuals of a race or family, and the same father and mother produce children of different temperaments, color of eyes and hair. See any family of the white race.

Take any or all fruits known as black; first the color is green, then white, next slight red which deepens daily to a final intense red or blackness in color. The fruit has simply increased in the red color matter until in its intensity we pronounce it black. Prove this fact by immersing a blood-clot in water—you will get a scarlet fluid reflecting the true color, red. The color of the blackest African is then simply concentrated red. The real color of the African is really purple and nothing else. Purple involves a mixture of red and blue, and implies the existence of blue in the blood. This is true, or whence come the blue veins of the white race and its blue eyes? Blue is an element of the blood; hence this purple color of the African. It is a significant fact that purple as a dress color originated in Africa; the Ethiopians and the Egyptians, who had the most delicate perception of color, adopted purple as a royal shade, and it was probably emblematic of the complexion of their kings and queens. Yellow is also a constituent of the blood as seen in the eyes, bile, jaundice and yellow fever. By a regular established law of physiology, an adequate quantity of red blood, blending, forms the purple of the blackest African complexion. The law by which this can be done is well-known to medical men and is beyond controversy. As in the animal kingdom, and in the anatomical structure of all vertebrae from fish to man, the Creator had but one plan; so in human races, running through all shades of complexion, there is but one color, modified and intensified from the purest white to the purest black.

WHAT OTHER CAUSE IS SOMETIMES GIVEN BY WRITERS FOR THE

COLOR OF THE AFRICAN AND HIS DESCENDANTS?—CLIMATE.* Instances are adduced in which individuals transplanted from one climate to another have changed the color of the skin in a marked degree. Thus people living near the equator and exposed to the intense heat of the sun's rays, are blacker than those living in the northern latitude of temperate zones. The Jews are a good example to illustrate our meaning. Descended from the stock, prohibited from intermarriage with the people of other nations, yet dispersed into every country of the globe, they have the color of every nation; fair in Briton and Germany, brown in France and Turkey, swarthy in Spain and Portugal, olive in Syria, copper-colored in Arabia, and black at Congo in Africa.†

CHAPTER IV.

Early Civilization of the Africans.‡

WHICH OF NOAH'S SONS IS MOST INTERESTING HISTORY TO THE PRESENT GENERATION OF HAMITIC ORIGIN?—Of the three sons, the history of the second, Ham, is fraught with more interest than that of either of the others.

HOW MANY SONS HAD HAM?—The sons of Ham were Cush, Mizriam, Phut and Canaan.

HOW MANY SONS HAD CUSH?—The sons of Cush were six in number: Seba, Havilah, Sabtah, Raamah, Sabtecha and Nimrod.

WHO WAS NIMROD?—The grandson of Ham; son of Cush. Nimrod first arose to national greatness as a monarch so that until this day his name is great among the princes of the earth. He was the founder of the great Assyrian Empire.

WHEN WAS THE FIRST PERIOD OF MUNICIPAL LAW?—When the separation took place the entire people began a new process in life as three distinct peoples with entirely different aims and interests. Shem went to Asia, Ham went to Africa and Japheth journeyed to Europe. The different races of the human family began, and at this time also began the period of municipal law. Previous to this time the people were governed by patriarchs. Their laws

* See esp. Brown, chap. 4, "Causes of Color," 78–83.
† The passage beginning with "Descended from" until "Congo in Africa" is verbatim from Brown (79). The original references from Brown are to "Smith on 'The Complexion of the Human Species'" and to "Pritchard."
‡ Most of the material in this chapter is taken from Perry 19–25. The Nimrod passage is quoted nearly verbatim from 22.

must have been few and simple, each father governing according to tradition or as it seemed best in his judgment.

WERE ETHIOPIA AND EGYPT EVER UNITED KINGDOMS?[*]—From all that we can gather from tradition, Cush went in a south-westerly direction, accompanied by his father, Ham. He settled a colony in Asia, near to Egypt, on the land terminating at the Isthmus of Suez, known to us as "the land of Midian." After remaining here a while, he entered Africa through the Isthmus, Ham settling on the delta or land formed by the mouths of the Nile, while Cush pushed up the Nile into the heart of Africa. Ancient historians agree that Cush left his brother Mizriam, Ham's second son, as ruler of the people in the infant colony, and he was known as the prince of Midian. When the colony at the delta of the Nile—Egypt—had grown in importance, Ham is supposed to have sent for his son Mizriam to assist him in the work of governing Egypt. Mizriam then left Midian in the hands of his brother Phut, joined his father Ham, and became co-ruler with him of the people.

That the rule of Cush extended from the Nilotic borders of Egypt in toward the interior of darkest Africa, and known as Ethiopia, is not to be disputed, all historians of ancient history agreeing on this point. In the early settlement of these countries, Ethiopia and Egypt were united kingdoms under the rule of three princes—father and two sons. Pliny relates that Ethiopia was originally divided into forty-five kingdoms. Diodorus Siculus affirms that the laws of Ethiopia agree with those of Egypt. This was accounted for by the Ethiopians who asserted that Egypt was first colonized by emigrants from their country, and they mention in proof, that the land of Egypt was for a long period entirely covered by water and was afterwards gradually filled in by accessions from the Nile of mud brought every year out of Ethiopia. This theory is confirmed by Herodotus, who designates Egypt as the gift of the Nile, and that the entire region, with the exception of Thebes, was once a vast morass.[†]

---

[*] This common Afrocentrist tenet can be traced back, inter alia, to Perry: "It seems, however, that with some writers (blinded by prejudice and influenced by prevailing opinion), there was a fixed purpose to locate places and explain difficulties in a way to exclude the probability that the frequent mention of 'Cush,' 'Cushites,' 'Ethiopia,' 'Ethiopians,' in the Holy Scriptures, has any reference to Negroes. But I shall undertake further on to prove with more satisfaction, that when the inspired writers of the Bible spoke of Cush and Cushites, of Ethiopia and the Ethiopians, they meant the land of Ham and the sons of Ham" (20). See also Perry 41–46.

[†] This entire paragraph is taken nearly verbatim from Delany (48). When Perry, Brown, and Delany refer to Pliny, Diodorus Siculus, and Herodotus, they cite common

The Ethiopians agreed with the Egyptians in most of their laws, their funerals, the deification of their princes, the colleges of their priests, circumcision, in their sacred and civil institutions, in their arts, science, learning and religion. Diodorus Siculus also asserts that not only the same kind of statutes, but also the same characters and hieroglyphics were used in Egypt and Ethiopia, since it is generally allowed that those were the repositories of Egyptian wisdom and literature.

The progress of Cush into the interior of Africa, toward the Niger, was easy because there was no opposition to his entrance. It was virgin soil, an unsettled country, and he was the pioneer in peopling of communities in Africa, and all the Soudan and Nigratia are today filled with the millions of his descendants.

WHAT WERE TWO GREAT CITIES OF THIS UNITED KINGDOM?—Meroe in Ethiopia, and Thebes in Egypt.[*]

WHERE WAS MEROE SITUATED, AND FOR WHAT WAS SHE CELEBRATED?—Meroe, the queen city of Ethiopia, has been celebrated for more than 2,000 years as the seat of all ancient greatness. It was situated at the junction of the Astaboras river and the Nile in Ethiopia. Flowing through Ethiopia the Nile forms great islands around which it scarcely flows in five days (Pliny). The island of Meroe was one of these great islands 340 miles in length and 115 miles in breadth, and on this island the city of Meroe was built. It is in the province of Atbar and lies between 13 degrees and 18 degrees of north latitude, forming a part of the modern kingdom of Sennaar, the southern part belonging to Abyssinia, a little below the present town of Shendy.

Meroe was the centre of trade between the north and south, east and west, and into the city poured all the caravans of Africa laden with frankincense

---

sources. As Moses writes in *Afrotopia:* "Since the 1820s, Afrocentrists have displayed remarkable exegetical power on those passages in Herodotus that are susceptible to interpretations as implying Egyptian or upper Nilotic origins for early Mediterranean civilization" (23–24). Moses also writes: "Classical black nationalists and Afrocentrists since the nineteenth century, including John Russwurm, Frances E. W. Harper, Martin Delany, Alexander Crummell, Edward Wilmot Blyden, Pauline Hopkins, W.E.B. Du Bois, and Marcus Garvey, were committed to a civilizing mission. They made references to Egyptian civilization hoping to focus the minds of black folk on noble and uplifting universal values—what Matthew Arnold called 'the best that has been known and said in the world.' They were not cultural relativists; they believed that some cultures were better than other cultures, and they were not amused by the spectacle of illiterate schoolboys insulting one another's mothers, just for fun" (35).
[*] Perry 25, 90–92; Brown 40, 44.

and gold and fine fabrics. Native products were thus exchanged for foreign luxuries.

CHAPTER V.

Progress in Religion and Government.

WHAT WAS THE FORM OF GOVERNMENT IN ETHIOPIA?—A KINGDOM. The rulers were selected from among the priestly caste. There was a custom which appears strange to civilized nations: the electors when weary of their ruler sent him a courier with orders for the ruler to die in any manner most satisfactory to himself. This absurd custom was resisted by Ergamenes, who lived in the reign of the second Ptolemy. He marched against the fortress of the priests and killed many of them. He founded a new religion.

Queens frequently reigned in Ethiopia, and royal women were treated with greater respect in the united kingdom than in any other ancient monarchy. Among the celebrated Ethiopian queens we may mention Candace, Aahmes (wife of Amoris of Egypt), and the queen of Sheba.*

HOW FAR DID THE RULE OF CUSH EXTEND?—From the Nilotic borders of Egypt to the interior of the country, the whole of which was called Ethiopia.

WHAT WAS THE RELIGIOUS CHARACTER OF THE ETHIOPIANS AND THE EGYPTIANS?—The religion of the Ethiopians and the Egyptians was a mixture of grand conceptions mingled with superstition. "No other ancient people were so firm in their belief in immortality, or felt its influence so strongly in their daily life; yet no other carried its idolatries to so debasing an extreme," says a writer. This contradiction is not confined to the ancient peoples of earth. We know that such contradictions exist everywhere, even among the professors of the religion of our Lord and Saviour—it is the difference simply which lies between ideal teaching and the personal character of those who receive it. Do we not worship idols today? Inordinate love of money and influence is the rock ahead forecasting the shipwreck of modern civilization.

The sacred books of the Egyptians and the Ethiopians contained the system adopted by the priests. Their fundamental principle was that God is one, unrepresented, invisible. But as God acts upon the world, his various attributes and modes of manifestation were represented in various forms.

* Both Perry (151–53) and Brown (39) write about Candace.

Some portion of his divine life was supposed to reside in plants and animals, and these were worshiped by the ignorant. To the wise, these animals and plants were merely symbols, but became objects of adoration to the unlearned. The priests perceived the power that this misconception gave their orders and refrained from spreading abroad the light which they possessed. Therefore the common people believed in eight gods of the first order, twelve of the second, and seven of the third; but these were worshiped under many titles, or as connected with different places.

The most interesting article of their mythology is the belief in the appearance of Osiris on the earth for the benefit of mankind under the title of Manifestor of Goodness and Truth; his death by the malice of the evil one; his burial and resurrection, and his office as judge of the dead.

Though many recognized the personality of one true God, they always represented him in three distinct persons, their idea of him being that he was a Three-One-God. This is illustrated in the person of Ham (Rameses I.) deified and worshiped as Jupiter Ammon. He is represented as the body of a man with the head of a ram seated on a great white throne of gold and ivory; in his left hand is a golden wand or sceptre, and in his right a thunderbolt; at his right side sat a phoenix with extended wings. This representation is symbolical; gold for purity; ivory for durability; the scepter, for authority, and the thunderbolt for power. A ram's head of two-fold significance combining the innocence of the sheep and the caution in the horns not to approach too near, illustrating the biblical declaration that "no man can look upon God's face and live;" and the phoenix illustrating the essential attributes of the Christian conception of God, as a self-created being without beginning and without end.[*]

CHAPTER VI.

Progress in Science, Art and Literature.

IN WHAT DID THE ETHIOPIANS EXCEL ALL OTHER NATIONS?—In wisdom and Literature.[†]

WHAT WERE THE PYRAMIDS?—Architectural structures built in Ethiopia and Egypt, begun under Ham, Cush and Mizriam.[‡]

---

[*] This paragraph is taken nearly verbatim from Delany 65–66.
[†] Delany 59. Perry writes that "it was in Ethiopia, the land of Cush, that the Sons of Ham began their career in art, literature, and science" (93).
[‡] See esp. Delany, chap. 10.

WHAT WERE THEIR USES?—They were sacred historical depositories for their bodies after death.

WHAT DO THEY SHOW?—Great advancement in science and the mechanical arts. They show the living reality of Ethiopian knowledge of mathematical accuracy in the science of geometry. No other power could have brought to Egypt's plains the great cubic rocks of thousands of tons weight, and placed them one above the other in regular symmetrical succession to a given height, decreasing from the first surface layer, finishing by a cap stone large enough for from twenty to forty persons to stand upon. Doubtless Euclid was induced to pursue his mathematical studies to the discovery of the forty-seventh problem, by dwelling among and studying, in other ages, these stupendous monuments.

HOW IS EACH MONUMENT PLACED?—Each is placed so as to exactly face the cardinal points, and the great pyramid is precisely upon the 30th parallel of latitude.

WHAT MAY BE SAID OF THE TEMPLES OF ETHIOPIA AND EGYPT?— They are the grandest architectural monuments in the world. That of Amun in a rich oasis twenty days' journey from Thebes, was one of the most famous of ancient oracles. Near it in a grove of palms rose a hot spring, the Fountain of the Sun. The oasis was a resting place for caravans which passed between Egypt and the interior regions of Nigritia or Soudan.

The science of medicine was practiced by the priests in even the remotest ages. The universal practice of embalming enabling them to acquaint themselves with the effects of various diseases by examination of the body after death. The Nile valley supplied drugs for all the world.

WHAT MAY BE SAID OF THE ETHIOPIANS IN LITERATURE?—They excelled all other nations in literature. Heliodorus says that the Ethiopians had two sorts of letters, the one called regal, the other vulgar; and that the regal resembled the sacerdotal characters of the Egyptians. The hieroglyphics on the Pyramids show that they understood ancient hieroglyphic characters as well as the Egyptians. Among the Ethiopians a hawk signified quickness or dispatch; the crocodile denoted malice; the eye the maintainer of justice, and the guard of the body; the open right hand represented plenty; and the left, closed, a secure possession of property. Diodorus attributes the invention of these characters to the Egyptians.

According to another writer the Ethiopians invented astronomy and astrology, and communicated these sciences to the Egyptians.

We can believe this because we know that the country of the African is very fit for making celestial observations. The Chaldeans were Hamites.

A learned writer states it as his conviction that the literature of the Israelites, in letters, government and religion, was derived from the Africans, as they must have carried with them the civilization of those peoples in their exodus. We must remember that the highest encomium upon Moses was that he "was skilled in all the wisdom of the Egyptians."

CHAPTER VII.

Restoration.

HOW HAVE THE BLACKS OF MODERN TIMES DEMONSTRATED THE FACT THAT THEY ARE DESCENDED FROM THE ONCE POWERFUL AND LEARNED ETHIOPIANS?—By the number of phenomenally intellectual men produced in Africa and America.

Name a few black men who are famous in science, art, literature, etc.[*]

Scientists.

Thomas Fuller, "The Virginia Calculator." (Native African enslaved.)
Benjamin Banneka—Astronomer.
Prof. Reason—Mathematician.
Prof. Kelly Miller—Mathematician.
Dr. Martin A. Delany—Physician, Ethnologist, Explorer.

Art.

Edmonia Lewis—Sculptor.
Meta Vaux Warrick—Sculptor.
William H. Simpson—Portrait Painter.
Edwin M. Bannister—Landscape Painter.
Henry Tanner—Landscape Painter.
Frederick Hemmings—Landscape Painter.
Samuel Coleridge Taylor—(Musician): Composer, Conductor.

Literature.

Phillis Wheatley—Poet.
Frederic Douglas—Orator, Editor, Author, Diplomat.
Frances Harper—Poet, Author.

[*] The following pan-African list includes famous African Americans and Africans. The original spellings have been retained. Notably absent from this list is Booker T. Washington.

Henry Highland Garnett—Learned Divine (Pure African descent.)

Dr. James McCune Smith—Physician, Orator, Author, Graduate of Glasgow University.

Dr. Alexander Crummell—Learned Divine, Graduate of Cambridge University.

Fanny J. Coppin—Educator, Writer, Orator.

T. McCants Stewart—Orator, Lawyer, Author, Diplomat.

Charles Lenox Redmond—Orator.

John M. Langston—Lawyer, Orator, Author, Politician.

Robert Elliott—Lawyer, Politician.

Ebenezer D. Bassett—Educator, Diplomat.

Rev. Tiyo Soga—Learned Divine, Orator Missionary. (Native Kaffir.)

Majola Agbebi—Learned Divine, Author, (Native West African.)

Dr. Blyden—Profound Scholar, Orator, Author (Native West African.)

Joseph J. Roberts—President Republic of Liberia.

Dr. Spurgeon—Liberian Charge d'Affaires.

Sir Edward Jordan—Editor, Politician (Mayor of Jamaica.)

George W. Williams—Historian, Soldier, Minister, Orator.

Prof. W. S. Scarborough—Educator, Author of Greek Text Books.

Robert Morris—Lawyer, Orator.

Clement G. Morgan—Lawyer, Orator, Politician.

Prof. Dubois—Philosopher, Educator, Author.

Bishops, Turner, Coppin, Derrick—Powerful Leaders in the A.M.E. Church.

Patriots (Revolutionary War).

Crispus Attucks.

Peter Salem.

Primus Hall.

Prince Whipple.

L. Latham.

James Armistead.

Patriots (Civil War).

Fifty-fourth Massachusetts Regiment—Fort Wagner, Olustee and other battles of the Civil War.

Fifty-fifth Massachusetts Regiment—Honey Hill, Olustee and other battles of the Civil War.

Eighth U.S. Colored Battery.

First North Carolina Colored Regiment.

Thirty-fifth U.S. Colored Regiment.
Thirty-second U.S. Colored Regiment.
Thirty-fourth U.S. Colored Regiment.
Sixth Regiment U.S. Troops.
Third and fourth U.S. Colored Regiments.

DO WE BELIEVE IT POSSIBLE THAT THE BIBLE PROPHECY CON-
CERNING ETHIOPIA WILL BE FULFILLED?—* We do, for even now the
time approaches. What reasons have we for so thinking?—The many significant happenings of the past few years: The establishment of the Liberian
Republic, the Anglo-Boer war in South Africa and the rapid opening up of
the Continent of Africa by civilized powers during the nineteenth century
and the rapid intellectual improvement of Africans and their descendants in
all parts of the world.

What is the obligation of the descendants of Africans in America?—To
help forward the time of restoration.

HOW MAY THIS BE DONE?—By becoming thoroughly familiar with the
meagre details of Ethiopian history, by fostering race pride and an international friendship with the Blacks of Africa.

Are we obliged to emigrate to Africa to do this successfully?—No.
Friendly intercourse and mutual aid and comfort are all that are necessary
at the present time. The future is in God's hands and will take care of itself.

EPILOGUE.

It is now several years since the first signs of cold indifference on the part
of former white friends, towards the social and political condition of the
black man, manifested itself openly and aggressively. Nothing is heard from
pulpit, press and platform but the growing charity and sympathy on the part
of southern whites towards the blacks of their section. Said "charity and
sympathy" seem to consist of an overwhelming desire to confine the Black
to the cornfield and domestic service. The crux of the position is found in
the words of Chas. H. Parkhurst in his sermon of April 28, 1901, after a visit
South:

"The less the Negro talks about civic rights under the constitution, particularly the right of suffrage, the better it will be for him and the sooner he will

* Psalms 68:31: "Princes shall come out of Egypt; Ethiopia shall soon stretch out her
hands unto God."

attain to all rights that justly belong to him . . . The Northern and Southern friends of the Negro are now counselling him to keep quiet upon the whole suffrage matter, to keep out of politics, not to talk about the constitution, not to insist upon his rights, but to attend industriously to the work of getting himself well ready—which he is not now—for what God and the country and the future have in store for him."

We have been quiet, we have grown so silent that we have become hateful to ourselves. Disfranchisement has been placed in full force at the South while at the North we have watched the narrow radius in which lie employment and advancement for the Black, growing narrower and narrower each month, until, perforce, we must break through the grim walls of ostracism or be crushed to death by want caused from lack of avenues for honest employment. The Propaganda of Silence is in full force. Newspapers and magazines have been subsidized or destroyed if the editors fearlessly advocated the cause of humanity. Every leading intellect has been intimidated while, per contrary, a horde of Southern writers, speakers and politicians are allowed to fill the air with their doleful clamor against a proscribed race, without a protest. Agitation by the black is rigidly barred, but the Southern white is allowed the front of the stage in presenting his grievances to a sympathetic public.

Among the many Southern white ladies engaged in the laudable (?) work of eliminating the black brother and assisting him into the valley of humiliation we find one Mrs. Jeannette Robinson Murphy; her work is an illustration of all the work of Southern whites against the Negro.* Since 1898 Mrs. Murphy has diligently canvassed the New England States, proselytizing the friends of the Blacks to the cause of the South, and inducing said friends to view the situation through Southern spectacles. Mrs. Murphy has appeared in the most aristocratic halls of amusement in our Northern cities and is being sustained by the richest and most influential members of our Northern aristocracy. We give an excerpt from Mrs. Murphy's book "Southern Thoughts for Northern Thinkers."

"Had the South been let alone and trusted it would have required but a few years more for the unnatural system of human bondage to have died of

---

* Mrs. Jeannette Robinson Murphy, dramatic soprano and lecturer, was born in Jefferson, Kentucky, but resided in New York, and was quite successful on the lecture platform. She was the author of some dialect work both in prose and in verse and published *Southern Thoughts for Northern Thinkers* and *African Music in America*. See *Biographical Dictionary of Authors*, vol. 15 of the *Library of Southern Literature* (1909).

itself a natural death, for it was no longer profitable, except in two or three states where the larger plantations could be successfully worked. . . .

"Just at the time when there seemed every probability that our Southern men would be able to solve their own problem satisfactorily, there came on the scene a new leader, a stranger to those fair parts. He chanced one glorious summer day to be walking up and down a lovely shaded lane beside a grand ancestral estate in far-famed old Virginia. He looked about him and saw countless broad acres, all gladly yielding their increase. He heard the merry shouts of laughter from hundreds of happy Negroes at work, broken occasionally by joyous religious bursts of song. He saw the courtliest, bravest race of knightly, stalwart men, growing up like their fathers before them, tall and straight and handsome; courteous men who set women up on their rightful pedestals and kept them there. He saw the fairest, tenderest women gladly dependent upon their natural protectors; he travelled all over the lovely Southland, and everywhere as far as his eye could reach were homes which were ruled by love alone, each home a perfect heaven in itself. Enviously he exclaimed, 'this will never do; these people love God and are perfectly happy. My power is threatened, and I must change all this and quickly, too, for I see these mothers are proud to possess large families of children to train for God's kingdom, and soon the hosts of good will outnumber my followers, and then I shall be hopelessly lost. I can scarcely credit my senses. If these Southerners have not taken these black savages whom I thought were forever mine, and even gone to Christianizing them, and they in turn are teaching the white babies to love and memorize God's Holy Word. I have never yet seen such noble men and women—I have never before found such stern sense of duty and principle as actuates their every motive.' . . . So spake his political majesty Satan, as he hurried away to execute his plans. Before leaving the South, however, he had promised large rewards to a few treacherous slaves who would do his bidding.

"Arriving at the cold, frozen North he knocked gently at the hearts of a few receptive, sympathetic, credulous souls, and calling himself, 'The Voice of the Lord,' he gained a royal entrance therein, and straightway those same misguided agents of his were filled with a burning zeal to abolish slavery and carry out, as they now believed, the Lord's will.

"These energetic abolitionists did not let the grass grow under their zealous feet, but began to sow the seeds of discontent among the very slaves in whose hearts Satan had already left his poison. They listened with itching ears to the lies of his runaway slaves—how they were beaten mercilessly, starved inhumanly and brutally overworked (as if anyone ever got any hard work out of an old-fashioned, free-from-care 'nigger,') and, worst of all, how they were tracked and torn to death by the fiercest of bloodhounds.

"Yes, these emissaries of Satan took the South's wealth, but had that great apostle of God, Abraham Lincoln, lived, this wrong would have been righted, for slavery must have been lawful under the constitution, else it would not have been necessary to add that controversial amendment, and so we feel deep down in our inmost hearts that the government of the United States still lawfully owes to the South millions of dollars.

"Generous Northerners seek in vain to catch the Southern viewpoint of the vexed Negro question.

"The whole trouble and difficulty lie in just one thing and nothing else. We are willing to give the Negro an all-round mental, moral, physical and spiritual education, but we insist upon the utter segregation and social isolation of the colored man. No proposed standing army can ever change the attitude of the white South upon this question. No qualifications or highest education of the Negro could ever make the true Southern man welcome that Negro into his family or hold out to him the tiniest tip of social recognition, for he believes that the mingling of a higher race with a lower one is an abomination unto the Lord. Around this pitiful point future wars and causes of war must lie . . .

"What often appears as cruelty to human beings is simply an outward expression of an instinctive racial gulf, which we think God fixed unalterably when He Himself first wisely segregated the Negro race in far-off Africa.

"As matters stand today the feelings of the Negroes are continually lacerated, because, forsooth, we will not call them 'Mr.' and 'Mrs.' and colored 'ladies' and 'gentlemen.'

"One's brain sickens and faints at the thought of America's future. There is one righteous solution, and that God alone knows.

"For all of the bitter feeling of today on the part of the young Southern Negroes toward their best true friends, their Southern white neighbors, and for all the blood to be shed in the future, we, in our narrow vision, can only thank two sources, that is, the misguided, interfering outsiders since the days before '60, as focused by Harriet Beecher Stowe, who gave the world a false impression of the treatment of slaves by the majority of generous, religious, true-bred gentlemen, their Southern masters, and a few tactless missionaries sent South since the war to lift up (?) the Negro.

"I have interviewed all my life great numbers of ex-slaves, and I have yet to find one old slave who will say that he or she was cruelly treated.

"Would it not be a good thing, in order to secure to posterity a true knowledge of the situation in those blessed old missionary slave days, to take down, ere it is too late, in the presence of just Northern witnesses, the sworn testimony of every old slave now living? My! what an everlasting exoneration our ancestors would have, even at this late day!

"Slaves were spoken of always as 'our people,' and were kept when possible under the same ownership. When colored parents must needs be separated, there were not often such heartbreaking scenes as those bloodcurdling tales (to be found in the books and tracts distributed throughout the North) would have us believe. Negro mothers are often unkind and cruel to their own children, though devoted, as a rule, to their white charges, whom they respect. Many a slave mother has said to her master, 'Ef you don't sell dat triflin' Jim o' mine 'way frum hyar, I's gwine to kill 'im,' and not infrequently the master had to protect children from their savage mothers' rage, and forcibly separate certain dangerous Negro families, for the safety of the lives of their members.

"The North does not understand nor love the sure-enough African in his present illiterate, irresponsible, shiftless state, and we of the South do not understand or care for the educated Negro.

"As the uneducated as well as the educated colored people are moving North to secure the social and political equality which we will never give them, it may not be many years before the northern section of the United States is overrun by them, and then, since they will not be properly appreciated, the ruptures will be sure to come, and if I were to turn prophet I should say, 'in that event it will be God pity the Negro and God pity the North, for a great race war will take place, and the few Negroes who do escape alive will fly back down home to their only friends, and they will long for the blessed old days when their jolly, easygoing fathers held the patient Southerners in bondage.'

"We lay it to the doors of unwise politicians exclusively for calling Confederates 'traitors' in the histories which I am told our Southern children living up North must now read.

"Instead of the South wasting any more of its hard-earned money upon the impossible higher education of the Negroes, let us give them as a whole domestic training and sound Bible teaching, employing white ministers to lead them, as in the old regime, and then later on expend all our surplus money and energy in colonizing the race somewhere as Abraham Lincoln suggested, and give it a chance to show if it is really capable of self-government and higher culture.

"As a temporary place of colonization we might try New England, since the historic underground railroad has already given the Negro a taste for travel, and the best and most acceptable charity that could be extended to him by the South would be a free ticket one way to such a colony at the welcoming North.

"Since writing the above, I have been inquiring into the attitude which Mrs. Harriet Beecher Stowe assumed toward the Negro race after she removed to her Southern home at Mandarin, Florida.

"It is said that she gave orders that no Negro was ever to enter her yard. Rumor also avers that shortly before her death she declared that if she had fully understood the Negro nature she would never have written 'Uncle Tom's Cabin,' and moreover, that she keenly regretted her part in bringing on the war."

Now is there anything in all this?

There is much in it. As an able white editor has boldly asserted, it means the acceptance of the docile domestic basis, supplemented by a little common school education, or deportation. The idea is to stop the flow of complaints against the white South and to cover its purposes against the Black from the just criticism of the nations of the earth.

Because of the desire and commands of our enemies, shall agitation stop, and shall we sit in silence while our traducers go unanswered? This question answers itself. We cannot cease from agitation while our wrongs are the sport of those who know how to silence our every complaint and plea for justice. NEVER SURRENDER THE BALLOT.*

The iron heel of oppression is everywhere; it has reached every section of this country, and every black citizen has a duty to perform. Cultured men and women of color in convention assembled sit in silence while one side of this burning question is discussed—the white side—and we are solemnly impressed with the magnitude of our wickedness and hopeless depravity by partisan white and colored speakers. It has reached the pass where the educated Black will handle any subject in his assemblies but politics. The South and its friends have said: "Not a word of complaint, no talk of lynching, not an offensive word, or it will go hard with you," and the race leaders have bowed to that decree in abject submission.

What are we going to do about it? STICK TO PRINCIPLE.

---

* Hopkins's call for agitation for full civil rights is repeated once more as the last sentence of this treatise. At her time, such a decided radical attitude antagonized such moderate African Americans as Booker T. Washington.

In replying to Mrs. Murphy's aspersions upon our race, we take first her allusion to the chivalry of Southern men.

We venture to assert that these gentlemen are responsible for all the evil that slavery wrought in the Southern home. The results of profligacy are the same in any case whether whites or blacks are the aggressors. But if this be true, and pity 'tis, 'tis true, it is but the result of conditions forced upon a helpless people, and not their choice. Tears and heart-burning are the portion of the Southern white woman, and like Sarah of old, she wreaks her vengeance on helpless Hagar.

Chivalrous Southern men desecrated the purity of the Southern home, and, incidentally, opened this question of racial purity.

For the sake of argument,[*] let us admit that there may be some foundation for the fears of the South that amalgamation may produce a race that will gradually supersede the present dominant factors in the government of this Republic. Who is to say that the type of the future American will not be represented by the descendants of men whose cosmopolitan genius makes them the property of all mankind?[†] The offspring of Samuel Coleridge Taylor, or of Henry Tanner, will, in all probability, unite with some one of their social set in the countries of their adoption. There were hundreds of Blacks, born in slavery and settled by their white fathers in the English Provinces, after being endowed with wealth. Their descendants have united with some of the best white families and are living in happiness among their countrymen.

These things are true, and, being true, who can tell when the drop of black blood will inadvertently filter back to the American channels from whence it started (especially if Americans continue to unite with Englishmen among whom there is very slight prejudice to color in marriage), and its possessors be placed by popular vote in the Presidential chair.

Anglo-Saxon blood is already hopelessly perverted, with that of other races, and in most cases to its great gain. Well, if it is so, what of it? The world moves on; old ideas and silly prejudices disappear in a fog of ridicule. All things are possible, if not probable.

---

[*] The passage from "For the sake of argument" until "All things are possible, if not probable" also appears in the earlier "Charles Winter Wood" article by Hopkins, writing as J. Shirley Shadrach (see "Charles Winter Wood," *Colored American Magazine* 5.5 [Sept. 1902]: 347).

[†] See my chapter "The Voices of the Dark Races" about the interrelation of the concept of the future American with Chesnutt's series of articles, Anna Julia Cooper, George Washington Williams, and other passages in Hopkins's writing.

With regard to the Abolitionists, we as their wards must speak a word in their defence. The present generation little understands the dangers and difficulties which these brave and good men faced. Let us not misunderstand their position; principle alone actuated them. Do not let us flatter ourselves that love for a black skin had anything to do with their acts for us. No; it was love of country and pride in the good name of the Republic simply. With true patriotism they sacrificed their fortunes to their principle in many cases. In penury and want they wrought. Oftentimes their home was an attic, a cot their bed, but withal their treatises on slavery were masterpieces of literature, for the Abolitionists embraced the flower of American intellectual culture. In their lives is a lesson for us in the present crisis of our racial history.

In a burst of eloquence as to the future of America, Mrs. Murphy deprecates the fact that blood will flow, and seems to take a savage pleasure in the thought that the Black will be the victim of a race war.

Blood will flow, but not by the seeking of the Black, and he will only participate in the fight when the government places in his hands arms for its protection. Meagre as is our intellectual capacity, we promise not to give the whites an excuse for the wholesale slaughter of our people which Mrs. Murphy evidently thirsts to behold. Blood will flow! When labor and capital become contending forces, the Black will float into the full enjoyment of citizenship.* Blood will flow, for humanity sweeps onward, and God's purposes never fail.

The testimony of ex-slaves as to good treatment received during bondage would be utterly worthless, as the oath of a black man is valueless in our courts of justice.

When we consider the fact that one of the safe guards of the institution of slavery lay in obliterating all family ties and in eliminating from the slave's life all family affection, it would be small cause for wonderment if the black mother were entirely devoid of feeling for her offspring. Mere vegetation without consciousness was the plan mapped out for modelling "good Negroes." Happily the plan failed, for our mothers are the bulwarks of the race whom we love, revere, and delight to honor.

Parental brutality was on the side of the fathers of the beautiful octoroons

---

* Hopkins's prominent phrase regarding the contending forces appears as the title of her novel *Contending Forces* and in the speech of Luke Sawyer (256). In the final installment of the "Dark Races" series, she writes: "The most serious questions of the hour are the Negro Problem and its fellow—Capital versus Labor. These are the factors which in a future generation will change the current of events and the deductions of science" (461).

who made the auction sales interesting, and at the same time filled the pockets of "the courtliest, bravest race of knightly, stalwart men," and also, incidentally "set women (white) upon their rightful pedestals and kept them there." These men were totally devoid of the feelings quite common to the brute creation for its offspring. If the springs of affection had failed sometimes among the blacks, small wonder when we consider that the master was the slave's god who could do no wrong, and that the white pastors of the plantations taught the slaves the duty of master-worship to the exclusion of God-worship.

In conclusion, Mrs. Murphy's arguments appear to the writer puerile and pointless in whatever light we may view them. As a representative of the most scholarly of living races she shows lamentable ignorance of the commonest scientific and historical facts. But more than all else it is borne in upon us by this attack that the foundation stones of the Republic are tottering. Woman, gentle, refined woman, who governs the home and whose influence is all potent with husband and father and brother and son and daughter, whose thoughts and examples are to rule our future governors and presidents, has stooped from her high pedestal to the mire of falsehood to crush a proscribed people lying helpless at the feet of Christendom.[*]

Ethiopia fell because of her arrogance and her stiff-necked idolatry. Scarcely a sign of her ancient splendor can be found today, and low in the dust of humiliation lie her suffering children. Egypt fell, and so did Greece. Rome fell. Why these happenings?[†]

Because Omnipotence was wearied by the injustice of man. History repeats itself. For God will visit us in judgment, and in the last hour when He seems

---

[*] In "Famous Women of the Negro Race: Phenomenal Vocalists," Hopkins writes: "Maligned and misunderstood, the Afro-American woman is falsely judged by other races. Nowhere on God's green earth are there nobler women, more self-sacrificing tender mothers, more gifted women in their chosen fields of work than among the millions of Negroes in the United States" (46).

[†] See Brown 43: "Every one knows that Rome got her civilization from Greece; that Greece again borrowed hers from Egypt, that thence she derived her earliest science and the form of her beautiful mythology." Brown also names as centers of civilization Thebes and Meroe and calls Meroe "the queenly city of Ethiopia, into which all Africa poured its caravans laden with ivory, frankincense, and gold" (44). He concludes from this: "So it is that we trace the light of Ethiopian civilization first into Egypt, thence into Greece, and Rome, whence, gathering new splendor on its way, it hath been diffusing itself all the world over." George Washington Williams writes that the Negro fell from his high state of civilization due to sin, "forgetfulness of God, idolatry" (History of the Negro Race 24).

to have left nothing undone that He could do for His vineyard, we still forget justice and judgment; none calling for justice, nor any in the high places of government pleading the cause of the poor, the very poorest of the poor, the despised and humiliated Negro.

Rome conquered the world, and was finally swallowed up by the world which she conquered. NEVER GIVE UP THE BALLOT.

Notes

RESTLESSNESS OF THE SPIRIT (1859–1900)

Background and Beginnings

1. Throughout history, appellations have been various, divergent, and often hotly debated. In this text the preferred choice is *African American*, the standard appellation since the 1990s. In some cases, *Negro, colored, colored American*, or *black* have been chosen to avoid ahistorical usage. They are employed with a full awareness of their historical context and the controversies surrounding them.

2. Information about James Monroe Whitfield can be found in Blyden Jackson (252); Laryea; and Sherman.

3. For information about the Paul family and their sometimes confusing genealogy, see Horton, *Black Bostonians*, 40ff.; Horton, *Free People,* 43–45. A detailed account of Susan Paul's life can be found in Lois Brown's introduction to Paul's *Memoir of James Jackson.*

4. James Oliver Horton writes about the pattern of family involvement over generations: "If one member of a family was involved in civil rights, anti-slavery, or general social reform, other family members were likely to take part" (*Free People* 48). See also Gatewood for a general discussion of prominent African American families.

5. The 1870 census showed that 37 percent of the African American population of Boston was born in the state of Massachusetts, whereas 36 percent were migrants from the South, mainly from Virginia, Maryland, and North Carolina (see Thernstrom 181).

6. Manuscript versions of both plays can be found in the Hopkins Papers, Fisk University Library Special Collections. There is no date given for "One Scene."

7. Collison describes the Boston of 1850: "The city shoreline bristled with docks, and hundreds of masts rose from Boston Harbor. A colossal spider's web of railroad tracks reached out from the center of the city toward the west, north, and south, connecting Boston to the manufacturing centers of Lowell, Worcester, and Lynn and to markets all through New England, the mid-Atlantic states, and the Midwest" (61).

Performances and *Peculiar Sam*

1. Subsequent references to the Hopkins Papers will be abbreviated HP, with folder abbreviated "f."

2. For information about Anna Madah and Emma Louise Hyers, who were considered by many to be the forerunners of the later celebrated singers Marie Selika and Sissieretta Jones, see Southern, *Music*, 244–55, and Southern, "An Early Black Concert Company." For information about Sam Lucas, see Southern, *Music* (esp. 237–42), and Holly.

3. According to Daniels, the social acceptance of a stenographer ranked in between "Menial and Common Labor Occupations" and "Professions and Business Proprietorships" in the category "Higher Grade Manual and Clerical Work" (Daniels 333–97). In his ascending scale "according to their estimation in the community" (345), stenographers ranked above such professions for women as dressmakers, milliners, bookbinders, printers, and telephone operators and below the top professions of clerks and copyists, bookkeepers, agents, and saleswomen. By percentage, 65 percent of all men and 76 percent of all women were employed in "Menial and Common Labor Occupations" (333–34); 25.5 percent of all men and 16 percent of all women were employed in "Higher Grade Manual and Clerical Work" (343–45); and 7.8 percent of men and 5.9 percent of women made their living in "Professions and Business Proprietorships" (357–59). Daniels was a white social worker in Boston at the South End's settlement for southern black migrants (Schneider 7).

4. In the biography of her father, Helen M. Chesnutt wrote that in the early 1880s Charles Waddell Chesnutt decided to learn stenography. In 1880, at the age of twenty-two, Chesnutt became principal of the Normal School at Fayetteville, N.C., but was looking for some means of earning his living in some other place (16). Therefore, he studied stenography. His dreams were realized when he went to New York and later to Cleveland, Ohio, where he established a successful business as court stenographer: "He was thus able to carry out the plans that he had made before leaving Fayetteville. He could earn his living by this magic gift of stenography, and make a slight start into the field of literature via the gate of journalism" (35).

NEGOTIATIONS IN RACE AND GENDER (1900–1905)

The *Colored American Magazine*

1. For general information about the *Colored American Magazine*, see Johnson and Johnson, *Propaganda* 1–16; Johnson and Johnson, "Away from Accommodation"; Bullock 106–18; Charles S. Johnson, "Rise"; Braithwaite, "Negro America's First Magazine"; Meier, "Booker T. Washington and the Negro Press"; Du Bois, "The Colored Magazine"; and Schneider 57–81.

2. For a discussion of the so-called "quality journals," the *Atlantic Monthly*, the *Century Magazine*, and *Harper's Monthly Magazine*, see Brodhead, *Cultures*, esp. 107–41.

3. "Writing always takes place within some completely concrete cultural situation," Brodhead argues, "a situation that surrounds it with some particular landscape

of institutional structures, affiliates it with some particular group from among the array of contemporary groupings, and installs it in some group-based world of understandings, practices, and values. But this setting provides writing with more than backdrop. A work of writing comes to its particular form of existence in interaction with the network of relations that surround it: in any actual instance, writing orients itself in or against some understanding of what writing is, does, and is good for that is culturally composed and derived" (*Cultures* 8).

4. In *Reconstructing Womanhood*, Carby puts the number of illiterate African Americans aged ten years and over at 45 percent out of a total African American population of 6,415,581 in 1900 (126). Carby has also gathered information from Elliott's "Story" about readers and agents (see especially 123–27).

The Use of Pseudonyms

1. Not every reader seems to have picked up this information, as William Braithwaite, who knew Hopkins, demonstrates in his 1947 article about the *Colored American Magazine* in which he mentions *Hagar's Daughter*, by Sarah A. Allen, and then praises *Contending Forces* as the outstanding contribution by Pauline E. Hopkins ("Negro America's" 24).

2. Harlan writes that Pickens's speech echoed Booker T. Washington's own graduation speech, and Washington later used Pickens to press a libel suit against William M. Trotter (*The Wizard of Tuskegee* 54–56).

3. This series, which will be analyzed later in more detail, was published in 1900 in the *Boston Evening Transcript*.

4. In January 1903 Du Bois spoke at the Boston Literary and Historical Association about the "Outlook for the Darker Races" (McHenry 182). Hopkins was certainly influenced by this speech.

5. Jane Sharp graduated from Boston Girls' High School in 1873 and might have been known to Hopkins from her own time at this school. There is, however, no reference to a personal acquaintance in the article.

Booker T. Washington and Famous Men

1. The development, various movements, use, and interconnection of scientific racism in the nineteenth century have been explored in numerous studies, among which I consider those by Fredrickson, Gossett, and Stanton especially helpful.

2. See Harlan, *Booker T. Washington: The Making of a Leader* and *Booker T. Washington: The Wizard of Tuskegee*.

3. For detailed information, see Harlan, *Wizard* 32–62, esp. 44–48; and Lewis, *Biography*, esp. 299–304. See also Scheiner, "President Theodore Roosevelt and the Negro, 1901–1908," esp. 172, for Booker T. Washington's influence on Theodore Roosevelt.

4. The Niagara Conference was called together in 1905 by Du Bois to assert equal political rights, economic opportunity, education, justice, and an end to segregation. The NAACP was founded in 1909 to advocate extending industrial opportunity and greater police protection for blacks (*Encyclopedia of American History* 660). It later grew into the leading race organization.

5. For information on Cooper, see Gabel and Hutchinson. Details about the work of Coppin, Wells-Barnett, and Terrell can be obtained from their autobiographies: *Reminiscences of School Life, and Hints on Teaching* (Coppin), *Crusade for Justice* (Wells-Barnett's autobiography edited by her daughter Alfreda M. Duster), and *A Colored Woman in a White World*, by Terrell.

6. See Gail Bederman's discussion of the ideologies of manliness, race, and civilization and its impact on male power, white supremacy, and evolutionary millennialism (esp. 26–41).

7. See Ashvill (463). In *Classical Black Nationalism*, Wilson J. Moses acknowledges the central role of Toussaint L'Ouverture in early African American writing: "As the nineteenth century progressed . . . references to Haiti became frequent in the rhetoric of black nationalism and Pan-Africanism. The leader of the revolt in its nationalist phase, Toussaint L'Ouverture, became a central figure in the black nationalist pantheon of heroes" (10).

8. See also Lois Brown for a discussion of these essays (169–206).

9. See Schneider (58); Harlan, *Booker T. Washington: Making of a Leader*, 291; and Meier (esp. 77–79).

10. My great thanks go to Alisha Knight from Washington College and Jessica Metzler from Florida State University for calling my attention to the discovery of these letters at Fisk and to Beth Howse from Special Collections at Fisk University for sending them to me.

11. In parenthetical citations I identify the letters by writer and addressee and by date if necessary (e.g., Freund-Dupree, Jan. 28, 1904 is the letter by John C. Freund to William Dupree dated Jan. 28, 1904). The page numbers in the long letter by Hopkins to Trotter are given in the original.

12. See Lewis, *When Harlem Was in Vogue*, 98–101. William L. Andrews examines the relationship between editor William Dean Howells and Charles W. Chesnutt as an example of "the kind of mixed blessings" that white patrons occasionally bestowed upon their African American protégés ("William Dean Howells" 328).

13. See Bethany Johnson for an excellent recent analysis of the *Voice of the Negro*; and Johnson and Johnson, *Propaganda*, 17–22. In his *The Wizard of Tuskegee*, Harlan writes about the *Voice of the Negro* and Booker T. Washington (see esp. 104). See also Harlan, "Booker T. Washington and *The Voice of the Negro*, 1904–1907," esp. 45–62.

14. *Booker T. Washington Papers* 7:329. See also Harlan, *Wizard*, 104, and Harlan, "Booker T. Washington and *The Voice*," 45–62.

15. For Washington's influence on African American magazines, see Johnson and Johnson, "Away from Accommodation"; Meier, "Booker T. Washington"; and Thornbrough, "More Light."

16. See Roscoe Conkling Simmons's letter to Booker T. Washington of December 13, 1904 (*Booker T. Washington Papers* 8:154–56), in which he writes, for example: "The world has long ago placed the laurel wreath of leadership, not only of a race, but of a thought, on your brow, and as long as I can see to write, none, shall disturb it" (155). This fulsome praise was caused by some unfavorable remarks about Washington in the *Voice of the Negro*. See also Braithwaite, "Negro America's First Magazine," 26; Meier, "Booker T. Washington," 70.

17. Martha H. Patterson makes this point with reference to *Winona* and contrasts it in her analysis with Booker T. Washington's anthology of the year 1900, *A New Negro for a New Century* (457).

The Black Woman's Era

1. For excellent information about the colored women's club movement, see especially Giddings, *When and Where I Enter*, 75–131; Stephanie J. Shaw's *What a Woman Ought to Be and to Do*; and Deborah Gray White's *Too Heavy a Load*, esp. 21–109, about the turn-of-the-century period. See also W. J. Moses, *Golden Age of Black Nationalism*, chap. 5 ("Black Bourgeois Feminism versus Peasant Values"), 103–31. Much-needed information is also given in *Forgotten Readers: Recovering the Lost History of African American Literary Societies*, by Elizabeth McHenry, esp. in her chapter "Reading, Writing, and Reform in the Woman's Era" (187–250). For information about the white women's club movement, see Ann Ruggles Gere's *Intimate Practice*.

2. These terms are examined in Barbara Welter's chapter "The Cult of True Womanhood, 1820–1860" in her *Dimity Convictions: The American Woman in the Nineteenth Century*: "four cardinal virtues—piety, purity, submissiveness and domesticity. Put them all together and they spelled mother, daughter, sister, wife—woman. Without them, no matter whether there was fame, achievement or wealth, all was ashes. With them she was promised happiness and power" (21).

3. In 1893 Frances Ellen Watkins Harper spoke at the Congress of Representative Women, saying: "Not the opportunity of discovering new worlds, but that of filling this old world with fairer and higher aims than the greed of gold and the lust of power, is hers. Through weary, wasting years men have destroyed, dashed in pieces, and overthrown, but to-day we stand on the threshold of woman's era, and woman's work is grandly constructive. In her hand are possibilities whose use or abuse must tell upon the political life of the nation, and send their influence for good or evil across the track of unborn ages" ("Woman's Political Future" 245).

4. Doreski analyses Hopkins's strategy: "Hopkins invested these life studies with the broader cultural ambitions of the national club movement. An insistence upon generational continuity as well as collective identity pervades each installment. Family or name recognition would be preserved while a historical race identity would be proposed. Hopkins sought to displace cultural ignorance with a schooled intelligence sharpened by fragile and incomplete citizenship" (21).

5. Information about these women can be obtained from *Black Women in America*,

ed. Darlene Clark Hine et al., an invaluable source of biographical and bibliographical information.

6. Harlan claims that Robert H. Terrell was one of Booker T. Washington's most influential lieutenants in Washington, D.C., and that his municipal judgeship was obtained through the help of Washington. Mary Church Terrell was a more reluctant and sometimes rebellious ally of Washington's. See Harlan, *Wizard*, esp. 94–95, and Terrell's own interpretation of her role in *A Colored Woman in a White World*.

7. In *Reconstructing Womanhood*, Carby names as one purpose of her study to show that in this period white women "allied themselves not with black women but with a racist patriarchal order against all black people" (6).

8. Hopkins writes about this convention in two articles: "Famous Women of the Negro Race. VIII. Educators (Concluded)" and "Famous Women of the Negro Race. IX. Club Life Among Colored Women." She refers to it once again in "Echoes from the Annual Convention of Northeastern Federation of Colored Women's Clubs."

9. See Gabler-Hover's central thesis that the betrayal of black women by white women in the Hagar novels reveals "the process of disavowal by which nineteenth-century white America denied the substantive cultural contribution of black Americans to American cultural identity" (5).

The Voices of the Dark Races

1. Rebecca Latimer Felton (1835–1930), a woman from Georgia, was a writer and the first woman to serve in the U.S. Senate. She gained prominence as a social reformer but also revealed a high degree of racism (see *Encyclopedia of Southern History*). Thomas Nelson Page (1853–1922) is considered by many to be the quintessence of nineteenth-century southern romanticism and an apologist for the Old South. The publication that the *Voice of the Negro* opposed was most likely *The Negro: The Southerner's Problem* (1904), which shows his belief in the natural inferiority of African Americans (see Holman). William Hannibal Thomas (1843–1935), an African American writer of mixed-race origin, was a nationally known critic of his own race. With his 1901 publication of *The American Negro*, he antagonized many prominent African Americans and especially many African American clubwomen (see John David Smith).

2. There is a growing body of writing about Africa and white European, white American, and black American attitudes toward Africa. See, for example, Brantlinger; Miller; Young; Sundquist; Moses, *Golden Age*, *Classical Black Nationalism*, and *Afrotopia*; Gruesser, *White on Black* and *Black on Black*. Recently, some controversy has centered around Mary Lefkovitz's *Not Out of Africa* (1996).

3. The importance of the Messiah coming out of Africa to redeem the African in the Western diaspora is traced, for example, by Moses in *Black Messiahs and Uncle Toms* and by Sundquist in *To Wake the Nations*, in reference to Du Bois's novel *Dark Princess*.

4. His reference to the concept of exceptionalism is based on Paul Gilroy, *Black Atlantic*.

5. The five parts—numbered I, II, III, IV, and VI—appear in the February, March, May, June, and July 1905 issues of the *Voice of the Negro*. Hopkins apparently misnumbered part VI.

6. J. F. Blumenbach was professor of medicine at the University of Göttingen and published "On the Natural Variety of Mankind" in 1775. He is called the father of craniology because he collected crania from all over the world and classified races accordingly. He also believed that climate contributed to racial differences. He did not, however, believe in racial superiority and inferiority (Gossett 37–39).

7. For a thorough investigation of the terms *civilization* and *culture* versus *barbarism* and *savagery*, and especially of the contribution of Johann Gottlieb Herder to the idea of the stages of human history toward perfection, see esp. Robert J. C. Young's chapter "Culture and the History of Difference" in his study *Colonial Desire: Hybridity in Theory, Culture and Race* (29–54).

8. Another example of this prevalent view of the essential differences between the races is an essay by James Weldon Johnson, included in Culp's *Twentieth Century Negro Literature*, in which he writes: "There are some things which the white race can do better than the Negro, and there are some things that the Negro can do better than the white race. . . . It is no fault of the Negro that he has not that daring and restless spirit, that desire for founding new empires, that craving for power over weaker races, which makes the white race a pioneer; neither is it the fault of the white race that it has not that buoyancy of spirit, that cheerful patience, that music in the soul, that faith in a Higher Power, which supports the Negro under hardships that would crush or make pessimists of almost any other race on earth" (73).

9. Sir James Brooke (1803–68) was made rajah for helping the sultan of Brunei to suppress rebel tribes.

10. The list is taken from David Levering Lewis's *W.E.B. Du Bois: A Reader* (527–50).

11. See Moses, *Afrotopia*, 44–135, for a detailed analysis of these and other texts and their historical and sociopolitical contexts.

12. The extreme form of racism based on the Bible can be found in Charles Carroll's book *"The Negro a Beast,"* in which he argues that the Negro is not human because he "is NOT a son of Ham" (81–100). For evidence of further negrophobia, see Fredrickson, *Black Image in the White Mind*, esp. his chapter "The Negro as Beast: Southern Negrophobia at the Turn of the Century" (256–82). For a general overview of early race theories, see Gossett, who offers an extremely helpful analysis of the general trends in eighteenth- and nineteenth-century anthropology and the scientific bases of race theories. See also the discussion of other white racist works in Robert Young's chapter "Egypt in America" in *Colonial Desire* (118–41).

13. Jeannette Robinson Murphy, a dramatic soprano and lecturer, was born in Jefferson, Kentucky, but resided in New York, and was quite successful on the lecture

platform. She was the author of some dialect work both in prose and verse and published *Southern Thoughts for Northern Thinkers* and *African Music in America*. See *Biographical Dictionary of Authors*, vol. 15 of the *Library of Southern Literature* (1907).

14. The text has been republished with an introduction by SallyAnn H. Ferguson and with critical commentary by Ferguson and Arlene Elder in *MELUS*. It has thus been made widely available to contemporary readers. An early source for this text was Count Arthur de Gobineau's *The Inequality of Human Races*, which was first published in French in 1853. An early American edition appeared in 1856 as *The Moral and Intellectual Diversity of Races*. This widely popular book argued for the inferiority of Negroes but also attributed artistic genius to mixed races. See Wilson Moses, *Afrotopia*, 259 n.77, and Gobineau, esp. 209.

15. Thomas Dixon (1864–1946) was a novelist, dramatist, and legislator who vigorously propagated ideas of white supremacy. His novel *The Leopard's Spots* was published in 1902. He is chiefly remembered for *The Clansman* (1905), which presents a sympathetic view of the Ku Klux Klan. It became the basis for D. W. Griffith's film *The Birth of a Nation* in 1915.

16. See Bruce 687. Excerpts of the *Westminster Review* and the *Kansas Review of Science* are reprinted in Simmons, 560–61, and *Atlantic Monthly* 51 (1883), 564–69.

17. For a longer discussion of environmentalism and innatism, see Fredrickson, *Black Image in the White Mind*, esp. 83, and William Stanton, *The Leopard's Spots*.

18. Bethany Johnson traces this debate about the use of the past in the service of the present back to Alexander Crummell and Frederick Douglass. Crummell, Johnson recapitulates, argued for a focus on the "broadest freedom of thought in a new and glorious present, and a still more magnificent future," while Douglass advocated the use of history to embrace the past and cultivate its memory (both qtd. in B. Johnson 29–30). A similar dichotomy can be traced in Du Bois and Booker T. Washington, a dichotomy that had its ramifications in many articles and editorials of the *Voice of the Negro*, as Johnson argues convincingly.

NEGOTIATIONS IN LITERATURE (1900–1905)

The Values of Race Literature

1. McHenry contends that "literature resurfaced as one of the practical tools black Americans envisioned using not only to reflect but also in fact to redefine themselves and their roles in the larger community" (188).

2. It can be assumed that Hopkins did not know of the two novels that today are taken as the first African American novel (*Our Nig*, by Harriet Wilson, 1859) and the first female slave novel (*Incidents in the Life of a Slave Girl*, by Harriet Jacobs, 1861).

3. See McHenry for a discussion of the prominence of these literary "luminaries" to inspire African American women writers in their own literary efforts (144–45).

4. Tate calls the literature and literary history of the generation between 1895

and 1920 "Talented-Tenth Poetics" and distinguishes it from the later "New Negro Poetics" (1920–40) and "Integrationist Poetics" (1941–68). See "Laying the Floor" (770–75).

5. "The Value of Race Literature" was reprinted in the *Massachusetts Review* 27 (1986) and in *With Pen and Voice*, ed. Shirley W. Logan. The quotations here are taken from the Logan collection because it is the more easily available text. Logan also treats the opening day of the conference and mentions the speeches by Josephine St. Pierre Ruffin and Anna Julia Cooper on that day (121–22).

6. Cooper's deprecating remarks about Howells take on an extra significance when we consider his role as patron of both Paul Laurence Dunbar and Charles W. Chesnutt as preferential treatment of male rather than female writers (see William Andrews, "William Dean Howells").

7. Barbara Christian writes about the most common stereotypes of the black woman: the contented mammy, the loose woman, the conjure woman, the tragic mulatta. See especially the first two chapters of her *Black Women Novelists* (3–61).

8. See Wonham, "Howells," 127. For a general discussion of Howells and dialect writing and language, race, and nationality, see Nettels (72–104).

9. A hundred years later, the first African American woman to win the Nobel Prize in literature, Toni Morrison, takes up this idea, traces its origins and uses, and writes about the "unspeakable things unspoken," the Africanist discourse in "American" literature, and includes in her analysis Howells's novel and works by Edgar Allan Poe, Mark Twain, and Ernest Hemingway. Her argument runs that her "American Africanism" should be seen as a term "for the denotative and connotative blackness that African peoples have come to signify, as well as the entire range of views, assumptions, readings, and misreadings that accompany Eurocentric learning about these people" (*Playing in the Dark* 6–7). See also Morrison's 1988 lecture "Unspeakable Things Unspoken: The Afro-American Presence in American Literature," which serves as a starting point for Wonham's collection *Criticism and the Color Line*. For a further discussion of the feminist side of this argument, see Tate, "Laying the Floor," esp. 775.

10. Charles W. Chesnutt gained immediate success with his two collections of short stories published in 1899, *The Conjure Woman* and *The Wife of His Youth and Other Stories of the Color Line*. At the time that McClellan wrote for Culp's *Twentieth Century Negro Literature*, Chesnutt had also published two novels, *The House Behind the Cedars* (1901) and *The Marrow of Tradition* (1901). His considerable fame certainly eclipsed the relative success of Hopkins's novel *Contending Forces*.

11. Recall the "Furnace Blasts. II" article analyzed earlier. Interracial marriage must be based on mutual consent, Hopkins contends in this article, in her answer to Mrs. Condict, and in her fiction.

12. McHenry cites the case of clubwoman and writer Mary Church Terrell unsuccessfully trying to publish some fiction. Firmly convinced of the power of the written

expression, Terrell detected a "conspiracy of silence" on the part of the American press to publish material that depicted the common and everyday humiliations of African Americans (247).

13. In "Tres-Passing in African American Literary Criticism," the concluding chapter of her *Passing and the Rise of the African American Novel*, Giulia Fabi gives an excellent and insightful overview of the theme of passing as treated by African American literary critics. She contends that "pre–Harlem Renaissance African American literature, especially the fiction of the color line, came to provide a negative touchstone both to measure the greater literary merits of later works and to argue the distinctiveness and relevance of specific thematic and critical agendas, such as the vernacular and the folk" (107). The fate of Hopkins at the hands of her critics thus becomes a specific example of the general point Fabi makes in this chapter.

14. In two chapters of his study *Victims and Heroes: Racial Violence in the African American Novel*, Jerry H. Bryant discusses twenty-four novels of racial violence between 1892 and 1922. Although I disagree with his assessment of writers such as Hopkins, Harper, and Griggs as minor, the canon of the novels he covers and their treatment offer insightful analyses and valuable information. See esp. 71–104 and 105–25 for a discussion of Chesnutt's *Marrow of Tradition* and Johnson's *Autobiography of an Ex-Colored Man*, the two writers and two novels he singles out for special praise.

15. I take this argument from Bryant, who uses it in order to distinguish between aesthetes (Langston Hughes, Rudolph Fisher, and Claude McKay) and moralists (Du Bois, Joshua Henry Jones, and Walter White) in the treatment of violence in the Harlem Renaissance (see 143–55).

16. A few more examples will illuminate the many directions criticism can take. In 1993 Carla L. Peterson demonstrated that a new set of questions would open new venues of investigation and bring new insights. She questions the possible reader responses to *Contending Forces* and then reads it as a historical romance because this form allowed Hopkins "to turn this genre back against itself, to critique its nationalist and imperialist ideology from a black feminist perspective" (180). Similarly based upon new critical and theoretical insights, Sean McCann discusses the novel as a melodrama. He discusses the figure of the tragic mulatta, the interplay of race and class matters, and the role of the minor characters, all of which had been sensitive issues for the reading public and critics for some time.

In their discussions of *Contending Forces*, other critics bring in ever new aspects, including those of homosexuality, the roles of black women, regionalism, point of view, and legal aspects. Siobhan Somerville reads homosexual desire in *Contending Forces* and claims maternity as a site of literary invention. Allison Berg takes a revisionary look at the history of black motherhood. Lisa Marcus says that Hopkins's fiction embodies a radical project "in its genealogical revision of America's national family tree" (119). In her opinion, such writers of mulatto fiction as Hopkins, Du Bois, and Cooper "were not surrendering to a fantasy of whiteness, but rather questioning the intersecting discourses of racial purity and female virtue" (127). Francesca Sawaya defends the assumption that Hopkins used the regionalist form "both to counter the racist regionalism of white Southern writers and to authorize their own political voices" (74). She interprets, for example, what is often considered the "loose or disorganized structure" of *Contending Forces* as representing "a regionalist logic" (78). Thomas Cassidy traces the voice of the omniscient yet unreliable narrator in *Contending Forces*. Kate McCullough claims that *Contending Forces* is not "merely a white bourgeois tale in blackface but a new narrative with a new kind of heroine, a narrative that reworks racial and gendered identity to claim a narrative space for the representation of a new version of African American womanhood" (27). Julie Cary Nerad is fascinated by this novel because its issues of race and sexual morality are connected to issues of property and inheritance. William E. Moddelmog reads *Contending Forces* as a romance of the law and discusses its treatment of the African American legal subject, the lynch law, and storytelling as well as the relationship between domesticity and the law.

17. The most sustained treatment of the novel is Janet Gabler-Hover's *Dreaming Black/Writing White: The Hagar Myth in American Cultural History*, a study in which Hopkins's novel is contextualized with some of the at least thirteen Hagar novels published between 1850 and 1913.

18. In the growing body of criticism of *Of One Blood*, the aspects of psychology, psychoanalysis, mysticism, blood and gender, melodrama, and melancholia are treated most frequently. In a well-researched and influential article, Thomas Otten concentrates on the connection between Hopkins and William James, Alfred Binet, Jean-Martin Charcot, Pierre Janet, and Hippolyte Bernheim and their scholarship on early psychology and psychoanalysis. In a more cautious article, Kevin Gaines points out and then tries to explain Hopkins's "contradictory declarations" on matters of civilization and racial equality ("Black Americans' Racial Uplift" 448). He draws parallels between *Of One Blood* and the "Dark Races" series. John Cullen Gruesser, in turn, sees the novel as Hopkins's attempt to "provide African-Americans with a usable, livable past" while being equally concerned "with addressing the issue of amalgamation and exposing the hypocrisy of contemporary American racial policies" (*"Of One Blood"* 75).

Cynthia Schrager argues that Hopkins was influenced "by accounts of the new psychology," which manifests itself in her interest in "mental healing, hypnosis, and multiple personality" (189). Deborah Horvitz reads *Of One Blood* as a "hysterical" text in which Hopkins racializes "the turn-of-the-century discourse on hysteria by considering its relevance to African American women and girls victimized by sexual trauma during and after slavery" (245). Jennie A. Kassanoff examines the "representative" African American in *Of One Blood*—"The interconnected corporeal issues of blood and gender that inform Hopkins's novel effectively deconstruct the monolith of the New Negro by questioning its contours and its limitations" (160)—and then writes about meanings of blood. Susan Gillman discusses Hopkins and the occult, the political implications of her Ethiopianism and Egyptology, and "her racial mysticism" ("Pauline Hopkins and the Occult" 70). And recently Dana Luciano has read the novel as a "powerful account of racial melancholia" and has reevaluated the role of Reuel as a melancholic mulatto character (149). New avenues of intertextual criticism are opened by Marla Harris in "Not Black and/or White: Reading Racial Difference in Heliodorus's *Ethiopica* and Pauline Hopkins's *Of One Blood*." In an intriguing intertextual conversation, she concentrates on the nature of identity and difference by using a Greek novel of the fourth century A.D. and Hopkins's novel as her examples.

Contending Forces of the Slave Past

1. See Allison Berg for a treatment of Lucy as a typical black surrogate mother, esp. 141–42.

2. See especially chapter 6, "The Color Factor," of Gatewood's *Aristocrats of Color*.

3. Lynching has been made the subject of numerous studies from the time of Hopkins onward. Hopkins was certainly familiar with Ida B. Wells's *On Lynchings: Southern Horrors*, her 1892 investigation of lynching. For a good overview of the literature about lynching, mob law, rape, and violence since then, see Bryant, Gunning, Trudier Harris, Bederman (45–76), Sundquist (406–54), and Giddings (17–31).

4. The resemblance between Will Smith and Arthur Lewis and Du Bois and Washington has been noticed by most readers of the novel. See Richard Yarborough, "Introduction," xxxvii–xxxix.

5. William Jonathan Northen (1835–1913), officeholder, educator, farmer, author, and religious leader, was born on the family plantation in Jones County, Georgia, enlisted in the Civil War, and became a teacher and an expert on agricultural matters after the war. He served three terms in the Georgia General Assembly and two terms in the Congress (1890–94) as a conservative Democrat. Backed by the Georgia Farmers Alliance, he passed several significant bills. Northen repeatedly recommended the enactment of a lynch law. Although there is no record of his speech in Boston in 1899, Hopkins calls him the model for the type of conservative unreconstructed white southerner who dons a liberal attitude toward his black "brother" while calling, at the same time, for total control of the African American population in the South (see *Dictionary of Georgia Biography* 751–52).

6. See, for example, Paul Laurence Dunbar's short story "Mr. Cornelius Johnson, Office-Seeker" (1899) and the roles politicians play in Du Bois's *Dark Princess* (1928), Charles W. Chesnutt's *The Marrow of Tradition* (1901), and Sutton E. Griggs's *Imperium in Imperio* (1899).

7. See Sean McCann for a discussion of the character of John Langley as embodying the failure of amalgamation.

8. Claire Pamplin is one of the critics who explain Hopkins's allegedly contradictory characterizations of good white and bad black blood as an outcome of the complex and contradictory age rather than as failure in characterization of the novelist

Hopkins: "Undeniably, Hopkins attributes the desirable characteristics in mulattoes to their 'white' blood. Perhaps difficult for readers to understand, nearly one hundred years after Hopkins wrote, is how she could have admired white ideals and supported African-American pride at the same time. Hopkins's white ideals and her black pride, in a delicate balance, defy the truism that the colonized subject desires to assume the identity of the colonizer. . . . Hopkins's subjects . . . reclaim their blackness by acknowledging its existence, while at the same time they attain their 'whiteness'— the social, economic, and political status—to which they have a legitimate claim. She presents the picture whole, as complex and contradictory as it is" (176).

Hagar's Beautiful Daughters

1. The terms *mulatta* and *mulatto* are often used to refer to people of mixed-race origin. It derives from *mule*, the infertile offspring of donkey and horse. *Quadroon* and *octoroon* usually designate people one-fourth or one-eighth African American. These terms have been kept in this study when historically appropriate and replaced by more neutral terms, such as person of mixed-race origin, if possible.

2. See Sollors's *Neither Black nor White Yet Both* for a chronological list of interracial literature (361–94).

3. Gabler-Hover describes this Miltonic pandemonium as "internal chaos . . . projected outward onto the national landscape" (142).

4. Hagar is the Egyptian slave that Sarah gave to her husband, Abraham, because she could not conceive a child. Hagar gives birth to Ishmael and then must suffer under the cruelty of the mistress. She flees into the desert and is rescued by God, who tells her that she should return to her mistress and promises her that her son will have many descendants (Genesis 16). After Sarah has borne Isaac to the elderly Abraham, Ishmael once makes fun of his half-brother, and Hagar and Ishmael are sent into the desert where they are rescued again by God (Genesis 21). For a treatment of the many biblical references in the novel, see Carby 153, Pamplin 175, and Gabler-Hover, esp. 29–31.

5. Gabler-Hover identifies this poem as the final stanza of a poem by Eliza Pointevent Nicholson, published in the November 1893 issue of *Cosmopolitan* (131).

6. For an in-depth analysis of the legal, social, political, cultural, literary, and other ramifications of miscegenation, see Sollors, *Interracialism*. Since Sollors's is one of the most recent of a great number of books on this subject, the articles included in this collection and the many references and expert bibliography will direct the reader to more titles.

7. J. Alexander Skeete was born in British Guiana in 1876. He studied art in Boston and was a renowned illustrator for the *Boston Herald* and other papers. See Elliott, "The Story," 48.

8. See Janet Gabler-Hover's well-researched study of *Hagar's Daughter* as the "direct response to the undermining of black female identity in nineteenth-century white

women's Hagar texts," and as a text that "reclaims Hagar for the empowerment of black women that forms a part of African American tradition" (123).

9. As Carby points out, Aurelia is clearly not meant to embody noble womanhood: "Aurelia was a female character who compromised her sexuality in two ways: she used her charms to lure men to gamble and lose their money to her father, and she adopted masculine characteristics" (*Reconstructing* 148). Benson values her as a reliable partner in card playing, and Sumner is obviously drawn to her sexually. As Carby says, Aurelia is "a perfect representation of the popular figure of the 'adventuress' who used her sexuality for her own ends and threatened men with her ambition" (149). Gabler-Hover analyses the personalities of the beautiful Jewel and the sexually promiscuous Aurelia as representative of the split that white Hagar writers make between a white and a black Hagar. "The white Hagar retains self-reliance but represses her sexuality; the black Hagar bears the mark of tabooed sexuality" (145).

10. One prominent example of this infiltration of an exclusive family are the descendants of Thomas Jefferson by his slave Sally Hemings. William Wells Brown makes his heroine Clotel a daughter of Thomas Jefferson, and the contemporary novels by Barbara Chase-Riboud treat the same topic. An extensive treatment of Thomas Jefferson and Sally Hemings can be found in Annette Gordon-Reed, *Thomas Jefferson and Sally Hemings: An American Controversy*.

11. Gabler-Hover reads the example of Elise as a fallen woman as a reversal of the usual Hagar pattern of "displacing illicit sexuality onto the black woman" (153). She also sees Elise's death by poison as a message that white women should fight together with black women instead of fight against them.

12. I would like to thank Janet Gabler-Hover for pointing this out to me.

13. See Carby, *Reconstructing*, 151–52; Gruesser, "Pauline Hopkins' *Hagar's Daughter*," 3; Pamplin 182. As Carby writes, "The last revelation, Jewel's blackness, was aimed directly at the punishment of Sumner and the hypocrisy of his philanthropy" (*Reconstructing* 152). Carby points out that the end "shifted the attention of her reader from individual to nation, from the acts of particular characters to systemic oppression, and rejected the possibility of a simple return to an acceptable moral order that a conventional 'happy ending' would have indicated" (152). Claire Pamplin argues that in the end "the question of race is not answerable. The question of equality is answerable, and of justice and inclusion. Hopkins believed that the answers begin with the fact that 'white' America must accept and embrace its own inner Africanness" (182).

14. For a discussion of this scene, see also Gabler-Hover (152–53).

Winona, Manhood, and Heroism

1. For an insightful and interesting discussion of the link between white manhood and nationalism, see Dana Nelson.

2. The most important source for Hopkins's treatment of John Brown must have been *The Life and Letters of John Brown, Liberator of Kansas, and Martyr of Virginia*,

edited by F. B. Sanborn in 1885, which contains a similarly positive view of the action of John Brown at Osawatomie, the figure of Luke Parsons (see esp. 285–87, where he claims to have been the man who shot Colonel Titus, and later references to Colonel Titus on 310–12), and some passages that Hopkins appropriated nearly verbatim. See especially page 295 for the description of Brown's camp. For more recent scholarship on Brown, see Stephen B. Oates's *To Purge This Land with Blood: A Biography of John Brown* (1984).

3. I am drawing here upon the scholarship about Bancroft and his school of historians by Kraus and Noble, and Huggins's criticism of it in "American Myths."

4. In *Victims and Heroes*, Bryant identifies the many warrior-heroes and Christian martyrs, the violent and nonviolent heroes who all assume readily recognized roles in the African American imagination and in real life. Bryant argues in the following way: "The labels of the forgiving Christian and the warrior oversimplify the variegated and often contradictory picture. But they lie at the two poles of the spectrum of the African American response to white violence that emerges in the nineteenth century. Both figures reflect admired values that give life worth. The violence of the warrior was retaliatory or self-defensive, and it meant manhood and self-respect. The nonviolence of the forgiving Christ meant a moral superiority that proved blacks worthy to enter the Christian civilization as full partners. Each image implied the desire for the respect and protection of the laws enjoyed by whites, freedom from white oppression and violence, safety and satisfaction" (54).

5. The reprint of *The Leopard's Spots* in 1967 features Dixon's original historical note, dated May 9, 1902. It must have appeared, therefore, shortly before or after Hopkins began her serial in the *Colored American Magazine*.

6. See Conlin 218, 243. Henry Clay is described in this way: "An outgoing, person-able, and handsome man, he charmed women with his good looks and wit, appealed to men with his willingness to sit down to a game of cards, share a bottle of whiskey, and, if, necessary, defend his honor with a dueling pistol" (218).

7. For a discussion of Haggard's African fantasies as antifeminist and racist, see Scheick 42–56. For a discussion of similarities between Haggard and Hopkins, see Wallinger, "Racial Contexts."

Of One Blood and the Future African American

1. Many critics have noted the link between classical Greek features and black an-cestry. To update this argument, Hopkins's reading of Egyptian civilization as African in origin predates Martin Bernal's argument in *Black Athena* by nearly one hundred years.

2. In the Hopkins chapter of his recent doctoral thesis "American Hearts: African American Writings on the Congo, 1890–1915," Ira Dworkin cites conclusive evidence that Hopkins drew heavily on the experiences and writings of William and Lucy Sheppard, African American missionaries to the Congo. He sees notable parallels and a shared discourse between Hopkins and the Sheppards about modern Africa and

African Americans in the diaspora (154–97, esp. 175–81). I agree with Dworkin that some African Americans knew Africa in ways other than as a literary trope, but I would still contend that most African Americans, including Hopkins, knew Africa only through reports by others rather than from firsthand experience.

3. To exemplify this point, see the following lament of a veteran African colonial officer about the boredom of life in his native England: "I'm tired of it too, dead-tired of doing nothing except play the squire in a country that is sick of squires. For a year or more I have been getting as restless as an old elephant who scents danger. I am always dreaming of Kukuanaland and Gogool and King Solomon's Mines. I can assure you I have become the victim of an almost unaccountable craving. I am sick of shooting pheasants and partridges, and want to have a go at some large game again. There, you know the feeling—when one has once tasted brandy and water, milk becomes insipid to the palate" (11). The example is taken from Henry Rider Haggard's popular novel *Allan Quatermain*, published in 1887.

4. It must remain conjecture that Pauline Hopkins knew of David Livingstone's encounter with a lion, as it is told by John S. Robertson in *David Livingstone: The Great Missionary Explorer*, published around 1883 (40ff.).

5. In "Voyage into the Heart of Africa: Pauline Hopkins and *Of One Blood*," my earlier interpretation of this novel, I took Reuel as describing this scene from his point of view instead of Charlie's. This mistake now strikes me as an unconscious move on my part to equate the positions of Charlie and Reuel at this stage in their expedition. There is fairly little up to now that is attributed to the perspective of Charlie, and there is no distancing in position between the two Americans.

6. Concerning the connections between Hopkins's Ethiopianism and her view of Egypt in this scene, Susan Gillman argues: "Hopkins's Ethiopianism is, then, not simply an elite black intellectual tradition combining the doctrine of uplift with the theme of ancient African cultural retentions and return. Neither does Hopkins's Egyptianist vision enshrine an imaginary African past at the expense of present problems and future solutions. Rather, Hopkins's transculturated 'Africa' is a fictional representation derived largely from factual sources and black history, not all of it glorious, and inclusive of both the contemporary U.S., and a diasporic, Pan-African future, itself contingent on colonial incursions in present-day Africa" ("Occult" 66).

7. Fabi applies the concept of race traveling as a literary device African American authors use to adapt and adopt the utopian dislocation of time and space in traditional white utopian fiction (*Passing* 46–47).

Folk Characters and Dialect Writing

1. See Carby, *Reconstructing*, 149–50; Carby, "Introduction," xxxix; Soitos 59–76; Gruesser, "Pauline Hopkins' *Hagar's Daughter*."

2. Venus is also a direct forerunner of Barbara Neeley's detective Blanche White in a series bearing the same title. Blanche White is a maid who, while solving mysterious

crimes, frequently muses about the fact that a maid always knows more about her employers than they would care to know.

3. See also Tate, *Domestic Allegories*, 204; Patterson 457–58.

Short Stories in the *Colored American Magazine*

1. For the sake of facility, all quotations from the text, unless otherwise noted, are taken from the Ammons collection.

2. Kevin K. Gaines observes that "many blacks saw passing as an act of betrayal and complicity in a racist social order" and mentions the close affinity between the use of the terms *to pass* and *to die* (*Uplifting the Race* 229).

3. Based upon a reading of Foucault, Samira Kawash talks about the intricate interplay between knowledge and power (see 129).

4. For treatment of Douglass's "The Heroic Slave," W. W. Brown's "Madison Washington," and Child's "Madison Washington" in comparison with Hopkins's "A Dash for Liberty," see Gruesser, "Taking Liberties," 98–118.

VOICES AND SILENCES (1905–1930)

On the Platform with Prominent Speakers

1. See L. Brown, "Essential Histories," 53. For information about the two societies, see Adelaide Cromwell (80–83). See McHenry for in-depth information about the Boston Literary and Historical Association (165–83).

2. In his biography of Trotter, Stephen Fox writes about the controversial organization of the Garrison centennial with two separate celebrations, one organized by Trotter and one by the Booker T. Washington group. In his record in the *Guardian*, Trotter mixes the two groups together and gives a list of speakers, including the Garrison-Villard family, as if they had been speaking at his celebration. See pages 97–100 for the Garrison centennial and pages 118–120 about the relationship between Trotter and the Garrison-Villard family.

The Late Years

1. See, for example, what Fox says about Trotter and Du Bois: "Du Bois, Trotter's nemesis, edited the *Crisis*, with freewheeling independence. In Trotter's opinion the *Crisis*, supposedly published in the general interest of the race, did not give fair coverage of the activities of the NERL [National Equal Rights League]. . . . Over the next few years the feud between the 'white' NAACP and the 'Colored' NERL smoldered, occasionally bursting into a spate of private mutual recriminations" (141). The Negro-American Political League was also called National Independent Political League, the National Independent Political Rights League, the National Independent

Equal Rights League, and was finally named the National Equal Rights League. It came into existence in 1908 and was continued mainly through Trotter's "stubborn presence as the corresponding secretary" (Fox 140).

2. Information about Chesnutt is taken from Helen M. Chesnutt; Andrews, *Literary Career*; Andrews, "Chesnutt"; Elder, *Hindered Hand*, 147–97; McElrath; Duncan; Sundquist, *To Wake the Nations*, 271–454; and Fabi, *Passing*, 48–55.

3. Information about Griggs can be obtained from Elder, *Hindered Hand*, 69–103; Elder, "Griggs"; Moses, "Literary Garveyism"; and Gloster, "Sutton E. Griggs."

4. Information about Dunbar can be found in Elder, *Hindered Hand*, 104–46; Braxton; and Gavin Jones (182–207).

5. The best sources of information about these authors are Tate, *Domestic Allegories*, and the introductions to the reprints of their works in the Schomburg Library of Nineteenth-Century Black Women Writers. These authors are also treated in the *Oxford Companion to African American Literature*, ed. Andrews.

6. For information about Dunbar-Nelson, see Dunbar-Nelson, *Works* and *Give Us Each Day*; Hull; Wallinger, "Dunbar-Nelson."

7. See Hutchinson, *Anna J. Cooper: A Voice from the South*, 148–49. For a treatment of the M Street High School controversy, see Gabel (46–59). For a dialogue between Du Bois and Cooper that never took place, see Wallinger, "Five Million."

8. This autobiographical sketch is called "The Third Step" and can be found in the Moorland-Spingarn Research Center at Howard University. Most biographical data are taken from Hutchinson and Gabel. I want to thank Paul Williams for sending me a copy of his "National Register of Historic Places Registration Form" (NPS Form 10–900, OMB No. 1024–0018), which includes a biographical sketch about Cooper. Paul Williams has successfully registered the Edwin P. Goodwin House, the former site of Frelinghuysen University (1800 Vermont Ave. N.W., Washington, D.C.), as a national historic place.

9. He evaluated, for example, Chesnutt's *The House Behind the Cedars* on the following grounds: "It is Mr. Chesnutt's most sustained treatment of the subject for which he has become best known, that is, the delicate and tragic situation of those who live on the border-line of the races; and it is the best work of fiction yet written by a member of the race in America" (*The Negro in Literature and Art* 79). Still, he sees *The Marrow of Tradition* as "too much a novel of purpose to satisfy the highest standard of art" (79).

10. The case argued here for Hopkins and a select number of her contemporaries can be widened indefinitely. In *Conflicting Stories*, Elizabeth Ammons analyzes and compares the lives and careers of Frances Harper, Sarah Orne Jewett, Kate Chopin, Edith Wharton, Willa Cather, Alice Dunbar-Nelson, Ellen Glasgow, Charlotte Perkins Gilman, Hopkins, Sui Sin Far, Gertrude Stein, Mary Austin, Humishuma or Mourning Dove, Anzia Yezierska, Jessie Redmon Fauset, Edith Summers Kelley, and Nella Larsen. All of them, at some time in their careers, suffered from lapses of visibility or fell silent. In her introduction to *Unruly Voice*, McKay compares the life of

Hopkins to that of Mary Ann Shadd Cary (1823–93), "the first North American black female editor, investigative reporter, and publisher" (9), and of Ida B. Wells-Barnett (1862–1931), prominent activist against lynching (9–12). As a group, they were "extraordinary women whose lives, through no fault of their own, fell short of what they might have been" (11).

11. I thank Ellen Garvey, who responded to my query on the H-Amstdy online discussion group, for identifying this poem as "John Brown," written by Eugene Ware, and appearing in his collection *Rhymes of Ironquill* (Topeka: Crane, 1895). Ware was a Kansas lawyer and legislator who published several books of poetry.

Bibliography

WORKS BY PAULINE E. HOPKINS

Novels

Contending Forces: A Romance Illustrative of Negro Life North and South. Boston: Colored Co-operative Publishing Company, 1900. Reprint, Miami: Mnemosyne, 1968. Reprint, with an afterword by Gwendolyn Brooks, Carbondale: Southern Illinois University Press, 1978. Reprint, with an introduction by Richard Yarborough. Schomburg Library of Nineteenth-Century Black Women Writers. New York: Oxford University Press, 1988.

The Magazine Novels of Pauline Hopkins. 1901–3. Intro. Hazel V. Carby. Schomburg Library of Nineteenth-Century Black Women Writers. New York: Oxford University Press, 1988.

Theater

Peculiar Sam; or, The Underground Railroad. 1879. Rpt. in *The Roots of African American Drama*. Ed. Leo Hamalian and James V. Hatch. Detroit, Mich.: Wayne State University Press, 1991. 100–123. Rpt. in *African American Theater*. Ed. Eileen Southern. New York: Garland, 1994.

Nonfiction

A Primer of Facts Pertaining to the Early Greatness of the African Race and the Possibility of Restoration by Its Descendants—with Epilogue. Cambridge, Mass.: P. E. Hopkins, 1905.

Serial Novels

Hagar's Daughter: A Story of Southern Caste Prejudice. Serialized in *Colored American Magazine* 2.5 (Mar. 1901): 337–52; 2.6 (Apr. 1901): 431–45; 3.1 (May 1901): 24–34; 3.2 (June 1901): 117–28; 3.3 (July 1901): 185–95; 3.4 (Aug. 1901): 262–72; 3.5 (Sept. 1901): 343–53; 3.6 (Oct. 1901): 425–35; 4.1 (Nov. 1901): 23–33; 4.2

(Dec. 1901): 113–24; 4.3 (Jan./Feb. 1902): 188–200; 4.4 (Mar. 1902): 281–91. Published as Sarah A. Allen. Rpt. in *The Magazine Novels* (1–284).

Of One Blood; or, The Hidden Self. Serialized in *Colored American Magazine* 6.1 (Nov. 1902): 29–40; 6.2 (Dec. 1902): 102–13; 6.3 (Jan. 1903): 191–200; 6.4 (Feb. 1903): 264–72; 6.5 (Mar. 1903): 339–48; 6.6 (May/June 1903): 423–32; 6.7 (July 1903): 492–501; 6.8 (Aug. 1903): 580–86; 6.9 (Sept. 1903): 643–47; 6.10 (Oct. 1903): 726–31; 6.11 (Nov. 1903): 802–7. Rpt. in *The Magazine Novels* (439–621).

Topsy Templeton. An incomplete serialized novel in *New Era Magazine* (Feb. 1916): 11–20, 48; (Mar. 1916): 75–84.

Winona: A Tale of Negro Life in the South and Southwest. Serialized in *Colored American Magazine* 5.1 (May 1902): 29–41; 5.2 (June 1902): 97–110; 5.3 (July 1902): 177–87; 5.4 (Aug. 1902): 257–68; 5.5 (Sept. 1902): 348–58; 5.6 (Oct. 1902): 522–31. Rpt. in *The Magazine Novels* (285–437).

Other Periodical Publications

"As the Lord Lives, He Is One of Our Mother's Children." *Colored American Magazine* 6.11 (Nov. 1903): 795–801. Rpt. in Ammons, *Short Fiction*, 276–86. Rpt. in Washington, *Invented Lives*, 130–46.

"Bro'r Abr'm Jimson's Wedding: A Christmas Story." *Colored American Magazine* 4.2 (Dec. 1901): 103–12. Rpt. in Ammons, *Short Fiction*, 107–25.

"Charles Winter Wood; or, From Bootblack to Professor." *Colored American Magazine* 5.5 (Sept. 1902): 345–48. Published as J. Shirley Shadrach.

"Converting Fanny." *New Era Magazine* (Feb. 1916): 33–34. Published as Sarah A. Allen.

"The Dark Races of the Twentieth Century." *Voice of the Negro.* "I. Oceania: The Dark-hued Inhabitants of New Guinea, the Bismarck Archipelago, New Hebrides, Solomon Islands, Fiji Islands, Polynesia, Samoa and Hawaii," 2.2 (Feb. 1905): 108–15; "II. The Malay Peninsula, Borneo, Java, Sumatra and the Philippines," 2.3 (Mar. 1905): 187–91; "III. The Yellow Race: Siam, China, Japan, Korea, Tibet," 2.5 (May 1905): 330–35; "IV. Africa: Abyssinians, Egyptians, Nilotic Class, Berbers, Kaffirs, Hottentots, Africans of Northern Tropics (Including Negroes of Central, Eastern and Western Africa), Negroes of the United States," 2.6 (June 1905): 415–18; "VI. The North American Indian.—Conclusion," 2.7 (July 1905): 459–63.

"A Dash for Liberty." *Colored American Magazine* 3.4 (Aug. 1901): 243–47. Rpt. in Ammons, *Short Fiction*, 89–98.

"Echoes from the Annual Convention of Northeastern Federation of Colored Women's Clubs." *Colored American Magazine* 6.10 (Oct. 1903): 709–13.

"Elijah William Smith: A Colored Poet of Early Days." *Colored American Magazine* 6.2 (Dec. 1902): 96–100.

"Famous Men of the Negro Race." A series published in the *Colored American Magazine.* "Toussaint L'Ouverture," 2.1 (Nov. 1900): 9–24; "Hon. Frederick Douglass,"

2.2 (Dec. 1900): 121–32; "William Wells Brown," 2.3 (Jan. 1901): 232–36; "Robert Browne Elliott," 2.4 (Feb. 1901): 294–301; "Edwin Garrison Walker," 2.5 (Mar. 1901): 358–66; "Lewis Hayden," 2.6 (Apr. 1901): 473–77; "Charles Lenox Remond," 3.1 (May 1901): 34–39; "Sergeant Wm. H. Carney," 3.2 (June 1901): 84–89; "Hon. John Mercer Langston," 3.3 (July 1901): 177–84; "Senator Blanche K. Bruce," 3.4 (Aug. 1901): 257–61; "Robert Morris," 3.5 (Sept. 1901): 337–42; "Booker T. Washington," 3.6 (Oct. 1901): 436–41.

"Famous Women of the Negro Race." A series published in the *Colored American Magazine.* "Phenomenal Vocalists," 4.1 (Nov. 1901): 45–53; "Sojourner Truth," 4.2 (Dec. 1901): 124–32; "Harriet Tubman," 4.3 (Jan./Feb. 1902): 210–23; "Some Literary Workers," 4.4 (Mar. 1902): 277–80; "Literary Workers (Concluded)," 4.5 (Apr. 1902): 366–71; "Educators," 5.1 (May 1902): 41–46; "Educators (Continued)," 5.2 (June 1902): 125–30; "Educators (Concluded)," 5.3 (July 1902): 206–13; "Club Life among Colored Women," 5.4 (Aug. 1902): 273–77; "Artists," 5.5 (Sept. 1902): 362–67; "Higher Education of Colored Women in White Schools and Colleges," 5.6 (Oct. 1902): 445–50.

"Furnace Blasts. I. The Growth of the Social Evil Among All Classes and Races in America." *Colored American Magazine* 6.4 (Feb. 1903): 259–63. Published as J. Shirley Shadrach.

"Furnace Blasts. II. Black or White—Which Should Be the Young Afro-American's Choice in Marriage." *Colored American Magazine* 6.5 (Mar. 1903): 348–52. Published as J. Shirley Shadrach.

"General Washington: A Christmas Story." *Colored American Magazine* 2.2 (Dec. 1900): 95–104. Rpt. in Ammons, *Short Fiction*, 69–82.

"Heroes and Heroines in Black: I. Neil Johnson, American Woodfolk, et al." *Colored American Magazine* 6.3 (Jan. 1903): 206–11.

"How a New York Newspaper Man Entertained a Number of Colored Ladies and Gentlemen at Dinner in the Revere House, Boston, and How the Colored American League Was Started." *Colored American Magazine* 7.3 (Mar. 1904): 151–60.

"Latest Phases of the Race Problem in America." *Colored American Magazine* 6.4 (Feb. 1903): 244–51. Published as Sarah A. Allen.

"Men of Vision: I. Mark Rene Demortie." *New Era Magazine* 1.1 (Feb. 1916): 35–39.

"Men of Vision: II. Leonard A. Grimes." *New Era Magazine* 1.2 (Mar. 1916): 99–105.

"Mr. Alan Kirkland Soga." *Colored American Magazine* 7.2 (Feb. 1904): 114–16. Published as Sarah A. Allen.

"Mr. M. Hamilton Hodges." *Colored American Magazine* 7.3 (Mar. 1904): 167–69. Published as Sarah A. Allen.

"Mrs. Jane E. Sharp's School for African Girls." *Colored American Magazine* 7.3 (Mar. 1904): 181–84.

"Munroe Rogers." *Colored American Magazine* 6.1 (Nov. 1902): 20–26.

"The Mystery Within Us." *Colored American Magazine* 1.1 (May 1900): 14–18. Rpt. in Ammons, *Short Fiction*, 21–26.

"A New Profession: The First Colored Graduate of the Y.M.C.A. Training School,

Springfield, Mass." *Colored American Magazine* 6.9 (Sept. 1903): 661–63. Published as Sarah A. Allen.

"The New York Subway." *Voice of the Negro* (Dec. 1904): 605, 608–12.

"Reminiscences of the Life and Times of Lydia Maria Child I." *Colored American Magazine* 6.4. (Feb. 1903): 279–84.

"Reminiscences of the Life and Times of Lydia Maria Child II." *Colored American Magazine* 6.5. (Mar. 1903): 353–57.

"A Retrospect of the Past [excerpt from *Contending Forces*]." *Colored American Magazine* 2.1 (Nov. 1900): 64–72.

"Rev. John Henry Dorsey." *Colored American Magazine* 5.6 (Oct. 1902): 411–17. Published as J. Shirley Shadrach.

Speech at the William Lloyd Garrison Centennial. *Guardian*, 16 Dec. 1905, 1, 4.

"Talma Gordon." *Colored American Magazine* 1.5 (Oct. 1900): 271–90. Rpt. in Ammons, *Short Fiction*, 49–68.

"The Test of Manhood." *Colored American Magazine* 6.2 (Dec. 1902): 113–19. Published as Sarah A. Allen. Rpt. in Ammons, *Short Fiction*, 205–17.

"Whittier, Friend of the Negro." *Colored American Magazine* 3.5 (Sept. 1901): 324–30.

"William Pickens, Yale University." *Colored American Magazine* 6.7 (July 1903): 517–21.

"Women's Department." *Colored American Magazine* 1.2 (June 1900): 118–23.

General Material from the *Colored American Magazine* and the *Voice of the Negro*

"Advertisements." *Colored American Magazine* 17.5 (Nov. 1909): opposite table of contents.

"Announcement." *Colored American Magazine* 1.1 (May 1900): n.p.

"Announcement for 1902." *Colored American Magazine* 4.5 (Apr. 1902): 413.

"Announcements." *Colored American Magazine* 3.6 (Oct. 1901): 479.

"Biographies of the Officers of the New Management of Our Magazine." *Colored American Magazine* 6.6 (May/June 1903): 443–49.

"Boston as the Paradise of the Negro." *Colored American Magazine* 7.5 (May 1904): 309–17.

"Editorial." *Colored American Magazine* 8.6 (June 1905): 342–43.

"Editorial and Publishers' Announcements." *Colored American Magazine* 1.1 (May 1900): 60–64.

"Editorial and Publishers' Announcements." *Colored American Magazine* 1.4 (Sept. 1900): 262.

"Editorial and Publishers' Announcements." *Colored American Magazine* 2.4 (Feb. 1901): 316–17.

"Editorial and Publishers' Announcements." *Colored American Magazine* 3.1. (May 1901): 78–79.

"Editorial and Publishers' Announcements." *Colored American Magazine* 4.4 (Mar. 1902): 335.

"Editorial and Publishers' Announcements." *Colored American Magazine* 6.5 (Mar. 1903): 398–400.

"Editorial and Publishers' Announcements." *Colored American Magazine* 6.6 (May/June 1903): 466–67.

"Editorial and Publishers' Announcements." *Colored American Magazine* 6.7 (July 1903): 546–47.

"In the Editor's Sanctum." *Colored American Magazine* 7.5 (May 1904): 382–83.

Letter from Cornelia A. Condict and Pauline Hopkins's reply. *Colored American Magazine* 6.5. (Mar. 1903): 398–400. Rpt. in *Norton Anthology of African American Literature*. Ed. Henry Louis Gates Jr. and Nellie Y. McKay. New York: Norton, 1997. 593–95.

"Our Christmas Number." *Voice of the Negro* 1.11 (Nov. 1904): 467.

"Pauline E. Hopkins." *Colored American Magazine* 2.3 (Jan. 1901): 218–19.

"Publishers' Announcements." *Colored American Magazine* 7.11 (Nov. 1904): 700.

"Publishers' Announcements." *Colored American Magazine* 8.3 (Mar. 1905): 164.

"Publishers' Announcements." *Colored American Magazine* 10.6 (June 1906): 434–35.

"The Voice of the Negro for 1905." *Voice of the Negro* 1.12 (Dec. 1904): n.p.

"The Voice of the Negro for July, 1905." *Voice of the Negro* 2.6 (June 1905): n.p.

"The Voice of the Negro for March." *Voice of the Negro* 2.2 (Feb. 1905): n.p.

"The Voice of the Negro for May, 1905." *Voice of the Negro* 2.5 (May 1905): n.p.

OTHER WORKS CITED

Ammons, Elizabeth. "Afterword: *Winona*, Bakhtin, and Hopkins in the Twenty-first Century." In Gruesser, *The Unruly Voice*, 211–19.

———. *Conflicting Stories: American Women Writers at the Turn into the Twentieth Century*. New York: Oxford University Press, 1991.

———. Introduction to *Short Fiction by Black Women*. Ed. Ammons. 3–20.

———, ed. *Short Fiction by Black Women, 1900–1920*. Schomburg Library of Nineteenth-Century Black Women Writers. New York: Oxford University Press, 1991.

Andrews, William L. "Chesnutt, Charles Waddell." In Andrews, *Oxford Companion*, 131–32.

———. *The Literary Career of Charles W. Chesnutt*. Baton Rouge: Louisiana State University Press, 1980.

———. "William Dean Howells and Charles W. Chesnutt: Criticism and Race Fiction in the Age of Booker T. Washington." *American Literature* 48 (1976): 327–39.

Andrews, William L., Frances Smith Foster, and Trudier Harris, eds. *The Oxford Companion to African American Literature*. New York: Oxford University Press, 1997.

Appiah, Anthony. "The Uncompleted Argument: Du Bois and the Illusion of Race."
    In *"Race," Writing, and Difference*. Ed. Henry Louis Gates Jr. Chicago: University
    of Chicago Press, 1986. 21–37.

Arroyo, Elizabeth Fortson. "Ruffin, Josephine St. Pierre." In Hine, *Black Women in
    America*, 994–97.

Ashvill, Gary. "Toussaint L'Ouverture." In Andrews, *Oxford Companion*, 463–64.

Baker, Houston A. *Workings of the Spirit: The Poetics of Afro-American Women's Writing*.
    Chicago: University of Chicago Press, 1991.

Baldwin, James. "Everybody's Protest Novel." In *Notes of a Native Son*. 1955. Reprint,
    Boston: Beacon, 1984. 13–23.

———. "Going to Meet the Man." In *Going to Meet the Man*. London: Michael Joseph,
    1965. 231–52.

Barber, J. Max. "Shall the Press Be Free?" *Voice of the Negro* 3.10 (Oct. 1906): 391.

Bederman, Gail. *Manliness and Civilization: A Cultural History of Gender and Race in
    the United States, 1880–1917*. Chicago: University of Chicago Press, 1995.

Berg, Allison. "Reconstructing Motherhood: Pauline Hopkins's *Contending Forces*."
    Studies in American Fiction 24.2 (1996): 131–50.

Bernal, Martin. *Black Athena: The Afroasiatic Roots of Classical Civilization*. New
    Brunswick, N.J.: Rutgers University Press, 1987.

Bernardi, Debra. "Narratives of Domestic Imperialism: The African-American Home
    in the *Colored American Magazine* and the Novels of Pauline Hopkins, 1900–
    1903." In *Separate Spheres No More: Gender Convergence in American Literature,
    1830–1930*. Ed. Monika M. Elbert. Tuscaloosa: University of Alabama Press, 2000.
    203–24.

Berzon, Judith R. *Neither White nor Black: The Mulatto Character in American Fiction*.
    New York: New York University Press, 1978.

Biographical Dictionary of Authors. Vol. 15 of *Library of Southern Literature*. Ed. Edwin
    Anderson Alderman et al. Atlanta: Martin and Hoyt, 1909–23.

Borne, O. S. "The Doctor's Great Discovery." *Colored American Magazine* 1.1 (May
    1900): 26–29.

Braithwaite, William Stanley. "Negro America's First Magazine." *Negro Digest* (Dec.
    1947): 21–26.

———. "The Negro in American Literature." Rpt. in Locke, *The New Negro*, 29–44.

Brantlinger, Patrick. *Rule of Darkness: British Literature and Imperialism, 1830–1914*.
    Ithaca: Cornell University Press, 1988.

Brawley, Benjamin Griffin. *The Negro Genius: A New Appraisal of the American Negro
    in Literature and the Fine Arts*. New York: Dodd and Mead, 1937.

———. "The Negro in American Fiction." In *The Negro in Literature and Art*. 185–99.

———. "The Negro in American Literature." In *The Negro in Literature and Art*.
    202–7.

———. "The Negro in Contemporary Fiction." In *The Negro in Literature and Art*.
    209–12.

———. *The Negro in Literature and Art in the United States*. 1930. Reprint, New York: Duffield, 1993.

———. "The Negro Literary Renaissance." 1927. Rpt. in Wintz, *Harlem Renaissance*, 4:57–64.

Braxton, Joanne M. "Dunbar, Paul Laurence." In Andrews, *Oxford Companion*, 240–41.

Brodhead, Richard. *Cultures of Letters: Scenes of Reading and Writing in Nineteenth-Century America*. Chicago: University of Chicago Press, 1993.

Brooks, Gwendolyn. Afterword to *Contending Forces: A Romance Illustrative of Negro Life North and South*, by Pauline Hopkins. Carbondale: Southern Illinois University Press, 1978. 403–9.

Brooks, Kristina. "Mammies, Bucks, and Wenches: Minstrelsy, Racial Pornography, and Racial Politics in Pauline Hopkins's *Hagar's Daughter*." In Gruesser, *The Unruly Voice*, 119–57.

Brooks, Peter. *The Melodramatic Imagination: Balzac, Henry James, Melodrama, and the Mode of Excess*. New Haven: Yale University Press, 1976.

Brown, Hallie Q. *Homespun Heroines and Other Women of Distinction*. Schomburg Library of Nineteenth-Century Women Writers. New York: Oxford University Press, 1988.

Brown, Lois, ed. *Memoir of James Jackson, the Attentive and Obedient Scholar, Who Died in Boston, October 31, 1833, Aged Six Years and Eleven Months. By His Teacher Miss Susan Paul*. Cambridge, Mass.: Harvard University Press, 2000.

Brown, Lois A. "Essential Histories / Determined Identities: Images of Race and Origin in the Works of Pauline Hopkins." Ph.D. diss., Boston College, 1993. DA 93-29279.

Brown, Lois Lamphere. " 'To Allow No Tragic End': Defensive Postures in Pauline Hopkins's *Contending Forces*." In Gruesser, *The Unruly Voice*, 50–70.

Brown, William Wells. *Clotel; or, The President's Daughter*. 1853. Reprint, with primary documents and introduction by Joan E. Cashin, Armonk, N.Y.: M. E. Sharpe, 1996.

———. *The Escape; or, A Leap for Freedom*. In Hamalian, *Roots of African American Drama*, 42–95.

———. "Madison Washington." In *The Black Man, His Antecedents, His Genius, and His Achievements*. 1863. Reprint, New York: Arno, 1969. 75–85.

———. *The Rising Son; or, The Antecedents and Advancement of the Colored Race*. 1874. Reprint, New York: Negro Universities Press, 1970.

Brown[e], Gertrude Dorsey. "A Case of Measure for Measure." In Ammons, *Short Fiction*, 375–419.

———. "Scrambled Eggs." In Ammons, *Short Fiction*, 328–53.

Bruce, Dickson D. "Ancient Africa and the Early American Historians, 1883–1915." *American Quarterly* 36.5 (1984): 684–99.

Bryant, Jerry H. *Victims and Heroes: Racial Violence in the African American Novel*. Amherst: University of Massachusetts Press, 1997.

Bullock, Penelope. *The Afro-American Press, 1838–1909*. Baton Rouge: Louisiana State University Press, 1981.

Burgess-Ware, M.[arie] Louise. "Bernice, the Octoroon." In Ammons, *Short Fiction*, 250–75.

Campbell, Jane. "Pauline Elizabeth Hopkins." In *Afro-American Writers before the Harlem Renaissance*. Vol. 50 of *Dictionary of Literary Biography*. Ed. Trudier Harris and Thadious M. Davis. Detroit, Mich.: Bruccoli Clark, 1986. 182–89.

Carby, Hazel V. Introduction to *The Magazine Novels of Pauline Hopkins*. Schomburg Library of Nineteenth-Century Black Women Writers. New York: Oxford University Press, 1988. xxix–l.

———. *Reconstructing Womanhood: The Emergence of the Afro-American Woman Novelist*. New York: Oxford University Press, 1987.

Carroll, Charles. *The Negro a Beast; or, In the Image of God*. 1900. Reprint, Miami: Mnemosyne, 1969.

Cassidy, Thomas. "Contending Contexts: Pauline Hopkins's *Contending Forces*." *African American Review* 32.4 (1998): 661–72.

Chesnutt, Charles W. *The Conjure Woman*. 1899. Reprint, Ann Arbor: University of Michigan Press, 1969.

———. "The Future American." Reprinted in *MELUS* 15.3 (1988): 96–107.

———. *The House Behind the Cedars*. 1901. Reprint, New York: Macmillan, 1969.

———. *The Marrow of Tradition*. 1901. Reprint, New York: AMS, 1972.

———. "The Wife of His Youth." In *The Wife of His Youth and Other Stories of the Color Line*. 1899. Reprint, Ridgewood, N.J.: Gregg Press, 1967. 1–24.

———. *The Wife of His Youth and Other Stories of the Color Line*. 1900. Reprint, Ann Arbor: University of Michigan Press, 1968.

Chesnutt, Helen Mary. *Charles Waddell Chesnutt: Pioneer of the Color Line*. Chapel Hill: University of North Carolina Press, 1952.

Child, Lydia Maria. "Madison Washington." In *The Freedman's Book*. 1865. Reprint, New York: Arno, 1968. 147–53.

Christian, Barbara. *Black Women Novelists: The Development of a Tradition, 1893–1976*. Westport, Conn.: Greenwood, 1987.

Collison, Gary. *Shadrach Minkins: From Fugitive Slave to Citizen*. Cambridge, Mass.: Harvard University Press, 1997.

Conlin, Joseph R. *The American Past: A Survey of American History*. San Diego: Harcourt Brace Jovanovich, 1984.

Cooper, Anna Julia. "Survey of Racial Attitudes of Negro Students." For a study published in 1932 by Dr. Charles S. Johnson. Anna Julia Cooper Papers. Moorland-Spingarn Research Center, Howard University, Washington, D.C.

———. "The Third Step." Anna Julia Cooper Papers. Moorland-Spingarn Research Center, Howard University, Washington, D.C.

———. *A Voice from the South*. 1892. Reprint, Schomburg Library of Nineteenth-Century Black Women Writers. New York: Oxford University Press, 1988.

Coppin, Fanny Jackson. *Reminiscences of School Life, and Hints on Teaching*. Vol. 13 of *Women in American Protestant Religion, 1800–1930*. New York: Garland, 1987.

Cromwell, Adelaide Hill. *The Other Brahmins: Boston's Black Upper Class, 1750–1950*. Fayetteville: University of Arkansas Press, 1994.

Culp, Donald W., ed. *Twentieth Century Negro Literature: A Cyclopedia of Thought on the Vital Topics Relating to the American Negro*. 1902. Reprint, New York: Arno, 1969.

Daniels, John. *In Freedom's Birthplace*. 1914. Reprint, New York: Arno Press, 1969.

Dearborn, Mary V. *Pocahontas's Daughters: Gender and Ethnicity in American Culture*. New York: Oxford University Press, 1986.

Delany, Martin R. *Principia of Ethnology: The Origin of Races and Color*. 1879. Reprint, Philadelphia: Harper and Brother, 1880.

Dictionary of American Biography. Ed. Allen Johnson and Dumas Malone. New York: Scribner's, 1960.

Dictionary of Georgia Biography. Ed. Kenneth Coleman and Charles Stephen Gurr. Athens: University of Georgia Press, 1983.

Dixon, Thomas, Jr. *The Clansman: An Historical Romance of the Ku Klux Klan*. 1905. Reprint, Ridgewood, N.J.: Gregg Press, 1967.

———. *The Leopard's Spots: A Romance of the White Man's Burden—1865–1900*. 1902. Reprint, Ridgewood, N.J.: Gregg Press, 1967.

Doreski, C. K. *Writing America Black: Race Rhetoric in the Public Sphere*. Cambridge, Mass.: Cambridge University Press, 1998.

Douglass, Frederick. "The Heroic Slave." 1853. In *Three Classic African-American Novels*. Ed. William L. Andrews. New York: Mentor, 1990. 23–69.

Du Bois, W.E.B. "The Colored Magazine in America." *Crisis* 5–6 (Nov. 1912): 33–35.

———. "The Conservation of Races." 1897. In *W.E.B. Du Bois: A Reader*. Ed. Andrew Paschal. New York: Collier, 1971. 19–31.

———. "Criteria of Negro Art." 1926. In *W.E.B. Du Bois: A Reader*. Ed. Andrew Paschal. New York: Collier, 1971. 86–96.

———. *Dark Princess: A Romance*. 1928. Reprint, with an introduction by Claudia Tate, Jackson: University Press of Mississippi, 1995.

———. "Industrial Education—Will It Solve the Negro Problem. VII. The Training of Negroes for Social Power." *Colored American Magazine* 7.5 (May 1904): 333–39.

———. "The Negro in Literature and Art." 1913. In *W.E.B. Du Bois: A Reader*. Ed. Andrew Paschal. New York: Collier, 1971. 81–86.

———. "The Negro Mind Reaches Out." In Locke, *The New Negro*, 385–414.

———. *The Souls of Black Folk*. In *Three Negro Classics*. New York: Avon, 1965. 206–389.

DuCille, Ann. *The Coupling Convention: Sex, Text, and Tradition in Black Women's Fiction*. New York: Oxford University Press, 1993.

———. "Where in the World Is William Wells Brown? Thomas Jefferson, Sally

Hemings, and the DNA of African-American Literary History." *American Literary History* 12.3 (2000): 443–62.

Dunbar, Paul Laurence. "Mr. Cornelius Johnson, Office-Seeker." In *Heath Anthology of American Literature*. Lexington, Mass.: Heath, 1990. 2:476–82.

Dunbar-Nelson, Alice. *Give Us Each Day: The Diary of Alice Dunbar-Nelson*. Ed. Gloria T. Hull. New York: Norton, 1984.

———. *The Works of Alice Dunbar-Nelson*. Ed. Gloria T. Hull. 3 vols. Schomburg Library of Nineteenth-Century Black Women Writers. New York: Oxford University Press, 1988.

Duncan, Charles. "The White and the Black: Charles W. Chesnutt's Narrator-Protagonists and the Limits of Authorship." *Journal of Narrative Technique* 28.2 (Spring 1998): 111–33.

Duster, Alfreda M., ed. *Crusade for Justice: The Autobiography of Ida B. Wells*. Negro American Biographies and Autobiographies. Chicago: University of Chicago Press, 1970.

Dworkin, Ira. "American Hearts: African American Writing on the Congo, 1890–1915." Ph.D. diss., City University of New York, 2003.

Elder, Arlene A. "Griggs, Sutton E." In Andrews, *Oxford Companion*, 328–29.

———. *The "Hindered Hand": Cultural Implications of Early African-American Fiction*. Westport, Conn.: Greenwood, 1978.

———. "*MELUS* Forum: 'The Future American Race': Charles W. Chesnutt's Utopian Illusion." *MELUS* 15.3 (1988): 121–29.

Elliott, R. S. "The Story of Our Magazine." *Colored American Magazine* 3.1 (May 1901): 43–77.

Encyclopedia of American History. Ed. Richard R. Morris. Updated and revised ed. New York: Harper, 1965.

Encyclopedia of Southern History. Ed. David C. Roller and Robert W. Twyman. Baton Rouge: Louisiana State University Press, 1979.

Fabi, M. Giulia. "Criticism." In Andrews, *Oxford Companion*, 184–87.

———. *Passing and the Rise of the African American Novel*. Urbana: University of Illinois Press, 2001.

Favor, Martin J. *Authentic Blackness: The Folk in the New Negro Renaissance*. Durham, N.C.: Duke University Press, 1999.

Ferguson, SallyAnn H. "*MELUS* Forum: Chesnutt's Genuine Blacks and Future Americans." *MELUS* 15.3 (1988): 109–19.

———, ed. "*MELUS* Forum: Charles W. Chesnutt's 'Future American.'" *MELUS* 15.3 (1988): 95–129.

Fox, Stephen R. *The Guardian of Boston: William Monroe Trotter*. Studies in American Negro Life. New York: Atheneum, 1970.

Franklin, John Hope. *From Slavery to Freedom: A History of Negro Americans*. 4th ed. New York: Knopf, 1974.

Fredrickson, George M. *The Black Image in the White Mind: The Debate on Afro-American Character and Destiny, 1817–1914*. New York: Harper, 1971.

Gabel, Leona C. *From Slavery to the Sorbonne and Beyond: The Life and Writings of Anna J. Cooper*. Northampton, Mass.: Smith College, 1982.

Gabler-Hover, Janet. *Dreaming Black/Writing White: The Hagar Myth in American Cultural History*. Lexington: University Press of Kentucky, 2000.

Gaines, Jane. "Fire and Desire: Race, Melodrama, and Oscar Micheaux." In *Black American Cinema*. Ed. Manthia Diawara. New York: Routledge, 1993. 48–70.

Gaines, Kevin K. "Black Americans' Racial Uplift Ideology as 'Civilizing Mission.'" In *Cultures of United States Imperialism*. Ed. Amy Kaplan and Donald E. Pease. Durham, N.C.: Duke University Press, 1993. 433–55.

———. *Uplifting the Race: Black Leadership, Politics, and Culture in the Twentieth Century*. Chapel Hill: University of North Carolina Press, 1996.

Gates, Henry Louis, Jr. *The Signifying Monkey: A Theory of Afro-American Literary Criticism*. New York: Oxford University Press, 1989.

Gatewood, Willard B. *Aristocrats of Color: The Black Elite, 1880–1920*. Bloomington and Indianapolis: Indiana University Press, 1990.

Gere, Anne Ruggles. *Intimate Practice: Literacy and Cultural Work in U.S. Women's Clubs, 1880–1920*. Urbana: University of Illinois Press, 1997.

Giddings, Paula. *When and Where I Enter: The Impact of Black Women on Race and Sex in America*. New York: Bantam, 1984.

Gillman, Susan. "The Mulatto, Tragic or Triumphant? The Nineteenth-Century American Race Melodrama." In *The Culture of Sentiment: Race, Gender, and Sentimentality in Nineteenth-Century America*. Ed. Shirley Samuels. New York: Oxford University Press, 1992. 221–43.

———. "Pauline Hopkins and the Occult: African-American Revisions of Nineteenth-Century Sciences." *American Literary History* 8.1 (1996): 57–82.

Gilroy, Paul. *The Black Atlantic: Modernity and Double Consciousness*. Cambridge, Mass.: Harvard University Press, 1993.

Glazener, Nancy. *Reading for Realism: The History of a U.S. Literary Institution, 1850–1910*. Durham, N.C.: Duke University Press, 1997.

Gloster, Hugh M. *Negro Voices in American Fiction*. 1948. Reprint, New York: Russell, 1965.

———. "Sutton E. Griggs: Novelist of the New Negro." In *The Black Novelist*. Ed. Robert Hemenway. Columbus, Ohio: Merrill, 1970. 11–22.

Gobineau, Arthur de. *The Inequality of Human Races*. Trans. Adrian Collins. London: Heinemann, 1915.

Gordon-Reed, Annette. *Thomas Jefferson and Sally Hemings: An American Controversy*. Charlottesville: University Press of Virginia, 1997.

Gossett, Thomas F. *Race: The History of an Idea in America*. Dallas: Southern Methodist University Press, 1963.

Greenblatt, Stephen. *Shakespearean Negotiations: The Circulation of Social Energy in Renaissance England*. Oxford: Clarendon Press, 1988.

Griggs, Sutton Elbert. *Imperium in Imperio*. 1899. Reprint, Miami: Mnemosyne, 1969.

Gruesser, John Cullen. *Black on Black: Twentieth-Century African American Writing about Africa*. Lexington: University Press of Kentucky, 2000.

————. "Pauline Hopkins' *Hagar's Daughter* and the Invention of the African American Detective Novel." *College English Notes* 26.2 (1999): 1–4.

————. "Pauline Hopkins' *Of One Blood*: Creating an Afrocentric Fantasy for a Black Middle Class Audience." In *Modes of the Fantastic: Selected Essays from the Twelfth International Conference on the Fantastic in the Arts*. Ed. Robert A. Latham and Robert A. Collins. Westport, Conn.: Greenwood, 1995. 74–83.

————. "Taking Liberties: Pauline Hopkins's Recasting of the *Creole* Rebellion." In Gruesser, *The Unruly Voice*, 98–118.

————. *White on Black: Contemporary Literature about Africa*. Urbana: University of Illinois Press, 1992.

————, ed. *The Unruly Voice: Rediscovering Pauline Elizabeth Hopkins*. Introduction by Nellie Y. McKay. Afterword by Elizabeth Ammons. Urbana: University of Illinois Press, 1996.

Gunning, Sandra. *Race, Rape, and Lynching: The Red Record of American Literature, 1890–1912*. New York: Oxford University Press, 1996.

Haggard, Henry Rider. *Allan Quatermain*. 1887. Reprint, London: Penguin, 1995.

Hamalian, Leo, and James V. Hatch, eds. *The Roots of African American Drama: An Anthology of Early Plays, 1858–1938*. Detroit: Wayne State University Press, 1991.

Hammond, Dorothy, and Alta Jablow. *The Africa That Never Was: Four Centuries of British Writing about Africa*. New York: Twayne, 1970.

Harlan, Louis R. *Booker T. Washington: The Making of a Leader, 1856–1901*. New York: Oxford University Press, 1972.

————. *Booker T. Washington: The Wizard of Tuskegee, 1901–1915*. New York: Oxford University Press, 1983.

————. "Booker T. Washington and *The Voice of the Negro*, 1904–1907." *Journal of Southern History* 45 (Feb. 1979): 45–62.

Harper, Frances E. W. *Iola Leroy, or Shadows Uplifted*. 1892. Reprint, with an introduction by Frances Smith Foster. Schomburg Library of Nineteenth-Century Black Women Writers. New York: Oxford University Press, 1988.

————. "Woman's Political Future." In Loewenberg, *Black Women*, 244–51.

Harris, Marla. "Not Black and/or White: Reading Racial Difference in Heliodorus's *Ethiopica* and Pauline Hopkins's *Of One Blood*." *African American Review* 35.3 (2001): 275–90.

Harris, Trudier. *Exorcising Blackness: Historical and Literary Lynching and Burning Rituals*. Bloomington: Indiana University Press, 1984.

Harris, William J. "Black Aesthetic." In Andrews, *Oxford Companion*, 67–70.

Higginbotham, Evelyn Brooks. "African-American Women's History and the Meta-language of Race." *Sings* 17.2 (1992): 251–74.

Higham, John. *Strangers in the Land: Patterns of American Nativism, 1860–1925*. Corrected and with a new preface. New York: Atheneum, 1973.

Hine, Darlene Clark, and Kathleen Thompson. *A Shining Thread of Hope: The History of Black Women in America*. New York: Broadway Books, 1998.

Hine, Darlene Clark, et al., eds. *Black Women in America: An Historical Encyclopedia*. 2 vols. Bloomington: Indiana University Press, 1993.

Holly, Ellistine Perkins. "Sam Lucas, 1840–1916: A Bibliographic Study." In *Feel the Spirit: Studies in Nineteenth-Century Afro-American Music*. Ed. George R. Keck and Sherrill V. Martin. Westport, Conn.: Greenwood, 1988. 83–103.

Holman, Harriet R. "Thomas Nelson Page (1853–1922)." In *Fifty Southern Writers before 1900: A Bio-Bibliographical Sourcebook*. Ed. Robert Bain and Joseph M. Flora. New York: Greenwood, 1987. 348–58.

Horton, James Oliver. *Free People of Color: Inside the African American Community*. Washington, D.C.: Smithsonian Institution Press, 1993.

Horton, James Oliver, and Lois E. Horton. *Black Bostonians: Family Life and Community Struggle in the Antebellum North*. New York: Holmes and Meier, 1979.

Horvitz, Deborah. "Hysteria and Trauma in Pauline Hopkins's *Of One Blood; or, The Hidden Self*." *African American Review* 33.2 (1999): 245–60.

Howells, William Dean. *An Imperative Duty*. 1891. Reprint, ed. David J. Nordloh et al., Bloomington: Indiana University Press, 1969.

Huggins, Nathan Irvin. "American Myths and Afro-American Claims." In *Revelations: American History, American Myths*. Ed. Brenda Smith Huggins. New York: Oxford University Press, 1995. 174–86.

————. *Harlem Renaissance*. New York: Oxford University Press, 1971.

Hughes, Langston. "The Negro Artist and the Racial Mountain." 1926. Rpt. in Wintz, *The Harlem Renaissance*, 2:166–68.

————. "Who's Passing for Who?" In *The Langston Hughes Reader*. New York: Braziller, 1958. 30–33.

Hull, Gloria T. *Color, Sex, and Poetry: Three Women Writers of the Harlem Renaissance*. Bloomington: Indiana University Press, 1987.

Hutchinson, Louise Daniel. *Anna Julia Cooper: A Voice from the South*. Washington, D.C.: Smithsonian Institution Press, 1981.

Jackson, Blyden. *The Long Beginning, 1746–1895*. Vol. 1 of *A History of Afro-American Literature*. Baton Rouge: Louisiana State University Press, 1989.

Jacobs, Harriet A. *Incidents in the Life of a Slave Girl*. 1861. Reprint, ed. Jean Fagan Yellin, Cambridge, Mass.: Harvard University Press, 1987.

James, William. "The Hidden Self." In *Essays in Psychology*. Cambridge, Mass.: Harvard University Press, 1983. 247–68.

JanMohamed, Abdul R. "The Economy of Manichean Allegory: The Function of

Racial Difference in Colonialist Literature." In *"Race," Writing, and Difference*. Ed.
    Henry Louis Gates Jr. Chicago: University of Chicago Press, 1986. 78–106.

Johnson, A. E. *Clarence and Corinne; or, God's Way*. Reprint, with an introduction by
    Hortense J. Spillers, New York: Oxford University Press, 1988.

———. *The Hazeley Family*. Reprint, with an introduction by Barbara Christian,
    New York: Oxford University Press, 1988.

Johnson, Abby Arthur, and Ronald Maberry Johnson. "Away from Accommodation:
    Radical Editors and Protest Journalism, 1900–1910." *Journal of Negro History* 62
    (1977): 325–38.

———. *Propaganda and Aesthetics: The Literary Politics of Afro-American Magazines
    in the Twentieth Century*. Amherst: University of Massachusetts Press, 1979.

Johnson, Bethany. "Freedom and Slavery in the *Voice of the Negro*: Historical Mem-
    ory and African-American Identity, 1904–1907." *Georgia Historical Quarterly* 84.1
    (2000): 29–71.

Johnson, Charles S. Introduction to *Ebony and Topaz: A Collectanea*. 1927. Rpt. in
    Wintz, *The Harlem Renaissance*, 2:9–11.

———. "The Negro Enters Literature." 1927. Rpt. in Wintz, *The Harlem Renaissance*,
    2:271–82.

———. "The Rise of the Negro Magazine." *Journal of Negro History* 13 (1928): 7–21

Johnson, James Weldon. "The Dilemma of the Negro Author." 1928. Rpt. in Wintz,
    The Harlem Renaissance, 2:247–51.

———. "Should the Negro Be Given an Education Different from That Given to the
    Whites?" In Culp, *Twentieth Century Negro Literature*, 72–75.

Jones, Gavin. *Strange Talk: The Politics of Dialect Literature in Gilded Age America*.
    Berkeley: University of California Press, 1999.

Kassanoff, Jennie A. " 'Fate Has Linked Us Together': Blood, Gender, and the Politics
    of Representation in Pauline Hopkins's *Of One Blood*." In Gruesser, *The Unruly
    Voice*, 158–81.

Kawash, Samira. *Dislocating the Color Line: Identity, Hybridity, and Singularity in
    African-American Literature*. Stanford, Calif.: Stanford University Press, 1997.

Kelley, Emma Dunham. *Megda*. 1891. Reprint, with an introduction by Molly Hite,
    New York: Oxford University Press, 1988.

Kelley-Hawkins, Emma D. *Four Girls at Cottage City*. 1898. Reprint, with an intro-
    duction by Deborah E. McDowell, New York: Oxford University Press, 1988.

Kilcup, Karen L. *Soft Canons: American Women Writers and Masculine Tradition*. Iowa
    City: University of Iowa Press, 1999.

Kraus, Michael. *The Writing of American History*. Norman: University of Oklahoma
    Press, 1953.

Laryea, Doris Lucas. "James Monroe Whitfield." In *Afro-American Writers before the
    Harlem Renaissance*. Vol. 50 of *Dictionary of Literary Biography*. Ed. Trudier Harris
    and Thadious M. Davis. Detroit, Mich.: Bruccoli Clark, 1986. 260–63.

Lears, T. J. Jackson. *No Place of Grace: Antimodernism and the Transformation of American Culture, 1880–1920.* New York: Pantheon, 1981.

Lefkovitz, Mary. *Not Out of Africa: How Afrocentrism Became an Excuse to Teach Myth as History.* New York: Basic, 1996.

Levine, Lawrence. *Black Culture and Black Consciousness: Afro-American Folk Thought from Slavery to Freedom.* New York: Oxford University Press, 1977.

Lewis, David Levering. *W.E.B. Du Bois: Biography of a Race.* New York: Henry Holt, 1993.

———. *When Harlem Was in Vogue.* New York: Penguin, 1997.

———, ed. *W.E.B. Du Bois: A Reader.* New York: Henry Holt, 1995.

Lewis, Walter I. Response to "The Negro as a Writer." In Culp, *Twentieth Century Negro Literature,* 272–74.

Locke, Alain. "The New Negro." In Locke, *The New Negro,* 3–16.

———, ed. *The New Negro.* 1925. Reprint, with an introduction by Arnold Rampersad, New York: Touchstone, 1992.

Loewenberg, Bert James, and Ruth Bogin, eds. *Black Women in Nineteenth-Century American Life: Their Words, Their Thoughts, Their Feelings.* University Park: Pennsylvania State University Press, 1976.

Logan, Rayford W. *The Betrayal of the Negro from Rutherford B. Hayes to Woodrow Wilson.* New, enlarged edition of *The Negro in American Life and Thought: The Nadir, 1877–1901.* New York: Collier, 1965.

Logan, Shirley Wilson. "Victoria Earle Matthews." In Logan, *With Pen and Voice,* 120–25.

———, ed. *With Pen and Voice: A Critical Anthology of Nineteenth-Century African-American Women.* Carbondale: Southern Illinois University Press, 1995.

Loggins, Vernon. *The Negro Author: His Development in America.* New York: Columbia University Press, 1931.

Lott, Eric. *Love and Theft: Blackface Minstrelsy and the American Working Class.* New York: Oxford University Press, 1993.

Luciano, Dana. "Passing Shadows: Melancholic Nationality and Black Critical Publicity in Pauline E. Hopkins's *Of One Blood.*" In *Loss: The Politics of Mourning.* Ed. David L. Eng and David Kazanjian. Berkeley: University of California Press, 2003. 148–87.

Marcus, Lisa. " 'Of One Blood': Reimagining American Genealogy in Pauline Hopkins's *Contending Forces.*" In *Speaking the Other Self: American Women Writers.* Ed. Jeanne Campbell Reesman. Athens: University of Georgia Press, 1997. 117–43.

Matthews, Victoria Earle. "Aunt Lindy." In *The Unforgetting Heart: An Anthology of Short Stories by African American Women (1859–1993).* Ed. Asha Kanwar. San Francisco: Aunt Lute Books, 1993. 11–15.

———. "The Value of Race Literature." *Massachusetts Review* 27.2 (1986): 170–91. Rpt. in Logan, *With Pen and Voice,* 126–48.

McCann, Sean. "'Bonds of Brotherhood': Pauline Hopkins and the Work of Melodrama." *English Literary History* 64 (1997): 789–822.

McClellan, George Marion. "The Negro as a Writer." In Culp, *Twentieth Century Negro Literature*, 275–86.

McCullough, Kate. "Slavery, Sexuality, and Genre: Pauline Hopkins and the Representation of Female Desire." In Gruesser, *The Unruly Voice*, 21–49.

McElrath, Joseph R., Jr. "Why Charles W. Chesnutt Is Not a Realist." *American Literary Realism* 32.2 (2000): 91–108.

McHenry, Elizabeth. *Forgotten Readers: Recovering the Lost History of African American Literary Societies*. Durham, N.C.: Duke University Press, 2002.

McKay, Nellie Y. Introduction to Gruesser, *The Unruly Voice*, 1–20.

Meier, August. "Booker T. Washington and the Negro Press." *Journal of Negro History* 38 (Jan. 1953): 67–90.

Miller, Christopher L. *Blank Darkness: Africanist Discourse in French*. Chicago: University of Chicago Press, 1985.

Moddelmog, William E. "Narrating Citizenship in Pauline Hopkins's *Contending Forces*." In *Reconstituting Authority: American Fiction in the Province of the Law, 1880–1920*. Ed. Moddelmog. Iowa City: University of Iowa Press, 2000. 89–125.

Morrison, Toni. *Playing in the Dark: Whiteness and the Literary Imagination*. Cambridge, Mass.: Harvard University Press, 1992.

———. "Unspeakable Things Unspoken: The Afro-American Presence in American Literature." In *Criticism and the Color Line: Desegregating American Literary Studies*. Ed. Henry B. Wonham. New Brunswick: Rutgers University Press, 1996. 16–29.

Moses, Wilson Jeremiah. *Afrotopia: The Roots of African American Popular History*. Cambridge, Mass.: Cambridge University Press, 1998.

———. *Black Messiahs and Uncle Toms: Social and Literary Manipulations of a Religious Myth*. University Park: Pennsylvania State University Press, 1982.

———. *The Golden Age of Black Nationalism*. Hamden, Conn.: Archon, 1978.

———. "Literary Garveyism: The Novels of Reverend Sutton E. Griggs." *Phylon* 40.3 (1979): 203–16.

———. "The Poetics of Ethiopianism: W.E.B. Du Bois and Literary Black Nationalism." *American Literature* 47.3 (1975): 411–26.

———, ed. *Classical Black Nationalism: From the American Revolution to Marcus Garvey*. New York: New York University Press, 1996.

Mossell, N. F. [Gertrude Bustill]. "Mizeriah Johnson: Her Arisings and Shinings." In Ammons, *Short Fiction*, 126–34.

———. *The Work of the Afro-American Woman*. 1894. 2nd ed., 1908. Reprint, with an introduction by Joanne Braxton. Schomburg Library of Nineteenth-Century Black Women Writers. New York: Oxford University Press, 1988.

Murphy, Jeannette Robinson. *Southern Thoughts for Northern Thinkers*. New York: Bandanna, 1904.

Neeley, Barbara. *Blanche on the Lam*. New York: Penguin, 1992.

Nelson, Dana. *National Manhood: Capitalist Citizenship and the Imagined Fraternity of White Men*. Durham, N.C.: Duke University Press, 1998.

Nerad, Julie Cary. " 'So strangely interwoven': The Property of Inheritance, Race, and Sexual Morality in Pauline Hopkins's *Contending Forces*." *African American Review* 35.3 (2001): 357–73.

Nettels, Elsa. *Language, Race, and Social Class in Howells's America*. Lexington: University Press of Kentucky, 1988.

Noble, David W. *Historians against History: The Frontier Thesis and the National Covenant in American Historical Writing since 1830*. Minneapolis: University of Minnesota Press, 1965.

Oates, Stephen B. *To Purge This Land with Blood: A Biography of John Brown*. 2nd ed. Amherst: University of Massachusetts Press, 1984.

Osborne, M. L. "A Wild Mountain Rose." *Colored American Magazine* 1.1 (May 1900): 5–9.

Ostendorf, Berndt. *Black Literature in White America*. Sussex: Harvester Press, 1982.

Otten, Thomas J. "Pauline Hopkins and the Hidden Self of Race." *English Literary History* 59 (1992): 227–56.

Pamplin, Claire. " 'Race' and Identity in Pauline Hopkins's *Hagar's Daughter*." In *Redefining the Political Novel: American Women Writers, 1797–1901*. Ed. Sharon M. Harris. Knoxville: University of Tennessee Press, 1995. 169–83.

Patterson, Martha H. " 'Kin' o' rough jestice fer a parson': Pauline Hopkins's *Winona* and the Politics of Reconstructing History." *African American Review* 32.3 (1998): 445–60.

Perkins, Linda M. "Heed Life's Demands: The Educational Philosophy of Fanny Jackson Coppin." *Journal of Negro Education* 51.3 (1982): 181–90.

Perry, Rufus L. *The Cushite; or, The Descendants of Ham*. Springfield, Mass.: Willey, 1893.

Peterson, Carla L. "Unsettled Frontiers: Race, History, and Romance in Pauline Hopkins's *Contending Forces*." In *Famous Last Words: Changes in Gender and Narrative Closure*. Ed. Alison Booth. Charlottesville: University Press of Virginia, 1993. 177–96.

Porter, Dorothy B. "Hopkins, Pauline Elizabeth." In *Dictionary of American Negro Biography*. Ed. Rayford W. Logan and Michael R. Winston. New York: Norton, 1982. 325–26.

Posnock, Ross. *Color and Culture: Black Writers and the Making of the Modern Intellectual*. Cambridge, Mass.: Harvard University Press, 1998.

Pratt, Mary Louise. *Imperial Eyes: Travel Writing and Transculturation*. New York: Routledge, 1992.

Rampersad, Arnold. Introduction to Locke, *The New Negro*, ix–xxiii.

Robertson, John S. *David Livingstone: The Great Missionary Explorer*. n.p. ca. 1883.

Roses, Lorraine Elena, and Ruth Elizabeth Randolph, eds. *Harlem's Glory: Black Women Writing, 1900–1950*. Cambridge, Mass.: Harvard University Press, 1996.

Sanborn, F. B., ed. *The Life and Letters of John Brown, Liberator of Kansas, and Martyr of Virginia*. 1885. Reprint, New York: Negro Universities Press, 1969.

Scales, Anne Bethel. "Beth's Triumph (A Two-Part Story)." *Colored American Magazine* 1.3 (Aug. 1900): 152–59; 1.4 (Sept. 1900): 238–44. Rpt. in Ammons, *Short Fiction*, 32–48.

Scheick, William J. *The Ethos of Romance at the Turn of the Century*. Austin: University of Texas Press, 1994.

Scheiner, Seth M. "President Theodore Roosevelt and the Negro, 1901–1908." *Journal of Negro History* 47 (1962): 169–82.

Schneider, Mark R. *Boston Confronts Jim Crow, 1890–1920*. Boston: Northeastern University Press, 1997.

Schomburg, Arthur A. "American Fiction before 1910." In Locke, *The New Negro*, 427–28.

———. "The Negro Digs Up His Past." In Locke, *The New Negro*, 231–37.

———. "A Select List of Negro-Americana and Africana." In Locke, *The New Negro*, 421–26.

Schrager, Cynthia D. "Pauline Hopkins and William James: The New Psychology and the Politics of Race." In Gruesser, *The Unruly Voice*, 182–209.

Shaw, Stephanie J. *What a Woman Ought to Be and to Do: Black Professional Women Workers during the Jim Crow Era*. Chicago: University of Chicago Press, 1996.

Sherman, Joan R. "Whitfield, James Monroe." In *Dictionary of American Negro Biography*. Ed. Rayford W. Logan and Michael R. Winston. New York: Norton, 1982. 650.

Shockley, Ann Allen. *Afro-American Women Writers, 1746–1933: An Anthology and Critical Guide*. Boston: Hall, 1988.

———. "Pauline Elizabeth Hopkins: A Biographical Excursion into Obscurity." *Phylon* 33 (Spring 1972): 22–26.

Simmons, William J. *Men of Mark: Eminent, Progressive and Rising*. 1887. Reprint, New York: Arno, 1968.

Smith, John David. *Black Judas: William Hannibal Thomas and The American Negro*. Athens: University of Georgia Press, 2000.

Soitos, Stephen F. *The Blues Detective: A Study of African American Detective Fiction*. Amherst: University of Massachusetts Press, 1996.

Sollors, Werner. *Neither Black nor White Yet Both: Thematic Explorations of Interracial Literature*. Cambridge, Mass.: Harvard University Press, 1997.

———, ed. *Interracialism: Black-White Intermarriage in American History, Literature, and Law*. New York: Oxford University Press, 2000.

Somerville, Siobhan. "Passing through the Closet in Pauline E. Hopkins's *Contending Forces*." *American Literature* 69.1 (1997): 139–66.

Southern, Eileen. "An Early Black Concert Company: The Hyers Sisters Combination." In *A Celebration of American Music*. Ed. Richard Crawford, R. Allen Lott, and Carol J. Oja. Ann Arbor: University of Michigan Press, 1990. 17–35.

———. *The Music of Black Americans: A History*. 3rd ed. New York: Norton, 1997.

————, ed. *Out of Bondage* and *Peculiar Sam; or, The Underground Railroad*. Vol. 9 of *African American Theater*. New York: Garland, 1994.

Stanton, William. *The Leopard's Spots: Scientific Attitudes toward Race in America, 1815–59*. Chicago: University of Chicago Press, 1960.

Stepan, Nancy Leys, and Sander L. Gilman. "Appropriating the Idioms of Science: The Rejection of Scientific Racism." In *The Bounds of Race: Perspectives on Hegemony and Resistance*. Ed. Dominick La Capra. Ithaca, N.Y.: Cornell University Press, 1991. 72–103.

Stewart, Georgia F. "Aunt 'Ria's Ten Dollars." In Ammons, *Short Fiction*, 83–88.

————. "The Wooing of Pastor Cummings." In Ammons, *Short Fiction*, 99–106.

Streitmatter, Rodger. "Josephine St. Pierre Ruffin: Driving Force in the Women's Club Movement." In *Raising Her Voice: African American Women Journalists Who Changed History*. Ed. Streitmatter. Lexington: University Press of Kentucky, 1994.

Sundquist, Eric J. *To Wake the Nations: Race in the Making of American Literature*. Cambridge, Mass.: Belknap Press of Harvard University Press, 1993.

Tate, Claudia. *Domestic Allegories of Political Desire: The Black Heroine's Text at the Turn of the Century*. New York: Oxford University Press, 1992.

————. "Hopkins, Pauline E." In Andrews, *Oxford Companion*, 366–67.

————. Introduction to *The Works of Katherine Davis Chapman Tillman*. Schomburg Library of Nineteenth-Century Black Women Writers. New York: Oxford University Press, 1991. 3–62.

————. "Laying the Floor, or the History of the Formation of the Afro-American Canon." In *The New Cavalcade: African American Writing from 1760 to the Present*. Ed. Arthur P. Davis, J. Saunders Redding, and Joyce Ann Joyce. Washington, D.C.: Howard University Press, 1992. 2:752–75.

————. "Pauline Hopkins: Our Literary Foremother." In *Conjuring: Black Women, Fiction, and Literary Tradition*. Ed. Marjorie Pryse and Hortense J. Spillers. Bloomington: Indiana University Press, 1985. 53–66.

Terrell, Mary Church. *A Colored Woman in a White World*. 1940. Reprint, with an introduction by Nellie Y. McKay. African-American Women Writers, 1910–1940. New York: Hall, 1996.

Thernstrom, Stephan. *The Other Bostonians: Poverty and Progress in the American Metropolis, 1880–1970*. Cambridge, Mass.: Harvard University Press, 1973.

Thornbrough, Emma L. "More Light on Booker T. Washington and the New York Age." *Journal of Negro History* 43 (1958): 34–49.

Tillman, Katherine. *The Works of Katherine Davis Chapman Tillman*. Schomburg Library of Nineteenth-Century Black Women Writers. New York: Oxford University Press, 1991.

Todd, Ruth D. "Florence Grey, a Three-Part Story." In Ammons, *Short Fiction*, 157–204.

————. "The Octoroon's Revenge." In Ammons, *Short Fiction*, 135–44.

Toll, Robert C. *Blacking Up: The Minstrel Show in Nineteenth-Century America.* New York: Oxford University Press, 1974.

Trotter, William Monroe, ed. *The Two Days Observance of the One Hundredth Anniversary of the Birth of Charles Sumner. By the Citizens of Boston and Vicinity. January Fifth and Sixth, 1911. At Faneuil Hall, Bowdoin Grammar School, Park Street Church and Other Places.* Boston: Boston Sumner Centenary Committee Publishers, 1911.

Twain, Mark [Samuel Langhorne Clemens]. *Pudd'nhead Wilson and Those Extraordinary Twins.* 1894. Reprint, ed. Malcolm Bradbury, London: Penguin, 1969.

Veeser, H. Aram. Introduction to *The New Historicism.* Ed. Veeser. New York: Routledge, 1989. ix–xvi.

Wallinger, Hanna. "Alice Dunbar-Nelson and the Color Line." In *Black Liberation in the Americas.* Ed. Chris Mulvey and Fritz Gysin. Hamburg: Lit Verlag, 2001. 121–32.

———. "The Five Million Women of My Race: Negotiations of Gender in W.E.B. Du Bois and Anna Julia Cooper." In *Soft Canons: American Women Writers and Masculine Tradition.* Ed. Karen L. Kilcup. Iowa City: University of Iowa Press, 1999. 262–80.

———. "Racial Contexts: Pauline E. Hopkins and *Of One Blood* and Henry Rider Haggard's *She.*" In *Text and Context: Essays in English and American Studies in Honour of Holger M. Klein.* Ed. Sabine Coelsch-Foisner and Wolfgang Görtschacher. Rheinfelden: Schäuble, 1998. 43–52.

———. "Voyage into the Heart of Africa: Pauline Hopkins and *Of One Blood.*" In *Black Imagination and the Middle Passage.* Ed. Maria Diedrich, Henry Louis Gates Jr., and Carl Pedersen. New York: Oxford University Press, 1999. 203–14.

Washington, Booker T. *Booker T. Washington Papers.* Ed. Louis R. Harlan and Raymond W. Smock. 13 vols. Urbana: University of Illinois Press, 1977.

———. "Industrial Education; Will It Solve the Negro Problem." *Colored American Magazine* 7.2 (1904): 87–95.

———. *Up from Slavery.* In *Three Negro Classics.* New York: Avon, 1965. 23–205.

Washington, Margaret Murray. "The Advancement of Colored Women." *Colored American Magazine* 8.4 (Apr. 1905): 183–89.

Washington, Mary Helen. Introduction to *Invented Lives: Narratives of Black Women, 1860–1960.* Ed. Washington. Garden City, N.Y.: Anchor, 1987. xv–liv.

———. Introduction to *A Voice from the South,* by Anna Julia Cooper. 1892. Reprint, Schomburg Library of Nineteenth-Century Black Women Writers. New York: Oxford University Press, 1988.

Webster's New Encyclopedic Dictionary. Springfield, Mass.: Merriam-Webster, 1993.

Wells, Ida B. *Southern Horrors: Lynch Law in All Its Phases.* 1892. Rpt. in *Selected Works of Ida B. Wells-Barnett.* Ed. Trudier Harris. Schomburg Library of Nineteenth-Century Black Women Writers. New York: Oxford University Press, 1991.

Welter, Barbara. *Dimity Convictions: The American Woman in the Nineteenth Century.* Athens: Ohio University Press, 1976.

White, Deborah Gray. *Too Heavy a Load: Black Women in Defense of Themselves, 1894–1994*. New York: Norton, 1999.

Williams, Fannie Barrier. "After Many Days: A Christmas Story." In Ammons, *Short Fiction*, 218–38.

———. "The Club Movement among the Colored Woman." *Voice of the Negro* (Mar. 1904): 99–102.

Williams, George Washington. *History of the Negro Race in America*. 1883. Reprint, New York: Arno, 1968.

Williams, Kenny Jackson. "Brawley, Benjamin." In Andrews, *Oxford Companion*, 95–96.

Williams, Linda. *Playing the Race Card: Melodramas of Black and White from Uncle Tom to O. J. Simpson*. Princeton: Princeton University Press, 2001.

Wilson, Harriet E. *Our Nig; or, Sketches from the Life of a Free Black*. 1859. Reprint, New York: Vintage, 1984.

Wintz, Cary D., ed. and introduction. *The Critics and the Harlem Renaissance*. Vol. 4 of *The Harlem Renaissance, 1920–1940*. Ed. Wintz. New York: Garland, 1996.

———. *The Politics and Aesthetics of "New Negro" Literature*. Vol. 2 of *The Harlem Renaissance, 1920–1940*. Ed. Wintz. New York: Garland, 1996.

Wolf, Amy. "Virtue, Housekeeping, and Domestic Space in Pauline Hopkins' *Contending Forces*." *Domestic Goddesses*. Ed. Kim Wells. August 23, 1999. http://www.womenwriters.net/domesticgoddess/wolf.htm.

Wonham, Henry B. "Howells, Du Bois, and the Effect of 'Common Sense': Race, Realism, and Nervousness in *An Imperative Duty* and *The Souls of Black Folk*." In Wonham, *Criticism and the Color Line*, 126–39.

Wonham, Henry B., ed. *Criticism and the Color Line: Desegregating American Literary Studies*. New Brunswick, N.J.: Rutgers University Press, 1996.

Wright, Richard. "Blueprint for Negro Writing." 1937. Rpt. in *The Black Aesthetic*. Ed. Addison Gayle. Garden City, N.Y.: Anchor-Doubleday, 1972. 315–26.

Yarborough, Richard. Introduction to *Contending Forces: A Romance Illustrative of Negro Life North and South*, by Pauline E. Hopkins. Reprint, Schomburg Library of Nineteenth-Century Black Women Writers. New York: Oxford University Press, 1988. xxvii–xlviii.

———. "Strategies of Black Characterization in *Uncle Tom's Cabin* and the Early Afro-American Novel." In *New Essays on* Uncle Tom's Cabin. Ed. Eric J. Sundquist. Cambridge, Mass.: Cambridge University Press, 1986. 45–84.

Yates, Josephine Silone. "Report of the National Federation of Colored Women's Clubs." *Colored American Magazine* 8.5 (May 1905): 258–62.

Young, Robert J. C. *Colonial Desire: Hybridity in Theory, Culture and Race*. London: Routledge, 1995.

Index

Page numbers for illustrations are in italics.